THE ART *of* DATE SELECTION

PERSONAL DATE SELECTION

The Art of Date Selection: Personal Date Selection

First Edition May 2007
Second Edition January 2008

The author can be reached at:

Mastery Academy of Chinese Metaphysics Sdn. Bhd. (611143-A)
19-3, The Boulevard, Mid Valley City,
59200 Kuala Lumpur, Malaysia.
Tel : +603-2284 8080
Fax : +603-2284 1218
Email : info@masteryacademy.com
Website: www.masteryacademy.com

Published by JY Books Sdn. Bhd. (659134-T)

INDEX

PREFACE

How often do we hear the words 'timing is everything' and 'do the right thing, at the right time'? Yet the answer to the question of when is the right time to do something is a persistently elusive one. When indeed is the right time for something, and if it is the right time, how will we know it is the right time?

Leave it to the Chinese to come up with an exacting answer to this seemingly murky metaphysical question indeed! The Art of Date Selection or Ze Ri Xue 擇日學 has been an integral part of Chinese Metaphysics since the era of the Three Kingdoms. By combining astronomy, astrology and historical observation, Chinese scholars were able to discern subtle energy patterns and cycles that co-related to certain events. These observations were then assimilated into the practice of Date Selection.

The philosophy of Date Selection is to schedule a particular activity to take place or be 'activated' at a point in time when the energies are most conducive for that particular activity. Since these energy patterns and cycles can be computed and calculated, it is a matter of determining the appropriate point in time to commence or embark upon the activity intended...and one would literally be 'doing the right thing, at the right time'.

As a Feng Shui consultant, Date Selection has been an intrinsic part of my consultative practice. Once we have advised our clients on the changes to be made to their property, we will also typically provide them with a date to commence renovations or move into the house as it were. We soon found that clients were requesting Date Selection services for many of their personal endeavours. Clearly, many people place a great premium on a 'good date' but I still sense that many do not know why a 'good date' is of significance!

It's not surprising that many people just know they have to have a good date but don't really know why. Most people who can read the Tong Shu or Chinese Almanac frequently don't know why a particular date is good or otherwise. Like so many things related to Chinese Metaphysics, more often than not, the answer to any 'why' question usually gets answered as 'it just is'. It doesn't help that there are virtually no books in English on this subject and the classical texts on Date Selection are not easy to understand.

The Art of Date Selection series was thus conceived. I have envisaged a simple series of books, designed to not just enable anyone to find a good date, but also understand WHY a good date is important.

實用擇日

From an educational standpoint, Date Selection is an important component of the advanced Feng Shui and BaZi (Chinese Destiny Analysis Astrology) courses. Thus, I have also written this book for students of Feng Shui and BaZi who wish to have a better understanding of Date Selection basics and how this field can complement their practice. For those who wish to delve deeper into this subject, a class on Date Selection may be the way to go.

Sometimes, many things may be beyond our control or are expensive to implement. Changing our house or office's Feng Shui may require costly renovations or changes may be difficult to implement. BaZi often requires individuals to be able to exercise tremendous self-discipline or some soul-searching, before they can effectively re-engineer their character, attitudes or perception towards something or someone. That is why Date Selection offers a third way if you like. It doesn't incur cost and it doesn't require hard changes. But it does demand a little patience and sometimes, waiting for a good point in time to do something.

Timing is everything. Time is of the essence. Be in the right place, at the right time, doing the right thing. And if you believe in these mantras and value your time, then Date Selection can be a powerful weapon in your hands. Go with the flow of the universe, work with prevailing energies of the day and don't go against the tide, and you would have taken the right step towards achieving success.

This is the first book in my Art of Date Selection series and I hope to be able to share with you more simple techniques and methods that you can use. Through this series, it is my hope that anybody, no matter what their level of knowledge of Chinese Metaphysics, will be able to achieve the aim of 'doing the right thing, at the right time'!

Joey Yap
San Francisco, USA
May 2007

Author's personal website: www.joeyyap.com
Academy website: www.masteryacademy.com | www.masteryjournal.com

實用擇日

MASTERY ACADEMY
OF CHINESE METAPHYSICS™

At www.masteryacademy.com, you will find some useful tools to ascertain key information about the Feng Shui of a property or for study of Astrology.

To learn more about your personal Destiny, you can use the Joey Yap BaZi Ming Pan Calculator to plot your Four Pillars of Destiny – you just need to have your date of birth (day, month, year) and time of birth. The Joey Yap Flying Star Calculator can be utilised to plot your home or office Flying Star chart. To find out your personal best directions, use the 8 Mansions Calculator.

For more information about BaZi, Xuan Kong or Flying Star Feng Shui, or if you wish to learn more about these subjects with Joey Yap, logon to the Mastery Academy of Chinese Metaphysics website at **www.masteryacademy.com**.

Chapter One: What's in a Date?

Date Selection is a classical Chinese practice, which predates to the era of the Han Dynasty (206 BC – 220 AD). Historical tomes and classical texts, including those from the age of the Three Kingdoms, contain many references to Date Selection and tell of Date Selection's strategic usage in areas of military warfare and state matters. But this is not a field of study unique to the Chinese. The ancient Greek, Indian and even Mayan civilisations all developed elaborate calendar systems, based on astrological and cosmological phenomena and movement, to guide their societies on the timing of events such as harvests and prayer rituals.

Chinese Date Selection as a field of study and practice originates from the metaphysical approach to life that the learned Chinese scholars took to all matters.

實用擇日

All Chinese Metaphysical studies converge on the aspiration of understanding the universe and the cosmos. This was achieved through long-term, careful observation and recording of astrological and cosmological events that took place in the Heavens (observed without help from a telescope!) and then co-relating those observations with events, natural phenomenon and socio-political occurrences that took place on Earth.

Through the eras of observation and recording, patterns were derived and these eventually formed the basis of many Chinese Metaphysical studies. The cyclical concept of time and energy, and the movement of the stars, found particular application in Feng Shui 風水, Purple Star Astrology 紫微斗數 (Zi Wei Dou Shu) and BaZi 八字(Four Pillars of Destiny Astrology), as well as Date Selection.

Originally utilised for matters relating to war and peace, Date Selection was eventually extended to key economic activities such as planting and harvesting of crops and further, to personal activities such as marriages, moving into a new house, travel and burial.

Date Selection reached its epoch in the era of Emperor Qian Long (1711-1799). Prior to the era of Qian Long, the Chinese used two calendars - one that the Emperor used (obviously more accurate) and one that was used by commoners and peasants. Both these calendars had contradictions and contained conflicting observations and conclusions.

One of Qian Long's academic undertakings was to commission a text that unified all the Chinese texts on astronomy and astrology, including star maps, planetary movements and astronomical phenomena, and further corroborate this information with Western astronomical data derived from the Jesuits. Qian Long's tome was called The Book of Unifying Times and Discerning Dimensions 協紀辨方書 (Xie Ji Bian Fang Shu). Today, it is a cornerstone classical text for the study of Date Selection and the basis for what we know as the Chinese Almanac or Tong Shu 通書.

The Tong Shu is one of the best-selling books of all time in Asia. It contains a plethora of information ranging from palmistry and face-reading to astronomical phenomenon, star positioning and calendar information. Produced annually, almost every Chinese household has a copy of the Tong Shu and usually, at least one family member knows how to read it. For most Asians, the Tong Shu is relied upon for Do-It-Yourself Date Selection, usually with help from a family member familiar with the ins and outs of reading the Tong Shu's calendar features.

Although it is frequently used to complement the fields of BaZi and Feng Shui, Date Selection is frequently practiced professionally as a specialist discipline these days. In Hong Kong and Taiwan, there are masters who only do Date Selection engagements. In the field of Chinese Metaphysics, Date Selection is regarded as a specialised area of study.

Date Selection has seen its usage expand vastly beyond its original 'war and peace' usage. With the increased sophistication of our lives and the movement of our economies beyond the simple agrarian societies of the past, Date Selection's use has been expanded beyond marriage, death and religious activities. Today, it is used for a range of personal and business activities, from marriage proposals, to job interviews, and even official openings.

Date Selection is a practice that continues to adapt and grow with society's needs and demands. Some of the more modern applications of Date Selection techniques include selecting dates to start a diet, to undergo IVF treatment and even to acquire a pet.

Whilst some traditional practitioners may see this as trivialising the practice of Date Selection, I think this shows the relevance of Date Selection. It is also indicative of how more and more people are appreciating the importance of attuning their activities and endeavours with the flow of the energies of the universe. In this age where time is a premium, no one wants to do something that is going to end in failure or prove to be a waste of time. Hence, Date Selection is in tandem with the 21st century dictates of society, which demands the ability to not only get things done more efficiently but also more effectively!

The Good Date: Is it just superstition?

Despite the awareness amongst Asians on the importance of a 'good date', there is frequently not much understanding as to the actual reason behind the importance of a 'good date'. Sometimes it is treated as a necessary superstition, other times it is simply seen as an observation of Chinese culture.

Part of this stems from the double-edged sword of the Tong Shu. With the advent of colour-coded printing, it became very easy for anyone, including a Feng Shui or BaZi practitioner who could read Chinese, to figure out what were general `good' and `bad' dates. But without proper training or understanding of the history of Date Selection, the various methods of Date Selection and a familiarity with the classical texts, some practitioners could not explain or justify why a particular day was good or bad. Hence, it was not possible to explain to a client 'why' a particular date was better than another date. And when something does not come with an explanation or logical justification, people tend to associate it with the randomness or superstition. And it is for this reason that Date Selection has become associated with superstition.

The concept behind Date Selection is simple: the objective is to carry out an activity at the point in which the energies in the universe are optimised for that particular endeavour. Through the infusion of these energies, a particular event can commence on a positive note and footing.

Chinese View of Time and the Universe

The Chinese viewpoint of time and the universe provides an explanation of how Date Selection techniques and methods were developed. To understand not only why Date Selection matters, but also its very foundation and basis (in other words, how do we know it really works?), we must first appreciate the philosophy behind the Chinese approach to Date Selection.

The conventional thinking of time is that it is linear and infinite in nature. This approach takes the viewpoint that events do not repeat themselves - once something has happened, it will not repeat itself. There is also a randomness to the Western perception of time - the idea that things occur sometimes without warning or at least, occur as a result of divine force or transcendent forces at work.

The Chinese viewpoint is different and naturally revolves around the Yin-Yang philosophy. What is void and unchanging (space) is in the same sphere as that which is moving and ever-changing (time). Space is Yin. Time is Yang. As such, Chinese philosophy sees time as moving forward and progressive in nature, and yet regards time as having a cyclical quality.

In other words, what comes around, will come around again! Positive energies and favourable moments do not zip in and out of our lives, but occur again and again. And there is nothing random in what occurs in the universe - it is all part of a pattern of energies that can be tracked, calculated, computed and pre-determined. In Chinese Metaphysics philosophy, there is no reference to transcendal power, thus, Chinese Metaphysics as a practice is entirely atheistic in nature.

Date Selection, at its most basic, is about using the information collated over the centuries by the Chinese scholars, astronomers and philosophers, to pin-point a window in time and the universe, when the energies are most conducive for an activity or endeavour. In simplified terms – go with the flow!

Heaven-Earth-Man and Date

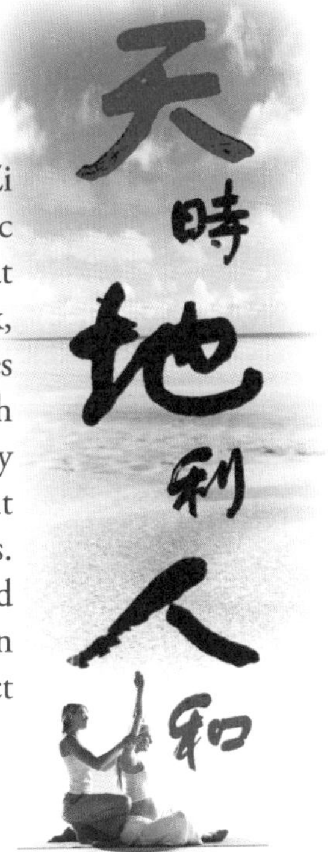

Those of you who have read my books on BaZi may be familiar with the concept of the Cosmic Trinity. The concept of the Cosmic Trinity is that Destiny is influenced by three forces: Heaven Luck, Earth Luck and Man Luck. Heaven Luck relates to a person's destiny, which is ascertained through analysing a person's BaZi or Purple Star astrology chart. Earth Luck relates to a person's environment and how that impacts on a person's life choices. Man Luck refers to individual choices made and personal endeavours undertaken to achieve certain goals. Each of these influences exerts a 33% impact on our lives.

Date Selection is viewed by Chinese Metaphysics experts as an aspect of Heaven Luck, although one could argue that since a person has to consciously make a choice to seek out a professional to help them select a good date, it also has a touch of Man Luck to it. It is generally accepted as Heaven Luck because it involves referencing a specific date and time (with certain planetary or star alignments) that is beyond the influence of Man.

Now, this probably sounds a bit confusing at this stage. Isn't Heaven Luck something that can't be changed? And if it can't be changed, then why bother selecting a date? Yes, Heaven Luck cannot be 'changed', but one can make choices and time certain decisions to maximise a positive outcome rather than a negative outcome.

A BaZi consult in the good old days focused on the person's life path only. A person was told their life would be of a certain path and that person was expected to just trundle down the path of life, as spelled-out by the astrologer. There was no question of if, but or can't-I-do this!

By contrast, the modern approach to a BaZi consult is less rigid and more orientated around the idea of making the right choices on the path of life. A person can learn what is the right and wrong decision to make at any point in life, and then seek to positively influence the outcomes of a potentially negative situation through the decisions or actions they take.

Similarly, by selecting a good date to commence a particular activity, the outcome of that activity can be influenced positively. By demarcating a point in time for the activity with the most beneficial energy patterns, based on the configuration of stars in the universe, it represents the epitome of 'doing the right thing, at the right time'. This does not represent 'changing' your Heaven Luck, but rather timing your activity so that you engage in your endeavour at the most beneficial point in time.

A Caesarean section birth is an example of timing one's Heaven Luck to maximise the outcome. A Caesarean section birth Date Selection requires both knowledge of Date Selection and BaZi. When professionally and properly done, it takes into account the unborn child's parents' BaZi before a date is selected. This is because the BaZi practitioner or Date Selection specialist must select a date that 'matches' the BaZi of the parents. If the parents are not destined to have a child that will become the next Prime Minister, then a BaZi practitioner or Date Selection specialist will not select a date that indicates such a destiny for the child.

But the BaZi practitioner or Date Selection specialist will select the most favourable, 'suitable' date based on the parents' BaZi and the type of destiny their child is likely to have. Thus, it involves adhering to the Heaven Luck of the parents, but attempting to select the best point in time for the child to be born to make the situation as advantageous as possible for the yet-to-be-born child.

Aspects of Date Selection

There are two key aspects to Date Selection and most techniques of Date Selection revolve around these two aspects: the first is the selection of a suitable day for the activity in question. This is what most people know as Date Selection. But in fact, Date Selection is not just about a good date. The other important aspect of Date Selection involves selecting the best time, within a particular date, in which to perform or undertake that particular activity. This is known as Time Selection. Classical techniques and methods within the school of study known as Date Selection focus almost entirely on selecting either the best date for a particular activity, or finding the best hour within a day, to commence the activity. I will be showing you simple, easy to use and safe methods to engage in both these aspects of Date Selection.

The very concept of Date Selection tells us that not all dates are created equal. Dates can be classified generally as bad dates (not usable for anything important), usable dates (can be used if there is no choice or for expediency purposes), good dates (generally good and usable by everyone for important personal activities and endeavours) and personalised good dates (a date that is not just generally good, but also specifically advantageous for a person and the activity they are undertaking, based on a combination of BaZi and Date Selection methods).

I will be showing you how to avoid using bad dates, how to find the good dates and most importantly, how to achieve a basic level of personalisation. Readers with a good knowledge of BaZi (Four Pillars of Destiny) or BaZi basics will of course be able to engage in a higher level of personalisation and utilise the entire BaZi and the Ten Gods 十神 (Shi Shen) to help with the personalisation of the date. However, do not be concerned if you have no BaZi knowledge at all as it is possible to still select a reasonably good and personalised date for yourself, without extensive BaZi knowledge. All you need to know is your Year of Birth.

This book is designed to be a simple book, for use by everyone and not just practitioners or professionals. Hence, my focus will be on showing you methods and techniques that you can use with minimum basic background knowledge. The goal will be to have you up and running, engaging in Date Selection for yourself, by the end of this book. Thus, primarily I will be focusing on safe and simple methods and techniques, such as the Gods and Killings 神煞 (Shen Sha), the 12 Day Officers 十二值神 (Shi Er Zhi Shen) and the 28 Constellations 二十八宿 (Er Shi Ba Su).

These are of course not the only techniques and methods for Date Selection. Other schools of Date Selection include the Star Head Method 斗首 (Dou Shou), Black Rabbit or Sun and Moon Method 烏兔 (Wu Tu), Grand Master Dong's

System 董公 (Dong Gong), Mystical Doors Method 奇門盾甲 (Qi Men Dun Jia), Six Ren System 六壬 (Liu Ren) and Purple White Method 紫白九星 (Zi Bai Jiu Xing).

There is also the Xuan Kong Da Gua Method 玄空大卦 (Xuan Kong Greater Hexagrams), which utilises the 64 Hexagrams together with the Four Pillars, to select the appropriate timing to activate Feng Shui. Finally, there is the Heavenly Stars Method 七政四餘天星 (Qi Zheng Si Yu Tian Xing), which is quite popular in Hong Kong. However, these require an extensive knowledge of Chinese Metaphysics, Feng Shui and BaZi and so are difficult to cover in a book for beginners.

However, with what you will learn in this book, you will be well-equipped to engage in Date Selection for your own personal activities and endeavours.

In this book, I will be focusing on Date Selection for personal activities and endeavours such as marriage dates, dates for business negotiations, and dates for travel and minor medical procedures. I have chosen to write about Date Selection for personal activities and endeavours first because moving house is not something people do all the time but starting a new job, or going for a job interview, or closing a business deal are activities we engage in frequently and on a regular basis. And because personal activities, like marriage and jobs, affect and impact a person's life significantly, it is all the more important that good dates are used for these activities and endeavours.

Feng Shui-related Date Selection - which relates to matters like dates for moving into a new home, commencing renovations or implementing a Feng Shui remedy will be dealt with in my next book in the *Art of Date Selection* series, ***Feng Shui Date Selection.***

The Power of a Good Date

You might be wondering now: does this mean that I cannot take action or do anything unless I have a good date? Well, with all things, moderation and practicality of course have to apply. By the end of this book, you'll appreciate the power of a good date, but you'll also discover that there aren't THAT many good dates in a month, or a year for that matter!

Of course, what is trivial to one person is of great importance to another and when more than one party is involved in the activity or endeavour in question (think weddings and business partnerships), it is not always easy to give an answer to the question I've posed above.

I will say this though; if the matter is something of great personal significance (marriage is of course the easiest example) or personal financial significance (starting a business), try to accommodate a good date. Some re-arrangement of schedules or changes to plans may be required but as you go through this book, you'll see that Date Selection is not an impractical art. I have found, in the course of my consulting work, that it is not the calendar that is inflexible, but people's minds that are carved in stone.

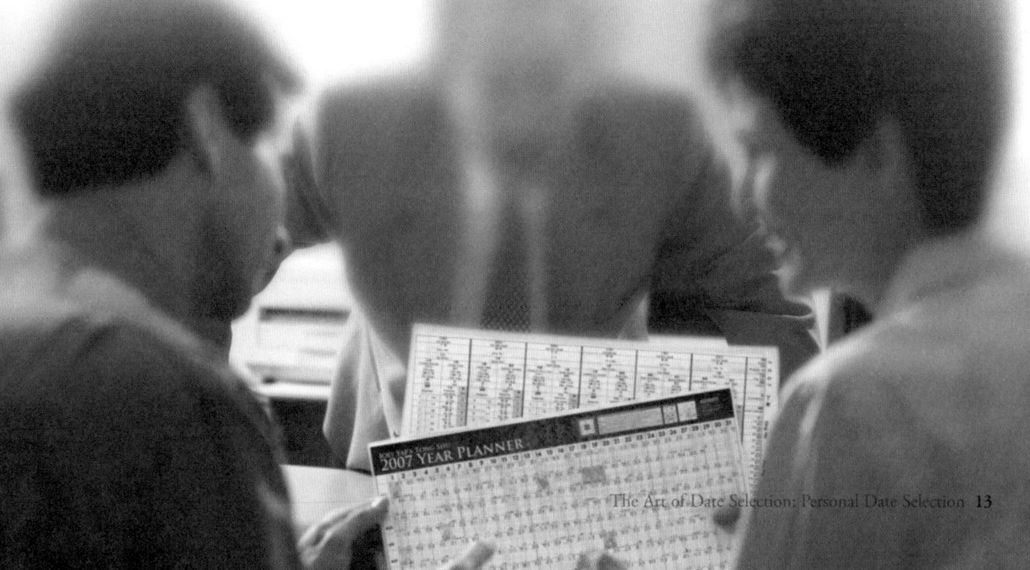

And if you cannot accommodate a good date for some reason, then endeavour to avoid using a bad date. Sometimes, it is not possible to start something off on a good footing, but you can also avoid starting off on a bad footing!

But if something requires very little sacrifice or change and involves only a slight inconvenience, versus the significant advantage you will gain through infusing your activity or endeavour of choice with positive energies and every chance of success, why not just go with the flow of the universe?

Chapter Two:
Date Selection Essentials

Before you can start doing your own Date Selection using the techniques outlined here, you need your basic tools and information. What are the tools you will need? First, a calendar. But not just any calendar. You need a Chinese Solar Calendar.

Secondly, if you are doing Date Selection for yourself, you will need to have your personal BaZi chart available on hand. If you are doing Date Selection for a friend or family member, then you will need their BaZi. For those of you who would like to delve deeper into BaZi or who would like to gain a better understanding of BaZi, my book ***BaZi - The Destiny Code*** provides an in-depth introduction to BaZi. In this section however, I will just provide you with the absolute bare essentials when it comes to using your BaZi for Date Selection.

The Chinese Calendar

Complex calendrical systems are common in many civilisations - the Gregorian calendar that we use daily was inherited from the Romans. But all major civilisations - from the Mayans to the Indians to the Chinese - have their own calendars, each with varying degrees of sophistication and usage.

Many Chinese do not know that the Chinese calendar system comprises of two types of calendars that are often used in tandem: a Solar calendar and a Lunar calendar. The Lunar calendar, as its name indicates, is derived from observations of the moon's movements and orbit around the Earth and is most commonly used for festivals and certain types of Chinese Metaphysical calculations, notably the Purple Star Method 紫微斗數 (Zi Wei Dou Shu) of destiny analysis.

The Solar Calendar, by contrast, was used for determining the dates to commence planting crops and begin harvests in the old days, and is also used for many Feng Shui and BaZi computations. The Chinese Solar calendar is the primary type of calendar used for Date Selection.

While the Lunar calendar has double months and missing months, and a constantly shifting transition point (hence, Chinese New Year never falls on the same day every year), the Solar calendar does not have missing months or double months or a shifting transition point. Therefore, each year transits on the same day, which is the first day of Spring 立春 (Li Chun). The first day of Spring in the Chinese Solar Calendar coincides with February 4th of the Western Gregorian Calendar every year.

立春

You might be wondering - why won't a normal calendar do for Date Selection? The reason you need to use a Chinese Solar calendar and not a normal Western Gregorian desktop calendar is because the Chinese Solar calendar will tell you which of the Five Elements are present on any particular day, in the form of a Day Pillar. You need this elemental information in order to engage in Date Selection.

JANUARY 2007 辛丑

SUNDAY	MONDAY	TUESDAY	WEDNESDAY	THURS
	乙未 1 十三	丙申 2 十四	丁酉 3 十五	戊戌
辛丑 7 十九	壬寅 8 二十	癸卯 9 廿一	甲辰 10 廿二	乙巳
戊申 14 廿六	己酉 15 廿七	庚戌 16 廿八	辛亥 17 廿九	壬子
乙卯 21 初三	丙辰 22 初四	丁巳 23 初五	戊午 24 初六	己未
壬戌 28 初十	癸亥 29 十一	甲子 30 十二	乙丑 31 十三	

The Day Pillar

Where do you get a Chinese Solar calendar?

There are several options: those of you who can read Chinese may want to use the Tong Shu although this can be quite complicated to use, even if you do read Chinese. You can use my bi-lingual Ten Thousand Year Calendar which displays the Gregorian Western calendar dates, alongside the Chinese Solar and Lunar Calendar information or if you want to make it really easy for yourself, use my Desktop Tong Shu Calendar. If you have access to Microsoft Outlook, the calendar function includes a Chinese Solar Calendar option and you can use that feature also.

Here is how you set up the Chinese Solar Calendar on Microsoft Outlook.

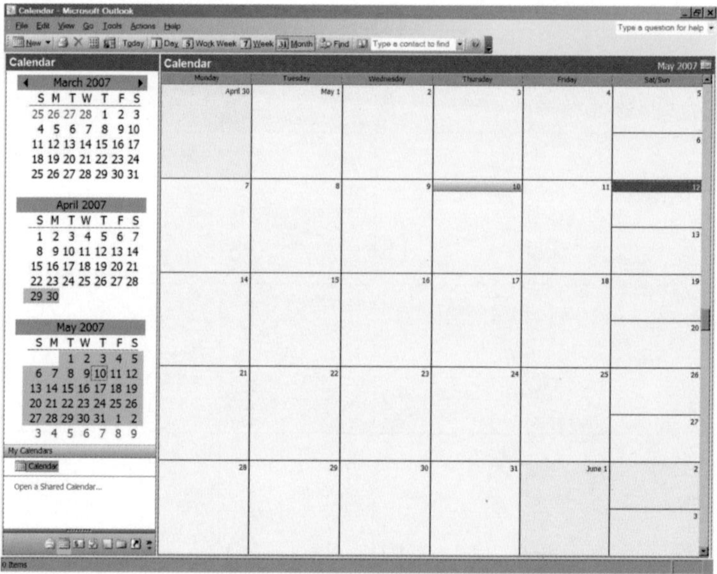

Go to the "Tools" Menu.

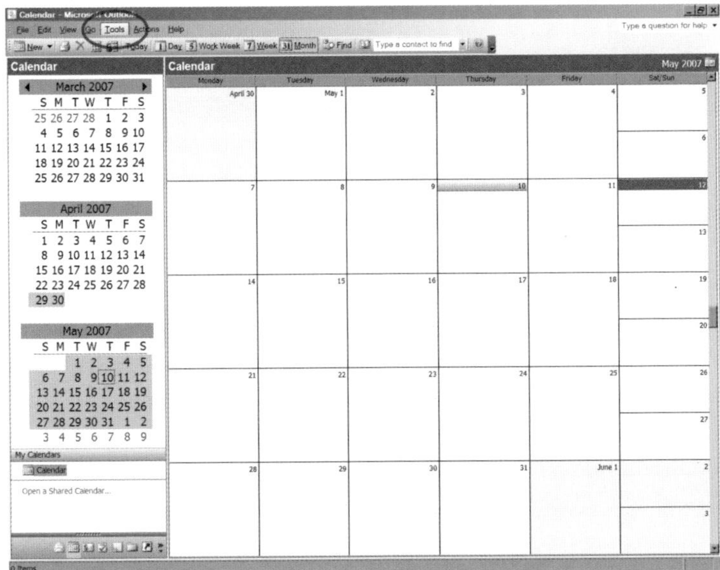

Then click on "Options" .

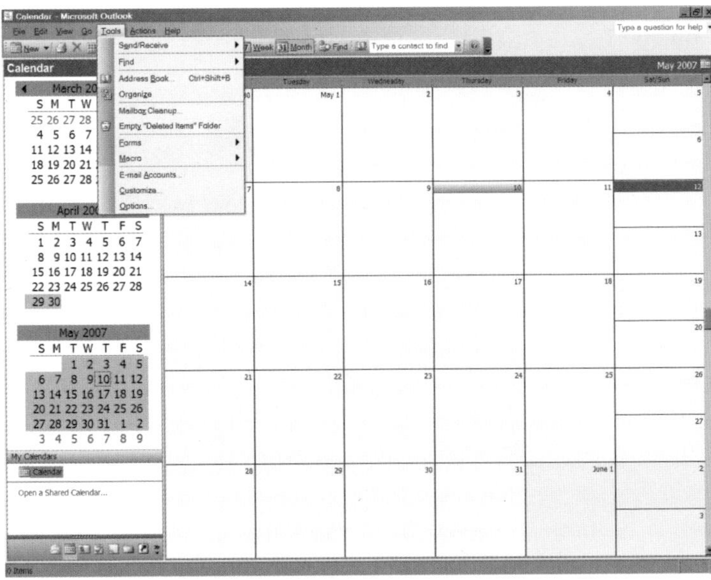

You will see the following Screen.
Click on "Calendar Options".

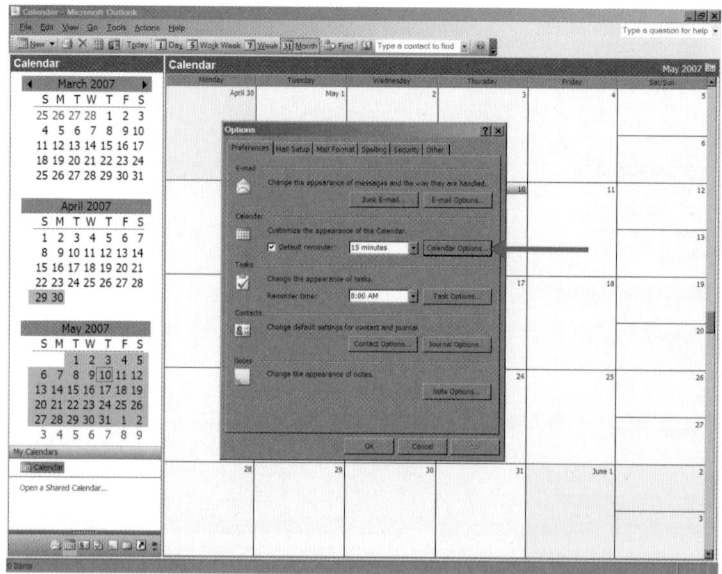

Under "Advanced Options",
activate "Enable Alternate Calendar".

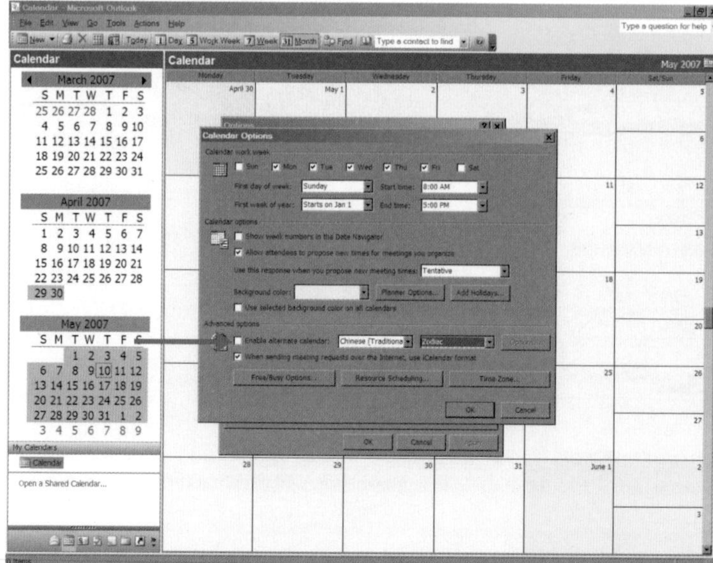

Now, select "Chinese (Traditional)" and select "Zodiac". And then click "OK".

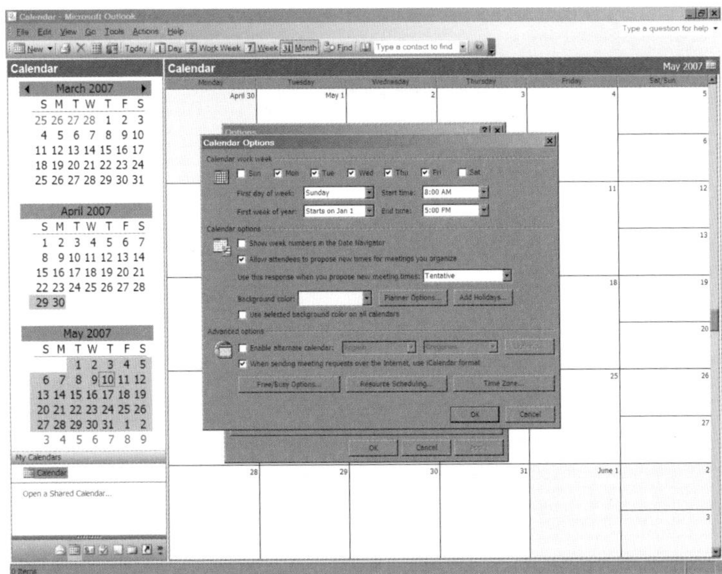

You are now set!
You will see the Day Pillars in your Calendar Pages.

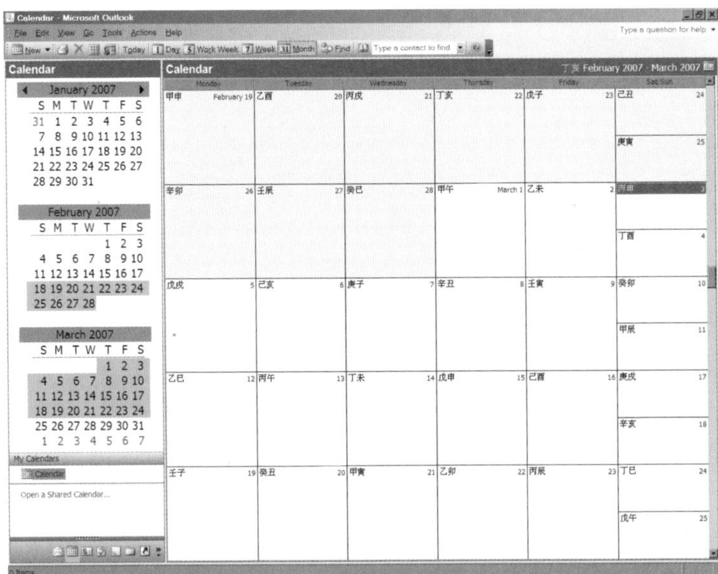

Assuming you already have a Chinese Solar Calendar on hand, the next thing you need to do is have your personal BaZi chart available and ready to be deciphered if you are selecting a date for yourself.

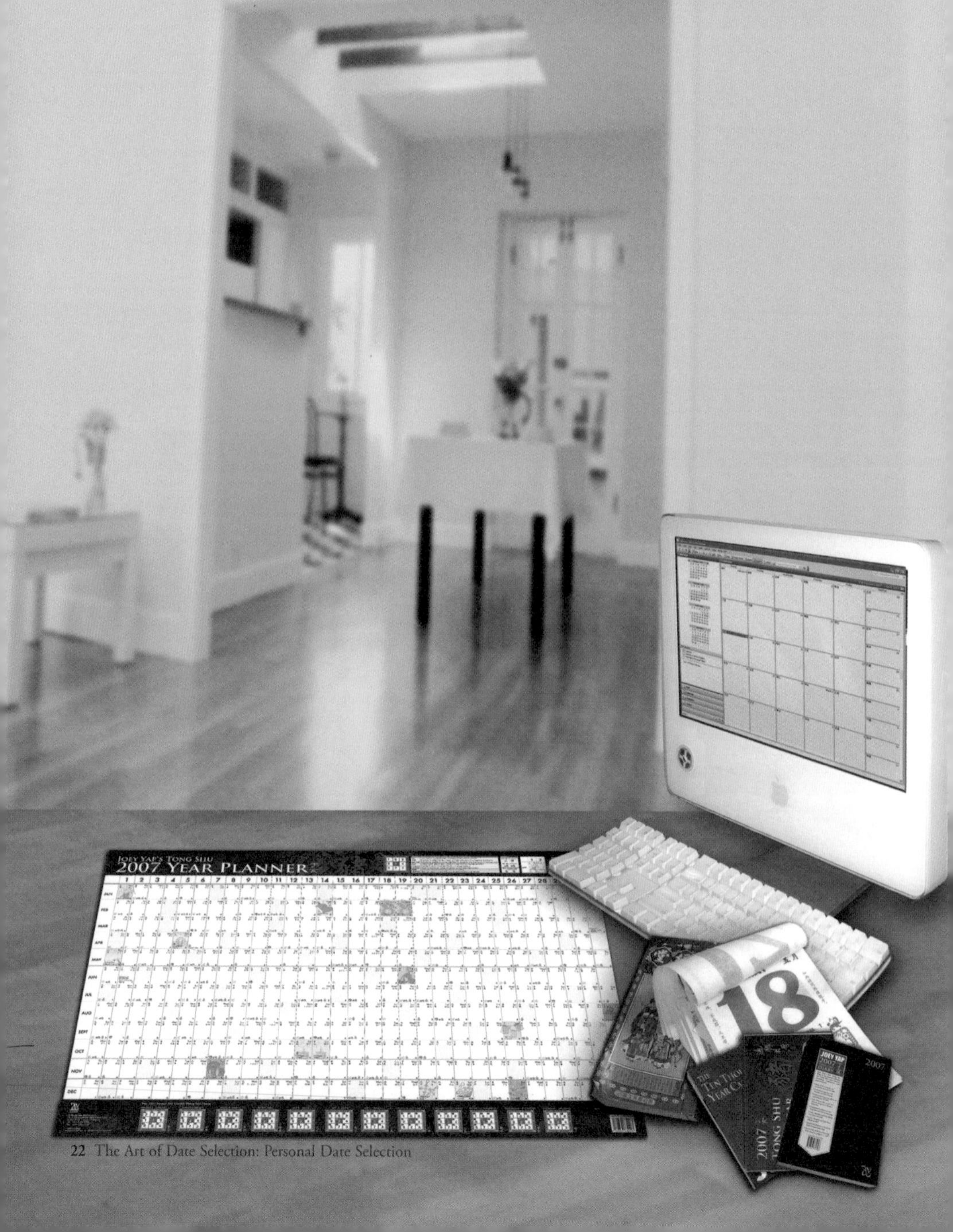

BaZi Basics

A person's BaZi chart, also known as their Four Pillars of Destiny, is an encoded representation of the elements present or dominant in the universe at the moment of their birth. Those elements are presented in the form of Four Pillars, hence the term 'Four Pillars of Destiny'.

時 Hour
日 Day
月 Month
年 Year
天干 Heavenly Stems
丙
Bing
Yang Fire
辛
Xin
Yin Metal
乙
Yi
Yin Wood
戊
Wu
Yang Earth
地支 Earthly Branches
申
Shen
Monkey
Yang Metal
巳
Si
Snake
Yin Fire
丑
Chou
Ox
Yin Earth
申
Shen
Monkey
Yang Metal
藏干 Hidden Stems
戊 庚 壬
庚 丙 戊
辛 己 癸
戊 庚 壬

Your BaZi is your personal Destiny Code. It contains information about your life. By understanding your personal Destiny Code, you are able to determine how best to walk the path that destiny has in store for you and to make the best of your personal talents and abilities.

The reason why Date Selection must involve BaZi is because truly effective Date Selection is about personalisation. When a Date Selection specialist is asked to select a date, they are paid not to find a generic good date that is good for anyone and everyone but to look for a date that is optimum for the activity and also optimum for the person who engages their services.

Hence, Date Selection is about finding a day that is good for a particular activity (activity personalisation), and also that person in particular (individual personalisation). It is about finding a date where the energies are in harmony with the activity in question, and also the person engaged in that particular activity.

There are 2 ways to obtain your personal BaZi chart.

You can manually plot a basic BaZi chart by yourself, using the Ten Thousand Year Calendar. Alternatively, you can use the computer software found at my website, **www.joeyyap.com** - click on the BaZi Ming Pan Software link. The latter obviously is a lot faster and makes life easier because it also provides you with your personal Luck Pillars. But it is worth manually plotting your own BaZi chart, as this will afford you an opportunity to familiarise yourself with the basic Chinese Astrology characters.

The technique for manually plotting a BaZi chart, including the Luck Pillars, is explained both in the Ten Thousand Year Calendar and in ***BaZi - The Destiny Code*** and you should refer to these books if you are interested in the technical aspects of BaZi chart plotting. I will focus here on explaining what are the key pieces of information in a BaZi chart that you will need to reference, to engage in Date Selection for yourself.

Every BaZi chart comprises of several components. There are the basic BaZi chart and the Luck Pillars.

Basic BaZi Chart

時 Hour	日 Day	月 Month	年 Year	
丙 Bing Yang Fire	辛 Xin Yin Metal	乙 Yi Yin Wood	戊 Wu Yang Earth	天干 Heavenly Stems
申 Shen Monkey Yang Metal	巳 Si Snake Yin Fire	丑 Chou Ox Yin Earth	申 Shen Monkey Yang Metal	地支 Earthly Branches
戊 庚 壬	庚 丙 戊	辛 己 癸	戊 庚 壬	藏干 Hidden Stems

Luck Pillars

80	70	60	50	40	30	20	10	0	
丙 Bing Yang Fire	丁 Ding Yin Fire	戊 Wu Yang Earth	己 Ji Yin Earth	庚 Geng Yang Metal	辛 Xin Yin Metal	壬 Ren Yang Water	癸 Gui Yin Water	甲 Jia Yang Wood	大運 Luck Pillars
辰 Chen Dragon Yang Earth	巳 Si Snake Yin Fire	午 Wu Horse Yang Fire	未 Wei Goat Yin Earth	申 Shen Monkey Yang Metal	酉 You Rooster Yin Metal	戌 Xu Dog Yang Earth	亥 Hai Pig Yin Water	子 Zi Rat Yang Water	

Within a BaZi chart, there are certain key reference points. The most important reference point is your personal Day Master. Look at the diagram below - the character that appears on the third column from the right, in the top box, is what we call your Day Master.

Day Master 日元

時 Hour	日 Day	月 Month	年 Year	
癸 Gui Yin Water	庚 Geng Yang Metal	癸 Gui Yin Water	戊 Wu Yang Earth	天干 Heavenly Stems
未 Wei Goat Yin Earth	子 Zi Rat Yang Water	亥 Hai Pig Yin Water	子 Zi Rat Yang Water	地支 Earthly Branches
乙 己 丁	癸	壬 甲	癸	藏干 Hidden Stems

For basic Date Selection techniques, the essential information that are needed from your BaZi are what we call the Year Pillar and Day Pillar. Of course, a Date Selection specialist will reference the full BaZi chart when selecting a date but at the basic level, just the Year Pillar and Day Pillar are needed.

What is a Year Pillar and what is a Day Pillar? Look at the diagram below.

時 Hour	日 Day (Day Pillar)	月 Month	年 Year (Year Pillar)	
癸 *Gui* Yin Water	庚 *Geng* Yang Metal	癸 *Gui* Yin Water	戊 *Wu* Yang Earth	天干 Heavenly Stems
未 *Wei* **Goat** Yin Earth	子 *Zi* **Rat** Yang Water	亥 *Hai* **Pig** Yin Water	子 *Zi* **Rat** Yang Water	地支 Earthly Branches
乙 己 丁	癸	壬 甲	癸	藏干 Hidden Stems

If you have your personal BaZi chart on hand, highlight or circle in red the following:

a) Your Day Master
b) Your Day Pillar
c) Your Year Pillar

All this may seem Greek to you but don't worry - keep on reading and it will all soon make sense.

Getting to know the Chinese Astrology 'Alphabet'

Now that you have the right tools and key basic information on hand, let's talk about what you need to know to learn the basic techniques. You will need to familiarise yourself a little with some of the Chinese Astrology terms that are commonly used in Date Selection.

Don't worry; there is no cause for panic. Learning these basic terms is like learning a new language - one must first familiarise oneself with the alphabet or the basic components of that language. So let's look at what are the basic components of Chinese Astrology that you need to know, to make use of Date Selection.

If you are familiar with BaZi or Feng Shui, you will be familiar with these basic components but it is worthwhile going through the following section, even if you have some knowledge of BaZi or Feng Shui.

I always tell my BaZi and Feng Shui students that they must not be psychologically 'put-off' by the fact that they have to learn a few Chinese characters. And it really is just a few - there are only 22 characters you need to learn. Most of us have no trouble learning the 26 letters of the alphabet so this should not be a problem!

What are these 22 Chinese characters? Essentially, they are the 10 Heavenly Stems, and the 12 Earthly Branches.

These are the 10 Heavenly Stems:

天干 Heavenly Stems	五行與陰陽屬性 Element and Polarity
甲 *Jia*	Yang Wood 陽木
乙 *Yi*	Yin Wood 陰木
丙 *Bing*	Yang Fire 陽火
丁 *Ding*	Yin Fire 陰火
戊 *Wu*	Yang Earth 陽土
己 *Ji*	Yin Earth 陰土
庚 *Geng*	Yang Metal 陽金
辛 *Xin*	Yin Metal 陰金
壬 *Ren*	Yang Water 陽水
癸 *Gui*	Yin Water 陰水

You will notice that the Heavenly Stems are the Yin and Yang variations of the 5 Elements: Wood, Fire, Earth, Metal and Water. Now, look at your personal BaZi chart - you will notice that your Day Master is in fact, one of the 10 Heavenly Stems.

Here are the 12 Earthly Branches:

Earthly Branches		Animal Sign	Element
子 *Zi*	Pronounced as 'Zh-er'	Rat	Yang Water
丑 *Chou*	Pronounced as 'Ch-o' as in the word 'go'	Ox	Yin Earth
寅 *Yin*	Pronounced as 'Yeen' as in the word 'seen'	Tiger	Yang Wood
卯 *Mao*	Pronounced as 'Mow' as in the word 'how'	Rabbit	Yin Wood
辰 *Chen*	Pronounced as 'Ch-earn' with a silent 'r'	Dragon	Yang Earth
巳 *Si*	Pronounced as 'Sir' with a silent 'r'	Snake	Yin Fire
午 *Wu*	Pronounced as 'Woo'	Horse	Yang Fire
未 *Wei*	Pronounced as 'Way'	Goat	Yin Earth
申 *Shen*	Pronounced as 'Sh-earn' with a silent 'r'	Monkey	Yang Metal
酉 *You*	Pronounced as 'YOU'	Rooster	Yin Metal
戌 *Xu*	Pronounced as 'Shoot' with a silent 't'	Dog	Yang Earth
亥 *Hai*	Pronounced as 'Hi' as in hi !	Pig	Yin Water

The 12 Earthly Branches correspond with what most people know as the 12 animal signs. You will notice that your BaZi comprises of Four Heavenly Stems and Four Earthly Branches.

	時 Hour	日 Day	月 Month	年 Year
天干 Heavenly Stems	辛 *Xin* Yin Metal	丙 *Bing* Yang Fire	丁 *Ding* Yin Fire	丙 *Bing* Yang Fire
地支 Earthly Branches	卯 *Mao* **Rabbit** Yin Wood	戌 *Xu* **Dog** Yang Earth	酉 *You* **Rooster** Yin Metal	辰 *Chen* **Dragon** Yang Earth
藏干 Hidden Stems	乙 *Yi*	丁 *Ding* 戊 *Wu* 辛 *Xin*	辛 *Xin*	癸 *Gui* 戊 *Wu* 乙 *Yi*

大運 Luck Pillars	82	72	62	52	42	32	22	12	2
Stem	丙 *Bing* Yang Fire	乙 *Yi* Yin Wood	甲 *Jia* Yang Wood	癸 *Gui* Yin Water	壬 *Ren* Yang Water	辛 *Xin* Yin Metal	庚 *Geng* Yang Metal	己 *Ji* Yin Earth	戊 *Wu* Yang Earth
Branch	午 *Wu* **Horse** Yang Fire	巳 *Si* **Snake** Yin Fire	辰 *Chen* **Dragon** Yang Earth	卯 *Mao* **Rabbit** Yin Wood	寅 *Yin* **Tiger** Yang Wood	丑 *Chou* **Ox** Yin Earth	子 *Zi* **Rat** Yang Water	亥 *Hai* **Pig** Yin Water	戌 *Xu* **Dog** Yang Earth
Hidden Stems	丁己	庚丙戊	癸戊乙	乙	戊甲丙	辛己癸	癸	壬甲	丁戊辛

實用擇日

More than just animals!

The Earthly Branches are used to represent many things in Chinese Metaphysics. At this point, you simply need to appreciate that the Earthly Branches can represent the year, month, day and hour. Of particular importance is understanding which Earthly Branches represent which month of the year, and which Hour in a day. For example, Tiger 寅 (Yin) can refer to the Tiger Month (February 4 - March 5) or the Tiger Hour (3-5am).

Here are the Earthly Branches and the Gregorian calendar months that they correspond to.

Earthly Branch of the month			
寅 Yin		**Tiger**	February 4th
卯 Mao		**Rabbit**	March 6th
辰 Chen		**Dragon**	April 5th
巳 Si		**Snake**	May 6th
午 Wu		**Horse**	June 6th
未 Wei		**Goat**	July 7th
申 Shen		**Monkey**	August 8th
酉 You		**Rooster**	September 8th
戌 Xu		**Dog**	October 8th
亥 Hai		**Pig**	November 7th
子 Zi		**Rat**	December 7th
丑 Chou		**Ox**	January 6th

實用擇日

An important point to note is that the Chinese Solar Calendar does not transit on the 31st or 30th of each Western month. So whilst the Western 2nd month (which is February) starts on the 1st of February, the Chinese Month, which is the Tiger Month, does not start on the 1st of February.

To determine the exact transition point for each month, you need to check the Tong Shu or the Ten Thousand Year Calendar. The black marker in my Ten Thousand Year Calendar will tell you when the transition point for each month is. As a general rule, the transition point is around the 4th or 5th of each month, give or take a day. However, for the purposes of Date Selection, it is always important to check to make sure you have considered the monthly transitions.

2004 甲申 Jia Shen Wood Monkey

閏二月小 Extra 2nd Mth Small				二月大 2nd Mth Big				正月小 1st Mth Small				月別 Month
				丁卯 Ding Mao				丙寅 Bing Yin				干支 Branches and Stems
				一白 One White				二黑 Two Black				九星 Nine Star
		清明 Clear and Bright		春分 Spring Equinox		驚蟄 Awakening of Worms		雨水 Rain Water		立春 Coming of Spring		節氣 Season
		十五 15th day		三十 30th day		十五 15th day		二十九 29th day		十四 14th day		
		18時 44 分 18hr 44min		14時 50 分 14hr 50min		13時 57 分 13hr 57min		15時 51 分 15hr 51min		19時 58 分 19hr 58min		朔 Constellation
		酉 You		未 Wei		未 Wei		申 Shen		戌 Xu		
國曆 Gregorian		干支 Branches and stems	星 Star	國曆 Gregorian		干支 Branches and stems	星 Star	國曆 Gregorian		干支 Branches and stems	星 Star	農曆 Solar Calender
3	21	己亥 Ji Hai	9	2	20	己巳 Ji Si	6	1	22	庚子 Geng Zi	4	初一 1st day
3	22	庚子 Geng Zi	1	2	21	庚午 Geng Wu	7	1	23	辛丑 Xin Chou	5	初二 2nd day
3	23	辛丑 Xin Chou	2	2	22	辛未 Xin Wei	8	1	24	壬寅 Ren Yin	6	初三 3rd day
3	24	壬寅 Ren Yin	3	2	23	壬申 Ren Shen	9	1	25	癸卯 Gui Mao	7	初四 4th day
3	25	癸卯 Gui Mao	4	2	24	癸酉 Gui You	1	1	26	甲辰 Jia Chen	8	初五 5th day
3	26	甲辰 Jia Chen	5	2	25	甲戌 Jia Xu	2	1	27	乙巳 Yi Si	9	初六 6th day
3	27	乙巳 Yi Si	6	2	26	乙亥 Yi Hai	3	1	28	丙午 Bing Wu	1	初七 7th day
3	28	丙午 Bing Wu	7	2	27	丙子 Bing Zi	4	1	29	丁未 Ding Wei	2	初八 8th day
3	29	丁未 Ding Wei	8	2	28	丁丑 Ding Chou	5	1	30	戊申 Wu Shen	3	初九 9th day
3	30	戊申 Wu Shen	9	2	29	戊寅 Wu Yin	6	1	31	己酉 Ji You	4	初十 10th day
3	31	己酉 Ji You	1	3	1	己卯 Ji Mao	7	2	1	庚戌 Geng Xu	5	十一 11th day
4	1	庚戌 Geng Xu	2	3	2	庚辰 Geng Chen	8	2	2	辛亥 Xin Hai	6	十二 12th day
4	2	辛亥 Xin Hai	3	3	3	辛巳 Xin Si	9	2	3	壬子 Ren Zi	7	十三 13th day
4	3	壬子 Ren Zi	4	3	4	壬午 Ren Wu	1	2	4	癸丑 Gui Chou	8	十四 14th day
4	4	癸丑 Gui Chou	5	3	5	癸未 Gui Wei	2	2	5	甲寅 Jia Yin	9	十五 15th day
4	5	甲寅 Jia Yin	6	3	6	甲申 Jia Shen	3	2	6	乙卯 Yi Mao	1	十六 16th day
4	6	乙卯 Yi Mao	7	3	7	乙酉 Yi You	4	2	7	丙辰 Bing Chen	2	十七 17th day
4	7	丙辰 Bing Chen	8	3	8	丙戌 Bing Xu	5	2	8	丁巳 Ding Si	3	十八 18th day
4	8	丁巳 Ding Si	9	3	9	丁亥 Ding Hai	6	2	9	戊午 Wu Wu	4	十九 19th day
4	9	戊午 Wu Wu	1	3	10	戊子 Wu Zi	7	2	10	己未 Ji Wei	5	二十 20th day
4	10	己未 Ji Wei	2	3	11	己丑 Ji Chou	8	2	11	庚申 Geng Shen	6	二十一 21st day

Monthly transition point marker

It is also important that you know the hours that each Earthly Branch represents in the 24 hours of the day. The Chinese only have 12 hours in a day so each Chinese Hour = 2 Western Hours.

Earthly Branches		Hour
子 *Zi*	**Rat**	11.00 pm - 1.00 am
丑 *Chou*	**Ox**	1.00 am - 3.00 am
寅 *Yin*	**Tiger**	3.00 am - 5.00 am
卯 *Mao*	**Rabbit**	5.00 am - 7.00 am
辰 *Chen*	**Dragon**	7.00 am - 9.00 am
巳 *Si*	**Snake**	9.00 am -11.00 am
午 *Wu*	**Horse**	11.00 am - 1.00 pm
未 *Wei*	**Goat**	1.00 pm - 3.00 pm
申 *Shen*	**Monkey**	3.00 pm - 5.00 pm
酉 *You*	**Rooster**	5.00 pm - 7.00 pm
戌 *Xu*	**Dog**	7.00 pm - 9.00 pm
亥 *Hai*	**Pig**	9.00 pm - 11.00 pm

The Four Pillars

In the Chinese calendar system, every year, month, day and hour has its own specific, dominant elemental energies. How do Chinese Metaphysical practitioners know what are the elemental energies dominant in a particular year, month, day and hour? By looking into the Tong Shu.

In the Tong Shu, the dominant elemental energies for every Year, Month, Day and Hour have been pre-calculated and are presented in the form of one Heavenly Stem, and one Earthly Branch. Together, these form what we call a Jia Zi or a 'pillar' in English terminology.

There are four types of pillars: Year Pillars, Month Pillars, Day Pillars and Hour Pillars. Thus, the information on the elemental energies for any particular point in time is captured and presented in the form of Four Pillars.

時 Hour	日 Day	月 Month	年 Year	
丙 Bing Yang Fire	辛 Xin Yin Metal	乙 Yi Yin Wood	戊 Wu Yang Earth	天干 Heavenly Stems
申 Shen Monkey Yang Metal	巳 Si Snake Yin Fire	丑 Chou Ox Yin Earth	申 Shen Monkey Yang Metal	地支 Earthly Branches
戊 庚 壬	庚 丙 戊	辛 己 癸	戊 庚 壬	藏干 Hidden Stems

That is why BaZi, which is the study of a person's destiny based on the elements prevailing at a person's time of birth, is also known as Four Pillars of Destiny.

實用擇日

In total, there are 60 different Jia Zi and these are used to tell us the elemental energies dominant in any year, month, day and hour. You don't need to memorise all these 60 Jia Zi by heart to use the Date Selection techniques in this book but I have included them here just for completeness and reference.

甲寅 *Jia Yin* Wood Tiger	甲辰 *Jia Chen* Wood Dragon	甲午 *Jia Wu* Wood Horse	甲申 *Jia Shen* Wood Monkey	甲戌 *Jia Xu* Wood Dog	甲子 *Jia Zi* Wood Rat
乙卯 *Yi Mao* Wood Rabbit	乙巳 *Yi Si* Wood Snake	乙未 *Yi Wei* Wood Goat	乙酉 *Yi You* Wood Rooster	乙亥 *Yi Hai* Wood Pig	乙丑 *Yi Chou* Wood Ox
丙辰 *Bing Chen* Fire Dragon	丙午 *Bing Wu* Fire Horse	丙申 *Bing Shen* Fire Monkey	丙戌 *Bing Xu* Fire Dog	丙子 *Bing Zi* Fire Rat	丙寅 *Bing Yin* Fire Tiger
丁巳 *Ding Si* Fire Snake	丁未 *Ding Wei* Fire Goat	丁酉 *Ding You* Fire Rooster	丁亥 *Ding Hai* Fire Pig	丁丑 *Ding Chou* Fire Ox	丁卯 *Ding Mao* Fire Rabbit
戊午 *Wu Wu* Earth Horse	戊申 *Wu Shen* Earth Monkey	戊戌 *Wu Xu* Earth Dog	戊子 *Wu Zi* Earth Rat	戊寅 *Wu Yin* Earth Tiger	戊辰 *Wu Chen* Earth Dragon
己未 *Ji Wei* Earth Goat	己酉 *Ji You* Earth Rooster	己亥 *Ji Hai* Earth Pig	己丑 *Ji Chou* Earth Ox	己卯 *Ji Mao* Earth Rabbit	己巳 *Ji Si* Earth Snake
庚申 *Geng Shen* Metal Monkey	庚戌 *Geng Xu* Metal Dog	庚子 *Geng Zi* Metal Rat	庚寅 *Geng Yin* Metal Tiger	庚辰 *Geng Chen* Metal Dragon	庚午 *Geng Wu* Metal Horse
辛酉 *Xin You* Metal Rooster	辛亥 *Xin Hai* Metal Pig	辛丑 *Xin Chou* Metal Ox	辛卯 *Xin Mao* Metal Rabbit	辛巳 *Xin Si* Metal Snake	辛未 *Xin Wei* Metal Goat
壬戌 *Ren Xu* Water Dog	壬子 *Ren Zi* Water Rat	壬寅 *Ren Yin* Water Tiger	壬辰 *Ren Chen* Water Dragon	壬午 *Ren Wu* Water Horse	壬申 *Ren Shen* Water Monkey
癸亥 *Gui Hai* Water Pig	癸丑 *Gui Chou* Water Ox	癸卯 *Gui Mao* Water Rabbit	癸巳 *Gui Si* Water Snake	癸未 *Gui Wei* Water Goat	癸酉 *Gui You* Water Rooster

Try to commit the names of the Heavenly Stems and Earthly Branches to memory as I will be referring to them throughout the book. You will also need to know which is the Stem and which is the Branch, when you look at a pillar. This is not too hard to figure out.

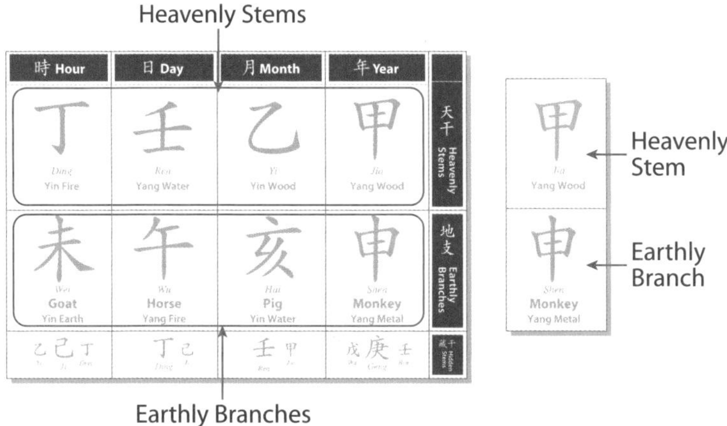

The Heavenly Stem is always on top, as Heaven is above. The Earthly Branch is always at the bottom, as Earth is always below Heaven. Easy, right?

Groupings and Connections in the Metaphysical Universe

Now that you have learnt about the individual Stems and Branches, you need to understand the groupings and relationships that the Stems and Branches have with each other.

Groupings refer to the ways in which the Stems and Branches are grouped together. Relationships refer to the ways in which Stems and Branches are connected or allied with each other, based on the Five Elements cycle.

實用擇日

Branch Groupings

The first grouping you need to know is based on the seasons. Each of the 12 Earthly Branches relates to one of the four seasons: Spring, Summer, Autumn and Winter.

春 Spring		
寅 Yin	卯 Mao	辰 Chen
Tiger	Rabbit	Dragon
Yang Wood	Yin Wood	Yang Earth

夏 Summer		
巳 Si	午 Wu	未 Wei
Snake	Horse	Goat
Yin Fire	Yang Fire	Yin Earth

秋 Autumn		
申 Shen	酉 You	戌 Xu
Monkey	Rooster	Dog
Yang Metal	Yin Metal	Yang Earth

冬 Winter		
亥 Hai	子 Zi	丑 Chou
Pig	Rat	Ox
Yin Water	Yang Water	Yin Earth

The 12 Earthly Branches can also be grouped according to the type of Branch they are, namely, Cardinals 四正, Graveyards 四墓 or Growth Stars 四生.

The Cardinals are the Branches that contain pure Qi. The Cardinals are as follows:

The Graveyards are Earthly Branches that contain Earth within what are known as the Hidden Stems. There are Four Graveyards:

Finally, we have the Growth Stars, also known as the Stables. They are as follows:

The most important grouping you must be aware of is the seasonal grouping so try to commit to memory which Earthly Branches are part of which season.

實用擇日

Branch Relationships

The first relationship between the Earthly Branches you will need to know is the Combination relationship. Combinations are based on which animals have an alliance with each other. There are two types of Combinations you need to be aware of: Six Combinations 六合 (Liu He) and Three Harmony Combinations 三合 (San He).

The Six Combination tells us which Earthly Branches combine with each other.

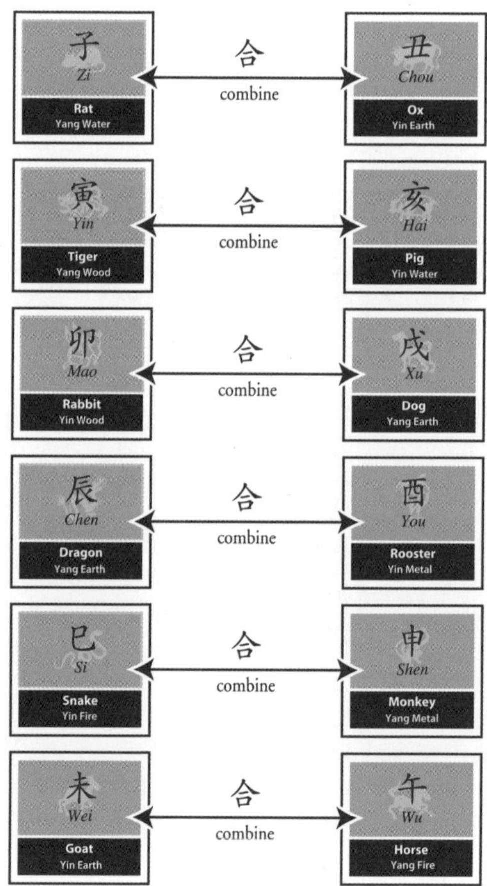

實用擇日

The Three Harmony Combination tells us which Earthly Branches combine based on elemental connections, and a triangulating formation on the Luo Pan.

Here are the Three Harmony Combinations.

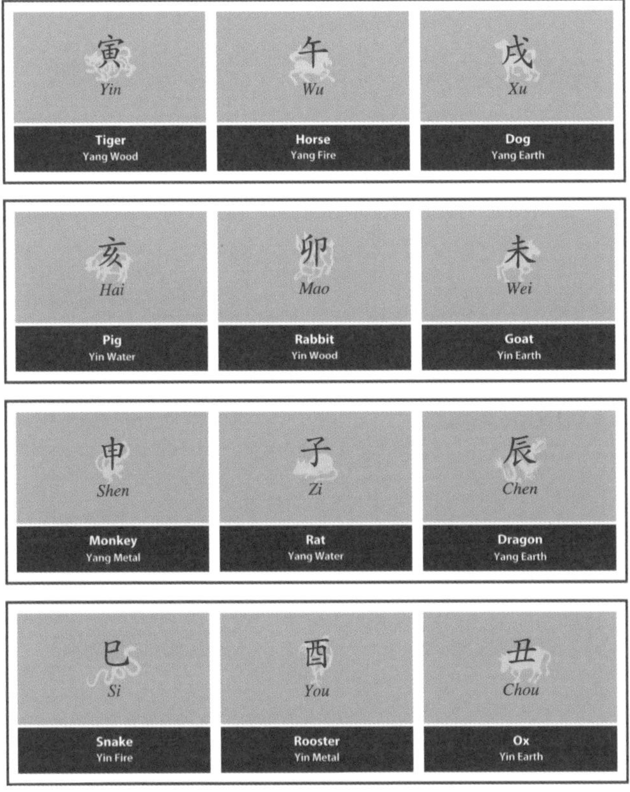

Try to commit these two groups of Combinations to memory if you can. If not, dog-ear this section of the book, for reference as you read through the rest of the chapters.

Now, Branches not only have alliance relationships, but they also are enemies, if you like, with certain branches. Certain Branches have an affinity with other Branches, and at the same time, they have negative vibes with some Branches. So if Combinations represent allies, then Clashes tell us about archenemies. How do you know which Branch clashes with which Branch? Look at the Six Clashes 六冲 (Liu Chong) table below:

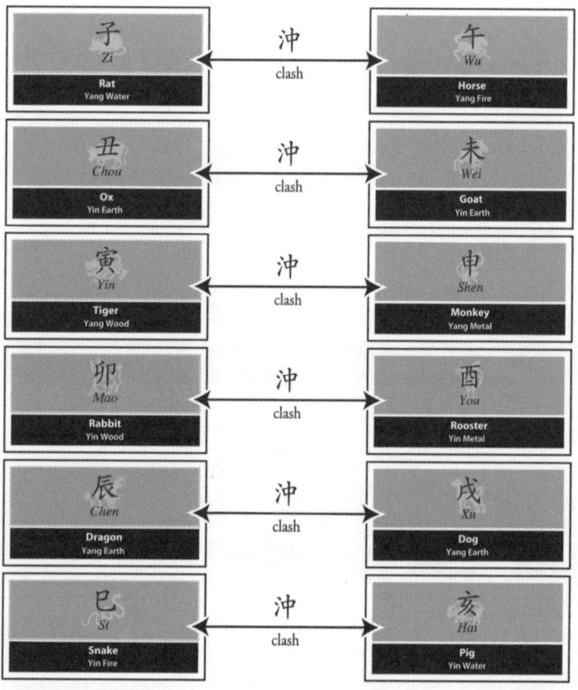

So, at any one time, an Earthly Branch has an alliance or Combination with a certain Earthly Branch, and is enemies or has a Clash with another Earthly Branch. For example, Dragon Combines with Rooster, but Clashes with Dog.

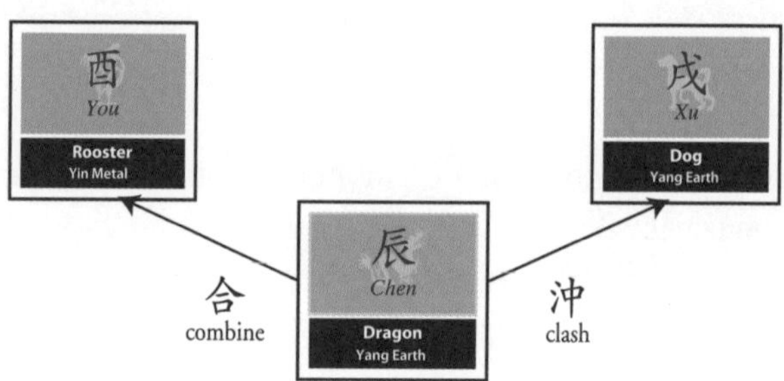

I must point out that although I have used the term 'alliance' and 'enemy', you should not impose any bias or prejudice on a Combination or Clash relationship. Never judge an elemental relationship as good or bad, favourable or unfavourable. Just take it as it is: a Clash or a Combination.

As you are not familiar with all these ideas, just focus at this point on knowing what Branch Clashes and Combines with your personal Year Pillar. In case you have forgotten, the Year Pillar is the Pillar on the far right of your personal BaZi chart.

Year Pillar

時 Hour	日 Day	月 Month	年 Year	
辛 Xin Yin Metal	壬 Ren Yang Water	丙 Bing Yang Fire	乙 Yi Yin Wood	天干 Heavenly Stems
亥 Hai Pig Yin Water	戌 Xu Dog Yang Earth	戌 Xu Dog Yang Earth	未 Wei Goat Yin Earth	地支 Earthly Branches
壬 甲	丁 戊 辛	丁 戊 辛	乙 己 丁	藏干 Hidden Stems

As you have a better grasp of the Combinations and Clashes, then you can look at other people's BaZi and do Date Selection for them. But for now, focus on your personal BaZi first.

You might be wondering why I've only asked you to look at your Year Pillar and focus on the Clash and Combination that involves your Year Pillar. What about the other Pillars?

In Date Selection, the Year Pillar is the most important reference point. This is because Qi moves from the right side of the BaZi chart, towards the left. So the Year Pillar in your personal BaZi is the pillar that forms your first line of defence against any adverse energies from the year. That is why the focus in Date Selection is the Year Pillar.

Stem Relationships

The Heavenly Stems also have relationships with each other - however, as this is a basic Date Selection book, you don't need to be too concerned with factoring in the relationships between the Stems. However, I have included them here, for your reference.

Each of the 10 Heavenly Stems has a Combination relationship with another Heavenly Stem. The Combination relationships are as follows:

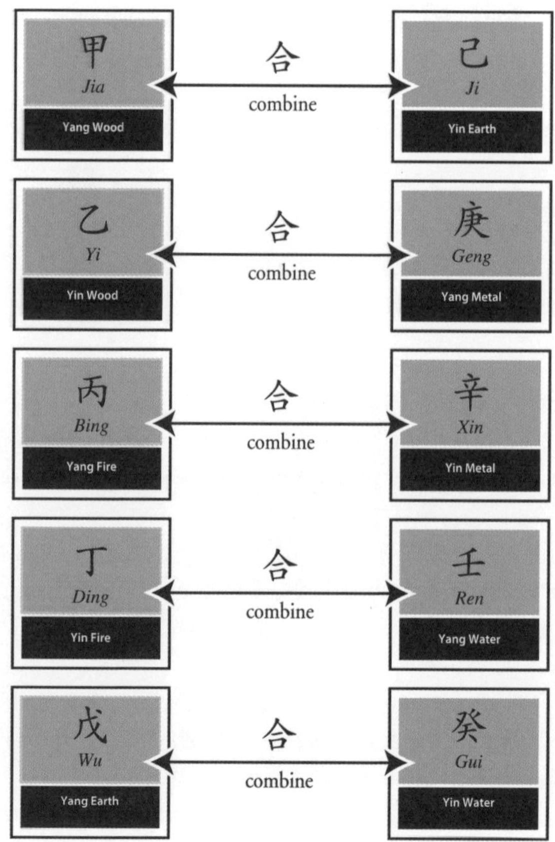

Some stems also have a Clash relationship with other stems. The Clash relationships are as follows:

Date Selection Basics

Okay, now that you have all the basic 'alphabet' and 'language' skills, you're ready to learn some techniques. Let me quickly recap what you need on hand to commence a Date Selection.

You'll need your personal BaZi chart on hand, and you need to know what is your Day Master and also, what Earthly Branches Clash and Combine with your Year Pillar.

Here's an example for you:

This person's personal Day Master is Ren 壬 Water. His year of birth is the Goat 未 (Wei), so his Year Pillar clashes with the Ox 丑 (Chou) and combines with the Horse 午 (Wu).

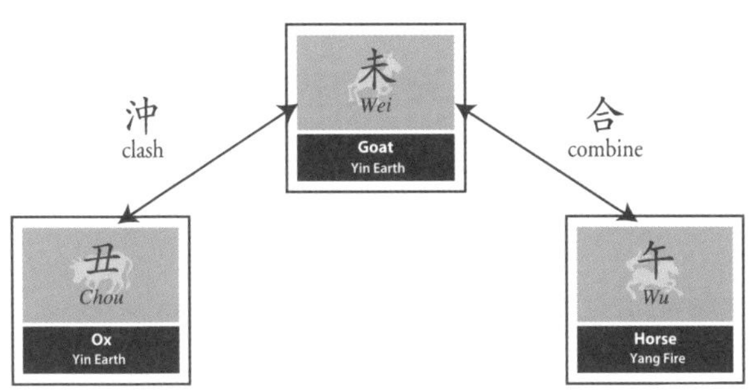

You'll need a Chinese Solar Calendar on hand to help you determine the elements in play on any particular day. I would also urge you to have some red pens or highlighters on hand, so you can mark out the negative dates and the usable dates.

Now, it's time to find some dates!

To make it easy for you to remember the basic BaZi information you will need on hand, I have included this worksheet. Make a photocopy and then fill in the basic BaZi information (your own or that of the person you are selecting a date for) into the spaces provided.

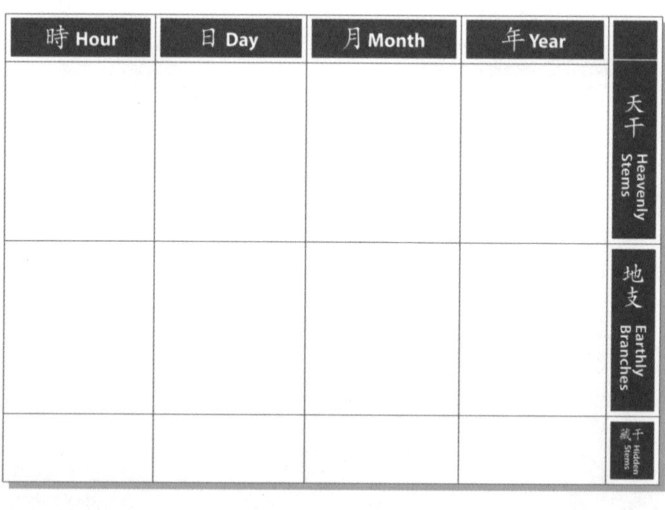

時 Hour	日 Day	月 Month	年 Year	
				天干 Heavenly Stems
				地支 Earthly Branches
				藏干 Hidden Stems

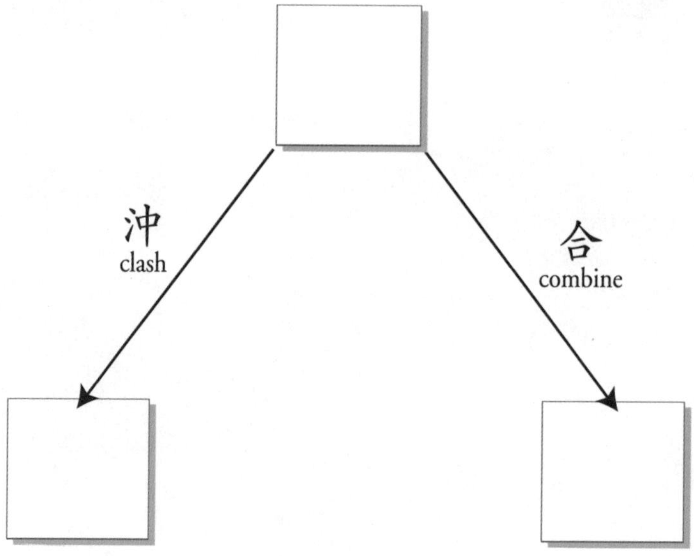

Chapter Three:
How to avoid the Bad Dates

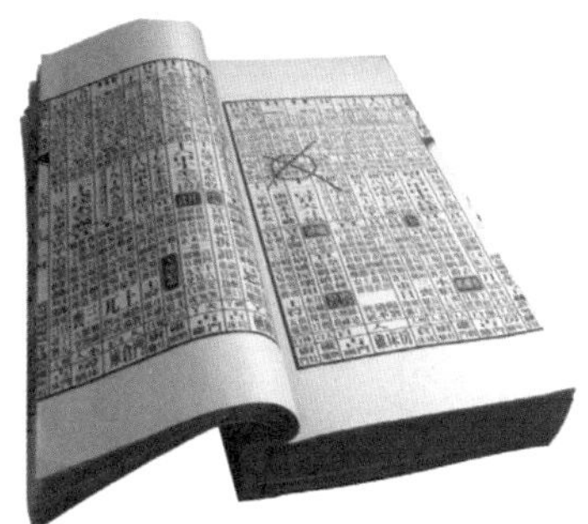

You might be wondering - why are we learning about the bad dates first? The Art of Date Selection is as much about the ability to select good dates as it is about the ability to avoid bad dates. The rationale behind this is that if you are uncertain whether or not a date is good, at least you should be certain if it is bad. Remember, commencing an activity on an average date is always better than commencing an activity on a bad date.

There are two types of bad dates that you should aim to avoid: General bad dates and Personal bad dates.

General bad dates are dates that are overall not suitable to undertake important personal or business activities. These are dates that would not augur well for everyone.

Personal bad dates by contrast are the dates that are not suited to you specifically. Your personal bad dates will not be the same as another person, whereas a general bad date is just bad for everybody.

Personal Date Selection was written as a beginner's book and designed for easy use. Therefore my aim will be to show you how to avoid a majority of the general bad dates and then show you some simple techniques to avoid personal bad dates. However, there are, as with all things, levels and depths to the techniques.

Those of you with some knowledge of BaZi, for example, will be able to apply a higher level of personalisation to your Date Selection efforts, compared to those who have little or no knowledge of BaZi. You will be able to apply your knowledge on the Ten Gods 十神 (Shi Shen) and favourable and unfavourable elements to your Date Selection efforts.

But as I said at the start, when it comes to Date Selection, being able to avoid bad dates is of overriding importance. So don't be too worried if you can't personalise your Date Selection efforts to a high level or add in the BaZi components. Your primary objective and focus should be to avoid bad dates and that's exactly what I'll be showing you how to do in this chapter.

General Bad Dates to Avoid

A. Year Breaker Days 歲破日

In every year, there is a governing Grand Duke 太歲 (Tai Sui) - the controlling or governing energy force of the year. The Grand Duke is recognisable via a star called Sui Xing 歲星 or Tai Sui (sometimes called Grand Duke Jupiter). But this is not actually a reference to the real astrological position of Jupiter, although it is related. Rather, it is a body of Qi. Frequently, many Chinese texts use the word 'Shen' which translates verbatim into God/Spirit. This often has a confusing effect. Lay people mistake it as a reference to a deity or god or spiritual figure. In fact, when the texts refer to Shen, it is a reference to a body of Qi.

Opposite the Tai Sui or Grand Duke of the year is what is known as the Year Breaker 歲破 (Sui Po). This is the star that opposes the governing star of the year. The energies are not complimentary but oppositional. Now, being the opposing star is a bit like being an opposition party - it is all about going against the prevailing order. There is a lot of tension, the situation is difficult and everyone feels uneasy. In short, it is an antagonistic rather than smooth situation.

The Year Breaker Day is a day that goes against the energies of the year and it is the first kind of general bad day that we want to avoid.

It is generally not beneficial to engage in important activities on a Year Breaker Day because this indicates you are commencing your activity or venture in opposition with the year.

If you have no choice but to start something on a Year Breaker Day, it is not the end of the world but you should expect some challenges, and niggling but minor problems for the project or event. That is why generally, it is okay for short-term activities to commence on a Year Breaker Day, but not long-term activities.

How do you know what are short-term and long-term activities? A renovation project to your kitchen is short term. Marriage is long term.

And why is it okay for short-term projects or activities but not long-term activities?

So, let's say you start a renovation project on a Year Breaker Day. Yes, you will have problems, mistakes will be made and things will have to keep being redone. For example, if you start a renovation on this date, expect workers to turn up late, the wrong sized doors to turn up and electrical wires or plumbing are punctured or cut by mistake. But as the activity is of a short-term nature, it will eventually come to an end - no matter how incompetent your workers are, eventually they will get there.

However should you engage in a long-term event, such as getting married on a Year Breaker Day, it means your marriage will be plagued by annoying problems and lingering issues throughout its lifespan. You can expect such 'joys' like a nosy mother-in-law or a spouse who doesn't live up to your expectations. It will not destroy the marriage but it will be tiresome for the entire duration of your life or your marriage.

Of course, there are always exceptions to the rule. Certain Year Breaker Days may have mitigating stars that reduce or eliminate the problems caused by the Year Breaker Days. Alternatively, a good hour can also be used to mitigate the effects of the Year Breaker Day. However, generally I would suggest you adhere to the basic rule and avoid Year Breaker Days where possible. Only use the Year Breaker Days if absolutely necessary or if a Date Selection specialist has indicated the date is usable.

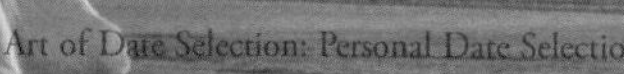

實用擇日

Finding the Year Breaker

Step 1: Ascertain the animal sign of the year

To do this, refer to the Ten Thousand Year Calendar. The animal sign of the year can be found in the Year Pillar, which can be found on the right side of the page.

三月大 3rd Mth Big				二月小 2nd Mth Small				正月小 1st Mth Small				月別 Month
甲辰 Jia Chen				癸卯 Gui Mao				壬寅 Ren Yin				干支 Branches and Stems
九紫 Nine Purple				一白 One White				二黑 Two Black				九星 Nine Star
立夏 Coming of Summer		穀雨 Grain Rain		清明 Clear and Bright		春分 Spring Equinox		驚蟄 Awakening of Worms		雨水 Rain Water		節氣 Season
二十 20th day		初四 4th day		十八 18th day		初三 3rd day		十七 17th day		初二 2nd day		
5時 21 分 5hr 21min		19時 8 分 19hr 8min		12時 6 分 12hr 6min		8時 9 分 8hr 9min		7時 19 分 7hr 19min		9時 11 分 9hr 11min		朔 Constellation
卯 Mao		戌 Xu		午 Wu		辰 Chen		辰 Chen		巳 Si		
國曆 Gregorian		干支 Branches and stems	星 Star	國曆 Gregorian		干支 Branches and stems	星 Star	國曆 Gregorian		干支 Branches and stems	星 Star	農曆 Lunar Calendar
4	17	辛巳 Xin Si	6	3	19	壬子 Ren Zi	4	2	18	癸未 Gui Wei	2	初一 1st day
4	18	壬午 Ren Wu	7	3	20	癸丑 Gui Chou	5	2	19	甲申 Jia Shen	3	初二 2nd day
4	19	癸未 Gui Wei	8	3	21	甲寅 Jia Yin	6	2	20	乙酉 Yi You	4	初三 3rd day
4	20	甲申 Jia Shen	9	3	22	乙卯 Yi Mao	7	2	21	丙戌 Bing Xu	5	初四 4th day
4	21	乙酉 Yi You	1	3	23	丙辰 Bing Chen	8	2	22	丁亥 Ding Hai	6	初五 5th day
4	22	丙戌 Bing Xu	2	3	24	丁巳 Ding Si	9	2	23	戊子 Wu Zi	7	初六 6th day
4	23	丁亥 Ding Hai	3	3	25	戊午 Wu Wu	1	2	24	己丑 Ji Chou	8	初七 7th day
4	24	戊子 Wu Zi	4	3	26	己未 Ji Wei	2	2	25	庚寅 Geng Yin	9	初八 8th day
4	25	己丑 Ji Chou	5	3	27	庚申 Geng Shen	3	2	26	辛卯 Xin Mao	1	初九 9th day
4	26	庚寅 Geng Yin	6	3	28	辛酉 Xin You	4	2	27	壬辰 Ren Chen	2	初十 10th day
4	27	辛卯 Xin Mao	7	3	29	壬戌 Ren Xu	5	2	28	癸巳 Gui Si	3	十一 11th day
4	28	壬辰 Ren Chen	8	3	30	癸亥 Gui Hai	6	3	1	甲午 Jia Wu	4	十二 12th day
4	29	癸巳 Gui Si	9	3	31	甲子 Jia Zi	7	3	2	乙未 Yi Wei	5	十三 13th day
4	30	甲午 Jia Wu	1	4	1	乙丑 Yi Chou	8	3	3	丙申 Bing Shen	6	十四 14th day
5	1	乙未 Yi Wei	2	4	2	丙寅 Bing Yin	9	3	4	丁酉 Ding You	7	十五 15th day
5	2	丙申 Bing Shen	3	4	3	丁卯 Ding Mao	1	3	5	戊戌 Wu Xu	8	十六 16th day
5	3	丁酉 Ding You	4	4	4	戊辰 Wu Chen	2	3	6	己亥 Ji Hai	9	十七 17th day
5	4	戊戌 Wu Xu	5	4	5	己巳 Ji Si	3	3	7	庚子 Geng Zi	1	十八 18th day
5	5	己亥 Ji Hai	6	4	6	庚午 Geng Wu	4	3	8	辛丑 Xin Chou	2	十九 19th day
5	6	庚子 Geng Zi	7	4	7	辛未 Xin Wei	5	3	9	壬寅 Ren Yin	3	二十 20th day
5	7	辛丑 Xin Chou	8	4	8	壬申 Ren Shen	6	3	10	癸卯 Gui Mao	4	二十一 21st day
5	8	壬寅 Ren Yin	9	4	9	癸酉 Gui You	7	3	11	甲辰 Jia Chen	5	二十二 22nd day
5	9	癸卯 Gui Mao	1	4	10	甲戌 Jia Xu	8	3	12	乙巳 Yi Si	6	二十三 23rd day
5	10	甲辰 Jia Chen	2	4	11	乙亥 Yi Hai	9	3	13	丙午 Bing Wu	7	二十四 24th day
5	11	乙巳 Yi Si	3	4	12	丙子 Bing Zi	1	3	14	丁未 Ding Wei	8	二十五 25th day
5	12	丙午 Bing Wu	4	4	13	丁丑 Ding Chou	2	3	15	戊申 Wu Shen	9	二十六 26th day
5	13	丁未 Ding Wei	5	4	14	戊寅 Wu Yin	3	3	16	己酉 Ji You	1	二十七 27th day
5	14	戊申 Wu Shen	6	4	15	己卯 Ji Mao	4	3	17	庚戌 Geng Xu	2	二十八 28th day
5	15	己酉 Ji You	7	4	16	庚辰 Geng Chen	5	3	18	辛亥 Xin Hai	3	二十九 29th day
5	16	庚戌 Geng Xu	8									三十 30th day

2007 丁亥 Ding Hai

Year Pillar

Fire Pig

Grand Duke 封齊

實用擇日

Alternatively, you can refer to the table below for the various years and their respective animal signs.

Animal signs for 2006 - 2053

Animal	Year of Birth	Year of Birth	Year of Birth	Year of Birth
Dog	2006 Fire Dog 丙戌 *Bing Xu*	2018 Earth Dog 戊戌 *Wu Xu*	2030 Metal Dog 庚戌 *Geng Xu*	2042 Water Dog 壬戌 *Ren Xu*
Pig	2007 Fire Pig 丁亥 *Ding Hai*	2019 Earth Pig 己亥 *Ji Hai*	2031 Metal Pig 辛亥 *Xin Hai*	2043 Water Pig 癸亥 *Gui Hai*
Rat	2008 Earth Rat 戊子 *Wu Zi*	2020 Metal Rat 庚子 *Geng Zi*	2032 Water Rat 壬子 *Ren Zi*	2044 Wood Rat 甲子 *Jia Zi*
Ox	2009 Earth Ox 己丑 *Ji Chou*	2021 Metal Ox 辛丑 *Xin Chou*	2033 Water Ox 癸丑 *Gui Chou*	2045 Wood Ox 乙丑 *Yi Chou*
Tiger	2010 Metal Tiger 庚寅 *Geng Yin*	2022 Water Tiger 壬寅 *Ren Yin*	2034 Wood Tiger 甲寅 *Jia Yin*	2046 Fire Tiger 丙寅 *Bing Yin*
Rabbit	2011 Metal Rabbit 辛卯 *Xin Mao*	2023 Water Rabbit 癸卯 *Gui Mao*	2035 Wood Rabbit 乙卯 *Yi Mao*	2047 Fire Rabbit 丁卯 *Ding Mao*
Dragon	2012 Water Dragon 壬辰 *Ren Chen*	2024 Wood Dragon 甲辰 *Jia Chen*	2036 Fire Dragon 丙辰 *Bing Chen*	2048 Earth Dragon 戊辰 *Wu Chen*
Snake	2013 Water Snake 癸巳 *Gui Si*	2025 Wood Snake 乙巳 *Yi Si*	2037 Fire Snake 丁巳 *Ding Si*	2049 Earth Snake 己巳 *Ji Si*
Horse	2014 Wood Horse 甲午 *Jia Wu*	2026 Fire Horse 丙午 *Bing Wu*	2038 Earth Horse 戊午 *Wu Wu*	2050 Metal Horse 庚午 *Geng Wu*
Goat	2015 Wood Goat 乙未 *Yi Wei*	2027 Fire Goat 丁未 *Ding Wei*	2039 Earth Goat 己未 *Ji Wei*	2051 Metal Goat 辛未 *Xin Wei*
Monkey	2016 Fire Monkey 丙申 *Bing Shen*	2028 Earth Monkey 戊申 *Wu Shen*	2040 Metal Monkey 庚申 *Geng Shen*	2052 Water Monkey 壬申 *Ren Shen*
Rooster	2017 Fire Rooster 丁酉 *Ding You*	2029 Earth Rooster 己酉 *Ji You*	2041 Metal Rooster 辛酉 *Xin You*	2053 Water Rooster 癸酉 *Gui You*

• *Please note that the date for the Chinese Solar Year starts on Feb 4. This means that if you were born on Feb 2 of 2002, you belong to the previous year 2001.*

2007 is the year of the Pig 亥 (Hai). 2008 is the year of the Rat 子 (Zi).

Step 2: Determine which animal clashes with the animal sign of the year

If you have not committed the Six Clashes to memory, check the table below. Find the animal sign of the year, and then check which animal Clashes with that animal sign.

For example, 2007 is the year of the Pig 亥 (Hai). The Pig clashes with the Snake 巳 (Si). So the Snake is the Year Breaker in 2007. All Snake Days in 2007 are Year Breaker Days and should not be used for important personal and business activities if possible.

2008 is the year of the Rat 子 (Zi). The Rat clashes with the Horse 午 (Wu). Accordingly, all Horse Days are Year Breaker Days in the year of the Rat.

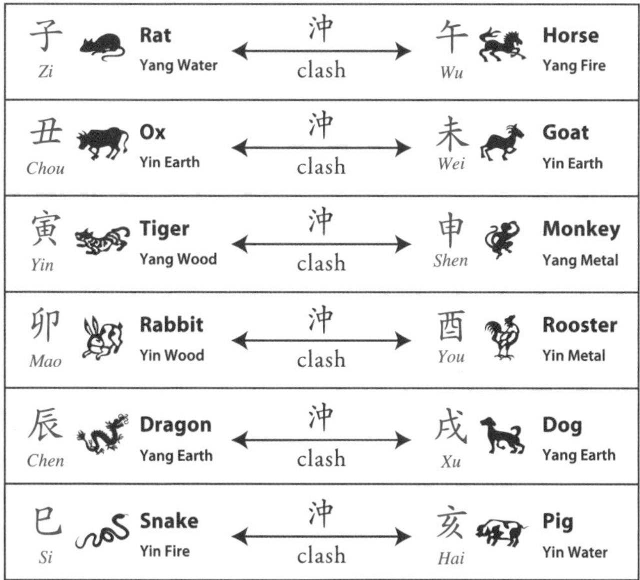

子 *Zi*	**Rat** Yang Water	沖 ←→ clash	午 *Wu*	**Horse** Yang Fire
丑 *Chou*	**Ox** Yin Earth	沖 ←→ clash	未 *Wei*	**Goat** Yin Earth
寅 *Yin*	**Tiger** Yang Wood	沖 ←→ clash	申 *Shen*	**Monkey** Yang Metal
卯 *Mao*	**Rabbit** Yin Wood	沖 ←→ clash	酉 *You*	**Rooster** Yin Metal
辰 *Chen*	**Dragon** Yang Earth	沖 ←→ clash	戌 *Xu*	**Dog** Yang Earth
巳 *Si*	**Snake** Yin Fire	沖 ←→ clash	亥 *Hai*	**Pig** Yin Water

Now, cross out all Year Breaker Days from your personal calendar.

As you go through this book, I suggest that you cross out all the negative days in your calendar. This will make it a lot easier for you to avoid picking a bad day to commence an important activity and make the process of selecting a good date a lot easier.

For example, 2007 is the year of the Pig 亥 (Hai). All Snake 巳 (Si) Days are Year Breaker Days. So cross out all Snake Days in 2007. I've done 3 months of examples for you here, using the Tong Shu Desktop Calendar.

AUGUST 2007 戊申

SUNDAY	MONDAY	TUESDAY	WEDNESDAY	THURSDAY	FRIDAY	SATURDAY
			丁卯 1 十九	戊辰 2 二十	己巳 歲破日 Year Breaker Day 3 廿一	庚午 4 廿二
辛未 5 廿三	壬申 6 廿四	癸酉 7 廿五	甲戌 8 廿六	乙亥 9 廿七	丙子 10 廿八	丁丑 11 廿九
戊寅 12 三十	己卯 13 七月初一	庚辰 14 初二	辛巳 歲破日 Year Breaker Day 15 初三	壬午 16 初四	癸未 17 初五	甲申 18 初六
乙酉 19 初七	丙戌 20 初八	丁亥 21 初九	戊子 22 初十	己丑 23 十一	庚寅 24 十二	辛卯 25 十三
壬辰 26 十四	癸巳 歲破日 Year Breaker Day 27 十五	甲午 28 十六	乙未 29 十七	丙申 30 十八	丁酉 31 十九	

SEPTEMBER 2007 己酉

SUNDAY	MONDAY	TUESDAY	WEDNESDAY	THURSDAY	FRIDAY	SATURDAY
						戊戌 1 二十
己亥 2 廿一	庚子 3 廿二	辛丑 4 廿三	壬寅 5 廿四	癸卯 6 廿五	甲辰 7 廿六	乙巳 歲破日 Year Breaker Day 8 廿七
丙午 9 廿八	丁未 10 廿九	戊申 11 八月初一	己酉 12 初二	庚戌 13 初三	辛亥 14 初四	壬子 15 初五
癸丑 16 初六	甲寅 17 初七	乙卯 18 初八	丙辰 19 初九	丁巳 歲破日 Year Breaker Day 20 初十	戊午 21 十一	己未 22 十二
庚申 23 十三	辛酉 24 十四	壬戌 25 十五	癸亥 26 十六	甲子 27 十七	乙丑 28 十八	丙寅 29 十九
丁卯 30 二十						

OCTOBER 2007 庚戌

SUNDAY	MONDAY	TUESDAY	WEDNESDAY	THURSDAY	FRIDAY	SATURDAY
	戊辰 1 廿一	己巳 歲破日 Year Breaker Day 2 廿二	庚午 3 廿三	辛未 4 廿四	壬申 5 廿五	癸酉 6 廿六
甲戌 7 廿七	乙亥 8 廿八	丙子 9 廿九	丁丑 10 三十	戊寅 11 九月初一	己卯 12 初二	庚辰 13 初三
辛巳 歲破日 Year Breaker Day 14 初四	壬午 15 初五	癸未 16 初六	甲申 17 初七	乙酉 18 初八	丙戌 19 初九	丁亥 20 初十
戊子 21 十一	己丑 22 十二	庚寅 23 十三	辛卯 24 十四	壬辰 25 十五	癸巳 歲破日 Year Breaker Day 26 十六	甲午 27 十七
乙未 28 十八	丙申 29 十九	丁酉 30 二十	戊戌 31 廿一			

B. Month Breaker Day 月破日

In addition to the Year Breaker Day, there is a Month Breaker Day 月破 (Yue Po). This is the day where the energies of the day are in conflict or in opposition with the energies of the month. The Month Breaker Day has amplified effects and is therefore considered a more dangerous day to use than a Year Breaker Day.

Month Breaker Days contain the star that goes against the energies of the Month and accordingly are very unsuitable days to embark on anything important or significant. The energies of the Month Breaker are considered more malevolent and negative than those of the Year Breaker.

Why is a Month Breaker Day more powerful than a Year Breaker Day?

The answer is proximity. The month Qi is closer to the day, than the year is to the day. A simple analogy to illustrate this concept is to look at the governor of the state versus the prime minister of the country. A person would be more fearful of the governor of the state because the governor can take immediate action against them, compared to the prime minister of the country who is far away in the capital.

It is for this reason that the Month Breaker is considered more dangerous than the Year Breaker. The month's energies are the dominant energies during the month and will have a more significant impact on the day. The year's energies, while having a generic effect, are more distant from the day compared to the month's energies. Obviously the influence of the month's energies impacts more significantly on the day than the year's energies. Accordingly, it is extremely important to avoid using Month Breaker Days for any important personal or business activities.

What kinds of outcomes are likely to beset activities that take place on a Month Breaker Day? If you get married on a Month Breaker Day, generally the marriage is difficult and complicated and if the relationship runs into problems, it is very easy for the marriage to unravel. In short, a vow that is made on this day is more likely to be an easily broken vow.

If you sign an important business contract or any kind of contract involving obligations on a Month Breaker Day, then the parties are likely to break their obligations. The contract is more likely to be already breached or broken at the point of signing. Official openings of businesses that take place on Month Breaker Days may also find the business goes downhill faster and if a partnership is involved, the partnership may break up soon after the official opening.

If you move into a house on a Month Breaker Day, you may expect issues with the landlord, or if you own the property, you may not stay long in the property since the bond you have with the house is not strong.

Month Breaker Days do have a use according to some of the old texts - for example, these days can be used to break down old things or tear down an old house. Some Date Selection specialists also favour the use of Month Breaker Days for medical procedures such as cutting out a tumour or removing cataracts.

Personally, I do not favour using Month Breaker Days this way. Health matters frequently involve complications and you certainly don't want complications on a Month Breaker Day! Only under very specific circumstances and subject to very stringent conditions would I consider the use of Month Breaker Days. And even then, it would only be when there are a significant number of positive stars on the day and a highly favourable and usable hour available to use.

This is because certain positive stars on the day can dissolve the energies of the Month Breaker, as can a good hour. But this involves a lot of skill and calculations and is not generally advisable for laypersons doing DIY Date Selection.

Hence, for beginners to Date Selection, it is not a good idea to use a Month Breaker Day for any important personal or business activities, even if it is a negative activity. Err on the side of caution and give the Month Breaker Days a miss.

Finding the Month Breaker Day

As the reference point of the Month Breaker Day is the month itself, the Month Breaker Day is dynamic and changes with each month. By contrast, the Year Breaker Day does not change for all 12 months of the year because the animal sign or Earthly Branch of the year does not change.

Step 1: Identify the Month Branch

Look at the table on the next page. It tells you which Earthly Branch represents which month in the Gregorian calendar. For example, if it is February, then the Month Branch is Tiger 寅 (Yin). If it is May, then the Month Branch is Snake 巳 (Si).

Remember to take into consideration the transit dates of the months. The Chinese Solar Calendar's monthly transition is not the same as that of the Western Gregorian calendar.

It is best to check the Ten Thousand Year Calendar for the actual transition dates. The table below should only be used as a general guide - always check the Ten Thousand Year calendar for the actual transit date of each month.

Branch	Animal	Date
寅 Yin	**Tiger**	February 4th
卯 Mao	**Rabbit**	March 6th
辰 Chen	**Dragon**	April 5th
巳 Si	**Snake**	May 6th
午 Wu	**Horse**	June 6th
未 Wei	**Goat**	July 7th
申 Shen	**Monkey**	August 8th
酉 You	**Rooster**	September 8th
戌 Xu	**Dog**	October 8th
亥 Hai	**Pig**	November 7th
子 Zi	**Rat**	December 7th
丑 Chou	**Ox**	January 6th

Step 2: Identify the Earthly Branch that clashes with the Month Branch

For example, let's say you are trying to find the Month Breaker for February, which is the Tiger 寅 (Yin) Month. Now, the Tiger clashes with the Monkey. Accordingly, during the entire Tiger Month, you cannot use any Monkey 申 (Shen) Days as these are the Month Breaker Days. Remember, the Tiger Month runs from February 4 to March 5 so when I say the 'entire' Tiger Month, I mean all the dates between these two dates.

Let's try another example. Let's say, you are trying to find the Month Breaker for May, which is the Snake 巳 (Si) Month. The Snake clashes with the Pig. Therefore in May, all Pig 亥 (Hai) Days are Month Breaker Days and should not be used for important activities.

Again, as you did with Year Breaker Days, cross out all the Month Breaker Days for the year on your calendar. I've done 3 months of examples for you here.

If you look at the ensuing examples, I've selected the months of February, March and April of 2007 to illustrate my point. In February, the Tiger Month is from Feb 4 – March 5. In March, the Rabbit 卯 (Mao) Month is from March 6 – April 4. In April, the Dragon 辰 (Chen) Month begins from April 5 and ends on May 5.

So for the Tiger Month, we will circle all the Monkey Days as the Month Breaker Days. In the Rabbit Month, we will circle all Rooster 酉 (You) Days as Month Breaker Days. And in the Dragon Month, we will circle all Dog 戌 (Xu) Days as Month Breaker Days. In addition, I've also marked out the Year Breaker Days for you!

FEBRUARY 2007 壬寅

SUNDAY	MONDAY	TUESDAY	WEDNESDAY	THURSDAY	FRIDAY	SATURDAY
				丙寅 1 十四	丁卯 2 十五	戊辰 歲破日 Year Breaker Day 3 十六
己巳 歲破日 Year Breaker Day 4 十七	庚午 5 十八	辛未 6 十九	壬申 月破日 Month Breaker Day 7 二十	癸酉 8 廿一	甲戌 9 廿二	乙亥 10 廿三
丙子 11 廿四	丁丑 12 廿五	戊寅 13 廿六	己卯 14 廿七	庚辰 15 廿八	辛巳 歲破日 Year Breaker Day 16 廿九	壬午 17 三十
癸未 歲破日 月破日 Year & Month Breaker Day 18 正月初一	甲申 月破日 Month Breaker Day 19 初二	乙酉 20 初三	丙戌 21 初四	丁亥 22 初五	戊子 23 初六	己丑 24 初七
庚寅 25 初八	辛卯 26 初九	壬辰 27 初十	癸巳 歲破日 Year Breaker Day 28 十一			

MARCH 2007 癸卯

SUNDAY	MONDAY	TUESDAY	WEDNESDAY	THURSDAY	FRIDAY	SATURDAY
				甲午 1 十二	乙未 2 十三	丙申 月破日 Month Breaker Day 3 十四
丁酉 4 十五	戊戌 5 十六	己亥 6 十七	庚子 7 十八	辛丑 8 十九	壬寅 9 二十	癸卯 10 廿一
甲辰 11 廿二	乙巳 歲破日 Year Breaker Day 12 廿三	丙午 13 廿四	丁未 14 廿五	戊申 15 廿六	己酉 月破日 Month Breaker Day 16 廿七	庚戌 17 廿八
辛亥 18 廿九	壬子 19 二月初一	癸丑 20 初二	甲寅 21 初三	乙卯 22 初四	丙辰 23 初五	丁巳 歲破日 Year Breaker Day 24 初六
戊午 25 初七	己未 26 初八	庚申 27 初九	辛酉 月破日 Month Breaker Day 28 初十	壬戌 29 十一	癸亥 30 十二	甲子 31 十三

APRIL 2007 甲辰

SUNDAY	MONDAY	TUESDAY	WEDNESDAY	THURSDAY	FRIDAY	SATURDAY
乙丑 1 十四	丙寅 2 十五	丁卯 3 十六	戊辰 4 十七	己巳 歲破日 Year Breaker Day 5 十	庚午 6 十九	辛未 7 二十
壬申 8 廿一	癸酉 9 廿二	甲戌 月破日 Month Breaker Day 10 廿三	乙亥 11 廿四	丙子 12 廿五	丁丑 13 廿六	戊寅 14 廿七
己卯 15 廿八	庚辰 16 廿九	辛巳 歲破日 Year Breaker Day 17 三月初	壬午 18 初二	癸未 19 初三	甲申 20 初四	乙酉 21 初五
丙戌 月破日 Month Breaker Day 22 初六	丁亥 23 初七	戊子 24 初八	己丑 25 初九	庚寅 26 初十	辛卯 27 十一	壬辰 28 十二
癸巳 歲破日 Year Breaker Day 29 十三	甲午 30 十四					

C. Day Breaker 日破

The Day Breaker 日破 (Ri Po) is the term used for the hour that clashes with the day. During this particular hour, the Qi is lost and it is the most inauspicious hour of the day. As a general rule of Date Selection, we do not like to use an hour that clashes with the day as this may end up negating any positive energies of the day, especially if it is an auspicious day.

There are some Date Selection specialist that take the view that a negative day can be neutralised by using the most negative hour of the day for an activity. This is flawed reasoning since it takes the viewpoint that two negatives can somehow make a positive. That may work in science but not with metaphysics I'm afraid. Using a negative hour on a negative day is without a doubt, not going to be a good start to any activity. Worse yet, you may find out you end up with a double whammy - twice the problems may beset your activity or endeavour.

The other reason why this approach is incorrect is derived from the understanding of Clashes and Combinations. Removing an element requires a Combination, not a Clash. Accordingly, a negative or inauspicious day can only be neutralised by a Combination, not a Clash.

Finding the Day Breaker

Step 1: Find out the Earthly Branch of the day in question.

To find out the Earthly Branch of the day in question, you can either use the Ten Thousand Year Calendar, a Tong Shu Desktop calendar or a simple calendaring program like Microsoft Outlook. I have shown you here how to find the Earthly Branch of the day in all three.

Let's say we wish to find out the Day Breaker for March 21 2007. Look at that date in the Ten Thousand Year Calendar, or the Tong Shu Desktop Calendar or Microsoft Outlook. The Earthly Branch of the Day Pillar is circled for you.

MARCH 2007 癸卯

SUNDAY	MONDAY	TUESDAY	WEDNESDAY	THURSDAY	FRIDAY	SATURDAY
				甲午 1 十二	乙未 2 十三	丙申 3 十四
丁酉 4 十五	戊戌 5 十六	己亥 6 十七	庚子 7 十八	辛丑 8 十九	壬寅 9 二十	癸卯 10 廿一
甲辰 11 廿二	乙巳 12 廿三	丙午 13 廿四	丁未 14 廿五	戊申 15 廿六	己酉 16 廿七	庚戌 17 廿八
辛亥 18 廿九	壬子 19 二月初一	癸丑 20 初二	甲寅 21 初三	乙卯 22 初四	丙辰 23 初五	丁巳 24 初六
戊午 25 初七	己未 26 初八	庚申 27 初九	辛酉 28 初十	壬戌 29 十一	癸亥 30 十二	甲子 31 十三

March 21, 2007 is a Tiger Day as the Earthly Branch of the Day Pillar is Tiger 寅 (Yin).

實用擇日

	三月大 3rd Mth Big		二月小 2nd Mth Small				正月小 1st Mth Small				月別 Month
	甲辰 Jia Chen		癸卯 Gui Mao				壬寅 Ren Yin				干支 Branches and Stems
	九紫 Nine Purple		一白 One White				二黑 Two Black				九星 Nine Star
mmer	穀雨 Grain Rain		清明 Clear and Bright		春分 Spring Equinox		驚蟄 Awakening of Worms		雨水 Rain Water		節氣 Season
y	初四 4th day		十八 18th day		初三 3rd day		十七 17th day		初二 2nd day		
in	19時8分 19hr 8min		12時6分 12hr 6min		8時9分 8hr 9min		7時19分 7hr 19min		9時11分 9hr 11min		朔 Constellation
	戌 Xu		午 Wu		辰 Chen		辰 Chen		巳 Si		
n	干支 Branches and stems	星 Star	國曆 Gregorian		干支 Branches and stems	星 Star	國曆 Gregorian		干支 Branches and stems	星 Star	農曆 Lunar Calendar
17	辛巳 Xin Si	6	3	19	壬子 Ren Zi	4	2	18	癸未 Gui Wei	2	初一 1st day
18	壬午 Ren Wu	7	3	20	癸丑 Gui Chou	5	2	19	甲申 Jia Shen	3	初二 2nd day
19	癸未 Gui Wei	8	3	21	甲寅 Jia Yin	6	2	20	乙酉 Yi You	4	初三 3rd day
20	甲申 Jia Shen	9	3	22	乙卯 Yi Mao	7	2	21	丙戌 Bing Xu	5	初四 4th day
21	乙酉 Yi You	1	3	23	丙辰 Bing Chen	8	2	22	丁亥 Ding Hai	6	初五 5th day
22	丙戌 Bing Xu	2	3	24	丁巳 Ding Si	9	2	23	戊子 Wu Zi	7	初六 6th day
23	丁亥 Ding Hai	3	3	25	戊午 Wu Wu	1	2	24	己丑 Ji Chou	8	初七 7th day
24	戊子 Wu Zi	4	3	26	己未 Ji Wei	2	2	25	庚寅 Geng Yin	9	初八 8th day
25	己丑 Ji Chou	5	3	27	庚申 Geng Shen	3	2	26	辛卯 Xin Mao	1	初九 9th day
26	庚寅 Geng Yin	6	3	28	辛酉 Xin You	4	2	27	壬辰 Ren Chen	2	初十 10th day
27	辛卯 Xin Mao	7	3	29	壬戌 Ren Xu	5	2	28	癸巳 Gui Si	3	十一 11th day
28	壬辰 Ren Chen	8	3	30	癸亥 Gui Hai	6	3	1	甲午 Jia Wu	4	十二 12th day
29	癸巳 Gui Si	9	3	31	甲子 Jia Zi	7	3	2	乙未 Yi Wei	5	十三 13th day
30	甲午 Jia Wu	1	4	1	乙丑 Yi Chou	8	3	3	丙申 Bing Shen	6	十四 14th day
1	乙未 Yi Wei	2	4	2	丙寅 Bing Yin	9	3	4	丁酉 Ding You	7	十五 15th day
2	丙申 Bing Shen	3	4	3	丁卯 Ding Mao	1	3	5	戊戌 Wu Xu	8	十六 16th day
3	丁酉 Ding You	4	4	4	戊辰 Wu Chen	2	3	6	己亥 Ji Hai	9	十七 17th day
4	戊戌 Wu Xu	5	4	5	己巳 Ji Si	3	3	7	庚子 Geng Zi	1	十八 18th day
5	己亥 Ji Hai	6	4	6	庚午 Geng Wu	4	3	8	辛丑 Xin Chou	2	十九 19th day
6	庚子 Geng Zi	7	4	7	辛未 Xin Wei	5	3	9	壬寅 Ren Yin	3	二十 20th day
7	辛丑 Xin Chou	8	4	8	壬申 Ren Shen	6	3	10	癸卯 Gui Mao	4	二十一 21st day
8	壬寅 Ren Yin	9	4	9	癸酉 Gui You	7	3	11	甲辰 Jia Chen	5	二十二 22nd day
9	癸卯 Gui Mao	1	4	10	甲戌 Jia Xu	8	3	12	乙巳 Yi Si	6	二十三 23rd day
10	甲辰 Jia Chen	2	4	11	乙亥 Yi Hai	9	3	13	丙午 Bing Wu	7	二十四 24th day
11	乙巳 Yi Si	3	4	12	丙子 Bing Zi	1	3	14	丁未 Ding Wei	8	二十五 25th day
12	丙午 Bing Wu	4	4	13	丁丑 Ding Chou	2	3	15	戊申 Wu Shen	9	二十六 26th day
13	丁未 Ding Wei	5	4	14	戊寅 Wu Yin	3	3	16	己酉 Ji You	1	二十七 27th day
14	戊申 Wu Shen	6	4	15	己卯 Ji Mao	4	3	17	庚戌 Geng Xu	2	二十八 28th day
15	己酉 Ji You	7	4	16	庚辰 Geng Chen	5	3	18	辛亥 Xin Hai	3	二十九 29th day
16	庚戌 Geng Xu	8									三十 30th day

2007 丁亥 Ding Hai Fire Pig Grand Duke 封齊

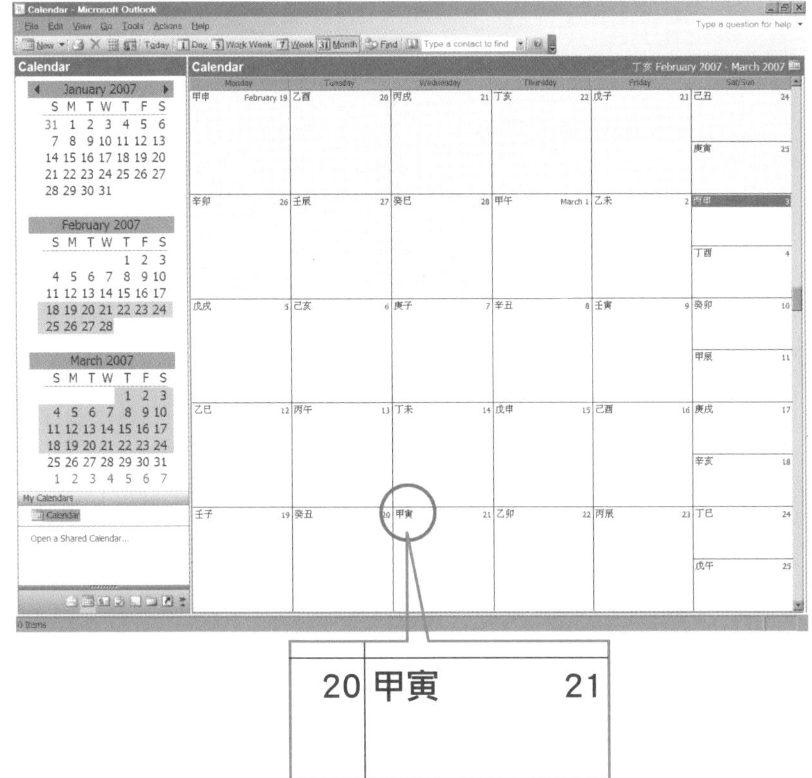

Calendar - Microsoft Outlook
File Edit View Go Tools Actions Help
Type a question for help
New Today Day Work Week Week Month Find
Type a contact to find
Calendar
January 2007
S M T W T F S
31 1 2 3 4 5 6
7 8 9 10 11 12 13
14 15 16 17 18 19 20
21 22 23 24 25 26 27
28 29 30 31
February 2007
S M T W T F S
1 2 3
4 5 6 7 8 9 10
11 12 13 14 15 16 17
18 19 20 21 22 23 24
25 26 27 28
March 2007
S M T W T F S
1 2 3
4 5 6 7 8 9 10
11 12 13 14 15 16 17
18 19 20 21 22 23 24
25 26 27 28 29 30 31
1 2 3 4 5 6 7
My Calendars
Calendar
Open a Shared Calendar...
0 Items
Calendar
丁亥 February 2007 - March 2007
Monday Tuesday Wednesday Thursday Friday Sat/Sun
甲申 February 19
乙酉 20
丙戌 21
丁亥 22
戊子 23
己丑 24
庚寅 25
辛卯 26
壬辰 27
癸巳 28
甲午 March 1
乙未 2
丙申 3
丁酉 4
戊戌 5
己亥 6
庚子 7
辛丑 8
壬寅 9
癸卯 10
甲辰 11
乙巳 12
丙午 13
丁未 14
戊申 15
己酉 16
庚戌 17
辛亥 18
壬子 19
癸丑 20
甲寅 21
乙卯 22
丙辰 23
丁巳 24
戊午 25
20 甲寅 21

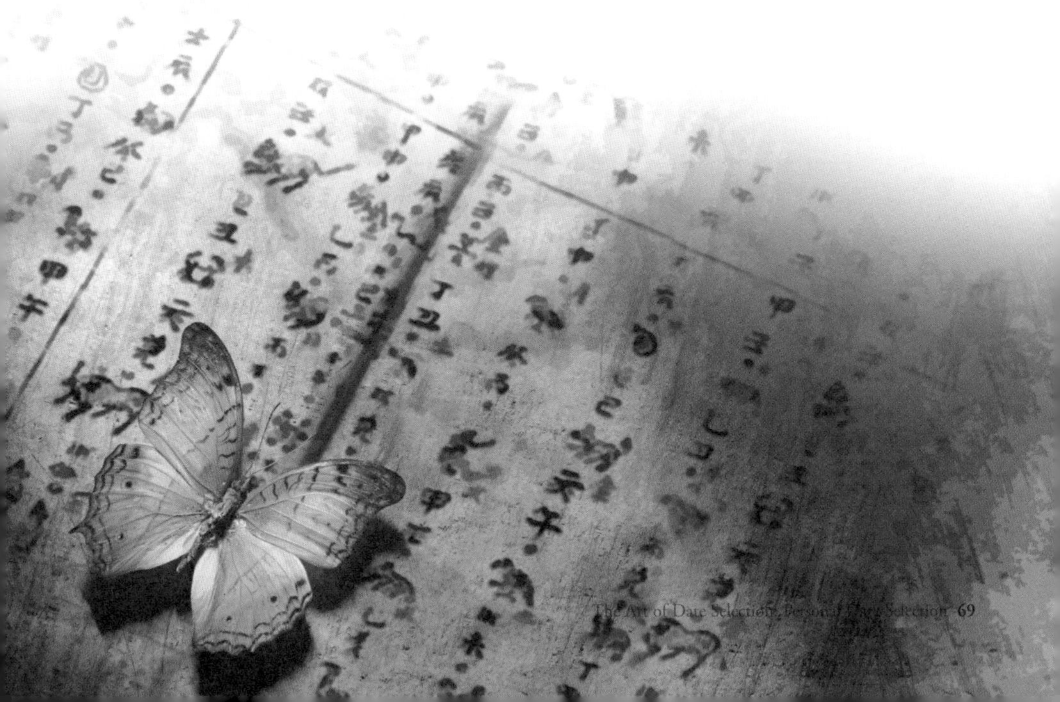

Step 2: Find out what Earthly Branch clashes with the Day Branch.

Let's say you are looking at a Tiger 寅 (Yin) Day, and you want to know what is the Day Breaker for a Tiger Day. Look at the Six Clashes table below. You will find the Monkey 申 (Shen) clashes with the Tiger. So during any Tiger Day, the Monkey Hour is the Day Breaker and should not be selected to commence any important activities.

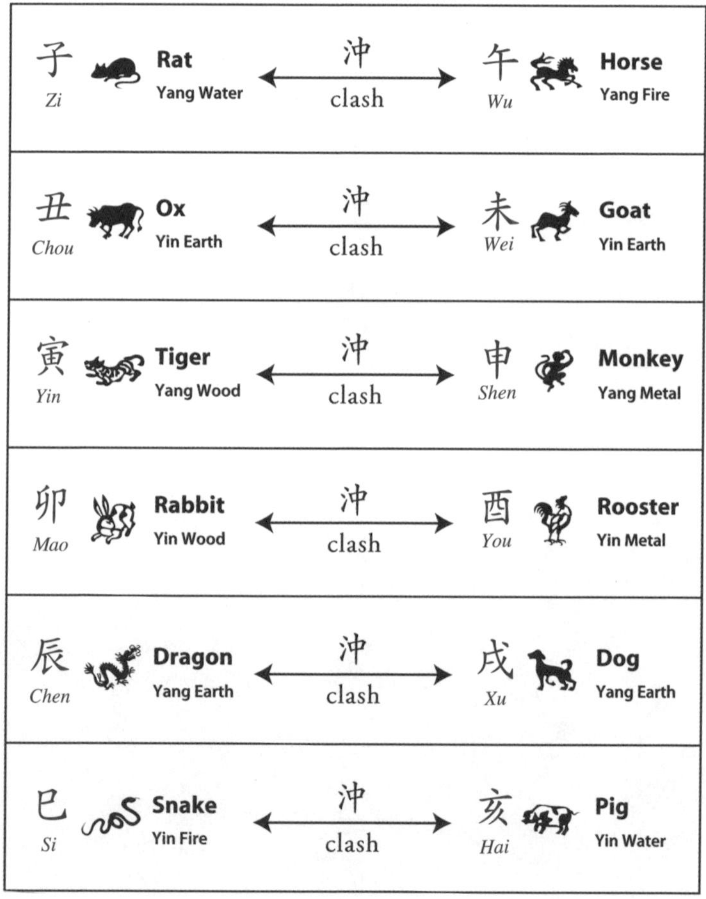

子 *Zi*	**Rat** Yang Water	沖 clash	午 *Wu*	**Horse** Yang Fire
丑 *Chou*	**Ox** Yin Earth	沖 clash	未 *Wei*	**Goat** Yin Earth
寅 *Yin*	**Tiger** Yang Wood	沖 clash	申 *Shen*	**Monkey** Yang Metal
卯 *Mao*	**Rabbit** Yin Wood	沖 clash	酉 *You*	**Rooster** Yin Metal
辰 *Chen*	**Dragon** Yang Earth	沖 clash	戌 *Xu*	**Dog** Yang Earth
巳 *Si*	**Snake** Yin Fire	沖 clash	亥 *Hai*	**Pig** Yin Water

Let's try another example - let's say it is a Rat 子 (Zi) Day and you want to find out what is the Day Breaker for a Rat Day. In the Six Clashes, the Rat clashes with the Horse 午 (Wu). Therefore, on all Rat Days, the Horse Hour cannot be used to commence any important activities.

Now, because the Day Breaker changes for every day, it's simply not practical to eliminate or calculate out all the Day Breakers in a given year or month. So with the Day Breaker, it is something that you should consider as part of your calculation to determine a suitable hour in which to commence an activity.

D. Three Killings Days 三煞

You have heard of Three Killings 三煞 (San Sha) with regard to Feng Shui. This is an annual inauspicious or negative direction. The Three Killings direction of the year normally is the direction where no renovation, striking of the wall or ground or drilling is encouraged, to avoid mishaps and calamities.

The Three Killings, when it comes to Personal Date Selection, has similarities to that of the Three Killings in Feng Shui, with regard to how the Three Killings are derived. But its application is different. In Feng Shui, the Three Killings is a direction or a location in relation to a property. In Date Selection, obviously it refers to certain months and days in a year.

Like the use of the word 'Shen', do not be overly alarmed by the use of the word 'Killings' here. There are, as I will soon share with you, instances when you can use the Monthly Three Killings Days. But remember, we prefer not to use bad days as a general rule in Date Selection!

Finding the Three Killings Days

The Three Killings is calculated with reference to the Three Harmony combination and with the Earthly Branch of the year as a reference point. The Three Killings is the element that is in elemental opposition to the Three Harmony combination of the year.

Just to quickly refresh your memory on the Three Harmony combination - the 12 Earthly Branches can be grouped according to four frames: the Fire frame, Wood frame, Metal frame and Water frame. The elemental frame is essentially the common element of the groups. This diagram shows you which Earthly Branches are grouped together, and the frame they are part of.

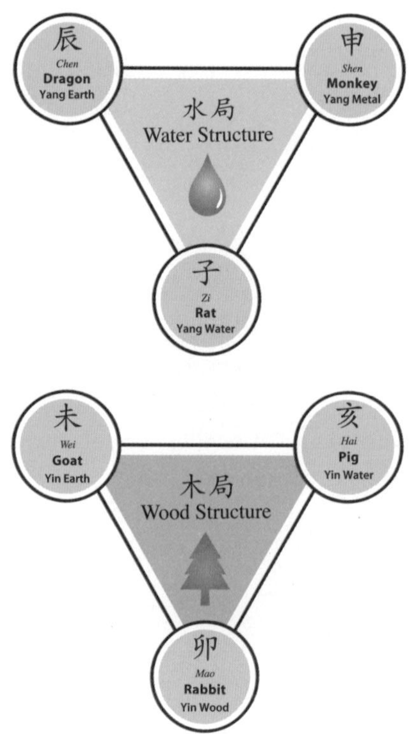

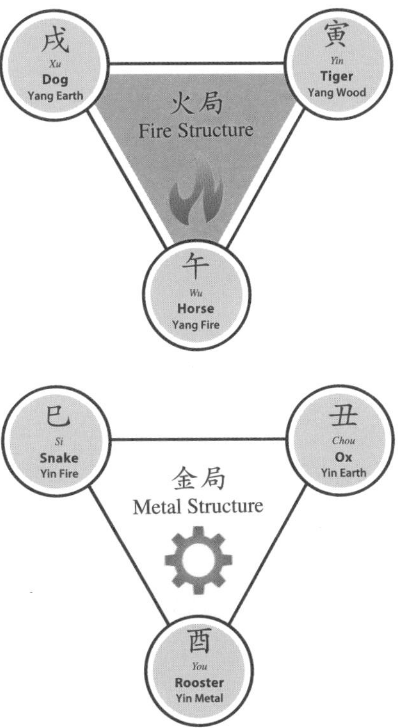

Now that we know which Earthly Branches or animal signs belong to which elemental grouping, all we have to do is figure out which elements oppose the groups.

An easy way to think about it is like rivalling groups. We want to find out in any year, which groups are against each other.

The grouping of Monkey-Rat-Dragon 申 子 辰 (Shen-Zi-Chen) forms the Water Frame. The Water Frame is opposed by Fire, as Fire and Water are obviously in opposition to each other in the study of the Five Elements. So we know that the Monkey-Rat-Dragon Water frame is opposed by the Fire grouping. What are the Earthly Branches or animal signs that are in the Fire grouping? The animals that form summer, the season of Fire - the Snake 巳 (Si), Horse 午 (Wu) and Goat 未 (Wei).

So we can say, in any year where the Earthly Branch or animal sign of the year is the Rat, Dragon OR Monkey, then the

Three Killings of those years will be the Snake, Horse and Goat Days.

Obviously, the other two oppositional groupings are Wood and Metal, since Metal clashes with Wood, in the study of the Five Elements. So, in any year where the Earthly Branch or animal sign belongs to the Metal frame grouping of Snake-Rooster-Ox 巳 酉 丑 (Si-You-Chou), we know the oppositional group is the Earthly Branches or animals signs that make up the Wood season, namely the Tiger 寅 (Yin), Rabbit 卯 (Mao) and Dragon 辰 (Chen) - the Three Killings for the Metal frame years.

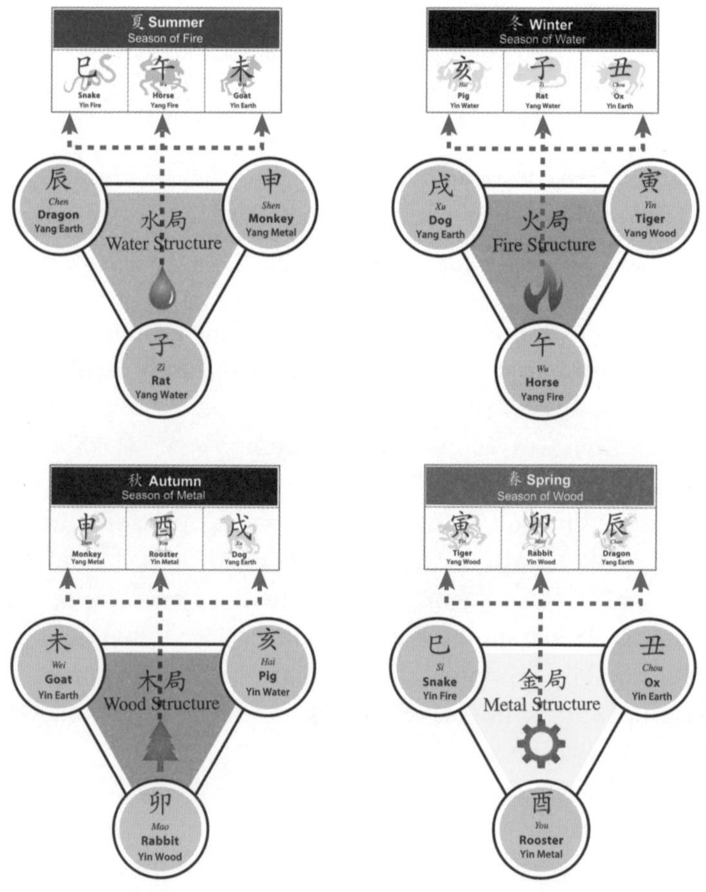

Let's take a few quick examples to help you work through this concept.

2006 is the Year of the Dog 戌 (Xu). The Dog belongs to the Fire frame or group, together with Tiger 寅 (Yin) and Horse 午 (Wu). The group that opposes the Fire frame is the Water frame. So in the Year of the Dog, the Three Killings Days are all Pig 亥 (Hai), Rat 子 (Zi) and Ox 丑 (Chou) Days, which are the Earthly Branches that make up the season of Water.

2007 is the Year of the Pig 亥 (Hai). The Pig is part of the Wood frame, together with the Rabbit 卯 (Mao) and the Goat 未 (Wei). The Wood frame is opposed by the Metal group. What Earthly Branches form part of the Metal group? The Monkey 申 (Shen), Rooster 酉 (You) and Dog 戌 (Xu) are the Earthly Branches that make up the Metal season. So in 2007, all Monkey, Rooster and Dog Days are Three Killings Days.

Why do we want to avoid Three Killings Days? In Date Selection, Three Killings really refers to three specific types of Killings or Sha, namely Robbery Sha, Calamity Sha and Annual Sha. Each of the Three Killings Days carries one of these types of Sha and violating each type of Sha or Killings carries a different, although obviously negative, outcome.

Determining which day carries which type of Three Killings

Now, before I move on to what are the implications the three types of Sha carry, let's look at how we determine which day carries which type of Killings. This table summarises the information for you.

Yearly Three Killings Table

Year 歲	Robbery Sha 劫煞	Calamity Sha 災煞	Annual Sha 歲煞
子 *Zi* **Rat** Yang Water	巳 *Si* **Snake** Yin Fire	午 *Wu* **Horse** Yang Fire	未 *Wei* **Goat** Yin Earth
丑 *Chou* **Ox** Yin Earth	寅 *Yin* **Tiger** Yang Wood	卯 *Mao* **Rabbit** Yin Wood	辰 *Chen* **Dragon** Yang Earth
寅 *Yin* **Tiger** Yang Wood	亥 *Hai* **Pig** Yin Water	子 *Zi* **Rat** Yang Water	丑 *Chou* **Ox** Yin Earth
卯 *Mao* **Rabbit** Yin Wood	申 *Shen* **Monkey** Yang Metal	酉 *You* **Rooster** Yin Metal	戌 *Xu* **Dog** Yang Earth
辰 *Chen* **Dragon** Yang Earth	巳 *Si* **Snake** Yin Fire	午 *Wu* **Horse** Yang Fire	未 *Wei* **Goat** Yin Earth
巳 *Si* **Snake** Yin Fire	寅 *Yin* **Tiger** Yang Wood	卯 *Mao* **Rabbit** Yin Wood	辰 *Chen* **Dragon** Yang Earth
午 *Wu* **Horse** Yang Fire	亥 *Hai* **Pig** Yin Water	子 *Zi* **Rat** Yang Water	丑 *Chou* **Ox** Yin Earth
未 *Wei* **Goat** Yin Earth	申 *Shen* **Monkey** Yang Metal	酉 *You* **Rooster** Yin Metal	戌 *Xu* **Dog** Yang Earth
申 *Shen* **Monkey** Yang Metal	巳 *Si* **Snake** Yin Fire	午 *Wu* **Horse** Yang Fire	未 *Wei* **Goat** Yin Earth
酉 *You* **Rooster** Yin Metal	寅 *Yin* **Tiger** Yang Wood	卯 *Mao* **Rabbit** Yin Wood	辰 *Chen* **Dragon** Yang Earth
戌 *Xu* **Dog** Yang Earth	亥 *Hai* **Pig** Yin Water	子 *Zi* **Rat** Yang Water	丑 *Chou* **Ox** Yin Earth
亥 *Hai* **Pig** Yin Water	申 *Shen* **Monkey** Yang Metal	酉 *You* **Rooster** Yin Metal	戌 *Xu* **Dog** Yang Earth

Step 1: Determine the Three Killings of the year, by referencing the Earthly Branch of the year.

Let's say it is the Year of the Monkey 申 (Shen). How do we determine the Three Killings Days of the year? The Monkey is part of the Water frame together with the Rat 子 (Zi) and Dragon 辰 (Chen). Water is opposed by Fire in the study of the Five Elements. So what animals form the Fire group or season of Fire? The Snake 巳 (Si), Horse 午 (Wu) and Goat 未 (Wei). So we know that the Three Killings for the year are the Snake, Horse and Goat.

Step 2: Refer to the table to determine which days carry which type of killings

The Yearly Three Killings table tells us which Earthly Branch carries which type of killings. So in our example of using the Year of the Monkey, we know the Three Killings Days are Snake, Horse and Goat. From the table, we know that all Snake Days are Robbery Sha Days, all Horse Days are Calamity Sha Days and all Goat Days are Annual Sha Days.

Let's do one more example. Let's say, it is the Year of the Dog 戌 (Xu). Now, the Dog belongs to the Fire frame, together with Tiger 寅 (Yin) and Horse 午 (Wu). What opposes Fire? Water of course. So what are the Earthly Branches that make up the Water group or season of water? The Pig 亥 (Hai), Rat 子 (Zi) and Ox 丑 (Chou). Now, look at the Yearly Three Killings table. You will see that in a Dog Year, all Pig Days are Robbery Sha Days, all Rat Days carry Calamity Sha and the Annual Sha Days are all the Ox Days.

Understanding the Three Killings Days

As with its application in Feng Shui, we do not want to violate Three Killings Days by selecting these days for important personal or business endeavours. But of course, as I have always said in my other books, it is one thing to know why something is a problem, but it is also important to understand what the problem is in order to take the appropriate action.

So what do each of the Three Killings mean?

Robbery Sha Days 劫煞日

As the name indicates, Robbery Sha Days are days when there is a high likelihood of being robbed, losing money or valuables and misplacing important personal effects. Now, those of you with familiarity of BaZi or knowledge of Feng Shui will notice that the Robbery Sha Days are made up of the grouping known as the Four Stables, which consists of the Tiger, Snake, Monkey and Pig.

If you have some knowledge of BaZi, you will also know that these stars are associated with travelling and mobility. Hence, this particular Three Killings Day involves problems caused during travelling, including being robbed, or mugged while going to work or a problem of losing items during travel. Do not bank in money on this day if possible and avoid travelling on Robbery Sha Three Killings Days!

Calamity Sha Days 災煞日

Calamity Sha Days usually bring about bodily harm, injuries, and illness. It is not a good day to have medical procedures done, especially by someone of the opposite sex.

Now if you know BaZi or Feng Shui, you will notice that the Calamity Sha Days are all the Cardinal or Peach Blossom Stars - the Horse, Rabbit, Rooster and Rat. So frequently, the problems are caused by relationships and the bodily harm usually caused by the opposite sex, along with scandals and sex-related problems.

Annual Sha Days 歲煞日

The Annual Sha Days are also Graveyard Stars, namely the Ox, Dragon, Dog and Goat. In BaZi, these four stars represent loneliness and a solitary nature, and an unmoving nature. This indicates procrastination, delay, and setbacks. Therefore these days usually result in problems of this nature. For Annual Sha Three Killings Days, it is best to avoid starting an important project that has a tight or pressing deadline, avoid submitting documents that require quick approval or instant replies and do not engage in property-related transactions.

As far as possible, the rule should be to avoid using the Three Killings Days.

However, you can also, if you have no choice, use the Three Killings Days provided the activity in question is not contrary to the type of Sha that influences the day and it is a long-term activity such as getting married or moving into a house. This is because the Three Killings Days only result in problems for the duration of the year. But that is for Date Selection experts who can also tailor the situation using other techniques and also, select a good hour. For beginners to Date Selection, I urge erring on the side of caution and where possible, avoid using any Three Killings Days.

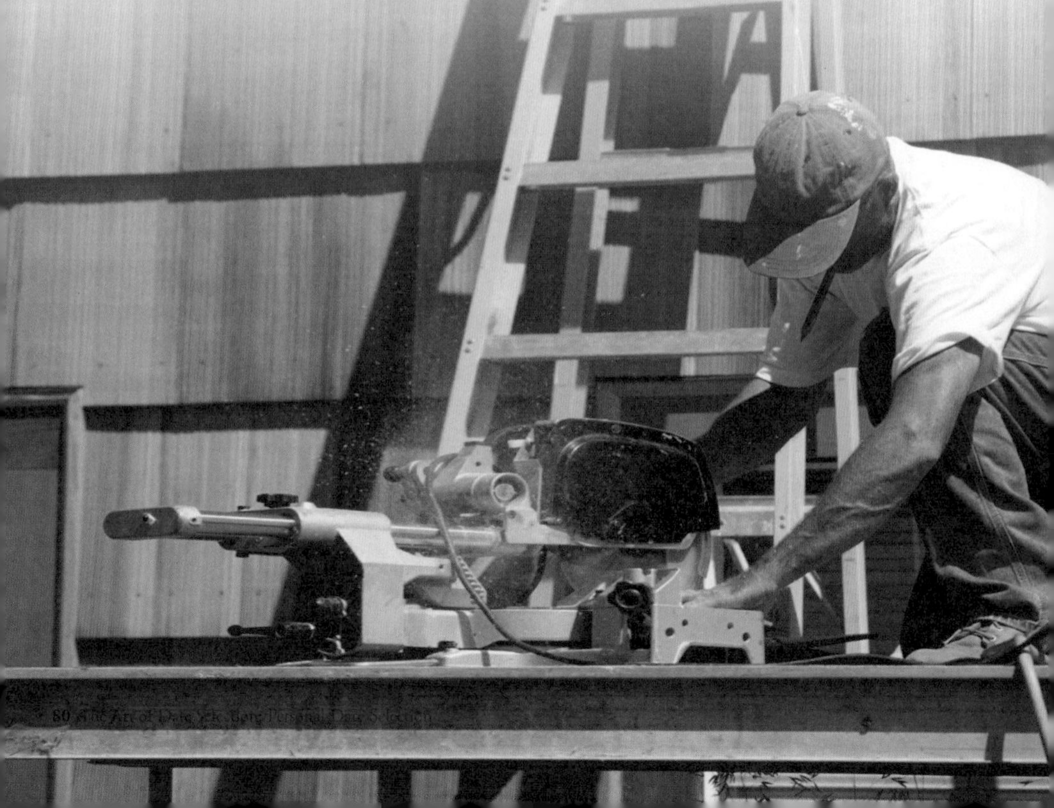

Monthly Three Killings Days 月三煞

In addition to Three Killings Days, certain days in the month may have a Three Killings relationship with the Earthly Branch of a given month. These are known as Monthly Three Killings Days. Like the Three Killings Days, Monthly Three Killings Days can also be divided into Robbery Sha, Calamity Sha and Month Sha.

The Monthly Three Killings are derived through the same method as the Yearly Three Killings. However, instead of basing it on the Earthly Branch or animal sign of the Year, we reference the Earthly Branch or animal sign of the month.

Once you know what the Earthly Branch or animal sign of the month is, determine which elemental Frame (Fire, Water, Metal or Wood) it belongs to, and then find the element that opposes that Frame. For example, in the Tiger 寅 (Yin) Month, the Monthly Three Killings are the Pig 亥 (Hai), the Rat 子 (Zi) and the Ox 丑 (Chou). This is because the Tiger belongs to the Fire frame, and the elements that oppose this frame are those that belong to the season of Water.

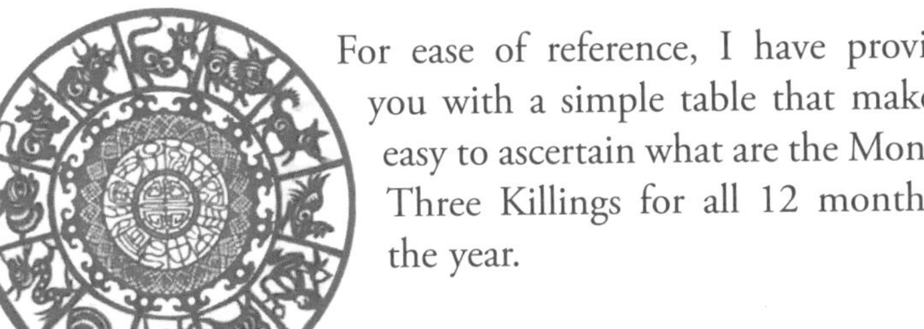

For ease of reference, I have provided you with a simple table that makes it easy to ascertain what are the Monthly Three Killings for all 12 months of the year.

Monthly Three Killings table

Month 月	Robbery Sha 劫煞	Calamity Sha 災煞	Annual Sha 歲煞
子 Zi Rat Yang Water	巳 Si Snake Yin Fire	午 Wu Horse Yang Fire	未 Wei Goat Yin Earth
丑 Chou Ox Yin Earth	寅 Yin Tiger Yang Wood	卯 Mao Rabbit Yin Wood	辰 Chen Dragon Yang Earth
寅 Yin Tiger Yang Wood	亥 Hai Pig Yin Water	子 Zi Rat Yang Water	丑 Chou Ox Yin Earth
卯 Mao Rabbit Yin Wood	申 Shen Monkey Yang Metal	酉 You Rooster Yin Metal	戌 Xu Dog Yang Earth
辰 Chen Dragon Yang Earth	巳 Si Snake Yin Fire	午 Wu Horse Yang Fire	未 Wei Goat Yin Earth
巳 Si Snake Yin Fire	寅 Yin Tiger Yang Wood	卯 Mao Rabbit Yin Wood	辰 Chen Dragon Yang Earth
午 Wu Horse Yang Fire	亥 Hai Pig Yin Water	子 Zi Rat Yang Water	丑 Chou Ox Yin Earth
未 Wei Goat Yin Earth	申 Shen Monkey Yang Metal	酉 You Rooster Yin Metal	戌 Xu Dog Yang Earth
申 Shen Monkey Yang Metal	巳 Si Snake Yin Fire	午 Wu Horse Yang Fire	未 Wei Goat Yin Earth
酉 You Rooster Yin Metal	寅 Yin Tiger Yang Wood	卯 Mao Rabbit Yin Wood	辰 Chen Dragon Yang Earth
戌 Xu Dog Yang Earth	亥 Hai Pig Yin Water	子 Zi Rat Yang Water	丑 Chou Ox Yin Earth
亥 Hai Pig Yin Water	申 Shen Monkey Yang Metal	酉 You Rooster Yin Metal	戌 Xu Dog Yang Earth

As the Monthly Three Killings Day is just a day that has a negative relationship with the month, the effects of using a Monthly Three Killings Day are quite transient and usually last only one month. Accordingly, it is generally acceptable to use if you must, a Monthly Three Killings Day, but only if it is for a long-term project or activity that you are undertaking.

However, for any short-term activities (such as a holiday or travelling or a spell in a holiday camp or student exchange) or a short-term project, avoid using the Monthly Three Killings Day to start your endeavour. Monthly Three Killings should

also not be used for starting any academic endeavours such as studying for an exam. Those of you who are contemplating embarking on a diet should avoid in particular the Disaster Sha Day (for obvious reasons, your diet will simply be disastrous for your health or go nowhere) and the Month Sha Day as these may have an adverse impact on your health.

It is considered acceptable to use a Monthly Three Killings Day for marriage, since in general, very few people have 52-hour marriages like Britney Spears! Of course, this is if you really cannot find a decent date and have a tight calendar or short window of time only. However, where avoidable, it is best not to use this day for a marriage.

As this book is on Date Selection for personal activities and endeavours, I have not discussed how the Three Killings Day and Monthly Three Killings Days impact on Feng Shui-related activities, such as moving into a new house or commencing renovations. This will be covered in my other book in the ***Art of Date Selection*** series, ***Feng Shui Date Selection***.

The 10 Ferocious and Big Disaster Days 十惡大敗日

The 10 Ferocious and Big Disaster Days 十惡大敗日 (Shi E Da Bai Ri) are also known as No Wealth Days 無祿日 (Wu Lu Ri). These are days that are considered negative for any activity that involves business trading or wealth generation. Therefore do not use these days for signing contracts, closing business deals, business trips or for official openings.

These 10 Days are derived with reference to the six groupings of the 60 Jia Zi. To calculate the 10 Ferocious and Big Disaster Days, you need some in-depth BaZi knowledge and understand how to use the Death and Emptiness tables. As this is quite a complex calculation, I have left this for Chapter 6. To make things simple for you right now, I have calculated in advance, the 10 Ferocious and Big Disaster Days for the years 2007-2017 for you here.

Year	丁亥 Ding Hai Day	己丑 Ji Chou Day
2007	February 22	February 24
	April 23	April 25
	June 22	June 24
	August 21	August 23
	October 20	October 22
	December 19	December 21
2008	February 17	February 19
	April 17	April 19
	June 16	June 18
	August 15	August 17
	October 14	October 16
	December 13	December 15
2009	February 11	February 13
	April 12	April 14
	June 11	June 13
	August 10	August 12
	October 9	October 11
	December 8	December 10

Year	丁亥 Ding Hai Day	己丑 Ji Chou Day
2010	February 6	February 8
	April 7	April 9
	June 6	June 8
	August 5	August 7
	October 4	October 6
	December 3	December 5
2011	February 1	February 3
	April 2	April 4
	June 1	June 3
	July 31	August 2
	September 29	October 1
	November 28	November 30
2012	January 27	January 29
	March 27	March 29
	May 26	May 28
	July 25	July 27
	September 23	September 25
	November 22	November 24
2013	January 21	January 23
	March 22	March 24
	May 21	May 28
	July 20	July 27
	September 18	September 20
	November 17	November 19

Year	丁亥 Ding Hai Day	己丑 Ji Chou Day
2014	March 26	March 28
	May 25	May 27
	July 24	July 26
	September 22	September 24
	November 21	November 23
2015	January 20	January 22
	March 21	March 23
	May 20	May 22
	July 19	July 21
	September 17	September 19
	November 16	November 18
2016	January 15	January17
	March 15	March 17
	May 14	May 16
	July 13	July 15
	September 11	September 13
	November 10	November 12
2017	January 9	January 11
	March 10	March 12
	May 9	May 11
	July 8	July 10
	September 6	September 8
	November 5	November 7

There are only a few 10 Ferocious and Big Disaster Days in each year. Using the tables above, you will be able to ascertain what those days are. On those days, avoid business ventures, business negotiation, expansion activity, official openings or maybe even something as simple as depositing money or cheques.

Four Separating Days 四離日

There are certain days in the Chinese Solar calendar where the Qi is stale and dead. These are known as the Four Separating Days 四離日 (Si Li Ri). The Qi is depleted on these days, the stars lack vitality and the energies are leftover at best. Using such days where the Qi is depleted and relying on leftover energies, means you are infusing your activity with at best, weak Qi, and at worse, totally unusable energies. Using any of the Four Separating Days results in important activities or endeavours lacking support or commencing on days that are not conducive to success.

The Four Separating Days are typically the transition point between Qi and elemental cycles of a certain season, which is why the Qi is considered stale and dead.

The Four Separating Days are:

One Day Before 前一天
Spring Equinox 春分
Summer Solstice 夏至
Autumn Equinox 秋分
Winter Solstice 冬至

So the Four Separating Days fall on March 20, June 20, September 22 and December 21. These days should not be used for any important personal activities or endeavours.

There are some Date Selection specialists who see a use for Separating Days. Typically they are used for problems like marital separation, dealing with stalkers or dealing with people who are harassing you. Separating Days are used to commence legal action (for example, seeking a restraining order against a stalker) or to end a relationship. Technically speaking, the Four Separating Days are not bad days per se, but neither are they good days so if you can choose another date, all the better. Also, as the types of activities that Separating Days are used for are not 'conventional' activities and are open to abuse, I generally do not advocate the use of Four Separating Days for any personal activities or endeavours.

Four Extinct Days 四絕日

In Chinese Metaphysical studies, Qi moves in upward and downward cycles. Accordingly at certain days in a year, the Qi cycle and energies of a particular element are at their lowest and weakest point. These days coincide with the ending or last day of each season.

The Four Extinct Days are

One Day Before 前一天
Coming of Spring 立春
Coming of Solstice 立夏
Coming of Equinox 立秋
Coming of Solstice 立冬

So the Four Extinct Days fall on February 3, May 5, August 8 and November 7. These days should not be used for any important personal activities or endeavours.

Briefly, the term 'season' here does not refer to the seasons as it is typically used in the context of climate or weather. So even if you are living in the Equator or South Pole, the Chinese Metaphysical concept of the seasons still applies. Season in the context of Chinese Metaphysical studies refers to different periods of Qi cycles, based on the orbit of the Earth around the Sun. A more thorough explanation of the concept of 'season' can be found in my book, ***BaZi - The Destiny Code.***

In the context of Date Selection, these 4 days in a year are called Extinct Days 四絕日 (Si Jue Ri). On each of these Extinct Days, a specific elemental Qi is very weak. So for example, on the last day of Winter, the energies of the Water element are at their weakest, as Winter is the season of Water.

Now, Extinct means 'to end'. Accordingly, any activity that you undertake on any of the Four Extinct Days will be doomed from the start and can only go one way and that is, down or to conclusion. The Four Extinct Days are not good days to use for any activity that involves growth or advancement such as marriage or important business transactions or contracts.

For example, if you get married on a Four Extinct Day, you may well find your marriage is NOT blessed with offspring! If you sign a contract on that day to expand a business, your business may instead stagnate or worse, decline.

Mark out the Four Extinct Days on your calendar for ease of reference and so that you will know not to use these days.

Making it personal

Now, I've covered quite extensively the various bad and negative dates that EVERYONE should try to avoid using where possible. But the true power of Date Selection is when it is personalised to the individual, according to their BaZi. This is how you ensure that you do not just avoid dates that are bad for everyone, but also avoid using dates that are not good for you personally and may affect you more significantly than the next person.

The personalisation of Date Selection involves many sophisticated techniques and requires quite an extensive understanding of BaZi. However, it is possible with the bare minimum knowledge of BaZi and equipped with your personal BaZi chart, to engage in some basic personalisation of Date Selection.

As we are on the topic of dates to avoid, I'm going to show you how to find your Personal Breaker, which is an extremely simple but effective method of Date Selection personalisation.

Personal Breaker 大耗日

The Personal Breaker 大耗 (Da Hao) is similar in concept to the Year and Month Breaker. The difference is of course in the word 'personal'. The Personal Breaker is the day that is not in sync with your personal BaZi if you like. It is the day where the energies of the day are against you personally. The Personal Breaker Day is found by referencing your Year of Birth with the respective dates.

You might be wondering why we use the year of birth or Year Pillar as a reference. It's quite simple. The Year Pillar in your BaZi is the pillar that feels the impact of any change in the energies first. This is the most external pillar in your BaZi. The energies of any month or year affect the year pillar of a person's BaZi first. This is because the energies move from the right side of the chart to the left, so it will always impact the Year Pillar first. The Year Pillar if you like, is your first line of defence.

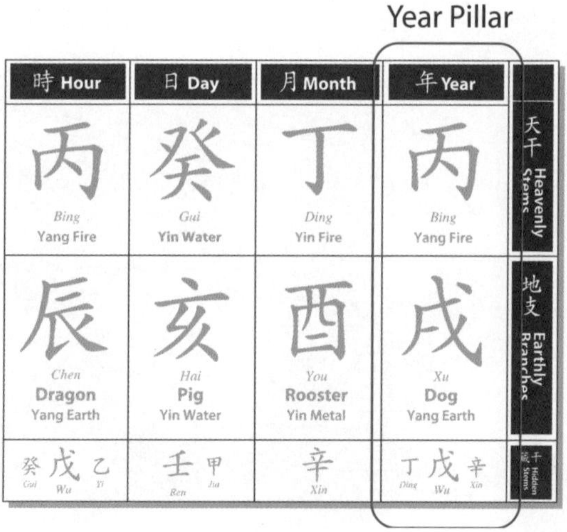

Year Pillar

時 Hour	日 Day	月 Month	年 Year	
丙 *Bing* Yang Fire	癸 *Gui* Yin Water	丁 *Ding* Yin Fire	丙 *Bing* Yang Fire	天干 Heavenly Stems
辰 *Chen* **Dragon** Yang Earth	亥 *Hai* **Pig** Yin Water	酉 *You* **Rooster** Yin Metal	戌 *Xu* **Dog** Yang Earth	地支 Earthly Branches
癸 *Gui* 戊 *Wu* 乙 *Yi*	壬 *Ren* 甲 *Jia*	辛 *Xin*	丁 *Ding* 戊 *Wu* 辛 *Xin*	藏干 Hidden Stems

For those of you familiar with BaZi, this is one of the reasons why in the study of BaZi, having good elements or a good Year Pillar is important - this indicates you will be insulated from the general negative impact of any annual energies. It also indicates that you get a good start in life as in the study of BaZi, your Year Pillar represents your family background or grandparents.

時 Hour	日 Day	月 Month	年 Year	
丙 Bing Yang Fire	癸 Gui Yin Water	丁 Ding Yin Fire	丙 Bing	天干 Heavenly Stems
辰 Chen Dragon Yang Earth	亥 Hai Pig Yin Water	酉 You Rooster Yin Metal	戌 Xu Dog Yang Earth	地支 Earthly Branches
癸 Gui 戊 Wu 乙 Yi	壬 Ren 甲 Jia	辛 Xin	丁 Ding 戊 Wu 辛 Xin	藏干 Hidden Stems

Family Background

In Date Selection studies (and in most classical Feng Shui applications), the year rather than the day is usually the point of reference. This is why the Personal Breaker relates to the person's year of birth rather than day of birth.

The Personal Breaker is important because it affords two important forms of personalisation. First, it helps you narrow down and further personalise the usable dates. It also helps you make a decision when you are considering using unfavourable or negative dates. If you have a choice between two negative but not entirely unusable dates, you should obviously avoid using the Personal Breaker Day.

Year Pillar

時 Hour	日 Day	月 Month	年 Year	
丙 *Bing* Yang Fire	癸 *Gui* Yin Water	丁 *Ding* Yin Fire	丙 *Bing* Yang Fire	天干 Heavenly Stems
辰 *Chen* Dragon Yang Earth	亥 *Hai* Pig Yin Water	酉 *You* Rooster Yin Metal	戌 *Xu* Dog Yang Earth	地支 Earthly Branches
癸 *Gui* 戊 *Wu* 乙 *Yi*	壬 *Ren* 甲 *Jia*	辛 *Xin*	丁 *Ding* 戊 *Wu* 辛 *Xin*	藏干 Hidden Stems

The Date you choose must not clash with the Year Pillar

It's fairly simple to identify your Personal Breaker Day. The Personal Breaker is the day that clashes with your personal animal sign or the Earthly Branch of your BaZi's Year Pillar. So, for example, if you are born in the year of the Rabbit 卯 (Mao), all Rooster 酉 (You) Days are against your animal sign and are therefore your Personal Breaker Days.

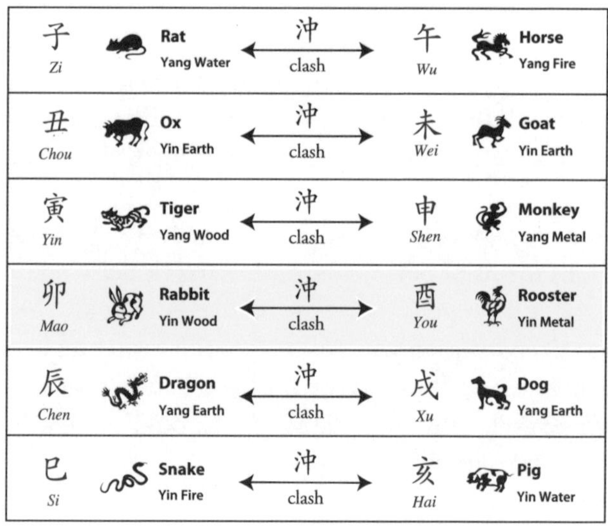

子 *Zi*	**Rat** Yang Water	沖 clash	午 *Wu*	**Horse** Yang Fire
丑 *Chou*	**Ox** Yin Earth	沖 clash	未 *Wei*	**Goat** Yin Earth
寅 *Yin*	**Tiger** Yang Wood	沖 clash	申 *Shen*	**Monkey** Yang Metal
卯 *Mao*	**Rabbit** Yin Wood	沖 clash	酉 *You*	**Rooster** Yin Metal
辰 *Chen*	**Dragon** Yang Earth	沖 clash	戌 *Xu*	**Dog** Yang Earth
巳 *Si*	**Snake** Yin Fire	沖 clash	亥 *Hai*	**Pig** Yin Water

This is because the Rooster clashes with the Rabbit in the theory of the Six Clashes 六沖. Let's try another example - let's say you are born in the year of the Horse 午 (Wu). What clashes with the Horse? The Rat 子 (Zi). Therefore, all Rat Days are against your Year Earthly Branch and so all Rat Days in the calendar are your Personal Breakers. Easy, right?

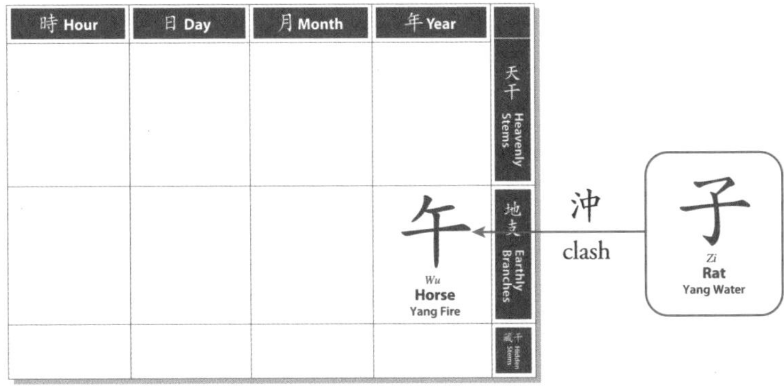

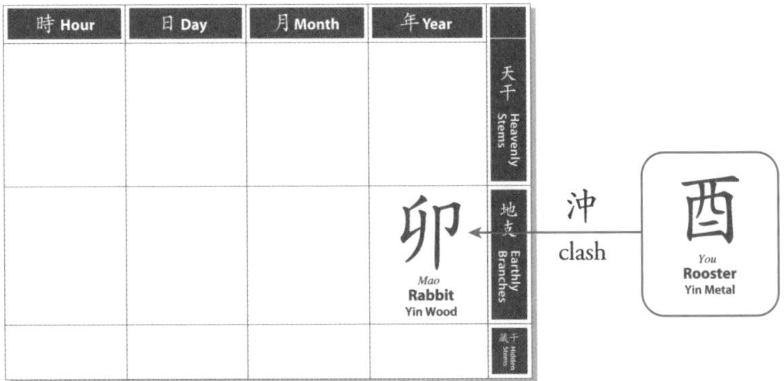

JUNE 2007 丙午

SUNDAY	MONDAY	TUESDAY	WEDNESDAY	THURSDAY	FRIDAY	SATURDAY
					丙寅 1 十六	丁卯 2 十七
戊辰 3 十八	己巳 歲破日 Year Breaker Day 4 十九	庚午 5 二十	辛未 6 廿一	壬申 7 廿二	癸酉 8 廿三	甲戌 9 廿四
乙亥 10 廿五	丙子 11 廿六	丁丑 12 廿七	戊寅 13 廿八	己卯 14 廿九	庚辰 15 五月初一	辛巳 歲破日 Year Breaker Day 16 初二
壬午 17 初三	癸未 18 初四	甲申 19 初五	乙酉 20 初六	丙戌 21 初七	丁亥 22 初八	戊子 23 初九
己丑 24 初十	庚寅 25 十一	辛卯 26 十二	壬辰 27 十三	癸巳 歲破日 Year Breaker Day 28 十四	甲午 29 十五	乙未 30 十六

Personal Breaker Days for a person born in the Year of the Horse

Now, it may be that a day that is your Personal Breaker Day may well be a good day according to the Tong Shu. How do you reconcile what seems like conflicting advice? Keep in mind that the Tong Shu's information is generic and assumes that additional calculations and methods of Date Selection will be factored in, including knowledge of the Personal Breaker.

On your Personal Breaker Day, all the energies of the day are against you whole-heartedly and you can just about be sure that if you do anything important on this date, it's not going to work out well, much less be successful. So, personal activities and endeavours should not be done on Personal Breaker Days.

What are personal activities? These are activities that relate to your private life, such as getting married, signing a contract or moving house. However, I generally also do not encourage starting work on a day that is your Personal Breaker as this indicates starting a job on not just the wrong foot, but with the entire company or organisation going against you from day one!

Getting a Good Day is a Challenge!

If you have been faithfully marking out all the negative and inauspicious dates in the year on your personal calendar and then also adding into the picture your Personal Breaker, you will pretty much soon realise that there aren't many truly good days in the year.

That is why getting a truly good day for an important activity is a challenge. And you know what, when you throw on the additional layers of personalisation, getting a good day becomes a serious challenge. It would not be an exaggeration to say that in 365 days, you may find that the really, really good days for you, the days that are 100 percent in tune with your personal BaZi, can be counted on one hand.

If you tried to build your entire schedule or personal life around just the good dates of the year, you'll find you won't or can't get much done. So, the answer is not to run around in fear, but to understand that you've simply got to prioritise. In

實用擇日

other words, what are the exceptions to the rule of totally avoiding bad days?

In general, if you have to decide between which of the Breakers to avoid, it is more important to avoid Month Breaker and Personal Breaker Days, than Year Breaker Days.

You will also want to make your decision based on the type of activity in question - for example, is it a short-term or long-term activity? When it comes to long-term activities, then Three Killings Days and Year Breaker Days are less significant. These can be safely ignored. If we are looking at a short-term project, I would pay particular attention to the Month Breakers, but be a bit less concerned with the Year Breaker because the Month Breaker impacts short-term projects more.

There is also a difference obviously between being flexible with something like say, a renovation, and being a little bit more picky with something more important personally, like getting married. You might not be so worried about going against your Personal Breaker with a renovation, but with a marriage, you must look to avoid the Personal Breaker Days of BOTH the bride and the groom.

Date Selection is a dynamic practice that needs a lot of consideration and understanding of the nature of the event, along with the BaZi of the persons whom the date is being selected for. It also has to be practical - for example, most people want to get married on a weekend rather than a weekday because it's more convenient. And who wants to start renovation work on a Sunday?

Nonetheless, I believe that in some instances, it is wise to wait. Sometimes, getting a good date is worth the wait, especially if what you are about to do is of great significance to you. In the next chapter, we'll look at how to find that gem of a day, in a month or year and find not just usable days, but good days in a year.

乙 壬 癸 丙
巳 辰 巳 戌
2.6
58
BAZI
THE
DESTINY
CODE
YOUR GUIDE TO THE
FOUR PILLARS OF DESTINY
JOEY YAP

Chapter Four:
A Few Good Dates

The Art of Date Selection begins with avoiding bad days. Now that you have worked out what are the bad days in the year, you will find you are left with a handful (at best) of usable dates in the whole year!

Why do I use the word 'usable' and not 'good'? Because the dates that are left over are just dates that are not 'bad dates'. That does not mean they are automatically 'good dates'. And with Date Selection, as far as possible, we do not want to go for the 'so-so' or 'okay' dates right? The whole point of the exercise is to find a good, if not superior date to kick off your activity or endeavour.

Accordingly, in this chapter, I'm going to share with you techniques and methods of determining which are the good dates, from the clutch of 'usable' dates you have in the yearly calendar.

What is a good date?

A good date is essentially one where the energies of the stars present in the constellation at the time, and the elements of the day are not just positive and in harmony with those of the Month and Year, but favourable specifically to the activity you have in mind. A superior good date is one that is not just all of the above, but is also elementally in tune with your Personal BaZi.

A number of the basic techniques outlined here are derived from an important classical text on Date Selection, The Book of Unifying Times and Discerning Dimensions 協紀辨方書 (Xie Ji Bian Fang Shu). This classical text, an academic work commissioned in the Qing Dynasty by Emperor Qian Long, is regarded as the cornerstone text on the subject of Date Selection. It contains extensive astronomical and calendrical information from centuries of Chinese scholarly works, corroborated against astronomical information known to the West during that era. The Book of Unifying Times and Discerning Dimensions is also the basis for the Chinese Almanac or Tong Shu.

吉日

Now, a date can be both good and bad. You must be thinking - wait a minute, how can it be both good and bad at the same time? Haven't we already eliminated all the bad days with the techniques in Chapter 3?

A day can actually have both positive and negative stars which dampen its positive effects. So the day is good because of its elemental relationship between the Earthly Branches but perhaps it has negative stars that weaken its positive effects. So while the date remains 'usable' and is not harmful to use, its positive attributes and energies are minimal at best.

As this is meant as a do-it-yourself Date Selection book, I want to keep things simple. But it is important to understand that there is a pecking order, even amongst the usable dates you have in hand. In short, not all usable dates are really that usable!

The focus of this chapter will be key basic Date Selection techniques to identify good dates, from the clutch of usable dates you have left over, after eliminating the bad dates. For those of you with the additional benefit of some BaZi knowledge, you will be able to further personalise the dates you select for specific personal and business activities.

All dates lead to the Tong Shu

Most Asians are familiar with requesting a good date from a learned or elderly member of our family - a grandmother is the usual choice. For most people who cannot read Chinese, the Tong Shu looks like a giant book of hieroglyphics and the idea of using it to obtain a date seems complicated. In reality, using the Tong Shu is a matter of being able to differentiate between the colours (the good dates are actually marked out in red and indicated in columns) and reading the instructions in the Tong Shu. It's a bit like using a dictionary - it's hard if you don't know how to use it.

But not everyone who can read a Tong Shu knows how to use it properly or can necessarily select anything more than a generic good date. The techniques that I will be discussing in this chapter will be techniques that you can use to help you obtain a date beyond the generic garden variety good date. By the end of this chapter, even if you have no idea now to read the Tong Shu, you will be able to select for yourself a good date, and personalise it for yourself.

The 12 Day Officers Method 建除十二值神

The 12 Day Officers 十二值神 (Shi Er Zhi Shen) is an entry level Date Selection technique that is essential for separating generic usable dates from the good usable dates. This method is also sometimes literally translated as The 12 Day Deities. The word 'Deity' 神 (Shen) here has no reference to a spirit or godly or transcendental figure of sorts. It is in fact a reference to the body of Qi that governs the energies of the day. Remember what I said in earlier chapters about how the word 'Shen' does not always reference a spirit or a god? So in this context, think of the 'Deity' as an officer if you like - a sort of person in charge for the day.

The concept of the 12 Day Officers is this: each day of the month is controlled by a governing officer. There are in total 12 officers, hence the technique is called the 12 Day Officers.

The 12 Day Officers are as follows:

1. Establish 建 (Jian)
2. Remove 除 (Chu)
3. Full 满 (Man)
4. Balance 平 (Ping)
5. Stable 定 (Ding)
6. Initiate 執 (Zhi)
7. Destruction 破 (Po)
8. Danger 危 (Wei)
9. Success 成 (Cheng)
10. Receive 收 (Shou)
11. Open 開 (Kai)
12. Close 閉 (Bi)

The names of the 12 Day Officers are derived from the twelve specific types of energy or Qi that govern a particular day. Now, before we delve into what each of these types of energies relate to and can be used for, and which should be avoided, we need to first be able to determine which Officer is in charge on any given date. This way, we can then determine what the prevailing energies of the day are and ascertain what is the best activity for that particular day, based on its Qi energies and attributes.

As always, you must know the Earthly Branch of the calendar month of the date you are referencing. So for example, if you are looking at dates in February, your reference point is the Tiger 寅 (Yin) Month. If you are looking at dates in August, your reference point is the Monkey 申 (Shen) Month. Here's a quick reminder of which Earthly Branch represents which Gregorian calendar month.

寅 Yin	Tiger	February 4th
卯 Mao	Rabbit	March 6th
辰 Chen	Dragon	April 5th
巳 Si	Snake	May 6th
午 Wu	Horse	June 6th
未 Wei	Goat	July 7th
申 Shen	Monkey	August 8th
酉 You	Rooster	September 8th
戌 Xu	Dog	October 8th
亥 Hai	Pig	November 7th
子 Zi	Rat	December 7th
丑 Chou	Ox	January 6th

Remember to check the exact transition day of the Chinese Solar month with the Ten Thousand Year Calendar. This chart is presented for convenience only.

Now, how do you work out which Officer is governing a particular day in a particular month? Just remember this simple rule: the first Day Officer in the pack is always the Establish 建 Day Officer. Thus, an Establish Day will always have the same Earthly Branch, as the reference month.

The 12 Day Officers Reference table below illustrates this clearly for you.

The 12 Day Officers Reference Table

月支 Month Branches / 日支 Day Branches	寅 *Yin* Tiger	卯 *Mao* Rabbit	辰 *Chen* Dragon	巳 *Si* Snake	午 *Wu* Horse	未 *Wei* Goat	申 *Shen* Monkey	酉 *You* Rooster	戌 *Xu* Dog	亥 *Hai* Pig	子 *Zi* Rat	丑 *Chou* Ox
寅 *Yin* Tiger Feb 4	建 *Jian* Establish	除 *Chu* Remove	滿 *Man* Full	平 *Ping* Balance	定 *Ding* Stable	執 *Zhi* Initiate	破 *Po* Destruction	危 *Wei* Danger	成 *Cheng* Success	收 *Shou* Receive	開 *Kai* Open	閉 *Bi* Close
卯 *Mao* Rabbit Mar 6	閉 *Bi* Close	建 *Jian* Establish	除 *Chu* Remove	滿 *Man* Full	平 *Ping* Balance	定 *Ding* Stable	執 *Zhi* Initiate	破 *Po* Destruction	危 *Wei* Danger	成 *Cheng* Success	收 *Shou* Receive	開 *Kai* Open
辰 *Chen* Dragon Apr 5	開 *Kai* Open	閉 *Bi* Close	建 *Jian* Establish	除 *Chu* Remove	滿 *Man* Full	平 *Ping* Balance	定 *Ding* Stable	執 *Zhi* Initiate	破 *Po* Destruction	危 *Wei* Danger	成 *Cheng* Success	收 *Shou* Receive
巳 *Si* Snake May 6	收 *Shou* Receive	開 *Kai* Open	閉 *Bi* Close	建 *Jian* Establish	除 *Chu* Remove	滿 *Man* Full	平 *Ping* Balance	定 *Ding* Stable	執 *Zhi* Initiate	破 *Po* Destruction	危 *Wei* Danger	成 *Cheng* Success
午 *Wu* Horse Jun 6	成 *Cheng* Success	收 *Shou* Receive	開 *Kai* Open	閉 *Bi* Close	建 *Jian* Establish	除 *Chu* Remove	滿 *Man* Full	平 *Ping* Balance	定 *Ding* Stable	執 *Zhi* Initiate	破 *Po* Destruction	危 *Wei* Danger
未 *Wei* Goat July 7	危 *Wei* Danger	成 *Cheng* Success	收 *Shou* Receive	開 *Kai* Open	閉 *Bi* Close	建 *Jian* Establish	除 *Chu* Remove	滿 *Man* Full	平 *Ping* Balance	定 *Ding* Stable	執 *Zhi* Initiate	破 *Po* Destruction
申 *Shen* Monkey Aug 8	破 *Po* Destruction	危 *Wei* Danger	成 *Cheng* Success	收 *Shou* Receive	開 *Kai* Open	閉 *Bi* Close	建 *Jian* Establish	除 *Chu* Remove	滿 *Man* Full	平 *Ping* Balance	定 *Ding* Stable	執 *Zhi* Initiate
酉 *You* Rooster Sept 8	執 *Zhi* Initiate	破 *Po* Destruction	危 *Wei* Danger	成 *Cheng* Success	收 *Shou* Receive	開 *Kai* Open	閉 *Bi* Close	建 *Jian* Establish	除 *Chu* Remove	滿 *Man* Full	平 *Ping* Balance	定 *Ding* Stable
戌 *Xu* Dog Oct 8	定 *Ding* Stable	執 *Zhi* Initiate	破 *Po* Destruction	危 *Wei* Danger	成 *Cheng* Success	收 *Shou* Receive	開 *Kai* Open	閉 *Bi* Close	建 *Jian* Establish	除 *Chu* Remove	滿 *Man* Full	平 *Ping* Balance
亥 *Hai* Pig Nov 7	平 *Ping* Balance	定 *Ding* Stable	執 *Zhi* Initiate	破 *Po* Destruction	危 *Wei* Danger	成 *Cheng* Success	收 *Shou* Receive	開 *Kai* Open	閉 *Bi* Close	建 *Jian* Establish	除 *Chu* Remove	滿 *Man* Full
子 *Zi* Rat Dec 7	滿 *Man* Full	平 *Ping* Balance	定 *Ding* Stable	執 *Zhi* Initiate	破 *Po* Destruction	危 *Wei* Danger	成 *Cheng* Success	收 *Shou* Receive	開 *Kai* Open	閉 *Bi* Close	建 *Jian* Establish	除 *Chu* Remove
丑 *Chou* Ox Jan 6	除 *Chu* Remove	滿 *Man* Full	平 *Ping* Balance	定 *Ding* Stable	執 *Zhi* Initiate	破 *Po* Destruction	危 *Wei* Danger	成 *Cheng* Success	收 *Shou* Receive	開 *Kai* Open	閉 *Bi* Close	建 *Jian* Establish

Let's take an example to help you understand this technique. Let's say you are looking at dates in February and you want to know which of the days in February are Establish 建 Days. February is the month of the Tiger 寅 (Yin). And since all

Establish Days share the same Earthly Branch as the month in reference, all Tiger Days in February (the Tiger Month) are Establish Days.

月支 Month Branches / 日支 Day Branches	寅 Yin Tiger	卯 Mao Rabbit	辰 Chen Dragon	巳 Si Snake	午 Wu Horse	未 Wei Goat	申 Shen Monkey	酉 You Rooster	戌 Xu Dog	亥 Hai Pig	子 Zi Rat	丑 Chou Ox
寅 Yin Tiger Feb 4	建 Jian Establish	除 Chu Remove	滿 Man Full	平 Ping Balance	定 Ding Stable	執 Zhi Initiate	破 Po Destruction	危 Wei Danger	成 Cheng Success	收 Shou Receive	開 Kai Open	閉 Bi Close
卯 Mao Rabbit Mar 6	閉 Bi Close	建 Jian Establish	除 Chu Remove	滿 Man Full	平 Ping Balance	定 Ding Stable	執 Zhi Initiate	破 Po Destruction	危 Wei Danger	成 Cheng Success	收 Shou Receive	開 Kai Open
辰 Chen Dragon Apr 5	開 Kai Open	閉 Bi Close	建 Jian Establish	除 Chu Remove	滿 Man Full	平 Ping Balance	定 Ding Stable	執 Zhi Initiate	破 Po Destruction	危 Wei Danger	成 Cheng Success	收 Shou Receive

FEBRUARY 2007 壬寅

SUNDAY	MONDAY	TUESDAY	WEDNESDAY	THURSDAY	FRIDAY	SATURDAY
				丙寅 1 十四	丁卯 2 十五	戊辰 3 十六
己巳 4 十七	庚午 5 十八	辛未 6 十九	壬申 7 二十	癸酉 8 廿一	甲戌 9 廿二	乙亥 10 廿三
丙子 11 廿四	丁丑 12 廿五	戊寅 建 Jian Establish 13 廿六	己卯 14 廿七	庚辰 15 廿八	辛巳 16 廿九	壬午 17 三十
癸未 18 正月初一	甲申 19 初二	乙酉 20 初三	丙戌 21 初四	丁亥 22 初五	戊子 23 初六	己丑 24 初七
庚寅 建 Jian Establish 25 初八	辛卯 26 初九	壬辰 27 初十	癸巳 28 十一			

The diagram above shows you all the Establish Days for the month of February 2007.

Let's take another example. Let's say you are looking at dates in July and you want to know which of the days in July are Establish Days. July is the month of the Goat 未 (Wei). And since all Establish Days share the same Earthly Branch as the month in reference, all Goat Days in July are Establish Days.

日支 Day Branches / 月支 Month Branches	寅 *Yin* **Tiger**	卯 *Mao* **Rabbit**	辰 *Chen* **Dragon**	巳 *Si* **Snake**	午 *Wu* **Horse**	未 *Wei* **Goat**	申 *Shen* **Monkey**	酉 *You* **Rooster**	戌 *Xu* **Dog**	亥 *Hai* **Pig**	子 *Zi* **Rat**	丑 *Chou* **Ox**
午 *Wu* **Horse** Jun 6	成 *Cheng* Success	收 *Shou* Receive	開 *Kai* Open	閉 *Bi* Close	建 *Jian* Establish	除 *Chu* Remove	滿 *Man* Full	平 *Ping* Balance	定 *Ding* Stable	執 *Zhi* Initiate	破 *Po* Destruction	危 *Wei* Danger
未 *Wei* **Goat** July 7	危 *Wei* Danger	成 *Cheng* Success	收 *Shou* Receive	開 *Kai* Open	閉 *Bi* Close	建 *Jian* Establish	除 *Chu* Remove	滿 *Man* Full	平 *Ping* Balance	定 *Ding* Stable	執 *Zhi* Initiate	破 *Po* Destruction
申 *Shen* **Monkey** Aug 8	破 *Po* Destruction	危 *Wei* Danger	成 *Cheng* Success	收 *Shou* Receive	開 *Kai* Open	閉 *Bi* Close	建 *Jian* Establish	除 *Chu* Remove	滿 *Man* Full	平 *Ping* Balance	定 *Ding* Stable	執 *Zhi* Initiate

Once you have found the Establish Day, then you have the starting point for the 12 Day Officers sequence. So, in the Tiger 寅 (Yin) Month, we know that the Tiger Day is governed by the Establish 建 Day Officer. Therefore, the Rabbit 卯 (Mao) Day is governed by the Remove 除 Day Officer, the Dragon 辰 (Chen) Day is governed by the Full 滿 Day Officer, and so on and so forth.

實用擇日

FEBRUARY 2007 壬寅

SUNDAY	MONDAY	TUESDAY	WEDNESDAY	THURSDAY	FRIDAY	SATURDAY
				丙寅 1 十四	丁卯 2 十五	戊辰 3 十六
己巳 平 *Ping* Balance 4 十七	庚午 定 *Ding* Stable 5 十八	辛未 執 *Zhi* Initiate 6 十九	壬申 破 *Po* Destruction 7 二十	癸酉 危 *Wei* Danger 8 廿一	甲戌 成 *Cheng* Success 9 廿二	乙亥 收 *Shou* Receive 10 廿三
丙子 開 *Kai* Open 11 廿四	丁丑 閉 *Bi* Close 12 廿五	戊寅 建 *Jian* Establish 13 廿六	己卯 除 *Chu* Remove 14 廿七	庚辰 滿 *Man* Full 15 廿八	辛巳 平 *Ping* Balance 16 廿九	壬午 定 *Ding* Stable 17 三十
癸未 執 *Zhi* Initiate 18 正月初一	甲申 破 *Po* Destruction 19 初二	乙酉 危 *Wei* Danger 20 初三	丙戌 成 *Cheng* Success 21 初四	丁亥 收 *Shou* Receive 22 初五	戊子 開 *Kai* Open 23 初六	己丑 閉 *Bi* Close 24 初七
庚寅 建 *Jian* Establish 25 初八	辛卯 除 *Chu* Remove 26 初九	壬辰 滿 *Man* Full 27 初十	癸巳 平 *Ping* Balance 28 十一			

This diagram shows you all the 12 Day Officers for every day of the month of February 2007. Note that February 4th 2007 is the transition point for the month.

So establishing the 12 Day Officers is pretty simple as you can see. Let's do another example just to familiarise you with how it works.

Let's say the date you are considering for a particular activity or venture is January 12, 2007.

January 12 is part of the Ox 丑 (Chou) Month. Now, look into the Ten Thousand Year Calendar or the Tong Shu Desktop Calendar.

月別 Month	十二月大 12th Mth Big				十一月大 11th Mth Big				十月小 10th Mth Small			
干支 Branches and Stems	辛丑 Xin Chou				庚子 Geng Zi				己亥 Ji Hai			
九星 Nine Star	三碧 Three Jade				四綠 Four Green				五黃 Five Yellow			
節氣 Season	立春 Coming of Spring		大寒 Greater Cold		小寒 Lesser Cold		冬至 Winter Solstice		大雪 Greater Snow		小雪 Lesser Snow	
	十七 17th day		初二 2nd day		十八 18th day		初三 3rd day		十七 17th day		初二 2nd day	
朔 Constellation	13時 20 分 13hr 20min		19時 2 分 19hr 2min		1時 42 分 1hr 42min		8時 24 分 8hr 24min		14時 28 分 14hr 28min		19時 3 分 19hr 3min	
	未 Wei		戌 Xu		丑 Chou		辰 Chen		未 Wei		戌 Xu	
農曆 Lunar Calendar	國曆 Gregorian		干支 Branches and stems	星 Star	國曆 Gregorian		干支 Branches and stems	星 Star	國曆 Gregorian		干支 Branches and stems	星 Star
初一 1st day	1	19	癸丑 Gui Chou	8	12	20	癸未 Gui Wei	5	11	21	甲寅 Jia Yin	7
初二 2nd day	1	20	甲寅 Jia Yin	9	12	21	甲申 Jia Shen	4	11	22	乙卯 Yi Mao	6
初三 3rd day	1	21	乙卯 Yi Mao	1	12	22	乙酉 Yi You	3\7	11	23	丙辰 Bing Chen	5
初四 4th day	1	22	丙辰 Bing Chen	2	12	23	丙戌 Bing Xu	8	11	24	丁巳 Ding Si	4
初五 5th day	1	23	丁巳 Ding Si	3	12	24	丁亥 Ding Hai	9	11	25	戊午 Wu Wu	3
初六 6th day	1	24	戊午 Wu Wu	4	12	25	戊子 Wu Zi	1	11	26	己未 Ji Wei	2
初七 7th day	1	25	己未 Ji Wei	5	12	26	己丑 Ji Chou	2	11	27	庚申 Geng Shen	1
初八 8th day	1	26	庚申 Geng Shen	6	12	27	庚寅 Geng Yin	3	11	28	辛酉 Xin You	9
初九 9th day	1	27	辛酉 Xin You	7	12	28	辛卯 Xin Mao	4	11	29	壬戌 Ren Xu	8
初十 10th day	1	28	壬戌 Ren Xu	8	12	29	壬辰 Ren Chen	5	11	30	癸亥 Gui Hai	7
十一 11th day	1	29	癸亥 Gui Hai	9	12	30	癸巳 Gui Si	6	12	1	甲子 Jia Zi	6
十二 12th day	1	30	甲子 Jia Zi	1	12	31	甲午 Jia Wu	7	12	2	乙丑 Yi Chou	5
十三 13th day	1	31	乙丑 Yi Chou	2	1	1	乙未 Yi Wei	8	12	3	丙寅 Bing Yin	4
十四 14th day	2	1	丙寅 Bing Yin	3	1	2	丙申 Bing Shen	9	12	4	丁卯 Ding Mao	3
十五 15th day	2	2	丁卯 Ding Mao	4	1	3	丁酉 Ding You	1	12	5	戊辰 Wu Chen	2
十六 16th day	2	3	戊辰 Wu Chen	5	1	4	戊戌 Wu Xu	2	12	6	己巳 Ji Si	1
十七 17th day	2	4	己巳 Ji Si	6	1	5	己亥 Ji Hai	3	12	7	庚午 Geng Wu	9
十八 18th day	2	5	庚午 Geng Wu	7	1	6	庚子 Geng Zi	4	12	8	辛未 Xin Wei	8
十九 19th day	2	6	辛未 Xin Wei	8	1	7	辛丑 Xin Chou	5	12	9	壬申 Ren Shen	7
二十 20th day	2	7	壬申 Ren Shen	9	1	8	壬寅 Ren Yin	6	12	10	癸酉 Gui You	6
二十一 21st day	2	8	癸酉 Gui You	1	1	9	癸卯 Gui Mao	7	12	11	甲戌 Jia Xu	5
二十二 22nd day	2	9	甲戌 Jia Xu	2	1	10	甲辰 Jia Chen	8	12	12	乙亥 Yi Hai	4
二十三 23rd day	2	10	乙亥 Yi Hai	3	1	11	乙巳 Yi Si	9	12	13	丙子 Bing Zi	3
二十四 24th day	2	11	丙子 Bing Zi	4	1	12	丙午 Bing Wu	1	12	14	丁丑 Ding Chou	2
二十五 25th day	2	12	丁丑 Ding Chou	5	1	13	丁未 Ding Wei	2	12	15	戊寅 Wu Yin	1
二十六 26th day	2	13	戊寅 Wu Yin	6	1	14	戊申 Wu Shen	3	12	16	己卯 Ji Mao	9
二十七 27th day	2	14	己卯 Ji Mao	7	1	15	己酉 Ji You	4	12	17	庚辰 Geng Chen	8
二十八 28th day	2	15	庚辰 Geng Chen	8	1	16	庚戌 Geng Xu	5	12	18	辛巳 Xin Si	7
二十九 29th day	2	16	辛巳 Xin Si	9	1	17	辛亥 Xin Hai	6	12	19	壬午 Ren Wu	6
三十 30th day	2	17	壬午 Ren Wu	1	1	18	壬子 Ren Zi	7				

2007 丁亥 Ding Hai Fire Pig

January 12, 2007

JANUARY 2007 辛丑

SUNDAY	MONDAY	TUESDAY	WEDNESDAY	THURSDAY	FRIDAY	SATURDAY
	乙未 1 十三	丙申 2 十四	丁酉 3 十五	戊戌 4 十六	己亥 5 十七	庚子 6 十八
辛丑 7 十九	壬寅 8 二十	癸卯 9 廿一	甲辰 10 廿二	乙巳 11 廿三	丙午 12 廿四	丁未 13 廿五
戊申 14 廿六	己酉 15 廿七	庚戌 16 廿八	辛亥 17 廿九	壬子 18 三十	癸丑 19 十二月初一	甲寅 20 初二
乙卯 21 初三	丙辰 22 初四	丁巳 23 初五	戊午 24 初六	己未 25 初七	庚申 26 初八	辛酉 27 初九
壬戌 28 初十	癸亥 29 十一	甲子 30 十二	乙丑 31 十三			

January 12, 2007 is a Bing Wu 丙午 Day.

Now, look at the 12 Day Officers table. You will see that the Horse 午 (Wu) Day in the Ox 丑 (Chou) Month is governed by the Initiate 執 Day Officer .

月支 Month Branches / 日支 Day Branches	寅 *Yin* Tiger	卯 *Mao* Rabbit	辰 *Chen* Dragon	巳 *Si* Snake	午 *Wu* Horse	未 *Wei* Goat	申 *Shen* Monkey	酉 *You* Rooster	戌 *Xu* Dog	亥 *Hai* Pig	子 *Zi* Rat	丑 *Chou* Ox
亥 *Hai* Pig Nov 7	平 *Ping* Balance	定 *Ding* Stable	執 *Zhi* Initiate	破 *Po* Destruction	危 *Wei* Danger	成 *Cheng* Success	收 *Shou* Receive	開 *Kai* Open	閉 *Bi* Close	建 *Jian* Establish	除 *Chu* Remove	満 *Man* Full
子 *Zi* Rat Dec 7	満 *Man* Full	平 *Ping* Balance	定 *Ding* Stable	執 *Zhi* Initiate	破 *Po* Destruction	危 *Wei* Danger	成 *Cheng* Success	收 *Shou* Receive	開 *Kai* Open	閉 *Bi* Close	建 *Jian* Establish	除 *Chu* Remove
丑 *Chou* Ox Jan 6	除 *Chu* Remove	満 *Man* Full	平 *Ping* Balance	定 *Ding* Stable	執 *Zhi* Initiate	破 *Po* Destruction	危 *Wei* Danger	成 *Cheng* Success	收 *Shou* Receive	開 *Kai* Open	閉 *Bi* Close	建 *Jian* Establish

Therefore, the Day Officer for January 12, 2007 is the Initiate Day Officer and January 12, 2007 is an Initiate Day.

Let's take another example. Let's say the day you are considering for your activity or venture is February 14, 2007. February 14 is part of the Tiger 寅 (Yin) Month. Now, look into the Ten Thousand Year Calendar at the month of February or the month of February in the Tong Shu Desktop Calendar.

月別 Month	十二月大 12th Mth Big				十一月大 11th Mth Big				十月小 10th Mth Small			
干支 Branches and Stems	辛丑 Xin Chou				庚子 Geng Zi				己亥 Ji Hai			
九星 Nine Star	三碧 Three Jade				四綠 Four Green				五黃 Five Yellow			
節氣 Season	立春 Coming of Spring		大寒 Greater Cold		小寒 Lesser Cold		冬至 Winter Solstice		大雪 Greater Snow		小雪 Lesser Snow	
	十七 17th day		初二 2nd day		十八 18th day		初三 3rd day		十七 17th day		初二 2nd day	
朔 Constellation	13時 20 分 13hr 20min		19時 2 分 19hr 2min		1時 42 分 1hr 42min		8時 24 分 8hr 24min		14時 28 分 14hr 28min		19時 3 分 19hr 3min	
	未 Wei		戌 Xu		丑 Chou		辰 Chen		未 Wei		戌 Xu	
農曆 Lunar Calendar	國曆 Gregorian		干支 Branches and stems	星 Star	國曆 Gregorian		干支 Branches and stems	星 Star	國曆 Gregorian		干支 Branches and stems	星 Star
初一 1st day	1	19	癸丑 Gui Chou	8	12	20	癸未 Gui Wei	5	11	21	甲寅 Jia Yin	7
初二 2nd day	1	20	甲寅 Jia Yin	9	12	21	甲申 Jia Shen	4	11	22	乙卯 Yi Mao	6
初三 3rd day	1	21	乙卯 Yi Mao	1	12	22	乙酉 Yi You	3\7	11	23	丙辰 Bing Chen	5
初四 4th day	1	22	丙辰 Bing Chen	2	12	23	丙戌 Bing Xu	8	11	24	丁巳 Ding Si	4
初五 5th day	1	23	丁巳 Ding Si	3	12	24	丁亥 Ding Hai	9	11	25	戊午 Wu Wu	3
初六 6th day	1	24	戊午 Wu Wu	4	12	25	戊子 Wu Zi	1	11	26	己未 Ji Wei	2
初七 7th day	1	25	己未 Ji Wei	5	12	26	己丑 Ji Chou	2	11	27	庚申 Geng Shen	1
初八 8th day	1	26	庚申 Geng Shen	6	12	27	庚寅 Geng Yin	3	11	28	辛酉 Xin You	9
初九 9th day	1	27	辛酉 Xin You	7	12	28	辛卯 Xin Mao	4	11	29	壬戌 Ren Xu	8
初十 10th day	1	28	壬戌 Ren Xu	8	12	29	壬辰 Ren Chen	5	11	30	癸亥 Gui Hai	7
十一 11th day	1	29	癸亥 Gui Hai	9	12	30	癸巳 Gui Si	6	12	1	甲子 Jia Zi	6
十二 12th day	1	30	甲子 Jia Zi	1	12	31	甲午 Jia Wu	7	12	2	乙丑 Yi Chou	5
十三 13th day	1	31	乙丑 Yi Chou	2	1	1	乙未 Yi Wei	8	12	3	丙寅 Bing Yin	4
十四 14th day	2	1	丙寅 Bing Yin	3	1	2	丙申 Bing Shen	9	12	4	丁卯 Ding Mao	3
十五 15th day	2	2	丁卯 Ding Mao	4	1	3	丁酉 Ding You	1	12	5	戊辰 Wu Chen	2
十六 16th day	2	3	戊辰 Wu Chen	5	1	4	戊戌 Wu Xu	2	12	6	己巳 Ji Si	1
十七 17th day	2	4	己巳 Ji Si	6	1	5	己亥 Ji Hai	3	12	7	庚午 Geng Wu	9
十八 18th day	2	5	庚午 Geng Wu	7	1	6	庚子 Geng Zi	4	12	8	辛未 Xin Wei	8
十九 19th day	2	6	辛未 Xin Wei	8	1	7	辛丑 Xin Chou	5	12	9	壬申 Ren Shen	7
二十 20th day	2	7	壬申 Ren Shen	9	1	8	壬寅 Ren Yin	6	12	10	癸酉 Gui You	6
二十一 21st day	2	8	癸酉 Gui You	1	1	9	癸卯 Gui Mao	7	12	11	甲戌 Jia Xu	5
二十二 22nd day	2	9	甲戌 Jia Xu	2	1	10	甲辰 Jia Chen	8	12	12	乙亥 Yi Hai	4
二十三 23rd day	2	10	乙亥 Yi Hai	3	1	11	乙巳 Yi Si	9	12	13	丙子 Bing Zi	3
二十四 24th day	2	11	丙子 Bing Zi	4	1	12	丙午 Bing Wu	1	12	14	丁丑 Ding Chou	2
二十五 25th day	2	12	丁丑 Ding Chou	5	1	13	丁未 Ding Wei	2	12	15	戊寅 Wu Yin	1
二十六 26th day	2	13	戊寅 Wu Yin	6	1	14	戊申 Wu Shen	3	12	16	己卯 Ji Mao	9
二十七 27th day	2	14	己卯 Ji Mao	7	1	15	己酉 Ji You	4	12	17	庚辰 Geng Chen	8
二十八 28th day	2	15	庚辰 Geng Chen	8	1	16	庚戌 Geng Xu	5	12	18	辛巳 Xin Si	7
二十九 29th day	2	16	辛巳 Xin Si	9	1	17	辛亥 Xin Hai	6	12	19	壬午 Ren Wu	6
三十 30th day	2	17	壬午 Ren Wu	1	1	18	壬子 Ren Zi	7				

February 14, 2007

FEBRUARY 2007 壬寅

SUNDAY	MONDAY	TUESDAY	WEDNESDAY	THURSDAY	FRIDAY	SATURDAY
				丙寅 1 十四	丁卯 2 十五	戊辰 3 十六
己巳 4 十七	庚午 5 十八	辛未 6 十九	壬申 7 二十	癸酉 8 廿一	甲戌 9 廿二	乙亥 10 廿三
丙子 11 廿四	丁丑 12 廿五	戊寅 13 廿六	己卯 14 廿七	庚辰 15 廿八	辛巳 16 廿九	壬午 17 三十
癸未 18 正月初一	甲申 19 初二	乙酉 20 初三	丙戌 21 初四	丁亥 22 初五	戊子 23 初六	己丑 24 初七
庚寅 25 初八	辛卯 26 初九	壬辰 27 初十	癸巳 28 十一			

It is a Ji Mao 己卯 Day.

Now look at the 12 Day Officers table. Any Rabbit 卯 (Mao) Day in the Tiger 寅 (Yin) Month is governed by the Remove 除 Day Officer. Therefore February 14, 2007 is a Remove Day.

月支 Month Branches / 日支 Day Branches	寅 Yin Tiger	卯 Mao Rabbit	辰 Chen Dragon	巳 Si Snake	午 Wu Horse	未 Wei Goat	申 Shen Monkey	酉 You Rooster	戌 Xu Dog	亥 Hai Pig	子 Zi Rat	丑 Chou Ox
寅 Yin Tiger Feb 4	建 Jian Establish	除 Chu Remove	滿 Man Full	平 Ping Balance	定 Ding Stable	執 Zhi Initiate	破 Po Destruction	危 Wei Danger	成 Cheng Success	收 Shou Receive	開 Kai Open	閉 Bi Close
卯 Mao Rabbit Mar 6	閉 Bi Close	建 Jian Establish	除 Chu Remove	滿 Man Full	平 Ping Balance	定 Ding Stable	執 Zhi Initiate	破 Po Destruction	危 Wei Danger	成 Cheng Success	收 Shou Receive	開 Kai Open
辰 Chen Dragon Apr 5	開 Kai Open	閉 Bi Close	建 Jian Establish	除 Chu Remove	滿 Man Full	平 Ping Balance	定 Ding Stable	執 Zhi Initiate	破 Po Destruction	危 Wei Danger	成 Cheng Success	收 Shou Receive

The Right Day for the Right Activity

Each of the 12 Day Officers or governing body of Qi has a use and function. So the trick in using this technique for Date Selection is to match the Day Officer or body of Qi to the activity that you have in mind. To do that, you will need to know what each Day Officer is specifically used for and why. I will refrain from the technical explanations as this is a beginners book. Let's just focus on understanding the qualities of each of the 12 types of days.

The qualities of the 12 Days in the 12 Day Officers Method vary from text to text. The following qualities of the 12 Days have been distilled from two classical texts: The Book of Unifying Times and Discerning Dimensions 協紀辨方書 (Xie Ji Bian Fang Shu) and The Philosophers of Huainan 淮南子 (Huai Nan Zi).

The 12 Day Officers are: Establish 建 (Jian), Remove 除 (Chu), Full 满 (Man), Balance 平 (Ping), Stable 定 (Ding), Initiate 執 (Zhi), Destruction 破 (Po), Danger 危 (Wei), Success 成 (Cheng), Receive 收 (Shou), Open 開 (Kai), Close 關 (Guan).

It is incorrect to classify these qualities of Qi in each of these days as entirely positive or negative and purely as superior or inferior, usable or unusable. Sometimes it is a question of how you use the energies of the day. Each Day can be said to have positive and negative aspects to it, with the exception of Success 成 and Destruction 破 Days. Success and Destruction Days are the only two days that can be said to have clear positive and negative energy attributes. So bear this in mind as you read through the attributes of the 12 Day Officers.

Establish Day 建日

Traditionally, the Establish Day was the date the Emperor would pray for a good harvest. In the modern context, an Establish Day is suitable for getting engaged or proposing marriage (but not marriage itself), starting a new job or assuming a new position at work, business transactions or dealings, or visiting friends.

In the old days, the term 'visiting friends' really meant visiting someone for negotiations. So a day that was suitable for 'visiting friends' in the old days would typically be used to discuss marriage, since finding a spouse for your child was usually considered 'important business'.

Today, the concept of 'visiting friends' has been updated to refer to activities such as the commencement of business negotiations or preliminary negotiations, discussions relating to business activities, and establishing communications with someone, with a view to doing business with them.

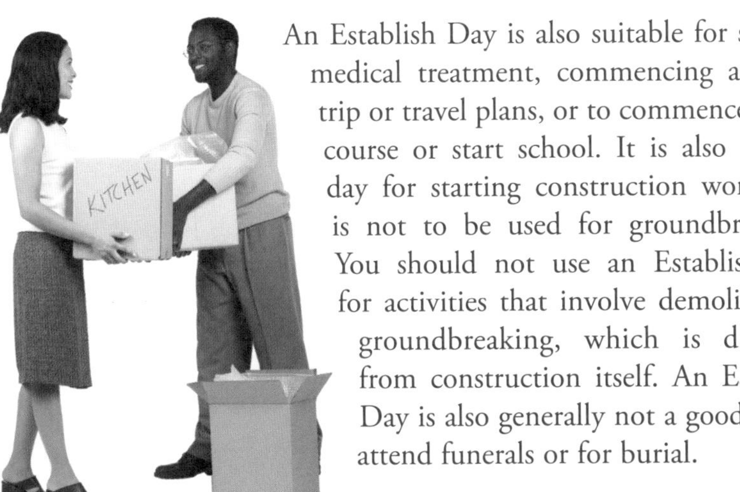

An Establish Day is also suitable for seeking medical treatment, commencing a major trip or travel plans, or to commence a new course or start school. It is also a good day for starting construction works but is not to be used for groundbreaking. You should not use an Establish Day for activities that involve demolition or groundbreaking, which is different from construction itself. An Establish Day is also generally not a good day to attend funerals or for burial.

Remove Day 除日

The Remove Day is usually used for cleansing activities or to rid something from the premises. In the old days, sometimes Remove Days were used for spiritual practice and removing bad karma, hence the reference to cleansing activities.

In the modern context, a Remove Day is a good day to use to end an abusive relationship, but can also be used to start going on a diet (you want to remove the fat right?). Remove Days are also good days to undergo medical procedures that involve removing something from your body. You can also use Remove Days to start demolition work and repair work on properties. It is also a good day for businesses to use to clear old or unwanted stock.

Naturally, we do not want to use a Remove Day for marriage. In the old days, getting married on a Remove Day was considered unfavourable because it would result in the early demise of the spouse. Today, it means separation or divorce. We also do not like to use Remove Days to adopt a child.

In the old days, Remove Days were not to be used for what is called 'buying livestock'. Farmers were not encouraged to farm animals on this day, as the animals would not reproduce well or would die easily or were short-lived. Today, very few people will find themselves buying a horse or cow. So, the equivalent activity would be buying or adopting a pet - avoid using a Remove Day to buy a pet or adopt a pet as this pet will be sickly or die or get lost easily.

Remove Days are also not good days to move into a new home as this indicates being evicted rather than moving by choice. A Remove Day is also a bad day to have an official opening unless your plan is to get rid of the business shortly after you start it! From a job standpoint, it is not a good day to start a job or assume a new job position at work. It is also generally not advisable to travel on a Remove Day as it indicates being turned away at the immigration points or having problems returning due to immigration hassles or problems on the return flight.

Full Day 満日

The Full Day is the day you use for when you want to have 'much' of something or plentiful and bountiful amounts of returns. It is good for signing agreements and official openings. This is a particularly good day to use if you are opening a chain of stores, or a franchise-concept store as you want to be able to tap into the multiplier effect of the Full Day.

You can also use the Full Day for a house-warming party and installing a new device or new equipment in your home or office. A Full Day is also a good day for debt-collection as you will be able to collect the sum 'in full'.

Although it is stipulated that Full Days can be used for matrimony, personally I don't select Full Days if possible for marriages. This is because in the old days, a Full Day signified more than one marriage and that was considered good - the more wives a man had, the richer he was. Today, having more than one wife is not permitted generally in law or by spouses! So it is best not to use a Full Day, unless you want to have lots of problems in the future.

The Full Day is a bit tricky in application when it comes to signing business agreements or activities that involve business transactions. You do have to scrutinise and understand the nature of the agreement or business activity or transaction very carefully. If it is something onerous (for example, you are signing a legal contract that is more about your obligations or responsibilities than say, money) then you may not want to choose a Full Day since that indicates a future full of more such obligations or responsibilities. On the other hand, if the contract is more commercial in nature and less obligation laden, then a Full Day could be usable.

Certainly, I do not advise signing any legal settlement agreement on such days (you may end up paying in full) or commencing any lawsuits on a Full Day since you may find you have your hands full of legal problems in the future.

In short, only use the Full Day if the activity in question is very positive and having too much of that outcome will not be detrimental.

The use of a Full Day to start a new job or assume a new job position is less than ideal. This is because arguably, you do not want the new job position to be 'full of responsibilities'.

It is also best not to use a Full Day for destroying or the demolition of buildings, and for burial.

Balance Day 平日

The Balance Day is a good day for marriage, construction, travelling (you will have a balanced journey) and business negotiations or commencing business communications. Activities that commence on a Balance Day will be favourable to both sides, with a win-win outcome for everyone. In some Date Selection texts, a Balance Day is classified as a negative day rather than a positive day. This is because since the day only produces a balanced outcome (as opposed to a superior or advantageous outcome), it is seen as not a useful day to choose since the point of Date Selection is to tilt the balance in one's favour, not create a win-win outcome.

Again, this comes back to the point about using the energies of the Day for the right activity rather than simply fixating on the superiority of the day. You should use a Balance Day to commence activities where you are in a less powerful position because this will help balance up the power situation or the odds for you. Of course, if you are in the superior position, this date doesn't do much for you. But if you are the David (and not the Goliath) in any situation, a Balance Day may well have its uses.

Date Selection specialists generally will not use a Balance Day to commence a legal action - such a lawsuit will be prolonged and will not produce an outcome that favours you, but one that is fair to both sides. We also do not like to use a Balance Day to commence activities that involve distribution of wealth, such as contesting a will or any division of assets. Balance Days are also not usable for burial.

實用擇日

Stable Day 定日

The Stable Day is a good day to start off or undertake activities that have a long-term aspect to them and for activities that you want to infuse with lasting effect or longevity. In short, it is a day to use for activities or actions that you want to go on in perpetuity or 'forever' - like marriage! Accordingly, it is a good day to use to seal an agreement for projects or matters that will span a long duration, or finalise something permanently. Hence this is a good day for official openings of businesses, commencing construction work on a property, hiring an important member of staff, buying a pet, getting married, house-warmings and seeking medical treatment (the cure will be permanent and lasting). It is not usually suitable to use a Stable Day for moving into a new house since this indicates you will keep moving. Similarly, we do not like to use Stable Days for funerals, travelling or getting buried.

When it comes to starting work on a project or a job, a Stable Day should only be used if you want to be on the project for the long-run or in that job for a long time. This is because the Stable Day indicates commencing something for the long run or long-term and generally in this day and age, people don't want to be tied down or stuck to one job or post in a company. If the project is one you want to get over and done with quickly or if the job is something you don't expect to stay at for the rest of your life, don't start work or a project on a Stable Day.

Initiate Day 執日

The Initiate Day is the day Date Selection specialists may select for activities that involve commencing or beginning something. Accordingly, an Initiate Day is a good day to accept work engagements or assignments, signing agreements, or to start up a new project or endeavour on a good footing. Anything that involves new beginnings or commencement should take place on an Initiate Day. That is why Initiate Days can also be used to start a new project, to open for business, to renovate your house or commence groundbreaking.

Having said that, Initiate Days are not considered by most classical Date Selection texts as a superior day. This is because it is the day before the Destruction Day. It would be more accurate to say it is a 'usable' or 'average' day and is usually only chosen in the absence of any other choice, due to a very restricted window in time for the activity or endeavour in question to commence or when there are positive stars present.

So what activities are Initiate Days not suitable for? Avoid moving into a new house and travelling on Initiate Days.

Destruction Day 破日

As the name suggests, Date Selection specialists use Destruction Days for activities that involve destroying something. Accordingly it is a good day to use to demolish a building or physical structures. It is said in the old books that Destruction Days can be used for removing something via a medical procedure although I would prefer not to use such a day.

Naturally, it is not a good idea to use a Destruction Day for important activities like marriage, engagements, opening a new business, commencing a trip or signing a contract - these are positive activities which obviously you do not want to infuse with destructive energies.

Danger Day 危日

All Danger Days contain danger stars and accordingly, such days are infused with much uncertainty. However, traditional Date Selection texts indicate that even Danger Days have some uses since there are usually positive stars present on Danger Days. Typically, Danger Days are used for religious worship, groundbreaking, bed positioning and dismantling objects.

Still, there is a danger component in the day so it is generally best to avoid dangerous or high risk sports activities and avoid being in very high places or at sea during Danger Days. It is also generally best to avoid commencing a long-distance journey on a Danger Day. This is not a suitable date for marriage or burial.

Success Day 成日

Of all the 12 Day Officers, the Success Day is the most auspicious and positive day of the lot. On Success Days, the energies are positive in all aspects and so are suitable for all activities that require positive starts and positive outcomes. Accordingly, it is good to use a Success Day to get married, propose marriage, submit a business proposal, seek medical treatment, begin construction of a property, move into a new house and for burial. The Success Day has a multiplier effect on the activities undertaken on the day so we always prefer to use it for positives, rather than negatives. Hence, we never use a Success Day for activities such as a lawsuit. The reasoning behind this is that you will end up having more lawsuits successfully!

You may be wondering why then I have included burial as the list of positive activities. Burials must be conducted on good days because this means that the deceased is buried in a good burial spot with favourable Feng Shui and the Feng Shui of that area is successfully activated. Their descendants can benefit from the positive energies of the burial location as the 'spot' is successfully activated.

Receive Day 收日

A Receive Day is a day to use to attain something, in particular, rewards. It is the day to use if you have to ask for something and get something in return. Typically, we like to use a Receive Day to start school, commence a course, close a deal, ask for a raise, propose marriage or start a new job - these are all activities for which a Receive Day is best utilised for. Receive Days are not good days to attend funerals, bury someone or seek medical treatment as you do not want to receive more of such activities. It is also not advisable to visit sick people on this day, unless you want to 'receive' their illness.

Open Day 開日

The Open Day, as its name suggests, is great for any activity that involves opening up your office or property or welcoming in guests. Use an Open Day for official openings, house-warming, starting or commencing work after Chinese New Year or a long-break, signing agreements, marriage and business engagements. It's also a good day to start a new job, assume a new job position at work or to start school or a course. Do not use Open Days for burial and groundbreaking.

Close Day 閉日

Qi is unmoving and at its lowest point on a Close Day as this is the last day of the 12 day cycle of the 12 Day Officers system. Accordingly you should never select a Close Day for any activity of great personal and business significance.

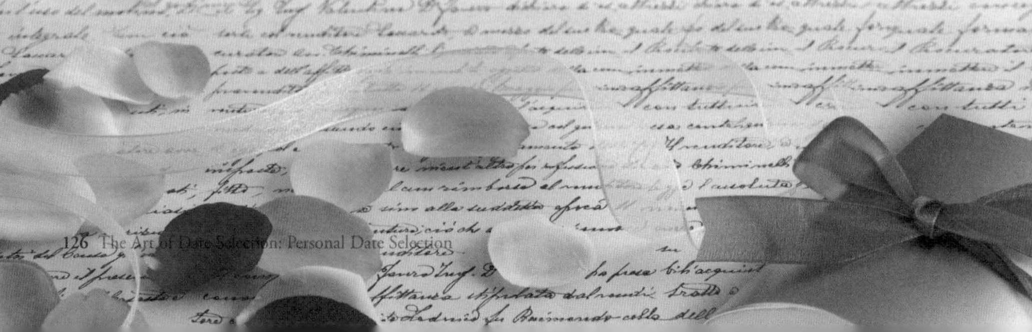

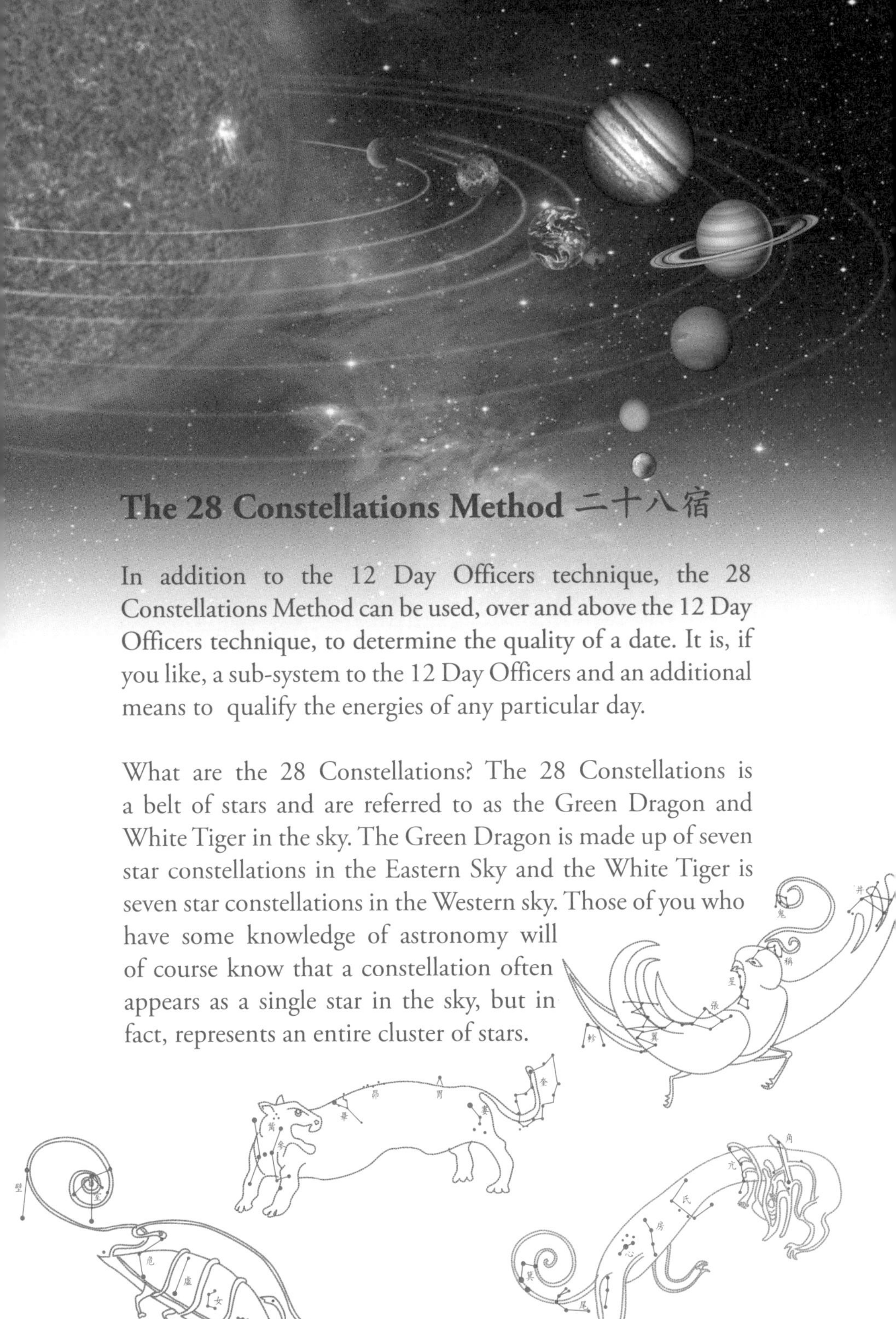

The 28 Constellations Method 二十八宿

In addition to the 12 Day Officers technique, the 28 Constellations Method can be used, over and above the 12 Day Officers technique, to determine the quality of a date. It is, if you like, a sub-system to the 12 Day Officers and an additional means to qualify the energies of any particular day.

What are the 28 Constellations? The 28 Constellations is a belt of stars and are referred to as the Green Dragon and White Tiger in the sky. The Green Dragon is made up of seven star constellations in the Eastern Sky and the White Tiger is seven star constellations in the Western sky. Those of you who have some knowledge of astronomy will of course know that a constellation often appears as a single star in the sky, but in fact, represents an entire cluster of stars.

實用擇日

The 28 Constellations Method is based on the concept that each day is represented by a single constellation of stars, and that particular body of energies. In the Tong Shu, the 28 Constellations Method is used to designate the daily star or 'star of the day'. Based on this system, the energies that affect us rotate on a 28-day cycle.

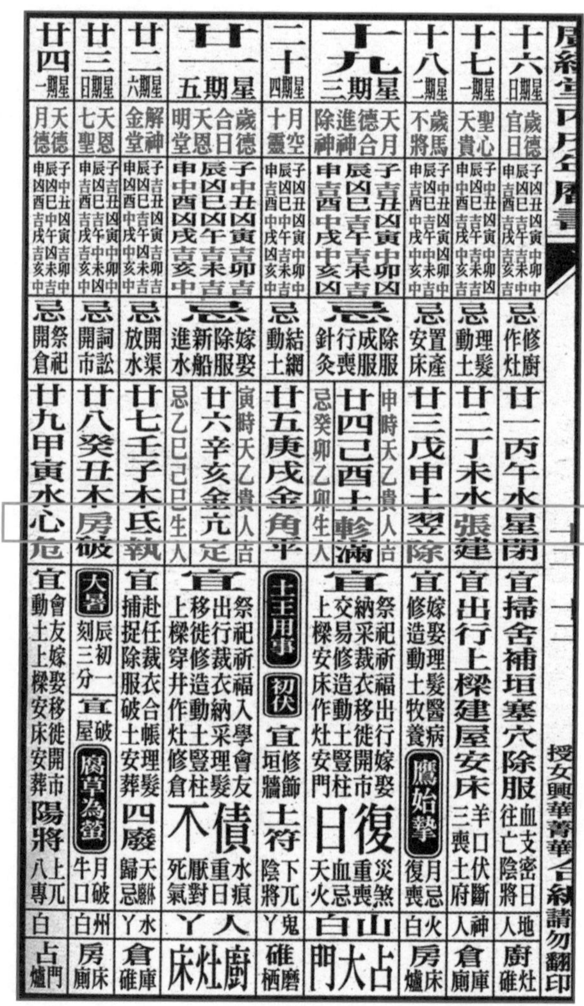

The 28 Constellations as it appears in a traditional Tong Shu

Some Date Selection specialists ignore the 28 Constellations Method and use the Gods and Killings Method in tandem with the 12 Day Officers as they are of the opinion that the alignment of the 28 Constellations can only be confirmed by actually observing the position of the stars using a telescope. Today, astronomical data is more accurate so I feel the 28 Constellations as a method can be explored further. However, this is a rather advanced approach to Date Selection, involving the study of astrology.

Generally, most Date Selection specialists do not really use the 28 Constellations as a main Date Selection system - it is typically used only as a refinement technique, to help further qualify the quality of the energies of a particular day, based on the position of the day star in the sky. A further point to note is that even though the 28 Constellations Method is documented in The Book of Unifying Time and Discerning Dimensions 協紀辨方書 (Xie Ji Bian Fang Shu), it is not emphasised as a definitive technique. Hence its usage as a back-up or corroborative method, rather than a primary method of Date Selection.

The rationale behind the 28 Constellations is that the 12 Day Officers cycle takes only 12 days to complete but the energies of each day will not necessarily always be the same every 12 days. Also, there are 60 Jia Zi or Day Pillars, each exerting a different elemental outcome, depending on how that day interacts with the Month and Year Earthly Branch.

So, the key point to remember about the 28 Constellations Method is it is an optional, additional layer that you can use to further qualify a particular date. In other words, to make sure a good date is really really good! If you would like to be sure you really have a good date, then check to make sure the date you have selected, using the 12 Day Officer technique also has a good daily star, based on the 28 Constellations Method. But if you can't be fussed, then don't worry - not working with the 28 Constellations is not going to cause your date of choice to suddenly go from good to unusable!

Using the 28 Constellations Method

星期 **Day of the week**		四 Thu	五 Fri	六 Sat	日 Sun	一 Mon	二 Tues	三 Wed
七曜 **7 Stars**		木 wood	金 metal	土 earth	日 sun	月 moon	火 fire	水 water
二十八宿 **The 28 Constellations**	東方青龍七宿 **Eastern Green Dragon 7 Constellations**	1 角 *Jiao* Horn	2 亢 *Kang* Neck	3 氐 *Di* Foundation	4 房 *Fang* House	5 心 *Xin* Heart	6 尾 *Wei* Tail	7 箕 *Ji* Basket
	北方玄武七宿 **Northern Black Tortoise 7 Constellations**	8 斗 *Dou* Dipper	9 牛 *Niu* Ox	10 女 *Nu* Weaving Maiden	11 虛 *Xu* Void	12 危 *Wei* Danger	13 室 *Shi* Room	14 壁 *Bi* Wall
	西方白虎七宿 **Western White Tiger 7 Constellations**	15 奎 *Kui* Astride	16 婁 *Lou* Mound	17 胃 *Wei* Stomach	18 昴 *Mao* Pleiades	19 畢 *Bi* Net	20 觜 *Zui* Beak	21 參 *Can* Orion
	南方朱雀七宿 **Southern Red Phoenix 7 Constellations**	22 井 *Jing* Well	23 鬼 *Gui* Ghost	24 柳 *Liu* Willow	25 星 *Xing* Star	26 張 *Zhang* Bow	27 翼 *Yi* Wing	28 軫 *Zhen* Carriage

The 28 Constellations Method is similar to that of the 12 Day Officers technique - the idea is to calculate and determine what energies are present in a day, based on the constellation in the sky. The sequence of stars used in the 28 Constellations Method is explained in the table below.

The starting point for the 28 Constellations system is always the Horn Star. This is the 1st star of the 28 Constellations and it always appears on a Thursday. I have calculated for you the dates the Horn Star appears for the years 2007-2020 in the following set of tables.

2007	2008	2009	2010	2011
January 4	January 3	January 1	January 28	January 27
February 1	January 31	January 29	February 25	February 24
March 1	February 28	February 26	March 25	March 24
March 29	March 27	March 26	April 22	April 21
April 26	April 24	April 23	May 20	May 19
May 24	May 22	May 21	June 17	June 16
June 21	June 19	June 18	July 15	July 14
July 19	July 17	July 16	August 12	August 11
August 16	August 14	August 13	September 9	September 8
September 13	September 11	September 10	October 7	October 6
October 11	October 9	October 8	November 4	December 29
November 8	November 6	November 5	November 2	
December 6	December 4	December 3	December 30	
		December 31		

2012	2013	2014	2015	2016
January 26	January 24	January 23	January 22	January 21
February 23	February 21	February 20	February 19	February 18
March 22	March 21	March 20	March 19	March 17
April 19	April 18	April 17	April 16	April 14
May 17	May 16	May 15	May 14	May 12
June 14	June 13	June 12	June 11	June 9
July 12	July 11	July 10	July 9	July 7
August 9	August 8	August 7	August 6	August 4
September 6	September 5	September 4	September 3	September 1
October 4	October 3	October 2	October 1	September 29
November 1	October 31	October 30	October 29	October 27
November 29	November 28	November 27	November 26	November 24
December 27	December 26	December 25	December 24	December 22

2017	2018	2019	2020
January 19	January 18	January 17	January 16
February 16	February 15	February 14	February 13
March 16	March 15	March 14	March 12
April 13	April 12	April 11	April 9
May 11	May 10	May 9	May 7
June 8	June 7	June 6	June 4
July 6	July 5	July 4	July 2
August 3	August 2	August 1	July 30
August 31	Augustt 30	August 29	August 27
September 28	September 27	September 26	September 24
October 26	October 25	October 24	October 22
November 23	November 22	November 21	November 19
December 21	December 20	December 19	December 17

Once you have established the Horn Star for the month, you simply follow the order of the table, backwards or forwards sequentially, through the other 27 stars, to the Daily Star you want to use.

To determine which Daily Star you should use, you have to know the qualities of each of the 28 Daily Stars in the 28 Constellations Method. The following narratives will give you some basic information about each of the 28 stars and the types of activities they support.

角

Horn 角 (Jiao)

The Horn Star is a positive and benevolent star - it heralds good tidings, increased wealth and appreciating assets. Hence, it is best to have present on days used for marriage, travelling and ground-breaking activities. However, the Horn Star should not be used for burial activities.

亢

Neck 亢 (Kang)

The Neck Star is a generally unfavourable star to have present for activities such as marriage, construction, burial and investments or commercial dealings. Using a day with this star indicates the activity will be infused with negativity, specifically, outcomes that result in a loss of wealth.

Foundation 氐 (Di)

This star has very specific uses and should only be present for activities that involve public speaking, property investment or major broadcasting events (such as the opening ceremony of the Olympics). For all other activities, this star is negative. In particular, avoid getting married or burying a family member on this day. According to the old texts, if one engages in renovation or construction on this day, the property may likely end up being a fire hazard.

House 房 (Fang)

The House Star is not a favourable star to have present for days when you intend to make an important financial investment. However, it is favourable and positive to have present for activities such as marriage, burial and long-distance travel. Used appropriately, it will bring wealth to the family. If utilized for burial, this star will produce descendents who are officers and ministers and if used for marriage, the couple will be blessed with offspring within 3 years. In short, this star is good for prayers, marriage, installing roof beams and migration. It is however bad for investment and visiting your tailor to order a set of new clothes!

Heart 心 (Xin)

The Heart Star is actually regarded as a negative star, despite its name. Its uses are highly limited and confined to traveling or harvesting commodities. Do not use a Heart Star Day to launch a lawsuit, break-ground or for burial as this star brings disputes and arguments and will most likely result in greater litigation (if used for a lawsuit) or squabbling heirs (if used for burial).

Tail 尾 (Wei)

This is an excellent star to have present for burial, door alignment and for Feng Shui water placement activities. On the personal activity level, this is a good star to have present for activities such as marriage, renovations and commencing construction of a building or structure. This star is also a favourable star to have present during contract signings. It ushers help from noble (helpful) people.

Basket 箕 (Ji)

This is a good star to have present for the construction of a building or structure, alignment of a new door, digging of a swimming pool, debt collection and receipt of monies. However, it is used predominantly for Feng Shui activities, rather than personal activities. It is not a suitable star to have present on a marriage date.

Dipper 斗 (Dou)

The Dipper is the star of Wealth and the star of Literary and Military success. In a modern context, this Star is ideal to have present during key Feng Shui alignment activities (such as the placement and alignment of a new door or a water feature) and is more suited for commercial endeavours rather than personal activities. It is best however not to start a new job or form a new business partnership on a day with this star present.

Ox 牛 (Niu)

This is a disaster star and so should not be present on any day used for important personal and business activities. Specifically, this is not a good star to have present during marriages and contract signings.

Weaving Maiden 女 (Nu)

This star is predominantly used for academic and literary pursuits, and is best used for private or internal activities. It is a good star to have present on days when you are starting a new course or commencing school. The Weaving Maiden is however unsuitable for public activities. Avoid legal issues or attending a funeral on a day with this star.

Void 虛 (Xu)

This star signals illness. It is considered a pure negative star that is not suitable for any activity of a personal or commercial nature. Try to avoid using a day that has this star for any important activities or endeavours.

Danger 危 (Wei)

The Danger star, as its name suggests, indicates bodily harm, danger at sea or near water and health problems. It is generally not usable for any important personal and commercial activities, with the exception of debt-collection.

Room 室 (Shi)

The Room star is a good and positive star to have present on a day when you intend to get married, start a new business or begin construction of a building or structure. It signifies the multiplication of assets, and many children and grandchildren of calibre!

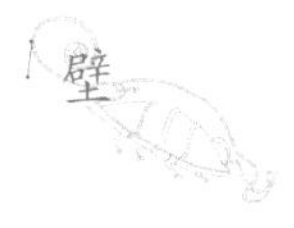

Wall 壁 (Bi)

A good star to have present during marriage, official openings, signing a contract and burial. It is a positive star that heralds prosperity and an increase in wealth. Avoid however commencing any travel in the South direction on days when this star is present.

Astride 奎 (Kui)

The presence of this star during an official opening indicates the business is likely to be plagued by legal problems and lots of obstacles and challenges in its early years of business. However, if this star is present on a day used for traveling or renovations, it brings about positive outcomes.

Mound 婁 (Lou)

This is a highly favourable star to have present during key business and personal activities. Days when this star is present are good for marriage, business deals, renovations, and building or adding extensions to a property. It is one of the few stars with no negative attributes.

The Mound star is ideal for building extra rooms or expanding your house, and is also the `guardian' star of wealth and prosperity. Accordingly, a household which has this star smiling upon them will find its occupants successful and even famous! A marriage `sanctified' by the presence of this star will produce good, healthy offspring. Hence, the Mound star is good for everything, especially marriage, business deals, commencing construction and renovation. Better still, there's no downside to this star!

Stomach 胃 (Wei)

A good star to have present on days used for marriage and burial as it heralds nobility, wealth, good health and happy events. It is a favourable star primarily for what are known as 'external' and 'public' matters and thus is not suitable on days when you intend to deal with family issues or private business matters.

As the harbinger of happy events, you can expect to be promoted both at work and in health - and enjoy good wealth prospects in your endeavours. Even if sombrely used for burial, the descendents of the deceased will hold high positions and status in society. A marriage that is blessed by the presence of the Stomach star will not only enjoy good wealth prospects, but also the company of filial children.

Hence, this star is good for burial, marriage, public matters and external matters (i.e. matters involving those outside the family). It is however bad for private or internal matters, which pertain to domestic issues.

Pleiades 昴 (Mao)

This is an extremely negative star and it is best not to use any day where this star is present for important personal or business activities. It is particularly important to avoid using a day when this star is present for marriage, debt-collection and commencing a lawsuit.

Net 畢 (Bi)

A good star to have present on days when the following activities take place: construction, land acquisition and marriage. It is a generally benevolent star that brings about harmonious outcomes, peaceful relationships and a day with this star present is generally a good day for most activities.

Beak 觜 (Zui)

It is considered a highly negative and unfavourable star to have present. Avoid engaging in any important personal and business activities on a day when this star is present. No good can come from any activities that commence on a day with this star present.

Orion 參 (Can)

Although this is a positive star, it is not a suitable star to have present on a day used for marriage or burial. However, for Feng Shui-related activities, travel, renovation and construction, this star is extremely favourable, heralding fame and achievements.

Well 井 (Jing)

The Well star has limited use. It is best utilised for Feng Shui activation activities like aligning the door or water placement but it can also be used for activities like ground-breaking or commencing a work project. When this star is present on a day, do not engage in activities like burial, signing contracts and marriage.

Ghost 鬼 (Gui)

The Ghost star is generally a negative star and should not be present on a day you intend to use to get married, travel to the West or construct a new building or home. It should only be present on a day used for burial activities.

Willow 柳 (Liu)

This star is not generally usable for any important activities. In particular, avoid starting a new job, starting business, acquiring assets, closing business deals or burial on a day with this star present. Feng Shui activation such as door alignment or water placement should be avoided on a day when this star is present.

Star 星 (Xing)

This star is a favourable star to have present on a marriage date. It is also favourable for negotiations, commencing an important project or official openings. This is not a favourable star to have present on a burial day.

Bow 張 (Zhang)

張

An extremely positive and auspicious star to have present during any commercial and personal activities and endeavours. This is one of the few stars that only has positive aspects. Open your new business, sign contracts and purchase assets on a day with this star present as this star has a multiplier effect on assets. It is also a good star to have present on a marriage date.

Wing 翼 (Yi)

翼

This star is unfavourable for most activities, particularly door alignment for Feng Shui purposes, burial and marriage. It is generally a negative star. Do not begin a new job or assume a new job position on a day with this star present.

Carriage 軫 (Zhen)

軫

This star is suitable for activities such as asset acquisition, marriage, investments, and if you are seeking approval or requisitioning something from someone. This is also a good star to have present on a day when you are starting school or commencing a course of study. It is only not usable for travelling, in particular, movement in the North direction.

Using the 28 Constellations Method with the 12 Day Officers

月支 Month Branches / 日支 Day Branches	寅 Yin Tiger	卯 Mao Rabbit	辰 Chen Dragon	巳 Si Snake	午 Wu Horse	未 Wei Goat	申 Shen Monkey	酉 You Rooster	戌 Xu Dog	亥 Hai Pig	子 Zi Rat	丑 Chou Ox
寅 Yin Tiger Feb 4	建 Jian Establish	除 Chu Remove	満 Man Full	平 Ping Balance	定 Ding Stable	執 Zhi Initiate	破 Po Destruction	危 Wei Danger	成 Cheng Success	收 Shou Receive	開 Kai Open	閉 Bi Close
卯 Mao Rabbit Mar 6	閉 Bi Close	建 Jian Establish	除 Chu Remove	満 Man Full	平 Ping Balance	定 Ding Stable	執 Zhi Initiate	破 Po Destruction	危 Wei Danger	成 Cheng Success	收 Shou Receive	開 Kai Open
辰 Chen Dragon Apr 5	開 Kai Open	閉 Bi Close	建 Jian Establish	除 Chu Remove	満 Man Full	平 Ping Balance	定 Ding Stable	執 Zhi Initiate	破 Po Destruction	危 Wei Danger	成 Cheng Success	收 Shou Receive

Let's say you want to move house or start a new business. Based on the 12 Day Officers technique, you know you want to use a Success 成 Day to move house. So you search through the calendar and find March 6 2007, which is a Success Day according to the 12 Day Officers technique. Now, you want to be sure that March 6 is really a good day to move house. So you want to double check the Daily Star, according to the 28 Constellations, to make sure it is really a good day.

MARCH 2007 癸卯

SUNDAY	MONDAY	TUESDAY	WEDNESDAY	THURSDAY	FRIDAY	SATURDAY
				甲午 1 十二	乙未 2 十三	丙申 3 十四
丁酉 4 十五	戊戌 5 十六	己亥 成 Cheng Success 6 十七	庚子 7 十八	辛丑 8 十九	壬寅 9 二十	癸卯 10 廿一
甲辰 11 廿二	乙巳 12 廿三	丙午 13 廿四	丁未 14 廿五	戊申 15 廿六	己酉 16 廿七	庚戌 17 廿八
辛亥 18 廿九	壬子 19 二月初一	癸丑 20 初二	甲寅 21 初三	乙卯 22 初四	丙辰 23 初五	丁巳 24 初六
戊午 25 初七	己未 26 初八	庚申 27 初九	辛酉 28 初十	壬戌 29 十一	癸亥 30 十二	甲子 31 十三

March 1 2007 is a Horn 角 Star Day. Counting forward 5 days (not including March 1 2007) brings you to the Tail 尾 Star Day. The Tail star, based on the 28 Constellations Method, is a good star for activities involving property purchase, weddings, and moving into a new house.

So, you know that March 6 is definitely a good date to use for moving house and starting a new business. Easy right?

Let's do another example.

Let's say you want to find a good day to commence work on a new project. Now you want to use an Initiate 執 Day to begin something new and infuse it with the right energies for success right? So you search through your calendar and you come across May 3 2007, an Initiate Day.

日支 Day Branches / 月支 Month Branches	寅 *Yin* Tiger	卯 *Mao* Rabbit	辰 *Chen* Dragon	巳 *Si* Snake	午 *Wu* Horse	未 *Wei* Goat	申 *Shen* Monkey	酉 *You* Rooster	戌 *Xu* Dog	亥 *Hai* Pig	子 *Zi* Rat	丑 *Chou* Ox
寅 *Yin* Tiger Feb 4	建 *Jian* Establish	除 *Chu* Remove	满 *Man* Full	平 *Ping* Balance	定 *Ding* Stable	執 *Zhi* Initiate	破 *Po* Destruction	危 *Wei* Danger	成 *Cheng* Success	收 *Shou* Receive	開 *Kai* Open	閉 *Bi* Close
卯 *Mao* Rabbit Mar 6	閉 *Bi* Close	建 *Jian* Establish	除 *Chu* Remove	满 *Man* Full	平 *Ping* Balance	定 *Ding* Stable	執 *Zhi* Initiate	破 *Po* Destruction	危 *Wei* Danger	成 *Cheng* Success	收 *Shou* Receive	開 *Kai* Open
辰 *Chen* Dragon Apr 5	開 *Kai* Open	閉 *Bi* Close	建 *Jian* Establish	除 *Chu* Remove	满 *Man* Full	平 *Ping* Balance	定 *Ding* Stable	執 *Zhi* Initiate	破 *Po* Destruction	危 *Wei* Danger	成 *Cheng* Success	收 *Shou* Receive

Now, you want to be doubly sure that this Initiate Day is really a good day to kick something off. So, let's find out the 28 Constellation Daily Star for May 3 2007.

April 26 2007 is the nearest Horn Star Day. So, counting forward to the 3rd of May (not including April 26 2007), we find that it is a Dipper 斗 Day, according to the 28 Constellations. The Dipper Day is a good day for digging a well, and building a house amongst other things. Generally the energies are positive for starting something new. Combined with the fact that it is an Initiate Day, means that this particular day is clearly a suitable day for the activity of commencing work on a new project.

For those who are industrious, you can label the entire calendar with all the 28 Constellations stars to make your annual Date Selection activities easier. But of course, you don't HAVE to do it. However, a little prep work sometimes goes a long way when it comes to making your Date Selection activities easier so I always tell my students - it's legwork that is well worth doing.

實用擇日

The right day, but is it the right time?

What I have covered in this chapter are simple Date Selection techniques. But these are enough techniques to help you not only avoid a bad date, but also chose a good date. Armed with these techniques and methods, you'll probably be able to give grandma a run for her money as far as doing family Date Selection is concerned - really!

十六	十七	十八	十九	二十	廿一	廿二	廿三	廿四
星期日	星期一	星期二	星期三	星期四	星期五	星期六	星期日	星期一
歲德 官日	聖心 天貴	歲馬 不將	天月 德合 進神 除神	月空 十靈	歲德 合日 天恩 明堂	解神 金堂	天恩 七聖	天德 月德
子凶 丑凶 寅中 卯中 辰凶 巳吉 午吉 未中 申吉 酉吉 戌吉 亥吉	子中 丑凶 寅中 卯凶 辰凶 巳吉 午吉 未吉 申中 酉吉 戌中 亥吉	子中 丑凶 寅凶 卯中 辰凶 巳吉 午中 未吉 申吉 酉中 戌中 亥中	子吉 丑凶 寅中 卯凶 辰凶 巳吉 午吉 未吉 申吉 酉中 戌中 亥凶	子凶 丑凶 寅中 卯中 辰凶 巳中 午吉 未吉 申吉 酉中 戌凶 亥中	子中 丑凶 寅吉 卯吉 辰凶 巳凶 午吉 未吉 申中 酉凶 戌吉 亥中	子吉 丑凶 寅吉 卯吉 辰凶 巳吉 午凶 未吉 申凶 酉中 戌中 亥中	子吉 丑凶 寅中 卯中 辰凶 巳吉 午中 未凶 申吉 酉吉 戌吉 亥中	子中 丑凶 寅吉 卯中 辰凶 巳中 午凶 未吉 申凶 酉吉 戌吉 亥中
忌 修廚 作灶	忌 理髮 動土	忌 置產 安床	忌 除服 成服 行喪 針灸	忌 結網 動土	忌 嫁娶 除服 新船 進水	忌 開渠 放水	忌 詞訟 開市	忌 祭祀 開倉
廿一丙午水星閉	廿二丁未水張建	廿三戊申土翌除	申時天乙貴人吉 廿四己酉土軫滿 忌癸卯乙卯生人	廿五庚戌金角平	寅時天乙貴人吉 廿六辛亥金亢定 忌乙巳己巳生人	廿七壬子木氐執	廿八癸丑木房破	廿九甲寅水心危
宜 掃舍補垣塞穴除服	宜 出行上樑建屋安床	宜 嫁娶理髮醫病 修造動土牧養 鷹始摯	宜 祭祀祈福出行嫁娶 納采裁衣移徙開市 交易修造動土豎柱 上樑安床作灶安門	土王用事 初伏 宜 修飾垣牆	宜 祭祀祈福入學會友 出行裁衣納采理髮 移徙修造動土豎柱 上樑穿井作灶修倉	宜 赴任裁衣合帳理髮 捕捉除服破土安葬	大暑 辰初一刻三分 宜 破屋 腐草為螢	宜 會友嫁娶移徙開市 動土上樑安床安葬
血支 密日 往亡 陰將	羊口 伏斷 三喪 土府	月忌 復喪	復日 災煞 重喪 血忌 天火	土符 下兀 陰將	不債 水痕 重日 厭對 死氣	四廢 天[illegible] 歸忌	月破 牛口	陽將 上兀 八專
地人	神人	火白	山白	鬼丫	人丫	水丫	州白	白
廚 灶碓	倉 庫廁	房 床爐	占大門	碓 磨栖	廚灶床	倉 庫碓	房 床廁	占 門爐

請勿翻印

Now, you're probably thinking: now that I have a date, does it matter what time I start? Definitely!

A Date Selection specialist will typically not just use the methods and techniques discussed in Chapter 3 and 4, but will plug in and superimpose additional techniques such as the Grand Master Dong's System (董公擇日), Star Head 斗首 (Dou Shou), Heavenly Stars 七政四餘 (Qi Zheng Si Yu) or 64 Hexagrams 玄空大卦 (Xuan Kong Da Gua). They will then zero in on a really good hour, using additional methods or Mystical Doors Method 奇門盾甲 (Qi Men Dun Jia) techniques, depending on the circumstances and activity in question.

Those of course are quite sophisticated methods, and this is a basics book so I'll keep it simple. In the next chapter, I'll show you a simple technique that you can use to pick a good hour to optimise further a good date and how to avoid hours that will neutralise the effects of your good date.

Chapter Five:
Time is of the Essence

Selecting a good date in which to commence an activity is the first step in making sure that you are starting off your venture or endeavour in the most positive and favourable way possible. But a day has 24 hours or 12 Chinese hours - when should you commence the activity in question? And does the time even matter?

Through the selection of a good date, 70 percent of the energies of the day are already on your side. By adding a suitable hour, you are adding icing to the cake and of course, enhancing the positive effect of the day. After all, it is all about doing the right thing, at the RIGHT TIME.

Date Selection specialists typically use hour selection to refine the outcome of the date chosen for the commencement of the activity or in certain instances, to improve an average date or negate an unfavourable date. Sometimes, the Date Selection specialist has no choice in the matter or the client has a very narrow window of time for the activity, such as an official opening or contract signing. Under specific circumstances, the use of a *good hour*, selected through certain techniques such as Mystical Doors Method 奇門盾甲 (Qi Men Dun Jia) or Nobleman Ascending Heavenly Gate Hour 貴人登天門 (Gui Ren Deng Tian Men), can help offset some of the negative aspects of the day.

However, the ideal situation with Date Selection is to have a good day, and top it off by commencing the activity at a good hour. In this chapter, I will focus on showing you on how to find a good hour to complement a good or usable date.

Telling the Time, the Chinese Way

Most of us are familiar with the 24 hours of the day. However, the Chinese 'clock' if you like, has only 12 hours. So in order to learn how to select a good hour to complement a good date, you need to learn how to tell the time, the Chinese way.

The hours of a day are demarcated according to the 12 Earthly Branches. Accordingly, each Chinese hour spans two normal Western hours. The table below shows you the 12 hours of the day, according to their Earthly Branches.

So, if you need to commence an activity at the Tiger 寅 (Yin) hour, then you have to start anywhere between 3-5am. If a suitable hour is the Horse 午 (Wu) hour, then begin or commence the activity anytime between 11am-1pm.

Time and Stars

For those of you who know how to read or use a Tong Shu, the page that is usually used to select an hour is like the one shown below. The Auspicious Hour Reference table contains all the 60 Day Pillars or 60 types of days and indicates the stars present in the solar system during every Chinese hour of the day, for every single one of the 60 Day Pillars or 60 types of days. The auspicious and negative stars in that hour are delineated through the use of red text (auspicious) and black text (negative). It also indicates what is the hour that clashes with that particular Day Pillar.

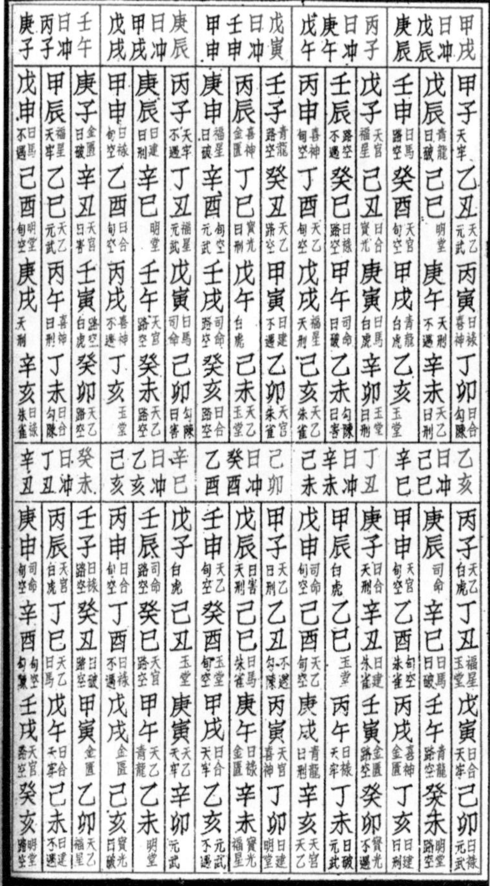

甲戌 日冲 戊辰 庚辰			丙子 日冲 庚午 戊午			戊寅 日冲 壬申 甲申			庚辰 日冲 甲戌 戊戌			壬午 日冲 丙子 庚子		
甲子 天牢	戊辰 青龍 日破	壬申 日馬 路空	戊子 天官 福星	壬辰 路空 不遇	丙申 喜神 旬空	壬子 青龍 路空	丙辰 喜神 金匱	庚申 福星 日破	丙子 天牢 不遇	庚辰 日建 日刑	甲申 日祿 旬空	庚子 金匱 日破	甲辰 福星 天牢	戊申 日馬 不遇
乙丑 天乙 元武	己巳 明堂	癸酉 天官 旬空	己丑 日合 寶光	癸巳 日祿 路空	丁酉 天乙 旬空	癸丑 天乙 路空	丁巳 寶光 日刑	辛酉 旬空 元武	丁丑 福星 元武	辛巳 明堂	乙酉 日合 旬空	辛丑 天官 日害	乙巳 天乙 元武	己酉 明堂 旬空
丙寅 日祿 喜神	庚午 天刑 不遇	甲戌 青龍 白虎	庚寅 日馬 白虎	甲午 司命 日破	戊戌 福星 天刑	甲寅 日建 不遇	戊午 白虎	壬戌 司命 路空	戊寅 日馬 司命	壬午 天官 路空	丙戌 喜神 不遇	壬寅 路空 白虎	丙午 喜神 日刑	庚戌 天刑
丁卯 日合 勾陳	辛未 天乙 日刑	乙亥 玉堂	辛卯 玉堂 日刑	乙未 勾陳 日害	己亥 天乙 朱雀	乙卯 天官 朱雀	己未 天乙 玉堂	癸亥 日合 路空	己卯 勾陳 日害	癸未 天乙 路空	丁亥 玉堂	癸卯 天乙 路空	丁未 日合 勾陳	辛亥 日祿 朱雀

乙亥 日冲 己巳 辛巳			丁丑 日冲 辛未 己未			己卯 日冲 癸酉 乙酉			辛巳 日冲 乙亥 己亥			癸未 日冲 丁丑 辛丑		
丙子 天乙 白虎	庚辰 司命	甲申 天官 旬空	庚子 日合 天刑	甲辰 白虎	戊申 司命 旬空	甲子 天乙 日刑	戊辰 日害 天刑	壬申 天乙 旬空	戊子 白虎	壬辰 司命 路空	丙申 日合 旬空	壬子 日祿 路空	丙辰 天官 白虎	庚申 司命 旬空
丁丑 福星 玉堂	辛巳 日馬 日破	乙酉 旬空 朱雀	辛丑 日建 朱雀	乙巳 玉堂	己酉 天乙 旬空	乙丑 不遇 勾陳	己巳 日馬 朱雀	癸酉 玉堂 旬空	己丑 玉堂	癸巳 天官 路空	丁酉 日祿 不遇	癸丑 日破 路空	丁巳 天乙 日馬	辛酉 旬空 勾陳
戊寅 日合 天牢	壬午 青龍 路空	丙戌 喜神 金匱	壬寅 金匱 路空	丙午 日祿 天牢	庚戌 青龍 日刑	丙寅 天官 喜神	庚午 日祿 金匱	甲戌 日合 天牢	庚寅 天乙 天牢	甲午 天乙 青龍	戊戌 金匱	甲寅 金匱	戊午 日合 天牢	壬戌 天官 路空
己卯 日祿 元武	癸未 明堂 路空	丁亥 日建 日刑	癸卯 寶光 不遇	丁未 日破 元武	辛亥 天官 天乙	丁卯 日建 明堂	辛未 寶光 福星	乙亥 元武 不遇	辛卯 元武	乙未 明堂	己亥 寶光 日破	乙卯 天乙 福星	己未 日建 不遇	癸亥 明堂 路空

A traditional 60 Jia Zi and Hour table in a Tong Shu

I have translated and re-formatted the table to make it easier for those who cannot read Chinese text to understand and use the Auspicious Hour Reference table. All you have to do is find the Day Pillar of the date you have selected and the translated table will tell you what are the stars present during each of the 12 hours of that day. To figure out what stars are auspicious and negative, just follow the simple red (auspicious) and black (negative) colour coding system!

To make things easy, I have arranged the tables according to the order of the Heavenly Stems rather than the 60 Jia Zi presentation method used in the Tong Shu. So you just have to find the relevant Heavenly Stem group (ie: Jia group, Bing group) and you will find all the hour tables.

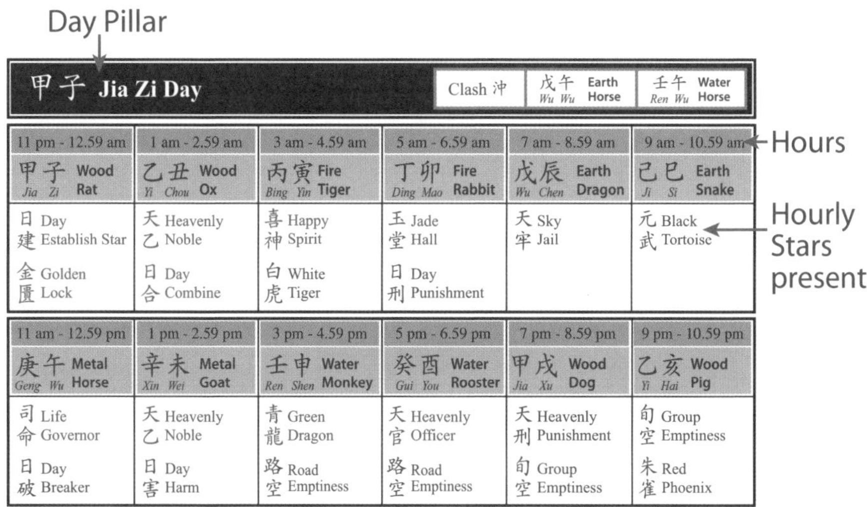

甲子 Jia Zi Day — Clash 沖: 戊午 Wu Wu Earth Horse; 壬午 Ren Wu Water Horse

11 pm - 12.59 am	1 am - 2.59 am	3 am - 4.59 am	5 am - 6.59 am	7 am - 8.59 am	9 am - 10.59 am
甲子 Jia Zi Wood Rat	乙丑 Yi Chou Wood Ox	丙寅 Bing Yin Fire Tiger	丁卯 Ding Mao Fire Rabbit	戊辰 Wu Chen Earth Dragon	己巳 Ji Si Earth Snake
日 Day 建 Establish Star	天 Heavenly 乙 Noble	喜 Happy 神 Spirit	玉 Jade 堂 Hall	天 Sky 牢 Jail	元 Black 武 Tortoise
金 Golden 匱 Lock	日 Day 合 Combine	白 White 虎 Tiger	日 Day 刑 Punishment		

11 am - 12.59 pm	1 pm - 2.59 pm	3 pm - 4.59 pm	5 pm - 6.59 pm	7 pm - 8.59 pm	9 pm - 10.59 pm
庚午 Geng Wu Metal Horse	辛未 Xin Wei Metal Goat	壬申 Ren Shen Water Monkey	癸酉 Gui You Water Rooster	甲戌 Jia Xu Wood Dog	乙亥 Yi Hai Wood Pig
司 Life 命 Governor	天 Heavenly 乙 Noble	青 Green 龍 Dragon	天 Heavenly 官 Officer	天 Heavenly 刑 Punishment	旬 Group 空 Emptiness
日 Day 破 Breaker	日 Day 害 Harm	路 Road 空 Emptiness	路 Road 空 Emptiness	旬 Group 空 Emptiness	朱 Red 雀 Phoenix

Auspicious Stars 吉星

Negative Stars 凶星

甲子 Jia Zi Day

Clash 沖: 戊午 *Wu Wu* Earth Horse | 壬午 *Ren Wu* Water Horse

11 pm - 12.59 am	1 am - 2.59 am	3 am - 4.59 am	5 am - 6.59 am	7 am - 8.59 am	9 am - 10.59 am
甲子 *Jia Zi* Wood Rat	乙丑 *Yi Chou* Wood Ox	丙寅 *Bing Yin* Fire Tiger	丁卯 *Ding Mao* Fire Rabbit	戊辰 *Wu Chen* Earth Dragon	己巳 *Ji Si* Earth Snake
日 Day 建 Establish Star 金 Golden 匱 Lock	天 Heavenly 乙 Noble 日 Day 合 Combine	喜 Happy 神 Spirit 白 White 虎 Tiger	玉 Jade 堂 Hall 日 Day 刑 Punishment	天 Sky 牢 Jail	元 Black 武 Tortoise

11 am - 12.59 pm	1 pm - 2.59 pm	3 pm - 4.59 pm	5 pm - 6.59 pm	7 pm - 8.59 pm	9 pm - 10.59 pm
庚午 *Geng Wu* Metal Horse	辛未 *Xin Wei* Metal Goat	壬申 *Ren Shen* Water Monkey	癸酉 *Gui You* Water Rooster	甲戌 *Jia Xu* Wood Dog	乙亥 *Yi Hai* Wood Pig
司 Life 命 Governor 日 Day 破 Breaker	天 Heavenly 乙 Noble 日 Day 害 Harm	青 Green 龍 Dragon 路 Road 空 Emptiness	天 Heavenly 官 Officer 路 Road 空 Emptiness	天 Heavenly 刑 Punishment 旬 Group 空 Emptiness	旬 Group 空 Emptiness 朱 Red 雀 Phoenix

甲寅 Jia Yin Day

Clash 沖: 戊申 *Wu Shen* Earth Monkey | 丙申 *Bing Shen* Fire Monkey

11 pm - 12.59 am	1 am - 2.59 am	3 am - 4.59 am	5 am - 6.59 am	7 am - 8.59 am	9 am - 10.59 am
甲子 *Jia Zi* Wood Rat	乙丑 *Yi Chou* Wood Ox	丙寅 *Bing Yin* Fire Tiger	丁卯 *Ding Mao* Fire Rabbit	戊辰 *Wu Chen* Earth Dragon	己巳 *Ji Si* Earth Snake
青 Green 龍 Dragon 旬 Group 空 Emptiness	天 Heavenly 乙 Noble 旬 Group 空 Emptiness	日 Day 建 Establish Star 天 Heavenly 刑 Punishment	朱 Red 雀 Phoenix	金 Golden 匱 Lock	寶 Precious 光 Light 日 Day 害 Harm

11 am - 12.59 pm	1 pm - 2.59 pm	3 pm - 4.59 pm	5 pm - 6.59 pm	7 pm - 8.59 pm	9 pm - 10.59 pm
庚午 *Geng Wu* Metal Horse	辛未 *Xin Wei* Metal Goat	壬申 *Ren Shen* Water Monkey	癸酉 *Gui You* Water Rooster	甲戌 *Jia Xu* Wood Dog	乙亥 *Yi Hai* Wood Pig
不 Non 遇 Eligible Day 白 White 虎 Tiger	天 Heavenly 乙 Noble 玉 Jade 堂 Hall	日 Day 馬 Horse 路 Road 空 Emptiness	天 Heavenly 官 Officer 路 Road 空 Emptiness	司 Life 命 Governor	日 Day 合 Combine 勾 Grappling 陳 Hook

甲辰 Jia Chen Day

Clash 沖: 戊戌 *Wu Xu* Earth Dog | 庚戌 *Geng Xu* Metal Dog

11 pm - 12.59 am	1 am - 2.59 am	3 am - 4.59 am	5 am - 6.59 am	7 am - 8.59 am	9 am - 10.59 am
甲子 *Jia Zi* Wood Rat	乙丑 *Yi Chou* Wood Ox	丙寅 *Bing Yin* Fire Tiger	丁卯 *Ding Mao* Fire Rabbit	戊辰 *Wu Chen* Earth Dragon	己巳 *Ji Si* Earth Snake
天 Sky 牢 Jail	天 Heavenly 乙 Noble 元 Black 武 Tortoise	日 Day 馬 Horse 旬 Group 空 Emptiness	勾 Grappling 陳 Hook 日 Day 害 Harm	日 Day 建 Establish Star 日 Day 刑 Punishment	明 Bright 堂 Hall

11 am - 12.59 pm	1 pm - 2.59 pm	3 pm - 4.59 pm	5 pm - 6.59 pm	7 pm - 8.59 pm	9 pm - 10.59 pm
庚午 *Geng Wu* Metal Horse	辛未 *Xin Wei* Metal Goat	壬申 *Ren Shen* Water Monkey	癸酉 *Gui You* Water Rooster	甲戌 *Jia Xu* Wood Dog	乙亥 *Yi Hai* Wood Pig
天 Heavenly 刑 Punishment 不 Non 遇 Eligible Day	天 Heavenly 乙 Noble 朱 Red 雀 Phoenix	金 Golden 匱 Lock 路 Road 空 Emptiness	日 Day 合 Combine 路 Road 空 Emptiness	白 White 虎 Tiger 日 Day 破 Breaker	玉 Jade 堂 Hall

甲午 Jia Wu Day

Clash 沖	戊子 Earth Wu Zi Rat	壬子 Water Ren Zi Rat

11 pm - 12.59 am	1 am - 2.59 am	3 am - 4.59 am	5 am - 6.59 am	7 am - 8.59 am	9 am - 10.59 am
甲子 Wood Jia Zi Rat	乙丑 Wood Yi Chou Ox	丙寅 Fire Bing Yin Tiger	丁卯 Fire Ding Mao Rabbit	戊辰 Earth Wu Chen Dragon	己巳 Earth Ji Si Snake
金匱 Golden Lock 日破 Day Breaker	天乙 Heavenly Noble 日害 Day Harm	日祿 Day Wealth 白虎 White Tiger	玉堂 Jade Hall	天牢 Sky Jail 旬空 Group Emptiness	元武 Black Tortoise 旬空 Group Emptiness
11 am - 12.59 pm	**1 pm - 2.59 pm**	**3 pm - 4.59 pm**	**5 pm - 6.59 pm**	**7 pm - 8.59 pm**	**9 pm - 10.59 pm**
庚午 Metal Geng Wu Horse	辛未 Metal Xin Wei Goat	壬申 Water Ren Shen Monkey	癸酉 Water Gui You Rooster	甲戌 Wood Jia Xu Dog	乙亥 Wood Yi Hai Pig
日建 Day Establish Star 不遇 Non Eligible Day	日合 Day Combine 勾陳 Grappling Hook	日馬 Day Horse 路空 Road Emptiness	天官 Heavenly Officer 路空 Road Emptiness	天刑 Heavenly Punishment	朱雀 Red Phoenix

甲申 Jia Shen Day

Clash 沖	戊寅 Earth Wu Yin Tiger	丙寅 Fire Bing Yin Tiger

11 pm - 12.59 am	1 am - 2.59 am	3 am - 4.59 am	5 am - 6.59 am	7 am - 8.59 am	9 am - 10.59 am
甲子 Wood Jia Zi Rat	乙丑 Wood Yi Chou Ox	丙寅 Fire Bing Yin Tiger	丁卯 Fire Ding Mao Rabbit	戊辰 Earth Wu Chen Dragon	己巳 Earth Ji Si Snake
青龍 Green Dragon	天乙 Heavenly Noble 明堂 Bright Hall	日祿 Day Wealth 日破 Day Breaker	朱雀 Red Phoenix	金匱 Golden Lock	日合 Day Combine 寶光 Precious Light
11 am - 12.59 pm	**1 pm - 2.59 pm**	**3 pm - 4.59 pm**	**5 pm - 6.59 pm**	**7 pm - 8.59 pm**	**9 pm - 10.59 pm**
庚午 Metal Geng Wu Horse	辛未 Metal Xin Wei Goat	壬申 Water Ren Shen Monkey	癸酉 Water Gui You Rooster	甲戌 Wood Jia Xu Dog	乙亥 Wood Yi Hai Pig
白虎 White Tiger 不遇 Non Eligible Day	天乙 Heavenly Noble 旬空 Group Emptiness	日建 Day Establish Star 路空 Road Emptiness	天官 Heavenly Officer 路空 Road Emptiness	司命 Life Governor	勾陳 Grappling Hook 日害 Day Harm

甲戌 Jia Xu Day

Clash 沖	戊辰 Earth Wu Chen Dragon	庚辰 Metal Geng Chen Dragon

11 pm - 12.59 am	1 am - 2.59 am	3 am - 4.59 am	5 am - 6.59 am	7 am - 8.59 am	9 am - 10.59 am
甲子 Wood Jia Zi Rat	乙丑 Wood Yi Chou Ox	丙寅 Fire Bing Yin Tiger	丁卯 Fire Ding Mao Rabbit	戊辰 Earth Wu Chen Dragon	己巳 Earth Ji Si Snake
天牢 Sky Jail	天乙 Heavenly Noble 元武 Black Tortoise	日祿 Day Wealth 喜神 Happy Spirit	日合 Day Combine 勾陳 Grappling Hook	青龍 Green Dragon 日破 Day Breaker	明堂 Bright Hall
11 am - 12.59 pm	**1 pm - 2.59 pm**	**3 pm - 4.59 pm**	**5 pm - 6.59 pm**	**7 pm - 8.59 pm**	**9 pm - 10.59 pm**
庚午 Metal Geng Wu Horse	辛未 Metal Xin Wei Goat	壬申 Water Ren Shen Monkey	癸酉 Water Gui You Rooster	甲戌 Wood Jia Xu Dog	乙亥 Wood Yi Hai Pig
天刑 Heavenly Punishment 不遇 Non Eligible Day	天乙 Heavenly Noble 日刑 Day Punishment	日馬 Day Horse 路空 Road Emptiness	天官 Heavenly Officer 旬空 Group Emptiness	青龍 Green Dragon 白虎 White Tiger	玉堂 Jade Hall

乙丑 Yi Chou Day

Clash 沖	己未 Ji Wei Earth Goat	癸未 Gui Wei Water Goat

11 pm - 12.59 am	1 am - 2.59 am	3 am - 4.59 am	5 am - 6.59 am	7 am - 8.59 am	9 am - 10.59 am
丙子 Bing Zi Fire Rat	丁丑 Ding Chou Fire Ox	戊寅 Wu Yin Earth Tiger	己卯 Ji Mao Earth Rabbit	庚辰 Geng Chen Metal Dragon	辛巳 Xin Si Metal Snake
天乙 Heavenly Noble 天刑 Heavenly Punishment	日建 Day Establish Star 朱雀 Red Phoenix	金匱 Golden Lock	日祿 Day Wealth 寶光 Precious Light	白虎 White Tiger	玉堂 Jade Hall 不遇 Non Eligible Day

11 am - 12.59 pm	1 pm - 2.59 pm	3 pm - 4.59 pm	5 pm - 6.59 pm	7 pm - 8.59 pm	9 pm - 10.59 pm
壬午 Ren Wu Water Horse	癸未 Gui Wei Water Goat	甲申 Jia Shen Wood Monkey	乙酉 Yi You Wood Rooster	丙戌 Bing Xu Fire Dog	丁亥 Ding Hai Fire Pig
天牢 Sky Jail 日害 Day Harm	路空 Road Emptiness 日破 Day Breaker	天乙 Heavenly Noble 天官 Heavenly Officer	勾陳 Grappling Hook	喜神 Happy Spirit 旬空 Group Emptiness	福星 Prosperity star 旬空 Group Emptiness

乙卯 Yi Mao Day

Clash 沖	己酉 Ji You Earth Rooster	丁酉 Ding You Fire Rooster

11 pm - 12.59 am	1 am - 2.59 am	3 am - 4.59 am	5 am - 6.59 am	7 am - 8.59 am	9 am - 10.59 am
丙子 Bing Zi Fire Rat	丁丑 Ding Chou Fire Ox	戊寅 Wu Yin Earth Tiger	己卯 Ji Mao Earth Rabbit	庚辰 Geng Chen Metal Dragon	辛巳 Xin Si Metal Snake
天乙 Heavenly Noble 日刑 Day Punishment	福星 Prosperity star 旬空 Group Emptiness	青龍 Green Dragon	日建 Day Establish Star 明堂 Bright Hall	日害 Day Harm 天刑 Heavenly Punishment	日馬 Day Horse 不遇 Non Eligible Day

11 am - 12.59 pm	1 pm - 2.59 pm	3 pm - 4.59 pm	5 pm - 6.59 pm	7 pm - 8.59 pm	9 pm - 10.59 pm
壬午 Ren Wu Water Horse	癸未 Gui Wei Water Goat	甲申 Jia Shen Wood Monkey	乙酉 Yi You Wood Rooster	丙戌 Bing Xu Fire Dog	丁亥 Ding Hai Fire Pig
金匱 Golden Lock 路空 Road Emptiness	寶光 Precious Light 路空 Road Emptiness	天乙 Heavenly Noble 白虎 White Tiger	玉堂 Jade Hall 日破 Day Breaker	日合 Day Combine 天牢 Sky Jail	福星 Prosperity star 元武 Black Tortoise

乙巳 Yi Si Day

Clash 沖	己亥 Ji Hai Earth Pig	辛亥 Xin Hai Metal Pig

11 pm - 12.59 am	1 am - 2.59 am	3 am - 4.59 am	5 am - 6.59 am	7 am - 8.59 am	9 am - 10.59 am
丙子 Bing Zi Fire Rat	丁丑 Ding Chou Fire Ox	戊寅 Wu Yin Earth Tiger	己卯 Ji Mao Earth Rabbit	庚辰 Geng Chen Metal Dragon	辛巳 Xin Si Metal Snake
天乙 Heavenly Noble 白虎 White Tiger	福星 Prosperity star 玉堂 Jade Hall	天牢 Sky Jail 日害 Day Harm	日祿 Day Wealth 旬空 Group Emptiness	司命 Life Governor	日建 Day Establish Star 不遇 Non Eligible Day

11 am - 12.59 pm	1 pm - 2.59 pm	3 pm - 4.59 pm	5 pm - 6.59 pm	7 pm - 8.59 pm	9 pm - 10.59 pm
壬午 Ren Wu Water Horse	癸未 Gui Wei Water Goat	甲申 Jia Shen Wood Monkey	乙酉 Yi You Wood Rooster	丙戌 Bing Xu Fire Dog	丁亥 Ding Hai Fire Pig
青龍 Green Dragon 路空 Road Emptiness	日建 Day Establish Star 路空 Road Emptiness	日合 Day Combine 日刑 Day Punishment	朱雀 Red Phoenix	喜神 Happy Spirit 金匱 Golden Lock	寶光 Precious Light 日破 Day Breaker

乙未 Yi Wei Day

Clash 沖: 己丑 Ji Chou Earth Ox | 癸丑 Gui Chou Water Ox

11 pm - 12.59 am	1 am - 2.59 am	3 am - 4.59 am	5 am - 6.59 am	7 am - 8.59 am	9 am - 10.59 am
丙子 Bing Zi Fire Rat	丁丑 Ding Chou Fire Ox	戊寅 Wu Yin Earth Tiger	己卯 Ji Mao Earth Rabbit	庚辰 Geng Chen Metal Dragon	辛巳 Xin Si Metal Snake
天乙 Heavenly Noble	福星 Prosperity star	金匱 Golden Lock	日祿 Day Wealth	旬空 Group Emptiness	日馬 Day Horse
日害 Day Harm	日刑 Day Punishment		寶光 Precious Light	白虎 White Tiger	不遇 Non Eligible Day

11 am - 12.59 pm	1 pm - 2.59 pm	3 pm - 4.59 pm	5 pm - 6.59 pm	7 pm - 8.59 pm	9 pm - 10.59 pm
壬午 Ren Wu Water Horse	癸未 Gui Wei Water Goat	甲申 Jia Shen Wood Monkey	乙酉 Yi You Wood Rooster	丙戌 Bing Xu Fire Dog	丁亥 Ding Hai Fire Pig
日合 Day Combine	日建 Day Establish Star	天官 Heavenly Officer	勾陳 Grappling Hook	青龍 Green Dragon	明堂 Bright Hall
路空 Road Emptiness	路空 Road Emptiness	司命 Life Governor		喜神 Happy Spirit	福星 Prosperity star

乙酉 Yi You Day

Clash 沖: 己卯 Ji Mao Earth Rabbit | 丁卯 Ding Mao Fire Rabbit

11 pm - 12.59 am	1 am - 2.59 am	3 am - 4.59 am	5 am - 6.59 am	7 am - 8.59 am	9 am - 10.59 am
丙子 Bing Zi Fire Rat	丁丑 Ding Chou Fire Ox	戊寅 Wu Yin Earth Tiger	己卯 Ji Mao Earth Rabbit	庚辰 Geng Chen Metal Dragon	辛巳 Xin Si Metal Snake
天乙 Heavenly Noble	福星 Prosperity star	青龍 Green Dragon	明堂 Bright Hall	日合 Day Combine	不遇 Non Eligible Day
司命 Life Governor	勾陳 Grappling Hook		日破 Day Breaker	天刑 Heavenly Punishment	朱雀 Red Phoenix

11 am - 12.59 pm	1 pm - 2.59 pm	3 pm - 4.59 pm	5 pm - 6.59 pm	7 pm - 8.59 pm	9 pm - 10.59 pm
壬午 Ren Wu Water Horse	癸未 Gui Wei Water Goat	甲申 Jia Shen Wood Monkey	乙酉 Yi You Wood Rooster	丙戌 Bing Xu Fire Dog	丁亥 Ding Hai Fire Pig
金匱 Golden Lock	寶光 Precious Light	天官 Heavenly Officer	日建 Day Establish Star	喜神 Happy Spirit	福星 Prosperity star
路空 Road Emptiness	路空 Road Emptiness	白虎 White Tiger	日刑 Day Punishment	天牢 Sky Jail	元武 Black Tortoise

乙亥 Yi Hai Day

Clash 沖: 己巳 Ji Si Earth Snake | 辛巳 Xin Si Metal Snake

11 pm - 12.59 am	1 am - 2.59 am	3 am - 4.59 am	5 am - 6.59 am	7 am - 8.59 am	9 am - 10.59 am
丙子 Bing Zi Fire Rat	丁丑 Ding Chou Fire Ox	戊寅 Wu Yin Earth Tiger	己卯 Ji Mao Earth Rabbit	庚辰 Geng Chen Metal Dragon	辛巳 Xin Si Metal Snake
天乙 Heavenly Noble	福星 Prosperity star	日合 Day Combine	日祿 Day Wealth	司命 Life Governor	日馬 Day Horse
白虎 White Tiger	玉堂 Jade Hall	天牢 Sky Jail	元武 Black Tortoise		日破 Day Breaker

11 am - 12.59 pm	1 pm - 2.59 pm	3 pm - 4.59 pm	5 pm - 6.59 pm	7 pm - 8.59 pm	9 pm - 10.59 pm
壬午 Ren Wu Water Horse	癸未 Gui Wei Water Goat	甲申 Jia Shen Wood Monkey	乙酉 Yi You Wood Rooster	丙戌 Bing Xu Fire Dog	丁亥 Ding Hai Fire Pig
青龍 Green Dragon	明堂 Bright Hall	天官 Heavenly Officer	旬空 Group Emptiness	喜神 Happy Spirit	日建 Day Establish Star
路空 Road Emptiness	路空 Road Emptiness	旬空 Group Emptiness	朱雀 Red Phoenix	金匱 Golden Lock	日刑 Day Punishment

丙寅 Bing Yin Day

Clash 沖	庚申 Geng Shen Metal Monkey	壬申 Ren Shen Water Monkey

11 pm - 12.59 am	1 am - 2.59 am	3 am - 4.59 am	5 am - 6.59 am	7 am - 8.59 am	9 am - 10.59 am
戊子 Earth Rat Wu Zi	己丑 Earth Ox Ji Chou	庚寅 Metal Tiger Geng Yin	辛卯 Metal Rabbit Xin Mao	壬辰 Water Dragon Ren Chen	癸巳 Water Snake Gui Si
天官 Heavenly Officer 福星 Prosperity star	明堂 Bright Hall	日建 Day Establish Star 天刑 Heavenly Punishment	朱雀 Phoenix	金匱 Golden Lock 路空 Road Emptiness	喜神 Happy Spirit 路空 Road Emptiness
11 am - 12.59 pm	**1 pm - 2.59 pm**	**3 pm - 4.59 pm**	**5 pm - 6.59 pm**	**7 pm - 8.59 pm**	**9 pm - 10.59 pm**
甲午 Wood Horse Jia Wu	乙未 Wood Goat Yi Wei	丙申 Fire Monkey Bing Shen	丁酉 Fire Rooster Ding You	戊戌 Earth Dog Wu Xu	己亥 Earth Pig Ji Hai
白虎 White Tiger	玉堂 Jade Hall	喜神 Happy Spirit 日破 Day Breaker	天乙 Heavenly Noble 元武 Black Tortoise	福星 Prosperity star 旬空 Group Emptiness	天乙 Heavenly Noble 旬空 Group Emptiness

丙辰 Bing Chen Day

Clash 沖	庚戌 Geng Xu Metal Dog	壬戌 Ren Xu Water Dog

11 pm - 12.59 am	1 am - 2.59 am	3 am - 4.59 am	5 am - 6.59 am	7 am - 8.59 am	9 am - 10.59 am
戊子 Earth Rat Wu Zi	己丑 Earth Ox Ji Chou	庚寅 Metal Tiger Geng Yin	辛卯 Metal Rabbit Xin Mao	壬辰 Water Dragon Ren Chen	癸巳 Water Snake Gui Si
天官 Heavenly Officer 天牢 Sky Jail	旬空 Group Emptiness 元武 Black Tortoise	日馬 Day Horse 司命 Life Governor	日害 Day Harm 勾陳 Grappling Hook	日建 Day Establish Star 路空 Road Emptiness	日祿 Day Wealth 路空 Road Emptiness
11 am - 12.59 pm	**1 pm - 2.59 pm**	**3 pm - 4.59 pm**	**5 pm - 6.59 pm**	**7 pm - 8.59 pm**	**9 pm - 10.59 pm**
甲午 Wood Horse Jia Wu	乙未 Wood Goat Yi Wei	丙申 Fire Monkey Bing Shen	丁酉 Fire Rooster Ding You	戊戌 Earth Dog Wu Xu	己亥 Earth Pig Ji Hai
天刑 Heavenly Punishment	朱雀 Red Phoenix	喜神 Happy Spirit 金匱 Golden Lock	天乙 Heavenly Noble 日合 Day Combine	福星 Prosperity star 日破 Day Breaker	天乙 Heavenly Noble 玉堂 Jade Hall

丙午 Bing Wu Day

Clash 沖	戊子 Wu Zi Earth Rat	庚子 Geng Zi Metal Rat

11 pm - 12.59 am	1 am - 2.59 am	3 am - 4.59 am	5 am - 6.59 am	7 am - 8.59 am	9 am - 10.59 am
戊子 Earth Rat Wu Zi	己丑 Earth Ox Ji Chou	庚寅 Metal Tiger Geng Yin	辛卯 Metal Rabbit Xin Mao	壬辰 Water Dragon Ren Chen	癸巳 Water Snake Gui Si
天官 Heavenly Officer 日破 Day Breaker	寶光 Precious Light 日害 Day Harm	旬空 Group Emptiness 白虎 White Tiger	玉堂 Jade Hall 旬空 Group Emptiness	不遇 Non Eligible Day 路空 Road Emptiness	日祿 Day Wealth 路空 Road Emptiness
11 am - 12.59 pm	**1 pm - 2.59 pm**	**3 pm - 4.59 pm**	**5 pm - 6.59 pm**	**7 pm - 8.59 pm**	**9 pm - 10.59 pm**
甲午 Wood Horse Jia Wu	乙未 Wood Goat Yi Wei	丙申 Fire Monkey Bing Shen	丁酉 Fire Rooster Ding You	戊戌 Earth Dog Wu Xu	己亥 Earth Pig Ji Hai
日建 Day Establish Star 日刑 Day Punishment	日合 Day Combine 勾陳 Grappling Hook	喜神 Happy Spirit 日馬 Day Horse	天乙 Heavenly Noble 明堂 Bright Hall	福星 Prosperity star 天刑 Heavenly Punishment	天乙 Heavenly Noble 朱雀 Red Phoenix

丙申 Bing Shen Day

Clash 沖: 庚寅 Metal Geng Yin Tiger | 壬寅 Water Ren Yin Tiger

11 pm - 12.59 am	1 am - 2.59 am	3 am - 4.59 am	5 am - 6.59 am	7 am - 8.59 am	9 am - 10.59 am
戊子 Earth Wu Zi Rat	己丑 Earth Ji Chou Ox	庚寅 Metal Geng Yin Tiger	辛卯 Metal Xin Mao Rabbit	壬辰 Water Ren Chen Dragon	癸巳 Water Gui Si Snake
天官 Heavenly Officer 福星 Prosperity star	明堂 Bright Hall	日馬 Day Horse 天刑 Heavenly Punishment	朱雀 Red Phoenix	金匱 Golden Lock 不遇 Non Eligible Day	日合 Day Combine 旬空 Group Emptiness

11 am - 12.59 pm	1 pm - 2.59 pm	3 pm - 4.59 pm	5 pm - 6.59 pm	7 pm - 8.59 pm	9 pm - 10.59 pm
甲午 Wood Jia Wu Horse	乙未 Wood Yi Wei Goat	丙申 Fire Bing Shen Monkey	丁酉 Fire Ding You Rooster	戊戌 Earth Wu Xu Dog	己亥 Earth Ji Hai Pig
白虎 White Tiger	玉堂 Jade Hall	日建 Day Establish Star 天牢 Sky Jail	天乙 Heavenly Noble 元武 Black Tortoise	福星 Prosperity star 司命 Life Governor	天乙 Heavenly Noble 日害 Day Harm

丙戌 Bing Xu Day

Clash 沖: 庚辰 Metal Geng Chen Dragon | 壬辰 Water Ren Chen Dragon

11 pm - 12.59 am	1 am - 2.59 am	3 am - 4.59 am	5 am - 6.59 am	7 am - 8.59 am	9 am - 10.59 am
戊子 Earth Wu Zi Rat	己丑 Earth Ji Chou Ox	庚寅 Metal Geng Yin Tiger	辛卯 Metal Xin Mao Rabbit	壬辰 Water Ren Chen Dragon	癸巳 Water Gui Si Snake
天官 Heavenly Officer 天牢 Sky Jail	元武 Black Tortoise	司命 Life Governor	日合 Day Combine 勾陳 Grappling Hook	青龍 Green Dragon 路空 Road Emptiness	日祿 Day Wealth 路空 Road Emptiness

11 am - 12.59 pm	1 pm - 2.59 pm	3 pm - 4.59 pm	5 pm - 6.59 pm	7 pm - 8.59 pm	9 pm - 10.59 pm
甲午 Wood Jia Wu Horse	乙未 Wood Yi Wei Goat	丙申 Fire Bing Shen Monkey	丁酉 Fire Ding You Rooster	戊戌 Earth Wu Xu Dog	己亥 Earth Ji Hai Pig
天刑 Heavenly Punishment 旬空 Group Emptiness	朱雀 Red Phoenix 旬空 Group Emptiness	喜神 Happy Spirit 日馬 Day Horse	天乙 Heavenly Noble 日害 Day Harm	日建 Day Establish Star 白虎 White Tiger	天乙 Heavenly Noble 玉堂 Jade Hall

丙子 Bing Zi Day

Clash 沖: 庚午 Metal Geng Wu Horse | 戊午 Earth Wu Wu Horse

11 pm - 12.59 am	1 am - 2.59 am	3 am - 4.59 am	5 am - 6.59 am	7 am - 8.59 am	9 am - 10.59 am
戊子 Earth Wu Zi Rat	己丑 Earth Ji Chou Ox	庚寅 Metal Geng Yin Tiger	辛卯 Metal Xin Mao Rabbit	壬辰 Water Ren Chen Dragon	癸巳 Water Gui Si Snake
天官 Heavenly Officer 福星 Prosperity star	日合 Day Combine 寶光 Precious Light	日馬 Day Horse 白虎 White Tiger	玉堂 Jade Hall 日刑 Day Punishment	路空 Road Emptiness 不遇 Non Eligible Day	日祿 Day Wealth 路空 Road Emptiness

11 am - 12.59 pm	1 pm - 2.59 pm	3 pm - 4.59 pm	5 pm - 6.59 pm	7 pm - 8.59 pm	9 pm - 10.59 pm
甲午 Wood Jia Wu Horse	乙未 Wood Yi Wei Goat	丙申 Fire Bing Shen Monkey	丁酉 Fire Ding You Rooster	戊戌 Earth Wu Xu Dog	己亥 Earth Ji Hai Pig
司命 Life Governor 日破 Day Breaker	勾陳 Grappling Hook 日害 Day Harm	喜神 Happy Spirit 旬空 Group Emptiness	天乙 Heavenly Noble 旬空 Group Emptiness	福星 Prosperity star 天刑 Heavenly Punishment	天乙 Heavenly Noble 朱雀 Red Phoenix

丁卯 Ding Mao Day

Clash 沖	辛酉 Xin You Metal Rooster	癸酉 Gui You Water Rooster

11 pm - 12.59 am	1 am - 2.59 am	3 am - 4.59 am	5 am - 6.59 am	7 am - 8.59 am	9 am - 10.59 am
庚子 Geng Zi Metal Rat	辛丑 Xin Chou Metal Ox	壬寅 Ren Yin Water Tiger	癸卯 Gui Mao Water Rabbit	甲辰 Jia Chen Wood Dragon	乙巳 Yi Si Wood Snake
司命 Life Governor	勾陳 Grappling Hook	青龍 Green Dragon 路空 Road Emptiness	日建 Day Establish Star 路空 Road Emptiness	天刑 Heavenly Punishment 日害 Day Harm	日馬 Day Horse 朱雀 Red Phoenix

11 am - 12.59 pm	1 pm - 2.59 pm	3 pm - 4.59 pm	5 pm - 6.59 pm	7 pm - 8.59 pm	9 pm - 10.59 pm
丙午 Bing Wu Fire Horse	丁未 Ding Wei Fire Goat	戊申 Wu Shen Earth Monkey	己酉 Ji You Earth Rooster	庚戌 Geng Xu Metal Dog	辛亥 Xin Hai Metal Pig
喜神 Happy Spirit 日祿 Day Wealth	寶光 Precious Light	白虎 White Tiger	天乙 Heavenly Noble 日破 Day Breaker	日合 Day Combine 旬空 Group Emptiness	天乙 Heavenly Noble 旬空 Group Emptiness

丁巳 Ding Si Day

Clash 沖	辛亥 Xin Hai Metal Pig	癸亥 Gui Hai Water Pig

11 pm - 12.59 am	1 am - 2.59 am	3 am - 4.59 am	5 am - 6.59 am	7 am - 8.59 am	9 am - 10.59 am
庚子 Geng Zi Metal Rat	辛丑 Xin Chou Metal Ox	壬寅 Ren Yin Water Tiger	癸卯 Gui Mao Water Rabbit	甲辰 Jia Chen Wood Dragon	乙巳 Yi Si Wood Snake
旬空 Group Emptiness 白虎 White Tiger	玉堂 Jade Hall 旬空 Group Emptiness	天牢 Sky Jail 路空 Road Emptiness	路空 Road Emptiness 不遇 Non Eligible Day	司命 Life Governor	日建 Day Establish Star 勾陳 Grappling Hook

11 am - 12.59 pm	1 pm - 2.59 pm	3 pm - 4.59 pm	5 pm - 6.59 pm	7 pm - 8.59 pm	9 pm - 10.59 pm
丙午 Bing Wu Fire Horse	丁未 Ding Wei Fire Goat	戊申 Wu Shen Earth Monkey	己酉 Ji You Earth Rooster	庚戌 Geng Xu Metal Dog	辛亥 Xin Hai Metal Pig
日祿 Day Wealth 喜神 Happy Spirit	明堂 Bright Hall	日合 Day Combine 天刑 Heavenly Punishment	天乙 Heavenly Noble 朱雀 Red Phoenix	金匱 Golden Lock	天官 Heavenly Officer 日破 Day Breaker

丁未 Ding Wei Day

Clash 沖	己丑 Ji Chou Earth Ox	辛丑 Xin Chou Metal Ox

11 pm - 12.59 am	1 am - 2.59 am	3 am - 4.59 am	5 am - 6.59 am	7 am - 8.59 am	9 am - 10.59 am
庚子 Geng Zi Metal Rat	辛丑 Xin Chou Metal Ox	壬寅 Ren Yin Water Tiger	癸卯 Gui Mao Water Rabbit	甲辰 Jia Chen Wood Dragon	乙巳 Yi Si Wood Snake
日害 Day Harm 天刑 Heavenly Punishment	朱雀 Red Phoenix 日破 Day Breaker	金匱 Golden Lock 路空 Road Emptiness	寶光 Precious Light 路空 Road Emptiness	白虎 White Tiger	日馬 Day Horse 玉堂 Jade Hall

11 am - 12.59 pm	1 pm - 2.59 pm	3 pm - 4.59 pm	5 pm - 6.59 pm	7 pm - 8.59 pm	9 pm - 10.59 pm
丙午 Bing Wu Fire Horse	丁未 Ding Wei Fire Goat	戊申 Wu Shen Earth Monkey	己酉 Ji You Earth Rooster	庚戌 Geng Xu Metal Dog	辛亥 Xin Hai Metal Pig
日合 Day Combine 天牢 Sky Jail	日建 Day Establish Star 元武 Black Tortoise	司命 Life Governor	天乙 Heavenly Noble 勾陳 Grappling Hook	青龍 Green Dragon	天乙 Heavenly Noble 明堂 Bright Hall

丁酉 Ding You Day

Clash 沖: 辛卯 Xin Mao Metal Rabbit; 癸卯 Gui Mao Water Rabbit

11 pm - 12.59 am	1 am - 2.59 am	3 am - 4.59 am	5 am - 6.59 am	7 am - 8.59 am	9 am - 10.59 am
庚子 Geng Zi Metal Rat	辛丑 Xin Chou Metal Ox	壬寅 Ren Yin Water Tiger	癸卯 Gui Mao Water Rabbit	甲辰 Jia Chen Wood Dragon	乙巳 Yi Si Wood Snake
司命 Life Governor	勾陳 Grappling Hook	青龍 Green Dragon 路空 Road Emptiness	明堂 Bright Hall 日破 Day Breaker	日合 Day Combine 天刑 Heavenly Punishment	旬空 Group Emptiness 朱雀 Red Phoenix

11 am - 12.59 pm	1 pm - 2.59 pm	3 pm - 4.59 pm	5 pm - 6.59 pm	7 pm - 8.59 pm	9 pm - 10.59 pm
丙午 Bing Wu Fire Horse	丁未 Ding Wei Fire Goat	戊申 Wu Shen Earth Monkey	己酉 Ji You Earth Rooster	庚戌 Geng Xu Metal Dog	辛亥 Xin Hai Metal Pig
日祿 Day Wealth 喜神 Happy Spirit	寶光 Precious Light	白虎 White Tiger	天乙 Heavenly Noble 日刑 Day Punishment	天牢 Sky Jail 日害 Day Harm	天官 Heavenly Officer 元武 Black Tortoise

丁亥 Ding Hai Day

Clash 沖: 辛巳 Xin Si Metal Snake; 癸巳 Gui Si Water Snake

11 pm - 12.59 am	1 am - 2.59 am	3 am - 4.59 am	5 am - 6.59 am	7 am - 8.59 am	9 am - 10.59 am
庚子 Geng Zi Metal Rat	辛丑 Xin Chou Metal Ox	壬寅 Ren Yin Water Tiger	癸卯 Gui Mao Water Rabbit	甲辰 Jia Chen Wood Dragon	乙巳 Yi Si Wood Snake
白虎 White Tiger	玉堂 Jade Hall	日合 Day Combine 路空 Road Emptiness	不遇 Non Eligible Day 路空 Road Emptiness	司命 Life Governor	日馬 Day Horse 日破 Day Breaker

11 am - 12.59 pm	1 pm - 2.59 pm	3 pm - 4.59 pm	5 pm - 6.59 pm	7 pm - 8.59 pm	9 pm - 10.59 pm
丙午 Bing Wu Fire Horse	丁未 Ding Wei Fire Goat	戊申 Wu Shen Earth Monkey	己酉 Ji You Earth Rooster	庚戌 Geng Xu Metal Dog	辛亥 Xin Hai Metal Pig
喜神 Happy Spirit 旬空 Group Emptiness	明堂 Bright Hall 旬空 Group Emptiness	日害 Day Harm 天刑 Heavenly Punishment	天乙 Heavenly Noble 朱雀 Red Phoenix	金匱 Golden Lock	天官 Heavenly Officer 日刑 Day Punishment

丁丑 Ding Chou Day

Clash 沖: 辛未 Xin Wei Metal Goat; 己未 Ji Wei Earth Goat

11 pm - 12.59 am	1 am - 2.59 am	3 am - 4.59 am	5 am - 6.59 am	7 am - 8.59 am	9 am - 10.59 am
庚子 Geng Zi Metal Rat	辛丑 Xin Chou Metal Ox	壬寅 Ren Yin Water Tiger	癸卯 Gui Mao Water Rabbit	甲辰 Jia Chen Wood Dragon	乙巳 Yi Si Wood Snake
日合 Day Combine 天刑 Heavenly Punishment	日建 Day Establish Star 朱雀 Red Phoenix	金匱 Golden Lock 路空 Road Emptiness	寶光 Precious Light 不遇 Non Eligible Day	白虎 White Tiger	玉堂 Jade Hall

11 am - 12.59 pm	1 pm - 2.59 pm	3 pm - 4.59 pm	5 pm - 6.59 pm	7 pm - 8.59 pm	9 pm - 10.59 pm
丙午 Bing Wu Fire Horse	丁未 Ding Wei Fire Goat	戊申 Wu Shen Earth Monkey	己酉 Ji You Earth Rooster	庚戌 Geng Xu Metal Dog	辛亥 Xin Hai Metal Pig
日祿 Day Wealth 天牢 Sky Jail	日破 Day Breaker 元武 Black Tortoise	司命 Life Governor 旬空 Group Emptiness	天乙 Heavenly Noble 旬空 Group Emptiness	青龍 Green Dragon 日刑 Day Punishment	天官 Heavenly Officer 天乙 Heavenly Noble

戊辰 Wu Chen Day

Clash 沖 壬戌 Ren Xu Water Dog | 丙戌 Bing Xu Fire Dog

11 pm - 12.59 am	1 am - 2.59 am	3 am - 4.59 am	5 am - 6.59 am	7 am - 8.59 am	9 am - 10.59 am
壬子 Ren Zi Water Rat	癸丑 Gui Chou Water Ox	甲寅 Jia Yin Wood Tiger	乙卯 Yi Mao Wood Rabbit	丙辰 Bing Chen Fire Dragon	丁巳 Ding Si Fire Snake
路空 Road Emptiness 天牢 Sky Jail	天乙 Heavenly Noble 路空 Road Emptiness	司命 Life Governor 不遇 Non Eligible Day	天官 Heavenly Officer 日害 Day Harm	日建 Day Establish Star 日刑 Day Punishment	日祿 Day Wealth 明堂 Bright Hall

11 am - 12.59 pm	1 pm - 2.59 pm	3 pm - 4.59 pm	5 pm - 6.59 pm	7 pm - 8.59 pm	9 pm - 10.59 pm
戊午 Wu Wu Earth Horse	己未 Ji Wei Earth Goat	庚申 Geng Shen Metal Monkey	辛酉 Xin You Metal Rooster	壬戌 Ren Xu Water Dog	癸亥 Gui Hai Water Pig
天刑 Heavenly Punishment	天乙 Heavenly Noble 朱雀 Red Phoenix	福星 Prosperity star 金匱 Golden Lock	日合 Day Combine 寶光 Precious Light	路空 Road Emptiness 日破 Day Breaker	玉堂 Jade Hall 路空 Road Emptiness

戊午 Wu Wu Day

Clash 沖 壬子 Ren Zi Water Rat | 甲子 Jia Zi Wood Rat

11 pm - 12.59 am	1 am - 2.59 am	3 am - 4.59 am	5 am - 6.59 am	7 am - 8.59 am	9 am - 10.59 am
壬子 Ren Zi Water Rat	癸丑 Gui Chou Water Ox	甲寅 Jia Yin Wood Tiger	乙卯 Yi Mao Wood Rabbit	丙辰 Bing Chen Fire Dragon	丁巳 Ding Si Fire Snake
金匱 Golden Lock 日破 Day Breaker	天乙 Heavenly Noble 路空 Road Emptiness	不遇 Non Eligible Day 白虎 White Tiger	天官 Heavenly Officer 玉堂 Jade Hall	喜神 Happy Spirit 天牢 Sky Jail	日祿 Day Wealth 元武 Black Tortoise

11 am - 12.59 pm	1 pm - 2.59 pm	3 pm - 4.59 pm	5 pm - 6.59 pm	7 pm - 8.59 pm	9 pm - 10.59 pm
戊午 Wu Wu Earth Horse	己未 Ji Wei Earth Goat	庚申 Geng Shen Metal Monkey	辛酉 Xin You Metal Rooster	壬戌 Ren Xu Water Dog	癸亥 Gui Hai Water Pig
日刑 Day Punishment	日合 Day Combine 勾陳 Grappling Hook	青龍 Green Dragon 日馬 Day Horse	明堂 Bright Hall	路空 Road Emptiness 天刑 Heavenly Punishment	朱雀 Red Phoenix 路空 Road Emptiness

戊申 Wu Shen Day

Clash 沖 壬寅 Ren Yin Water Tiger | 甲寅 Jia Yin Wood Tiger

11 pm - 12.59 am	1 am - 2.59 am	3 am - 4.59 am	5 am - 6.59 am	7 am - 8.59 am	9 am - 10.59 am
壬子 Ren Zi Water Rat	癸丑 Gui Chou Water Ox	甲寅 Jia Yin Wood Tiger	乙卯 Yi Mao Wood Rabbit	丙辰 Bing Chen Fire Dragon	丁巳 Ding Si Fire Snake
青龍 Green Dragon 路空 Road Emptiness	天乙 Heavenly Noble 路空 Road Emptiness	日馬 Day Horse 日破 Day Breaker	天官 Heavenly Officer 朱雀 Red Phoenix	金匱 Golden Lock 喜神 Happy Spirit	日祿 Day Wealth 日合 Day Combine

11 am - 12.59 pm	1 pm - 2.59 pm	3 pm - 4.59 pm	5 pm - 6.59 pm	7 pm - 8.59 pm	9 pm - 10.59 pm
戊午 Wu Wu Earth Horse	己未 Ji Wei Earth Goat	庚申 Geng Shen Metal Monkey	辛酉 Xin You Metal Rooster	壬戌 Ren Xu Water Dog	癸亥 Gui Hai Water Pig
白虎 White Tiger	天乙 Heavenly Noble 玉堂 Jade Hall	日建 Day Establish Star 天牢 Sky Jail	元武 Black Tortoise	司命 Life Governor 路空 Road Emptiness	日害 Day Harm 路空 Road Emptiness

戊戌 Wu Xu Day

Clash 沖	壬辰 Water Ren Chen Dragon	丙辰 Fire Gui Chou Dragon

11 pm - 12.59 am	1 am - 2.59 am	3 am - 4.59 am	5 am - 6.59 am	7 am - 8.59 am	9 am - 10.59 am
壬子 Water Ren Zi Rat	癸丑 Water Gui Chou Ox	甲寅 Wood Jia Yin Tiger	乙卯 Wood Yi Mao Rabbit	丙辰 Fire Bing Chen Dragon	丁巳 Fire Ding Si Snake
路 Road 空 Emptiness 天 Sky 牢 Jail	天 Heavenly 乙 Noble 路 Road 空 Emptiness	司 Life 命 Governor 不 Non 遇 Eligible Day	日 Day 合 Combine 勾 Grappling 陳 Hook	喜 Happy 神 Spirit 日 Day 破 Breaker	明 Bright 堂 Hall 旬 Group 空 Emptiness

11 am - 12.59 pm	1 pm - 2.59 pm	3 pm - 4.59 pm	5 pm - 6.59 pm	7 pm - 8.59 pm	9 pm - 10.59 pm
戊午 Earth Wu Wu Horse	己未 Earth Ji Wei Goat	庚申 Metal Geng Shen Monkey	辛酉 Metal Xin You Rooster	壬戌 Water Ren Xu Dog	癸亥 Water Gui Hai Pig
天 Heavenly 刑 Punishment	天 Heavenly 乙 Noble 日 Day 刑 Punishment	福 Prosperity 星 star 日 Day 馬 Horse	寶 Precious 光 Light 日 Day 害 Harm	日 Day 建 Establish Star 路 Road 空 Emptiness	金 Golden 匱 Lock 路 Road 空 Emptiness

戊子 Wu Zi Day

Clash 沖	壬午 Water Ren Wu Horse	甲午 Wood Jia Wu Horse

11 pm - 12.59 am	1 am - 2.59 am	3 am - 4.59 am	5 am - 6.59 am	7 am - 8.59 am	9 am - 10.59 am
壬子 Water Ren Zi Rat	癸丑 Water Gui Chou Ox	甲寅 Wood Jia Yin Tiger	乙卯 Wood Yi Mao Rabbit	丙辰 Fire Bing Chen Dragon	丁巳 Fire Ding Si Snake
日 Day 建 Establish Star 路 Road 空 Emptiness	日 Day 合 Combine 路 Road 空 Emptiness	日 Day 馬 Horse 不 Non 遇 Eligible Day	天 Heavenly 官 Officer 日 Day 刑 Punishment	司 Life 命 Governor 天 Sky 牢 Jail	日 Day 祿 Wealth 元 Black 武 Tortoise

11 am - 12.59 pm	1 pm - 2.59 pm	3 pm - 4.59 pm	5 pm - 6.59 pm	7 pm - 8.59 pm	9 pm - 10.59 pm
戊午 Earth Wu Wu Horse	己未 Earth Ji Wei Goat	庚申 Metal Geng Shen Monkey	辛酉 Metal Xin You Rooster	壬戌 Water Ren Xu Dog	癸亥 Water Gui Hai Pig
司 Life 命 Governor 旬 Group 空 Emptiness	天 Heavenly 乙 Noble 日 Day 害 Harm	福 Prosperity 星 star 青 Green 龍 Dragon	明 Bright 堂 Hall	路 Road 空 Emptiness 天 Heavenly 刑 Punishment	路 Road 空 Emptiness 朱 Red 雀 Phoenix

戊寅 Wu Yin Day

Clash 沖	壬申 Water Ren Shen Monkey	甲申 Wood Jia Shen Monkey

11 pm - 12.59 am	1 am - 2.59 am	3 am - 4.59 am	5 am - 6.59 am	7 am - 8.59 am	9 am - 10.59 am
壬子 Water Ren Zi Rat	癸丑 Water Gui Chou Ox	甲寅 Wood Jia Yin Tiger	乙卯 Wood Yi Mao Rabbit	丙辰 Fire Bing Chen Dragon	丁巳 Fire Ding Si Snake
青 Green 龍 Dragon 路 Road 空 Emptiness	天 Heavenly 乙 Noble 路 Road 空 Emptiness	日 Day 建 Establish Star 不 Non 遇 Eligible Day	天 Heavenly 官 Officer 朱 Red 雀 Phoenix	喜 Happy 神 Spirit 金 Golden 匱 Lock	寶 Precious 光 Light 日 Day 刑 Punishment

11 am - 12.59 pm	1 pm - 2.59 pm	3 pm - 4.59 pm	5 pm - 6.59 pm	7 pm - 8.59 pm	9 pm - 10.59 pm
戊午 Earth Wu Wu Horse	己未 Earth Ji Wei Goat	庚申 Metal Geng Shen Monkey	辛酉 Metal Xin You Rooster	壬戌 Water Ren Xu Dog	癸亥 Water Gui Hai Pig
白 White 虎 Tiger	天 Heavenly 乙 Noble 玉 Jade 堂 Hall	福 Prosperity 星 star 日 Day 破 Breaker	旬 Group 空 Emptiness 元 Black 武 Tortoise	司 Life 命 Governor 路 Road 空 Emptiness	日 Day 合 Combine 路 Road 空 Emptiness

己巳 Ji Si Day

Clash 沖	癸亥 Water Gui Hai Pig	丁亥 Fire Ding Hai Pig

11 pm - 12.59 am	1 am - 2.59 am	3 am - 4.59 am	5 am - 6.59 am	7 am - 8.59 am	9 am - 10.59 am
甲子 Wood Jia Zi Rat	乙丑 Wood Yi Chou Ox	丙寅 Fire Bing Yin Tiger	丁卯 Fire Ding Mao Rabbit	戊辰 Earth Wu Chen Dragon	己巳 Earth Ji Si Snake
天 Heavenly 乙 Noble 白 White 虎 Tiger	玉 Jade 堂 Hall 不 Non 遇 Eligible Day	天 Heavenly 官 Officer 天 Sky 牢 Jail	元 Black 武 Tortoise	司 Life 命 Governor	日 Day 建 Establish Star 勾 Grappling 陳 Hook
11 am - 12.59 pm	**1 pm - 2.59 pm**	**3 pm - 4.59 pm**	**5 pm - 6.59 pm**	**7 pm - 8.59 pm**	**9 pm - 10.59 pm**
庚午 Metal Geng Wu Horse	辛未 Metal Xin Wei Goat	壬申 Water Ren Shen Monkey	癸酉 Water Gui You Rooster	甲戌 Wood Jia Xu Dog	乙亥 Wood Yi Hai Pig
日 Day 祿 Wealth 青 Green 龍 Dragon	福 Prosperity 星 star 明 Bright 堂 Hall	日 Day 合 Combine 路 Road 空 Emptiness	路 Road 空 Emptiness 朱 Red 雀 Phoenix	金 Golden 匱 Lock 旬 Group 空 Emptiness	日 Day 馬 Horse 日 Day 破 Breaker

己未 Ji Wei Day

Clash 沖	癸丑 Water Gui Chou Ox	乙丑 Wood Yi Chou Ox

11 pm - 12.59 am	1 am - 2.59 am	3 am - 4.59 am	5 am - 6.59 am	7 am - 8.59 am	9 am - 10.59 am
甲子 Wood Jia Zi Rat	乙丑 Wood Yi Chou Ox	丙寅 Fire Bing Yin Tiger	丁卯 Fire Ding Mao Rabbit	戊辰 Earth Wu Chen Dragon	己巳 Earth Ji Si Snake
天 Heavenly 乙 Noble 日 Day 害 Harm	日 Day 馬 Horse 日 Day 破 Breaker	天 Heavenly 官 Officer 喜 Happy 神 Spirit	寶 Precious 光 Light	白 White 虎 Tiger	日 Day 馬 Horse 玉 Jade 堂 Hall
11 am - 12.59 pm	**1 pm - 2.59 pm**	**3 pm - 4.59 pm**	**5 pm - 6.59 pm**	**7 pm - 8.59 pm**	**9 pm - 10.59 pm**
庚午 Metal Geng Wu Horse	辛未 Metal Xin Wei Goat	壬申 Water Ren Shen Monkey	癸酉 Water Gui You Rooster	甲戌 Wood Jia Xu Dog	乙亥 Wood Yi Hai Pig
日 Day 合 Combine 天 Sky 牢 Jail	日 Day 建 Establish Star 元 Black 武 Tortoise	司 Life 命 Governor 路 Road 空 Emptiness	勾 Grappling 陳 Hook 路 Road 空 Emptiness	青 Green 龍 Dragon	明 Bright 堂 Hall 不 Non 遇 Eligible Day

己酉 Ji You Day

Clash 沖	癸卯 Water Gui Mao Rabbit	乙卯 Wood Yi Mao Rabbit

11 pm - 12.59 am	1 am - 2.59 am	3 am - 4.59 am	5 am - 6.59 am	7 am - 8.59 am	9 am - 10.59 am
甲子 Wood Jia Zi Rat	乙丑 Wood Yi Chou Ox	丙寅 Fire Bing Yin Tiger	丁卯 Fire Ding Mao Rabbit	戊辰 Earth Wu Chen Dragon	己巳 Earth Ji Si Snake
天 Heavenly 乙 Noble 司 Life 命 Governor	不 Non 遇 Eligible Day 勾 Grappling 陳 Hook	天 Heavenly 官 Officer 旬 Group 空 Emptiness	明 Bright 堂 Hall 旬 Group 空 Emptiness	日 Day 合 Combine 天 Heavenly 刑 Punishment	朱 Red 雀 Phoenix
11 am - 12.59 pm	**1 pm - 2.59 pm**	**3 pm - 4.59 pm**	**5 pm - 6.59 pm**	**7 pm - 8.59 pm**	**9 pm - 10.59 pm**
庚午 Metal Geng Wu Horse	辛未 Metal Xin Wei Goat	壬申 Water Ren Shen Monkey	癸酉 Water Gui You Rooster	甲戌 Wood Jia Xu Dog	乙亥 Wood Yi Hai Pig
日 Day 祿 Wealth 金 Golden 匱 Lock	福 Prosperity 星 star 寶 Precious 光 Light	天 Heavenly 乙 Noble 路 Road 空 Emptiness	日 Day 建 Establish Star 路 Road 空 Emptiness	日 Day 害 Harm 天 Sky 牢 Jail	日 Day 馬 Horse 元 Black 武 Tortoise

己亥 Ji Hai Day

Clash 沖	癸巳 Gui Si Water Snake	丁巳 Ding Si Fire Snake

11 pm - 12.59 am	1 am - 2.59 am	3 am - 4.59 am	5 am - 6.59 am	7 am - 8.59 am	9 am - 10.59 am
甲子 Jia Zi Wood Rat	乙丑 Yi Chou Wood Ox	丙寅 Bing Yin Fire Tiger	丁卯 Ding Mao Fire Rabbit	戊辰 Wu Chen Earth Dragon	己巳 Ji Si Earth Snake
天 Heavenly 乙 Noble 白 White 虎 Tiger	玉 Jade 堂 Hall 不 Non 遇 Eligible Day	日 Day 合 Combine 天 Sky 牢 Jail	元 Black 武 Tortoise	司 Life 命 Governor 旬 Group 空 Emptiness	日 Day 馬 Horse 日 Day 破 Breaker
11 am - 12.59 pm	**1 pm - 2.59 pm**	**3 pm - 4.59 pm**	**5 pm - 6.59 pm**	**7 pm - 8.59 pm**	**9 pm - 10.59 pm**
庚午 Geng Wu Metal Horse	辛未 Xin Wei Metal Goat	壬申 Ren Shen Water Monkey	癸酉 Gui You Water Rooster	甲戌 Jia Xu Wood Dog	乙亥 Yi Hai Wood Pig
日 Day 祿 Wealth 青 Green 龍 Dragon	福 Prosperity 星 star 明 Bright 堂 Hall	天 Heavenly 乙 Noble 日 Day 害 Harm	朱 Red 雀 Phoenix 路 Road 空 Emptiness	金 Golden 匱 Lock	日 Day 祿 Wealth 不 Non 遇 Eligible Day

己丑 Ji Chou Day

Clash 沖	癸未 Gui Wei Water Goat	己未 Ji Wei Earth Goat

11 pm - 12.59 am	1 am - 2.59 am	3 am - 4.59 am	5 am - 6.59 am	7 am - 8.59 am	9 am - 10.59 am
甲子 Jia Zi Wood Rat	乙丑 Yi Chou Wood Ox	丙寅 Bing Yin Fire Tiger	丁卯 Ding Mao Fire Rabbit	戊辰 Wu Chen Earth Dragon	己巳 Ji Si Earth Snake
日 Day 合 Combine 天 Heavenly 刑 Punishment	日 Day 建 Establish Star 不 Non 遇 Eligible Day	喜 Happy 神 Spirit 天 Heavenly 官 Officer	寶 Precious 光 Light	白 White 虎 Tiger	玉 Jade 堂 Hall
11 am - 12.59 pm	**1 pm - 2.59 pm**	**3 pm - 4.59 pm**	**5 pm - 6.59 pm**	**7 pm - 8.59 pm**	**9 pm - 10.59 pm**
庚午 Geng Wu Metal Horse	辛未 Xin Wei Metal Goat	壬申 Ren Shen Water Monkey	癸酉 Gui You Water Rooster	甲戌 Jia Xu Wood Dog	乙亥 Yi Hai Wood Pig
日 Day 祿 Wealth 天 Sky 牢 Jail	福 Prosperity 星 star 日 Day 破 Breaker	天 Heavenly 乙 Noble 路 Road 空 Emptiness	路 Road 空 Emptiness 勾 Grappling 陳 Hook	青 Green 龍 Dragon 日 Day 刑 Punishment	日 Day 馬 Horse 不 Non 遇 Eligible Day

己卯 Ji Mao Day

Clash 沖	癸酉 Gui You Water Rooster	乙酉 Yi You Wood Rooster

11 pm - 12.59 am	1 am - 2.59 am	3 am - 4.59 am	5 am - 6.59 am	7 am - 8.59 am	9 am - 10.59 am
甲子 Jia Zi Wood Rat	乙丑 Yi Chou Wood Ox	丙寅 Bing Yin Fire Tiger	丁卯 Ding Mao Fire Rabbit	戊辰 Wu Chen Earth Dragon	己巳 Ji Si Earth Snake
天 Heavenly 乙 Noble 日 Day 刑 Punishment	不 Non 遇 Eligible Day 勾 Grappling 陳 Hook	天 Heavenly 官 Officer 喜 Happy 神 Spirit	日 Day 建 Establish Star 明 Bright 堂 Hall	日 Day 害 Harm 天 Heavenly 刑 Punishment	日 Day 馬 Horse 朱 Red 雀 Phoenix
11 am - 12.59 pm	**1 pm - 2.59 pm**	**3 pm - 4.59 pm**	**5 pm - 6.59 pm**	**7 pm - 8.59 pm**	**9 pm - 10.59 pm**
庚午 Geng Wu Metal Horse	辛未 Xin Wei Metal Goat	壬申 Ren Shen Water Monkey	癸酉 Gui You Water Rooster	甲戌 Jia Xu Wood Dog	乙亥 Yi Hai Wood Pig
日 Day 祿 Wealth 金 Golden 匱 Lock	寶 Precious 光 Light 福 Prosperity 星 star	天 Heavenly 乙 Noble 旬 Group 空 Emptiness	玉 Jade 堂 Hall 旬 Group 空 Emptiness	日 Day 合 Combine 天 Sky 牢 Jail	元 Black 武 Tortoise 不 Non 遇 Eligible Day

庚午 Geng Wu Day

Clash 沖	甲子 Jia Zi Wood Rat	丙子 Bing Zi Fire Rat

11 pm - 12.59 am	1 am - 2.59 am	3 am - 4.59 am	5 am - 6.59 am	7 am - 8.59 am	9 am - 10.59 am
丙子 Bing Zi Fire Rat	丁丑 Ding Chou Fire Ox	戊寅 Wu Yin Earth Tiger	己卯 Ji Mao Earth Rabbit	庚辰 Geng Chen Metal Dragon	辛巳 Xin Si Metal Snake
金匱 Golden Lock 日破 Day Breaker	天乙 Heavenly Noble 日害 Day Harm	日馬 Day Horse 白虎 White Tiger	玉堂 Jade Hall	天牢 Sky Jail	元武 Black Tortoise

11 am - 12.59 pm	1 pm - 2.59 pm	3 pm - 4.59 pm	5 pm - 6.59 pm	7 pm - 8.59 pm	9 pm - 10.59 pm
壬午 Ren Wu Water Horse	癸未 Gui Wei Water Goat	甲申 Jia Shen Wood Monkey	乙酉 Yi You Wood Rooster	丙戌 Bing Xu Fire Dog	丁亥 Ding Hai Fire Pig
天官 Heavenly Officer 路空 Road Emptiness	日合 Day Combine 路空 Road Emptiness	日祿 Day Wealth 青龍 Green Dragon	明堂 Bright Hall	喜神 Happy Spirit 旬空 Group Emptiness	旬空 Group Emptiness 朱雀 Red Phoenix

庚申 Geng Shen Day

Clash 沖	甲寅 Jia yin Wood Tiger	戊寅 Wu Yin Earth Tiger

11 pm - 12.59 am	1 am - 2.59 am	3 am - 4.59 am	5 am - 6.59 am	7 am - 8.59 am	9 am - 10.59 am
丙子 Bing Zi Fire Rat	丁丑 Ding Chou Fire Ox	戊寅 Wu Yin Earth Tiger	己卯 Ji Mao Earth Rabbit	庚辰 Geng Chen Metal Dragon	辛巳 Xin Si Metal Snake
青龍 Green Dragon 不遇 Non Eligible Day	天乙 Heavenly Noble 旬空 Group Emptiness	日馬 Day Horse 天刑 Heavenly Punishment	天乙 Heavenly Noble 朱雀 Red Phoenix	金匱 Golden Lock	日合 Day Combine 寶光 Precious Light

11 am - 12.59 pm	1 pm - 2.59 pm	3 pm - 4.59 pm	5 pm - 6.59 pm	7 pm - 8.59 pm	9 pm - 10.59 pm
壬午 Ren Wu Water Horse	癸未 Gui Wei Water Goat	甲申 Jia Shen Wood Monkey	乙酉 Yi You Wood Rooster	丙戌 Bing Xu Fire Dog	丁亥 Ding Hai Fire Pig
天官 Heavenly Officer 白虎 White Tiger	路空 Road Emptiness	日建 Day Establish Star 天牢 Sky Jail	元武 Black Tortoise	司命 Life Governor 不遇 Non Eligible Day	日害 Day Harm 勾陳 Grappling Hook

庚戌 Geng Xu Day

Clash 沖	甲辰 Jia Chen Wood Dragon	戊辰 Wu Chen Earth Dragon

11 pm - 12.59 am	1 am - 2.59 am	3 am - 4.59 am	5 am - 6.59 am	7 am - 8.59 am	9 am - 10.59 am
丙子 Bing Zi Fire Rat	丁丑 Ding Chou Fire Ox	戊寅 Wu Yin Earth Tiger	己卯 Ji Mao Earth Rabbit	庚辰 Geng Chen Metal Dragon	辛巳 Xin Si Metal Snake
不遇 Non Eligible Day 天牢 Sky Jail	天乙 Heavenly Noble 元武 Black Tortoise	司命 Life Governor 旬空 Group Emptiness	日合 Day Combine 旬空 Group Emptiness	青龍 Green Dragon 日破 Day Breaker	明堂 Bright Hall

11 am - 12.59 pm	1 pm - 2.59 pm	3 pm - 4.59 pm	5 pm - 6.59 pm	7 pm - 8.59 pm	9 pm - 10.59 pm
壬午 Ren Wu Water Horse	癸未 Gui Wei Water Goat	甲申 Jia Shen Wood Monkey	乙酉 Yi You Wood Rooster	丙戌 Bing Xu Fire Dog	丁亥 Ding Hai Fire Pig
天官 Heavenly Officer 路空 Road Emptiness	天乙 Heavenly Noble 路空 Road Emptiness	日祿 Day Wealth 日馬 Day Horse	寶光 Precious Light 日害 Day Harm	日建 Day Establish Star 不遇 Non Eligible Day	玉堂 Jade Hall

庚子 Geng Zi Day

Clash 沖 | 甲午 Jia Wu Wood Horse | 丙午 Bing Wu Fire Horse

11 pm - 12.59 am	1 am - 2.59 am	3 am - 4.59 am	5 am - 6.59 am	7 am - 8.59 am	9 am - 10.59 am
丙子 Bing Zi Fire Rat	丁丑 Ding Chou Fire Ox	戊寅 Wu Yin Earth Tiger	己卯 Ji Mao Earth Rabbit	庚辰 Geng Chen Metal Dragon	辛巳 Xin Si Metal Snake
日 Day 建 Establish Star	天 Heavenly 乙 Noble	日 Day 馬 Horse	玉 Jade 堂 Hall	天 Sky 牢 Jail	旬 Group 空 Emptiness
不 Non 遇 Eligible Day	日 Day 合 Combine	白 White 虎 Tiger	日 Day 刑 Punishment	旬 Group 空 Emptiness	元 Black 武 Tortoise

11 am - 12.59 pm	1 pm - 2.59 pm	3 pm - 4.59 pm	5 pm - 6.59 pm	7 pm - 8.59 pm	9 pm - 10.59 pm
壬午 Ren Wu Water Horse	癸未 Gui Wei Water Goat	甲申 Jia Shen Wood Monkey	乙酉 Yi You Wood Rooster	丙戌 Bing Xu Fire Dog	丁亥 Ding Hai Fire Pig
天 Heavenly 乙 Noble	天 Heavenly 乙 Noble	青 Green 龍 Dragon	明 Bright 堂 Hall	喜 Happy 神 Spirit	朱 Red 雀 Phoenix
路 Road 空 Emptiness	路 Road 空 Emptiness	日 Day 祿 Wealth		不 Non 遇 Eligible Day	

庚寅 Geng Yin Day

Clash 沖 | 甲申 Jia Shen Wood Monkey | 戊申 Wu Shen Earth Monkey

11 pm - 12.59 am	1 am - 2.59 am	3 am - 4.59 am	5 am - 6.59 am	7 am - 8.59 am	9 am - 10.59 am
丙子 Bing Zi Fire Rat	丁丑 Ding Chou Fire Ox	戊寅 Wu Yin Earth Tiger	己卯 Ji Mao Earth Rabbit	庚辰 Geng Chen Metal Dragon	辛巳 Xin Si Metal Snake
青 Green 龍 Dragon	天 Heavenly 乙 Noble	日 Day 建 Establish Star	朱 Red 雀 Phoenix	金 Golden 匱 Lock	寶 Precious 光 Light
不 Non 遇 Eligible Day	明 Bright 堂 Hall	天 Heavenly 刑 Punishment			日 Day 害 Harm

11 am - 12.59 pm	1 pm - 2.59 pm	3 pm - 4.59 pm	5 pm - 6.59 pm	7 pm - 8.59 pm	9 pm - 10.59 pm
壬午 Ren Wu Water Horse	癸未 Gui Wei Water Goat	甲申 Jia Shen Wood Monkey	乙酉 Yi You Wood Rooster	丙戌 Bing Xu Fire Dog	丁亥 Ding Hai Fire Pig
天 Heavenly 官 Officer	玉 Jade 堂 Hall	日 Day 馬 Horse	元 Black 武 Tortoise	司 Life 命 Governor	日 Day 合 Combine
路 Road 空 Emptiness	路 Road 空 Emptiness	天 Sky 牢 Jail		不 Non 遇 Eligible Day	勾 Grappling 陳 Hook

庚辰 Geng Chen Day

Clash 沖 | 甲戌 Jia Xu Wood Dog | 戊戌 Wu Xu Earth Dog

11 pm - 12.59 am	1 am - 2.59 am	3 am - 4.59 am	5 am - 6.59 am	7 am - 8.59 am	9 am - 10.59 am
丙子 Bing Zi Fire Rat	丁丑 Ding Chou Fire Ox	戊寅 Wu Yin Earth Tiger	己卯 Ji Mao Earth Rabbit	庚辰 Geng Chen Metal Dragon	辛巳 Xin Si Metal Snake
天 Sky 牢 Jail	福 Prosperity 星 star	日 Day 馬 Horse	勾 Grappling 陳 Hook	日 Day 建 Establish Star	明 Bright 堂 Hall
不 Non 遇 Eligible Day	元 Black 武 Tortoise	司 Life 命 Governor	日 Day 害 Harm	日 Day 刑 Punishment	

11 am - 12.59 pm	1 pm - 2.59 pm	3 pm - 4.59 pm	5 pm - 6.59 pm	7 pm - 8.59 pm	9 pm - 10.59 pm
壬午 Ren Wu Water Horse	癸未 Gui Wei Water Goat	甲申 Jia Shen Wood Monkey	乙酉 Yi You Wood Rooster	丙戌 Bing Xu Fire Dog	丁亥 Ding Hai Fire Pig
天 Heavenly 官 Officer	天 Heavenly 乙 Noble	日 Day 祿 Wealth	日 Day 合 Combine	喜 Happy 神 Spirit	玉 Jade 堂 Hall
路 Road 空 Emptiness	路 Road 空 Emptiness	旬 Group 空 Emptiness	旬 Group 空 Emptiness	不 Non 遇 Eligible Day	

辛未 Xin Wei Day

Clash 沖: 乙丑 Wood Ox (Yi Chou) | 丁丑 Fire Ox (Ding Chou)

11 pm - 12.59 am	1 am - 2.59 am	3 am - 4.59 am	5 am - 6.59 am	7 am - 8.59 am	9 am - 10.59 am
戊子 Wu Zi Earth Rat	己丑 Ji Chou Earth Ox	庚寅 Geng Yin Metal Tiger	辛卯 Xin Mao Metal Rabbit	壬辰 Ren Chen Water Dragon	癸巳 Gui Si Water Snake
日害 Day Harm	日破 Day Breaker	天乙 Heavenly Noble	寶光 Precious Light	路空 Road Emptiness	天官 Heavenly Officer
天刑 Heavenly Punishment	朱雀 Red Phoenix	金匱 Golden Lock		白虎 White Tiger	路空 Road Emptiness

11 am - 12.59 pm	1 pm - 2.59 pm	3 pm - 4.59 pm	5 pm - 6.59 pm	7 pm - 8.59 pm	9 pm - 10.59 pm
甲午 Jia Wu Wood Horse	乙未 Yi Wei Wood Goat	丙申 Bing Shen Fire Monkey	丁酉 Ding You Fire Rooster	戊戌 Wu Xu Earth Dog	己亥 Ji Hai Earth Pig
日合 Day Combine	日建 Day Establish Star	喜神 Happy Spirit	日祿 Day Wealth	青龍 Green Dragon	明堂 Bright Hall
天牢 Sky Jail	元武 Black Tortoise	司命 Life Governor	不遇 Non Eligible Day	旬空 Group Emptiness	旬空 Group Emptiness

辛酉 Xin You Day

Clash 沖: 乙卯 Wood Rabbit (Yi Mao) | 己卯 Earth Rabbit (Ji Mao)

11 pm - 12.59 am	1 am - 2.59 am	3 am - 4.59 am	5 am - 6.59 am	7 am - 8.59 am	9 am - 10.59 am
戊子 Wu Zi Earth Rat	己丑 Ji Chou Earth Ox	庚寅 Geng Yin Metal Tiger	辛卯 Xin Mao Metal Rabbit	壬辰 Ren Chen Water Dragon	癸巳 Gui Si Water Snake
司命 Life Governor	勾陳 Grappling Hook	天乙 Heavenly Noble	明堂 Bright Hall	日合 Day Combine	天官 Heavenly Officer
旬空 Group Emptiness	旬空 Group Emptiness	青龍 Green Dragon	日破 Day Breaker	路空 Road Emptiness	路空 Road Emptiness

11 am - 12.59 pm	1 pm - 2.59 pm	3 pm - 4.59 pm	5 pm - 6.59 pm	7 pm - 8.59 pm	9 pm - 10.59 pm
甲午 Jia Wu Wood Horse	乙未 Yi Wei Wood Goat	丙申 Bing Shen Fire Monkey	丁酉 Ding You Fire Rooster	戊戌 Wu Xu Earth Dog	己亥 Ji Hai Earth Pig
天乙 Heavenly Noble	寶光 Precious Light	喜神 Happy Spirit	日建 Day Establish Star	日害 Day Harm	日馬 Day Horse
金匱 Golden Lock		白虎 White Tiger	不遇 Non Eligible Day	天牢 Sky Jail	元武 Black Tortoise

辛亥 Xin Hai Day

Clash 沖: 乙巳 Wood Snake (Yi Si) | 己巳 Earth Snake (Ji Si)

11 pm - 12.59 am	1 am - 2.59 am	3 am - 4.59 am	5 am - 6.59 am	7 am - 8.59 am	9 am - 10.59 am
戊子 Wu Zi Earth Rat	己丑 Ji Chou Earth Ox	庚寅 Geng Yin Metal Tiger	辛卯 Xin Mao Metal Rabbit	壬辰 Ren Chen Water Dragon	癸巳 Gui Si Water Snake
白虎 White Tiger	玉堂 Jade Hall	日合 Day Combine	元武 Black Tortoise	司命 Life Governor	天乙 Heavenly Noble
		天牢 Sky Jail	旬空 Group Emptiness	路空 Road Emptiness	日破 Day Breaker

11 am - 12.59 pm	1 pm - 2.59 pm	3 pm - 4.59 pm	5 pm - 6.59 pm	7 pm - 8.59 pm	9 pm - 10.59 pm
甲午 Jia Wu Wood Horse	乙未 Yi Wei Wood Goat	丙申 Bing Shen Fire Monkey	丁酉 Ding You Fire Rooster	戊戌 Wu Xu Earth Dog	己亥 Ji Hai Earth Pig
天乙 Heavenly Noble	明堂 Bright Hall	喜神 Happy Spirit	日祿 Day Wealth	金匱 Golden Lock	日建 Day Establish Star
青龍 Green Dragon		日害 Day Harm	不遇 Non Eligible Day		日刑 Day Punishment

辛丑 Xin Chou Day

Clash 沖: 乙未 Yi Wei Wood Goat | 丁未 Ding Wei Fire Goat

11 pm - 12.59 am	1 am - 2.59 am	3 am - 4.59 am	5 am - 6.59 am	7 am - 8.59 am	9 am - 10.59 am
戊子 Wu Zi Earth Rat	己丑 Ji Chou Earth Ox	庚寅 Geng Yin Metal Tiger	辛卯 Xin Mao Metal Rabbit	壬辰 Ren Chen Water Dragon	癸巳 Gui Si Water Snake
日 Day 合 Combine 天 Heavenly 刑 Punishment	日 Day 建 Establish Star 朱 Red 雀 Phoenix	天 Heavenly 乙 Noble 金 Golden 匱 Lock	寶 Precious 光 Light	路 Road 空 Emptiness 白 White 虎 Tiger	天 Heavenly 官 Officer 路 Road 空 Emptiness

11 am - 12.59 pm	1 pm - 2.59 pm	3 pm - 4.59 pm	5 pm - 6.59 pm	7 pm - 8.59 pm	9 pm - 10.59 pm
甲午 Jia Wu Wood Horse	乙未 Yi Wei Wood Goat	丙申 Bing Shen Fire Monkey	丁酉 Ding You Fire Rooster	戊戌 Wu Xu Earth Dog	己亥 Ji Hai Earth Pig
天 Heavenly 乙 Noble 天 Sky 牢 Jail	元 Black 武 Tortoise 日 Day 破 Breaker	喜 Happy 神 Spirit 司 Life 命 Governor	日 Day 祿 Wealth 不 Non 遇 Eligible Day	青 Green 龍 Dragon 日 Day 刑 Punishment	日 Day 馬 Horse 明 Bright 堂 Hall

辛卯 Xin Mao Day

Clash 沖: 乙酉 Yi You Wood Rooster | 己酉 Ji You Earth Rooster

11 pm - 12.59 am	1 am - 2.59 am	3 am - 4.59 am	5 am - 6.59 am	7 am - 8.59 am	9 am - 10.59 am
戊子 Wu Zi Earth Rat	己丑 Ji Chou Earth Ox	庚寅 Geng Yin Metal Tiger	辛卯 Xin Mao Metal Rabbit	壬辰 Ren Chen Water Dragon	癸巳 Gui Si Water Snake
司 Life 命 Governor 日 Day 刑 Punishment	勾 Grappling 陳 Hook	天 Heavenly 乙 Noble 青 Green 龍 Dragon	日 Day 建 Establish Star 明 Bright 堂 Hall	路 Road 空 Emptiness 天 Heavenly 刑 Punishment	天 Heavenly 官 Officer 路 Road 空 Emptiness

11 am - 12.59 pm	1 pm - 2.59 pm	3 pm - 4.59 pm	5 pm - 6.59 pm	7 pm - 8.59 pm	9 pm - 10.59 pm
甲午 Jia Wu Wood Horse	乙未 Yi Wei Wood Goat	丙申 Bing Shen Fire Monkey	丁酉 Ding You Fire Rooster	戊戌 Wu Xu Earth Dog	己亥 Ji Hai Earth Pig
金 Golden 匱 Lock 旬 Group 空 Emptiness	寶 Precious 光 Light 旬 Group 空 Emptiness	青 Green 龍 Dragon 白 White 虎 Tiger	日 Day 建 Establish Star 不 Non 遇 Eligible Day	日 Day 合 Combine 天 Sky 牢 Jail	元 Black 武 Tortoise

辛巳 Xin Si Day

Clash 沖: 乙亥 Yi Hai Wood Pig | 己亥 Ji Hai Earth Pig

11 pm - 12.59 am	1 am - 2.59 am	3 am - 4.59 am	5 am - 6.59 am	7 am - 8.59 am	9 am - 10.59 am
戊子 Wu Zi Earth Rat	己丑 Ji Chou Earth Ox	庚寅 Geng Yin Metal Tiger	辛卯 Xin Mao Metal Rabbit	壬辰 Ren Chen Water Dragon	癸巳 Gui Si Water Snake
白 White 虎 Tiger	玉 Jade 堂 Hall	天 Heavenly 乙 Noble 天 Sky 牢 Jail	元 Black 武 Tortoise	司 Life 命 Governor 路 Road 空 Emptiness	天 Heavenly 官 Officer 路 Road 空 Emptiness

11 am - 12.59 pm	1 pm - 2.59 pm	3 pm - 4.59 pm	5 pm - 6.59 pm	7 pm - 8.59 pm	9 pm - 10.59 pm
甲午 Jia Wu Wood Horse	乙未 Yi Wei Wood Goat	丙申 Bing Shen Fire Monkey	丁酉 Ding You Fire Rooster	戊戌 Wu Xu Earth Dog	己亥 Ji Hai Earth Pig
天 Heavenly 乙 Noble 青 Green 龍 Dragon	明 Bright 堂 Hall	日 Day 合 Combine 旬 Group 空 Emptiness	日 Day 祿 Wealth 不 Non 遇 Eligible Day	金 Golden 匱 Lock	寶 Precious 光 Light 日 Day 破 Breaker

壬申 Ren Shen Day

Clash 沖	丙寅 Bing Yin Fire Tiger	庚寅 Geng Yin Metal Tiger

11 pm - 12.59 am	1 am - 2.59 am	3 am - 4.59 am	5 am - 6.59 am	7 am - 8.59 am	9 am - 10.59 am
庚子 Geng Zi Metal Rat	辛丑 Xin Chou Metal Ox	壬寅 Ren Yin Water Tiger	癸卯 Gui Mao Water Rabbit	甲辰 Jia Chen Wood Dragon	乙巳 Yi Si Wood Snake
青龍 Green Dragon	天官 Heavenly Officer 明堂 Bright Hall	日馬 Day Horse 日破 Day Breaker	天乙 Heavenly Noble 路空 Road Emptiness	福星 Prosperity star 金匱 Golden Lock	天乙 Heavenly Noble 日合 Day Combine

11 am - 12.59 pm	1 pm - 2.59 pm	3 pm - 4.59 pm	5 pm - 6.59 pm	7 pm - 8.59 pm	9 pm - 10.59 pm
丙午 Bing Wu Fire Horse	丁未 Ding Wei Fire Goat	戊申 Wu Shen Earth Monkey	己酉 Ji You Earth Rooster	庚戌 Geng Xu Metal Dog	辛亥 Xin Hai Metal Pig
喜神 Happy Spirit 白虎 White Tiger	天官 Heavenly Officer 玉堂 Jade Hall	日建 Day Establish Star 不遇 Non Eligible Day	元武 Black Tortoise	司命 Life Governor 旬空 Group Emptiness	日馬 Day Horse 旬空 Group Emptiness

壬戌 Ren Xu Day

Clash 沖	丙辰 Bing Chen Fire Dragon	甲辰 Jia Chen Wood Dragon

11 pm - 12.59 am	1 am - 2.59 am	3 am - 4.59 am	5 am - 6.59 am	7 am - 8.59 am	9 am - 10.59 am
庚子 Geng Zi Metal Rat	辛丑 Xin Chou Metal Ox	壬寅 Ren Yin Water Tiger	癸卯 Gui Mao Water Rabbit	甲辰 Jia Chen Wood Dragon	乙巳 Yi Si Wood Snake
旬空 Group Emptiness 天牢 Sky Jail	天官 Heavenly Officer 旬空 Group Emptiness	司命 Life Governor 路空 Road Emptiness	日合 Day Combine 路空 Road Emptiness	福星 Prosperity star 日破 Day Breaker	天乙 Heavenly Noble 明堂 Bright Hall

11 am - 12.59 pm	1 pm - 2.59 pm	3 pm - 4.59 pm	5 pm - 6.59 pm	7 pm - 8.59 pm	9 pm - 10.59 pm
丙午 Bing Wu Fire Horse	丁未 Ding Wei Fire Goat	戊申 Wu Shen Earth Monkey	己酉 Ji You Earth Rooster	庚戌 Geng Xu Metal Dog	辛亥 Xin Hai Metal Pig
喜神 Happy Spirit 天刑 Heavenly Punishment	天官 Heavenly Officer 朱雀 Red Phoenix	日馬 Day Horse 不遇 Non Eligible Day	寶光 Precious Light 日害 Day Harm	日建 Day Establish Star 白虎 White Tiger	日祿 Day Wealth 玉堂 Jade Hall

壬子 Ren Zi Day

Clash 沖	丙午 Bing Wu Fire Horse	庚午 Geng Wu Metal Horse

11 pm - 12.59 am	1 am - 2.59 am	3 am - 4.59 am	5 am - 6.59 am	7 am - 8.59 am	9 am - 10.59 am
庚子 Geng Zi Metal Rat	辛丑 Xin Chou Metal Ox	壬寅 Ren Yin Water Tiger	癸卯 Gui Mao Water Rabbit	甲辰 Jia Chen Wood Dragon	乙巳 Yi Si Wood Snake
金匱 Golden Lock 日建 Day Establish Star	日合 Day Combine 天官 Heavenly Officer	日馬 Day Horse 路空 Road Emptiness	天乙 Heavenly Noble 路空 Road Emptiness	福星 Prosperity star 天牢 Sky Jail	天乙 Heavenly Noble 元武 Black Tortoise

11 am - 12.59 pm	1 pm - 2.59 pm	3 pm - 4.59 pm	5 pm - 6.59 pm	7 pm - 8.59 pm	9 pm - 10.59 pm
丙午 Bing Wu Fire Horse	丁未 Ding Wei Fire Goat	戊申 Wu Shen Earth Monkey	己酉 Ji You Earth Rooster	庚戌 Geng Xu Metal Dog	辛亥 Xin Hai Metal Pig
司命 Life Governor 日破 Day Breaker	天官 Heavenly Officer 日害 Day Harm	青龍 Green Dragon 不遇 Non Eligible Day	明堂 Bright Hall	天刑 Heavenly Punishment	日祿 Day Wealth 朱雀 Red Phoenix

壬寅 Ren Yin Day

Clash 沖	庚申 Metal Geng Shen Monkey	丙申 Fire Bing Shen Monkey

11 pm - 12.59 am	1 am - 2.59 am	3 am - 4.59 am	5 am - 6.59 am	7 am - 8.59 am	9 am - 10.59 am
庚子 Metal Geng Zi Rat	辛丑 Metal Xin Chou Ox	壬寅 Water Ren Yin Tiger	癸卯 Water Gui Mao Rabbit	甲辰 Wood Jia Chen Dragon	乙巳 Wood Yi Si Snake
青 Green 龍 Dragon	天 Heavenly 官 Officer 明 Bright 堂 Hall	日 Day 建 Establish Star 路 Road 空 Emptiness	天 Heavenly 乙 Noble 路 Road 空 Emptiness	福 Prosperity 星 star 旬 Group 空 Emptiness	天 Heavenly 乙 Noble 日 Day 刑 Punishment

11 am - 12.59 pm	1 pm - 2.59 pm	3 pm - 4.59 pm	5 pm - 6.59 pm	7 pm - 8.59 pm	9 pm - 10.59 pm
丙午 Fire Bing Wu Horse	丁未 Fire Ding Wei Goat	戊申 Earth Wu Shen Monkey	己酉 Earth Ji You Rooster	庚戌 Metal Geng Xu Dog	辛亥 Metal Xin Hai Pig
喜 Happy 神 Spirit 白 White 虎 Tiger	天 Heavenly 官 Officer 玉 Jade 堂 Hall	日 Day 馬 Horse 天 Sky 牢 Jail	元 Black 武 Tortoise	司 Life 命 Governor	日 Day 馬 Horse 勾 Grappling 陳 Hook

壬辰 Ren Chen Day

Clash 沖	丙戌 Fire Bing Xu Dog	甲戌 Wood Jia Xu Dog

11 pm - 12.59 am	1 am - 2.59 am	3 am - 4.59 am	5 am - 6.59 am	7 am - 8.59 am	9 am - 10.59 am
庚子 Metal Geng Zi Rat	辛丑 Metal Xin Chou Ox	壬寅 Water Ren Yin Tiger	癸卯 Water Gui Mao Rabbit	甲辰 Wood Jia Chen Dragon	乙巳 Wood Yi Si Snake
天 Sky 牢 Jail	天 Heavenly 官 Officer 元 Black 武 Tortoise	日 Day 馬 Horse 路 Road 空 Emptiness	天 Heavenly 乙 Noble 路 Road 空 Emptiness	福 Prosperity 星 star 日 Day 刑 Punishment	天 Heavenly 乙 Noble 明 Bright 堂 Hall

11 am - 12.59 pm	1 pm - 2.59 pm	3 pm - 4.59 pm	5 pm - 6.59 pm	7 pm - 8.59 pm	9 pm - 10.59 pm
丙午 Fire Bing Wu Horse	丁未 Fire Ding Wei Goat	戊申 Earth Wu Shen Monkey	己酉 Earth Ji You Rooster	庚戌 Metal Geng Xu Dog	辛亥 Metal Xin Hai Pig
喜 Happy 神 Spirit 天 Heavenly 刑 Punishment	天 Heavenly 官 Officer 旬 Group 空 Emptiness	金 Golden 匱 Lock 不 Non 遇 Eligible Day	日 Day 合 Combine 寶 Precious 光 Light	日 Day 破 Breaker 白 White 虎 Tiger	日 Day 祿 Wealth 玉 Jade 堂 Hall

壬午 Ren Wu Day

Clash 沖	丙子 Fire Bing Zi Rat	庚子 Metal Geng Zi Rat

11 pm - 12.59 am	1 am - 2.59 am	3 am - 4.59 am	5 am - 6.59 am	7 am - 8.59 am	9 am - 10.59 am
庚子 Metal Geng Zi Rat	辛丑 Metal Xin Chou Ox	壬寅 Water Ren Yin Tiger	癸卯 Water Gui Mao Rabbit	甲辰 Wood Jia Chen Dragon	乙巳 Wood Yi Si Snake
金 Golden 匱 Lock 日 Day 破 Breaker	天 Heavenly 官 Officer 日 Day 害 Harm	路 Road 空 Emptiness 白 White 虎 Tiger	天 Heavenly 乙 Noble 路 Road 空 Emptiness	福 Prosperity 星 star 天 Sky 牢 Jail	天 Heavenly 乙 Noble 元 Black 武 Tortoise

11 am - 12.59 pm	1 pm - 2.59 pm	3 pm - 4.59 pm	5 pm - 6.59 pm	7 pm - 8.59 pm	9 pm - 10.59 pm
丙午 Fire Bing Wu Horse	丁未 Fire Ding Wei Goat	戊申 Earth Wu Shen Monkey	己酉 Earth Ji You Rooster	庚戌 Metal Geng Xu Dog	辛亥 Metal Xin Hai Pig
喜 Happy 神 Spirit 日 Day 刑 Punishment	日 Day 合 Combine 勾 Grappling 陳 Hook	日 Day 馬 Horse 不 Non 遇 Eligible Day	明 Bright 堂 Hall 旬 Group 空 Emptiness	天 Heavenly 刑 Punishment	日 Day 祿 Wealth 朱 Red 雀 Phoenix

癸酉 Gui You Day

Clash 沖	丁卯 Ding Mao Fire Rabbit	辛卯 Xin Mao Metal Rabbit

11 pm - 12.59 am	1 am - 2.59 am	3 am - 4.59 am	5 am - 6.59 am	7 am - 8.59 am	9 am - 10.59 am
壬子 Ren Zi Water Rat	癸丑 Gui Chou Water Ox	甲寅 Jia Yin Wood Tiger	乙卯 Yi Mao Wood Rabbit	丙辰 Bing Chen Fire Dragon	丁巳 Ding Si Fire Snake
日 Day 祿 Wealth 路 Road 空 Emptiness	路 Road 空 Emptiness 勾 Grappling 陳 Hook	青 Green 龍 Dragon	福 Prosperity 星 star 日 Day 破 Breaker	日 Day 合 Combine 天 Heavenly 刑 Punishment	天 Heavenly 乙 Noble 朱 Red 雀 Phoenix
11 am - 12.59 pm	**1 pm - 2.59 pm**	**3 pm - 4.59 pm**	**5 pm - 6.59 pm**	**7 pm - 8.59 pm**	**9 pm - 10.59 pm**
戊午 Wu Wu Earth Horse	己未 Ji Wei Earth Goat	庚申 Geng Shen Metal Monkey	辛酉 Xin You Metal Rooster	壬戌 Ren Xu Water Dog	癸亥 Gui Hai Water Pig
金 Golden 匱 Lock	寶 Precious 光 Light 不 Non 遇 Eligible Day	白 White 虎 Tiger	日 Day 建 Establish Star 日 Day 刑 Punishment	天 Heavenly 官 Officer 旬 Group 空 Emptiness	日 Day 馬 Horse 旬 Group 空 Emptiness

癸亥 Gui Hai Day

Clash 沖	丁巳 Ding Si Fire Snake	乙巳 Yi Si Wood Snake

11 pm - 12.59 am	1 am - 2.59 am	3 am - 4.59 am	5 am - 6.59 am	7 am - 8.59 am	9 am - 10.59 am
壬子 Ren Zi Water Rat	癸丑 Gui Chou Water Ox	甲寅 Jia Yin Wood Tiger	乙卯 Yi Mao Wood Rabbit	丙辰 Bing Chen Fire Dragon	丁巳 Ding Si Fire Snake
日 Day 祿 Wealth 路 Road 空 Emptiness	玉 Jade 堂 Hall 路 Road 空 Emptiness	日 Day 合 Combine 天 Sky 牢 Jail	天 Heavenly 乙 Noble 元 Black 武 Tortoise	天 Heavenly 官 Officer 司 Life 命 Governor	日 Day 馬 Horse 勾 Grappling 陳 Hook
11 am - 12.59 pm	**1 pm - 2.59 pm**	**3 pm - 4.59 pm**	**5 pm - 6.59 pm**	**7 pm - 8.59 pm**	**9 pm - 10.59 pm**
戊午 Wu Wu Earth Horse	己未 Ji Wei Earth Goat	庚申 Geng Shen Metal Monkey	辛酉 Xin You Metal Rooster	壬戌 Ren Xu Water Dog	癸亥 Gui Hai Water Pig
青 Green 龍 Dragon	明 Bright 堂 Hall 不 Non 遇 Eligible Day	天 Heavenly 刑 Punishment 日 Day 害 Harm	朱 Red 雀 Phoenix	天 Heavenly 官 Officer 路 Road 空 Emptiness	日 Day 建 Establish Star 路 Road 空 Emptiness

癸丑 Gui Chou Day

Clash 沖	丁未 Ding Wei Fire Goat	辛未 Xin Wei Metal Goat

11 pm - 12.59 am	1 am - 2.59 am	3 am - 4.59 am	5 am - 6.59 am	7 am - 8.59 am	9 am - 10.59 am
壬子 Ren Zi Water Rat	癸丑 Gui Chou Water Ox	甲寅 Jia Yin Wood Tiger	乙卯 Yi Mao Wood Rabbit	丙辰 Bing Chen Fire Dragon	丁巳 Ding Si Fire Snake
日 Day 合 Combine 路 Road 空 Emptiness	日 Day 建 Establish Star 路 Road 空 Emptiness	金 Golden 匱 Lock 旬 Group 空 Emptiness	天 Heavenly 乙 Noble 旬 Group 空 Emptiness	天 Heavenly 官 Officer 白 White 虎 Tiger	天 Heavenly 乙 Noble 玉 Jade 堂 Hall
11 am - 12.59 pm	**1 pm - 2.59 pm**	**3 pm - 4.59 pm**	**5 pm - 6.59 pm**	**7 pm - 8.59 pm**	**9 pm - 10.59 pm**
戊午 Wu Wu Earth Horse	己未 Ji Wei Earth Goat	庚申 Geng Shen Metal Monkey	辛酉 Xin You Metal Rooster	壬戌 Ren Xu Water Dog	癸亥 Gui Hai Water Pig
日 Day 害 Harm 天 Sky 牢 Jail	不 Non 遇 Eligible Day 日 Day 破 Breaker	司 Life 命 Governor	勾 Grappling 陳 Hook	天 Heavenly 官 Officer 路 Road 空 Emptiness	日 Day 馬 Horse 路 Road 空 Emptiness

癸卯 Gui Mao Day

Clash 沖	辛酉 Metal Rooster (Xin You)	丁酉 Fire Rooster (Ding You)

11 pm - 12.59 am	1 am - 2.59 am	3 am - 4.59 am	5 am - 6.59 am	7 am - 8.59 am	9 am - 10.59 am
壬子 Water Rat Ren Zi	癸丑 Water Ox Gui Chou	甲寅 Wood Tiger Jia Yin	乙卯 Wood Rabbit Yi Mao	丙辰 Fire Dragon Bing Chen	丁巳 Fire Snake Ding Si
喜 Happy 神 Spirit 路 Road 空 Emptiness	路 Road 空 Emptiness 勾 Grappling 陳 Hook	青 Green 龍 Dragon	天 Heavenly 乙 Noble 福 Prosperity 星 star	喜 Happy 神 Spirit 日 Day 害 Harm	日 Day 馬 Horse 朱 Red 雀 Phoenix
11 am - 12.59 pm	**1 pm - 2.59 pm**	**3 pm - 4.59 pm**	**5 pm - 6.59 pm**	**7 pm - 8.59 pm**	**9 pm - 10.59 pm**
戊午 Earth Horse Wu Wu	己未 Earth Goat Ji Wei	庚申 Metal Monkey Geng Shen	辛酉 Metal Rooster Xin You	壬戌 Water Dog Ren Xu	癸亥 Water Pig Gui Hai
金 Golden 匱 Lock	寶 Precious 光 Light 不 Non 遇 Eligible Day	白 White 虎 Tiger	玉 Jade 堂 Hall 日 Day 破 Breaker	日 Day 合 Combine 路 Road 空 Emptiness	元 Black 武 Tortoise 路 Road 空 Emptiness

癸巳 Gui Si Day

Clash 沖	丁亥 Fire Pig (Ding Hai)	乙亥 Wood Pig (Yi Hai)

11 pm - 12.59 am	1 am - 2.59 am	3 am - 4.59 am	5 am - 6.59 am	7 am - 8.59 am	9 am - 10.59 am
壬子 Water Rat Ren Zi	癸丑 Water Ox Gui Chou	甲寅 Wood Tiger Jia Yin	乙卯 Wood Rabbit Yi Mao	丙辰 Fire Dragon Bing Chen	丁巳 Fire Snake Ding Si
日 Day 祿 Wealth 路 Road 空 Emptiness	玉 Jade 堂 Hall 路 Road 空 Emptiness	日 Day 害 Harm 天 Sky 牢 Jail	天 Heavenly 乙 Noble 元 Black 武 Tortoise	天 Heavenly 官 Officer 司 Life 命 Governor	日 Day 建 Establish Star 勾 Grappling 陳 Hook
11 am - 12.59 pm	**1 pm - 2.59 pm**	**3 pm - 4.59 pm**	**5 pm - 6.59 pm**	**7 pm - 8.59 pm**	**9 pm - 10.59 pm**
戊午 Earth Horse Wu Wu	己未 Earth Goat Ji Wei	庚申 Metal Monkey Geng Shen	辛酉 Metal Rooster Xin You	壬戌 Water Dog Ren Xu	癸亥 Water Pig Gui Hai
青 Green 龍 Dragon 旬 Group 空 Emptiness	明 Bright 堂 Hall 不 Non 遇 Eligible Day	日 Day 合 Combine 天 Heavenly 刑 Punishment	朱 Red 雀 Phoenix	金 Golden 匱 Lock 路 Road 空 Emptiness	日 Day 馬 Horse 日 Day 破 Breaker

癸未 Gui Wei Day

Clash 沖	丁丑 Fire Ox (Ding Chou)	辛丑 Metal Ox (Xin Chou)

11 pm - 12.59 am	1 am - 2.59 am	3 am - 4.59 am	5 am - 6.59 am	7 am - 8.59 am	9 am - 10.59 am
壬子 Water Rat Ren Zi	癸丑 Water Ox Gui Chou	甲寅 Wood Tiger Jia Yin	乙卯 Wood Rabbit Yi Mao	丙辰 Fire Dragon Bing Chen	丁巳 Fire Snake Ding Si
日 Day 祿 Wealth 路 Road 空 Emptiness	日 Day 破 Breaker 路 Road 空 Emptiness	金 Golden 匱 Lock	天 Heavenly 乙 Noble 福 Prosperity 星 star	天 Heavenly 官 Officer 白 White 虎 Tiger	天 Heavenly 乙 Noble 日 Day 馬 Horse
11 am - 12.59 pm	**1 pm - 2.59 pm**	**3 pm - 4.59 pm**	**5 pm - 6.59 pm**	**7 pm - 8.59 pm**	**9 pm - 10.59 pm**
戊午 Earth Horse Wu Wu	己未 Earth Goat Ji Wei	庚申 Metal Monkey Geng Shen	辛酉 Metal Rooster Xin You	壬戌 Water Dog Ren Xu	癸亥 Water Pig Gui Hai
日 Day 合 Combine 天 Sky 牢 Jail	日 Day 建 Establish Star 不 Non 遇 Eligible Day	司 Life 命 Governor 旬 Group 空 Emptiness	旬 Group 空 Emptiness 勾 Grappling 陳 Hook	天 Heavenly 官 Officer 路 Road 空 Emptiness	明 Bright 堂 Hall 路 Road 空 Emptiness

Using the Auspicious Hour Reference table 四神吉星

Okay, now let's walk you through the process of selecting a suitable hour to commence your activity or endeavour, using the Auspicious Hour Reference tables that I have provided on the previous pages.

Step 1: Determine the Day Pillar

What is the Day Pillar of the date you have selected? This is the basic piece of information you need. Accordingly, before you select the hour, you must first have pre-selected the date for your activity or endeavour, based on the techniques discussed in Chapters 3 and 4.

Let's say you have selected October 9, 2007 for your activity or endeavour. So we need to know what the Day Pillar for October 9, 2007 is.

If you use the Tong Shu Desktop Calendar, the Day Pillar of each date is found on the top left hand corner.

OCTOBER 2007 庚戌

SUNDAY	MONDAY	TUESDAY	WEDNESDAY	THURSDAY	FRIDAY	SATURDAY
	戊辰 1 廿一	己巳 2 廿二	庚午 3 廿三	辛未 4 廿四	壬申 5 廿五	癸酉 6 廿六
甲戌 7 廿七	乙亥 8 廿八	丙子 9 廿九	丁丑 10 三十	戊寅 11 九月初一	己卯 12 初二	庚辰 月破日 Month Breaker Day 13 初三
辛巳 14 初四	壬午 15 初五	癸未 16 初六	甲申 17 初七	乙酉 18 初八	丙戌 19 初九	丁亥 20 初十
戊子 21 十一	己丑 22 十二	庚寅 23 十三	辛卯 24 十四	壬辰 月破日 Month Breaker Day 25 十五	癸巳 歲破日 Year Breaker Day 26 十六	甲午 27 十七
乙未 28 十八	丙申 29 十九	丁酉 30 二十	戊戌 31 廿一			

Day Pillar

實用擇日

If you use the Ten Thousand Year Calendar, this is how you find the Day Pillar.

2007 丁亥 Ding Hai Fire Pig

Grand Duke 封齊

九月大 9th Mth Big				八月大 8th Mth Big				七月小 7th Mth Small			
庚戌 Geng Xu				己酉 Ji You				戊申 Wu Shen			
三碧 Three Jade				四綠 Four Green				五黃 Five Yellow			
立冬 Coming of Winter		霜降 Frosting		寒露 Cold Dew		秋分 Autumn Equinox		白露 White Dew		處暑 Heat Ends	
二十九 29th day		十四 14th day		二十九 29th day		十三 13th day		二十七 27th day		十一 11th day	
3時25分 3hr 25min		3時17分 3hr 17min		0時13分 0hr 13min		17時53分 17hr 53min		8時31分 8hr 31min		20時9分 20hr 9min	
寅 Yin		寅 Yin		子 Zi		酉 You		辰 Chen		戌 Xu	
國曆 Gregorian		干支 Branches and stems	星 Star	國曆 Gregorian		干支 Branches and stems	星 Star	國曆 Gregorian		干支 Branches and stems	星 Star
10	11	戊寅 Wu Yin	7	9	11	戊申 Wu Shen	1	8	13	己卯 Ji Mao	3
10	12	己卯 Ji Mao	6	9	12	己酉 Ji You	9	8	14	庚辰 Geng Chen	2
10	13	庚辰 Geng Chen	5	9	13	庚戌 Geng Xu	8	8	15	辛巳 Xin Si	1
10	14	辛巳 Xin Si	4	9	14	辛亥 Xin Hai	7	8	16	壬午 Ren Wu	9
10	15	壬午 Ren Wu	3	9	15	壬子 Ren Zi	6	8	17	癸未 Gui Wei	8
10	16	癸未 Gui Wei	2	9	16	癸丑 Gui Chou	5	8	18	甲申 Jia Shen	7
10	17	甲申 Jia Shen	1	9	17	甲寅 Jia Yin	4	8	19	乙酉 Yi You	6
10	18	乙酉 Yi You	9	9	18	乙卯 Yi Mao	3	8	20	丙戌 Bing Xu	5
10	19	丙戌 Bing Xu	8	9	19	丙辰 Bing Chen	2	8	21	丁亥 Ding Hai	4
10	20	丁亥 Ding Hai	7	9	20	丁巳 Ding Si	1	8	22	戊子 Wu Zi	3
10	21	戊子 Wu Zi	6	9	21	戊午 Wu Wu	9	8	23	己丑 Ji Chou	2
10	22	己丑 Ji Chou	5	9	22	己未 Ji Wei	8	8	24	庚寅 Geng Yin	1
10	23	庚寅 Geng Yin	4	9	23	庚申 Geng Shen	7	8	25	辛卯 Xin Mao	9
10	24	辛卯 Xin Mao	3	9	24	辛酉 Xin You	6	8	26	壬辰 Ren Chen	8
10	25	壬辰 Ren Chen	2	9	25	壬戌 Ren Xu	5	8	27	癸巳 Gui Si	7
10	26	癸巳 Gui Si	1	9	26	癸亥 Gui Hai	4	8	28	甲午 Jia Wu	6
10	27	甲午 Jia Wu	9	9	27	甲子 Jia Zi	3	8	29	乙未 Yi Wei	5
10	28	乙未 Yi Wei	8	9	28	乙丑 Yi Chou	2	8	30	丙申 Bing Shen	4
10	29	丙申 Bing Shen	7	9	29	丙寅 Bing Yin	1	8	31	丁酉 Ding You	3
10	30	丁酉 Ding You	6	9	30	丁卯 Ding Mao	9	9	1	戊戌 Wu Xu	2
10	31	戊戌 Wu Xu	5	10	1	戊辰 Wu Chen	8	9	2	己亥 Ji Hai	1
11	1	己亥 Ji Hai	4	10	2	己巳 Ji Si	7	9	3	庚子 Geng Zi	9
11	2	庚子 Geng Zi	3	10	3	庚午 Geng Wu	6	9	4	辛丑 Xin Chou	8
11	3	辛丑 Xin Chou	2	10	4	辛未 Xin Wei	5	9	5	壬寅 Ren Yin	7
11	4	壬寅 Ren Yin	1	10	5	壬申 Ren Shen	4	9	6	癸卯 Gui Mao	6
11	5	癸卯 Gui Mao	9	10	6	癸酉 Gui You	3	9	7	甲辰 Jia Chen	5
11	6	甲辰 Jia Chen	8	10	7	甲戌 Jia Xu	2	9	8	乙巳 Yi Si	4
11	7	乙巳 Yi Si	7	10	8	乙亥 Yi Hai	1	9	9	丙午 Bing Wu	3
11	8	丙午 Bing Wu	6	10	9	丙子 Bing Zi	9	9	10	丁未 Ding Wei	2
11	9	丁未 Ding Wei	5	10	10	丁丑 Ding Chou	8				

Day Pillar

You can also access the Chinese Solar Calendar using Windows Outlook. Simply set your calendar to Chinese Solar Calendar and the Day Pillar for every day of the year will be displayed in your Outlook Calendar.

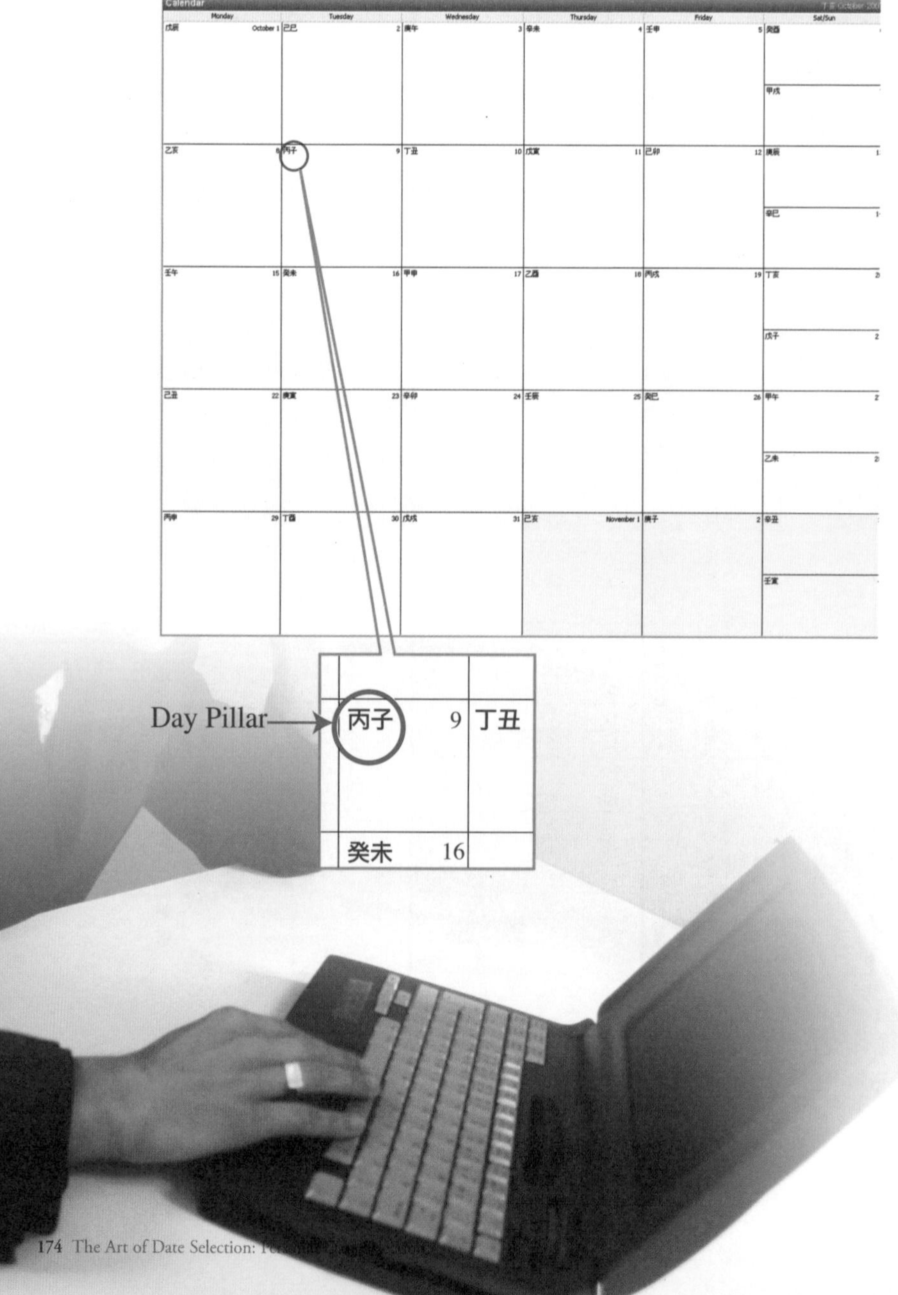

Step 2: Cross-reference the Day Pillar with the Auspicious Hour Reference tables

October 9, 2007 is a Bing Zi Day. Refer to the Auspicious Hour Reference tables, under the Bing group, and find the Bing Zi 丙子 Day.

丙子 Bing Zi Day			Clash 沖	庚午 Geng Wu Metal Horse	戊午 Wu Wu Earth Horse
11 pm - 12.59 am	1 am - 2.59 am	3 am - 4.59 am	5 am - 6.59 am	7 am - 8.59 am	9 am - 10.59 am
戊子 Wu Zi Earth Rat	己丑 Ji Chou Earth Ox	庚寅 Geng Yin Metal Tiger	辛卯 Xin Mao Metal Rabbit	壬辰 Ren Chen Water Dragon	癸巳 Gui Si Water Snake
天 Heavenly 官 Officer	日 Day 合 Combine	日 Day 馬 Horse	玉 Jade 堂 Hall	路 Road 空 Emptiness	日 Day 祿 Wealth
福 Prosperity 星 star	寶 Precious 光 Light	白 White 虎 Tiger	日 Day 刑 Punishment	不 Non 遇 Eligible Day	路 Road 空 Emptiness
11 am - 12.59 pm	1 pm - 2.59 pm	3 pm - 4.59 pm	5 pm - 6.59 pm	7 pm - 8.59 pm	9 pm - 10.59 pm
甲午 Jia Wu Wood Horse	乙未 Yi Wei Wood Goat	丙申 Bing Shen Fire Monkey	丁酉 Ding You Fire Rooster	戊戌 Wu Xu Earth Dog	己亥 Ji Hai Earth Pig
司 Life 命 Governor	勾 Grappling 陳 Hook	喜 Happy 神 Spirit	天 Heavenly 乙 Noble	福 Prosperity 星 star	天 Heavenly 乙 Noble
日 Day 破 Breaker	日 Day 害 Harm	旬 Group 空 Emptiness	旬 Group 空 Emptiness	天 Heavenly 刑 Punishment	朱 Red 雀 Phoenix

Now you will be able to determine which hour has positive auspicious stars and which hour has negative stars, and what those specific stars are - using the table. Remember, red stars are good, black stars are bad!

Step 3: Selecting the Hour

When selecting the right hour, obviously the first step is to eliminate the negative hours first. This is exactly the same process we applied to selecting a good date, remember? So what hours should you avoid? Avoid using any hour that contains only negative stars as this will negate any positive effects of the day.

You should also avoid using an hour that clashes with the Stem or Branch of the day you have selected. So for example, for the Bing Zi 丙子 Day, the Horse 午(Wu) Hour should not be used as the Rat and Horse form a Clash. For those of you who have some BaZi knowledge, you should avoid an hour with Ren 壬 Water on top, as Ren and Bing is a Heavenly Stems Clash.

In case you have forgotten the Six Clashes, have a look at the Six Clashes table below:

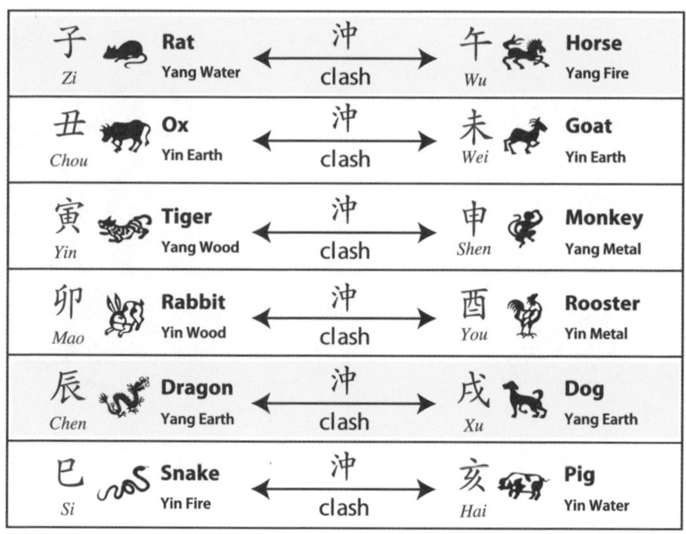

子 *Zi*	Rat	Yang Water	沖 clash	午 *Wu*	Horse	Yang Fire
丑 *Chou*	Ox	Yin Earth	沖 clash	未 *Wei*	Goat	Yin Earth
寅 *Yin*	Tiger	Yang Wood	沖 clash	申 *Shen*	Monkey	Yang Metal
卯 *Mao*	Rabbit	Yin Wood	沖 clash	酉 *You*	Rooster	Yin Metal
辰 *Chen*	Dragon	Yang Earth	沖 clash	戌 *Xu*	Dog	Yang Earth
巳 *Si*	Snake	Yin Fire	沖 clash	亥 *Hai*	Pig	Yin Water

Now that you know how to avoid the negative hours, what principles should guide you to find a good hour? You want an hour that contains auspicious stars so the best hours to use to commence your activity or endeavour are the hours that contain red stars. But of course, sometimes you have to consider practicality. A good hour may be in the middle of the night, so sometimes you have to widen your scope a little.

If the hour contains one good auspicious star and one negative, the specific qualities of the auspicious star must be taken into consideration before selecting the hour. If the auspicious star's qualities and energies correspond with the activity in question, it is usually usable.

Let's take a look at our Bing Zi Day example.

丙子 Bing Zi Day			Clash 沖	庚午 Geng Wu Metal Horse	戊午 Wu Wu Earth Horse
11 pm - 12.59 am	1 am - 2.59 am	3 am - 4.59 am	5 am - 6.59 am	7 am - 8.59 am	9 am - 10.59 am
戊子 Wu Zi Earth Rat	己丑 Ji Chou Earth Ox	庚寅 Geng Yin Metal Tiger	辛卯 Xin Mao Metal Rabbit	壬辰 Ren Chen Water Dragon	癸巳 Gui Si Water Snake
天 Heavenly 官 Officer	日 Day 合 Combine	日 Day 馬 Horse	玉 Jade 堂 Hall	路 Road 空 Emptiness	日 Day 祿 Wealth
福 Prosperity 星 star	寶 Precious 光 Light	白 White 虎 Tiger	日 Day 刑 Punishment	不 Non 遇 Eligible Day	路 Road 空 Emptiness
11 am - 12.59 pm	1 pm - 2.59 pm	3 pm - 4.59 pm	5 pm - 6.59 pm	7 pm - 8.59 pm	9 pm - 10.59 pm
甲午 Jia Wu Wood Horse	乙未 Yi Wei Wood Goat	丙申 Bing Shen Fire Monkey	丁酉 Ding You Fire Rooster	戊戌 Wu Xu Earth Dog	己亥 Ji Hai Earth Pig
司 Life 命 Governor	勾 Grappling 陳 Hook	喜 Happy 神 Spirit	天 Heavenly 乙 Noble	福 Prosperity 星 star	天 Heavenly 乙 Noble
日 Day 破 Breaker	日 Day 害 Harm	旬 Group 空 Emptiness	旬 Group 空 Emptiness	天 Heavenly 刑 Punishment	朱 Red 雀 Phoenix

From the table above, it is clear that the best general hour for the Bing Zi 丙子 Day would be the Rat 子 (Zi) Hour because there are two positive stars present: The Heavenly Officer 天官 (Tian Guan) and Prosperity Star 福星 (Fu Xing). But this depends on the activity in question as well. If it is a marriage

實用擇日

registration ceremony, the Monkey 申 (Shen) Hour, where the Happy Spirit Star 喜神 (Xi Shen) is present, obviously facilitates this activity better and is definitely more practical than the Rat Hour, which is 11pm-1am.

When it comes to selecting the hour, it is important to always consider the type of activity in question because this will then guide you in determining what kind of stars you want present in the hour.

Auspicious Stars and Negative Stars appearing at the Hour

In some cases, a particular hour may contain both auspicious and negative stars. When this happens, you need to determine whether those auspicious stars are suitable for your activity and also, whether or not you can safely ignore the negative stars. Understanding the quality of the auspicious and negative stars that appear at the hour will help you determine if an hour that contains both auspicious and negative stars can be used.

Remember, the aim is to try and select an hour that contains stars that are not just auspicious, but helpful to the particular activity or endeavour in question. In this section, I will explain the qualities of some of the more important stars and when they can be used for what types of activities and endeavours.

Auspicious Stars 吉星

Heavenly Officer 天官 (Tian Guan)
This is an Officer Nobleman Star. It denotes helpful people who are higher in position or who are of a higher status than you, i.e.: your boss or a government officer or minister or judge.

Golden Lock 金匱 (Jin Gui)
This is a Wealth Star. It is a good star to have present in the hour for most activities.

Heavenly Noble 天乙 (Tian Yi)
This is also a Nobleman Star but denotes a mentor or a helpful person or friend of the same level or of a slightly higher status. Generally a good star to have present.

Happy Spirit 喜神 (Xi Shen)
This is a good star to have present for happy events such as celebrations or a marriage.

Jade Hall 玉堂 (Yu Tang)
This star is particularly auspicious for asset acquisition. Select the hour that contains this star if you are going to engage in activities that involve business dealings, financial or money matters or transactions involving assets.

Day Combine 日合 (Ri He)
A favourable star to have present for activities that require talking or communication or persuasion.

Day Horse 日馬 (Ri Ma)
This is the Travelling Star for the Day. It brings about good tidings for travels - select the hour that contains this star to commence a journey.

Prosperity Star 福星 (Fu Xing)
This star is particularly good for money related matters - it is ideal to have it present when you want to engage in activities that have a bearing on your finances or commercial activities, like signing a contract.

實用擇日

Negative Stars 凶星

These are stars that we generally do not want present in the hour selected to commence an activity or venture. Try to avoid selecting an hour with any of these stars present. I have also added some details on what are the specific negative aspects of these stars, to help you further understand why they should not be used and what activities they should not be used for.

Day Breaker 日破 (Ri Po)
This star dissolves and negates all positive effects of the day - avoid selecting or using an hour that contains this star for any activity of importance.

Black Tortoise 元武 (Yuan Wu)
If an hour containing a Black Tortoise Star is used, your activity or endeavour will be influenced by negative energies that can bring about theft, robbery or loss or misplacement of items. If you have to submit documents or important items, do not use an hour that contains this star.

Group Emptiness 旬空 (Xun Kong)
Any hour that has this star should not be used for marriage in particular. The energies of this star denote missing items or missing documents.

White Tiger 白虎 (Bai Hu)
Injuries, cuts and bodily harm are likely to occur if you choose to commence your activity or endeavour at an hour that contains the White Tiger Star. It is very important to avoid selecting an hour that contains the White Tiger Star if you plan to engage in activities pertaining to your health or medical procedures.

Red Phoenix 朱雀 (Zhu Que)

This star denotes arguments and disputes, and is particularly negative if negotiations or legal disputes are involved. It is not good to select an hour that contains the Red Phoenix if you are making a submission to request for something, such as a decision or a contract.

Grappling Hook 勾陳 (Gou Chen)

This star denotes being deceived or cheated. This star is not usable for activities such as marriage, business dealings or signing a contract.

Day Punishment 日刑 (Ri Xing)

This star strains communication and causes injuries and harm. It also indicates the possibility of betrayal. Do not select an hour where this star is present if your activity or endeavour involves communications, such as a product launch.

Finding the Golden Hour

It is not easy to find a good hour with only auspicious stars, as most hours will contain some good and some bad stars. The trick here is to be able to figure out what to do if you find the hour you want to use has a negative star. The key is to discern the TYPE of activity you want to undertake, and then understand the EFFECT of the negative stars present. For example, let's say you plan to sign a contract at a certain hour but there is a negative White Tiger 白虎 (Bai Hu) Star in that hour. The White Tiger Star affects medical or health related situations adversely, but doesn't impact on commercial transactions or dealings. So it's safe to use an hour with a White Tiger Star to sign the contract!

But at the basic level, focus your attention on two important principles: avoiding a clashing hour and finding auspicious stars for the specific activity in question. This will ensure you select an hour that is at the very least safe and does not negate the date you have selected.

In the next chapter, I will show you how to find good dates for a selection of personal activities and endeavours, with examples and step-by-step instructions on how to select a date for certain key personal activities and endeavours.

實用擇日

Chapter Six: Practical Date Selection

Now, all the calculations you have to do to select a good date may seem a bit intimidating initially. Which is why I've included this chapter - by showing you practical uses for Date Selection, so that you will have a better understanding of what Date Selection can be used for and how it is done in practice by professionals.

Where helpful and relevant, and for certain (more) important types of activities, I have included examples of the process of selecting a date so you will be able to better understand how the calculations are done. I have included a variety of examples, involving personal activities and endeavours, so that you can appreciate how Date Selection is done for these activities and how to select dates for yourself for these activities.

The Gods and Killings 神煞 (Shen Sha) method

These days, with so many translations of the Tong Shu available (and of course, the colour coding system used in the Tong Shu), it is not hard to separate the generic good days from the decidedly bad days, with very little knowledge of Date Selection. That is why in addition to the methods discussed in Chapters 3, 4 and 5, you need to take into account the daily positive stars, or what is known as the Gods and Killings 神煞 (Shen Sha) method.

The Gods and Killings Method (don't let this name spook you as it has nothing to do with spirits, gods or any kind of killing!), is basically a system to determine if the governing star of the day is positive or negative. By ascertaining if the daily star is positive or unfavourable, we can then further qualify the quality of the day in question and determine whether it is really a good or bad day.

You might be wondering - why didn't I mention this in the earlier chapters? Isn't this an important method that deserves a detailed explanation? Yes and no. While the Gods and Killings Method is important, you also have to remember that there are hundreds of stars in the constellations of space at any one time. Listing all these stars requires an entire book by itself before we can even discuss the method of determining which date each star falls on!

The Gods and Killings Method is one example of where the method should not over-shadow the purpose. It is much more important to understand which daily stars should be present for certain types of activities, rather than just focusing on having an entire list of stars at one's disposal, with no idea how to use them or when they should appear.

The goal of this book is to make the Art of Date Selection simple and comprehensible but more importantly, practical and easy to use. So rather than throwing lots of star names at you, I'm simply going to give you the stars that are relevant to a particular type of activity or endeavour. This way, you simply need to identify the type of activity or endeavour in question and refer to the relevant section to determine what stars you need to have present on the date you select.

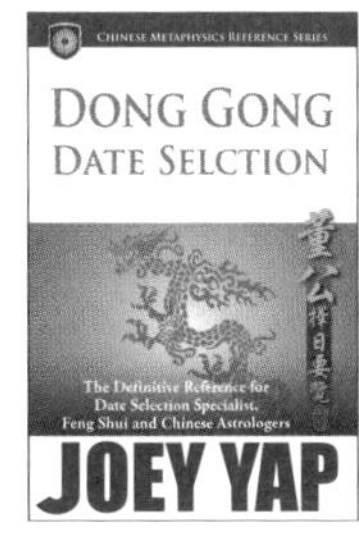

In addition to the Gods and Killings Method, there are also additional qualifying methods that are deployed in Date Selection, designed to further ensure the date selected is truly a suitable date for that particular activity. Typically, a Date Selection specialist will employ the basic methods outlined in Chapters 2, 3 and 4, add in the Gods and Killings Method for the daily and monthly stars, and further qualify the day using Grand Master Dong's System 董公 (Dong Gong), which takes into account in the Melodic Five Elements 納音 (Na Yin) of the day. Then of course, there is finding a really good hour.

However do not worry too much about these qualifying methods for now but focus on making use of the methods I have discussed in Chapters 2, 3 and 4.

實用擇日

A word on how the pros do it!

When you are doing Date Selection, it is easy to get caught up in the calculations and forget the basics and fundamentals. The most important rule to remember is the one I told you about at the start of Chapter 3: the Art of Date Selection is as much about avoiding bad dates as it is about selecting a good one.

It is quite rare for Date Selection specialists to use generic bad days, or to even attempt to qualify bad days or render them usable through additional refinement techniques. So as long as you make it a point NOT to use a bad day, you have won half the battle in the task of selecting a good date. If you can then go on to select a good date from the clutch of usable and neutral dates, you would have already gone the extra mile to infuse your activities or endeavour with the right kind of positive energies and a good start.

Throughout your Date Selection efforts, you should always assume that Year Breaker, Month Breaker and Personal Breaker Days are not to be used, under any circumstances, for any important activity of a personal or business nature. Unless it is indicated to the contrary here, these dates should always be avoided, even if it is a 'good day' under the 12 Day Officers method.

Do remember to take into account the transition dates for each month, as you read through these examples. This is particularly important when the 12 Day Officer technique is used to select a date.

1. Selecting a Marriage Date

For Date Selection specialists, selecting marriage dates is probably the most typical type of Date Selection they do on a daily basis! You may be wondering: Why is a good date important for marriage? Many people do not really understand why a good date for marriage is important. Chinese couples, for example, will frequently seek a good date, often out of superstition or respect for cultural practices, but without really understanding why it is so important.

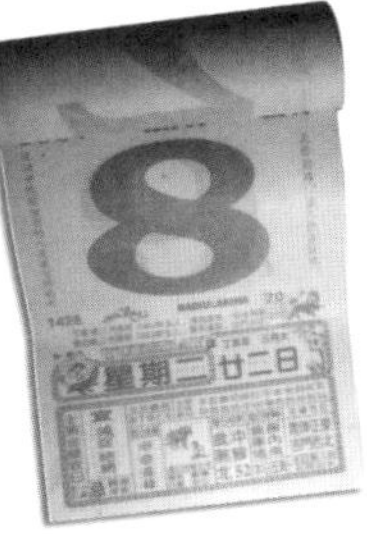

It is this lack of understanding of the value of a good marriage date that leads to the common assumption that it is more to do with symbolism and auspiciousness, rather than any practical basis. Hence the popularity of dates containing the number 8 and getting married in the 8th month.

Marriage, as an activity, involves legal commitment, personal commitment, accepting obligations and responsibilities (in sickness and in health, remember?) and also acceptance into a new family. Hence, the purpose of a good marriage date, in the context of the field of Date Selection, is to ensure the process of marriage proceeds smoothly and without incident, that the parties are bound by their vows and legal commitment to each other, and that the spouse is accepted by the family.

Selecting a good marriage date is not just about starting off on the right foot - it also ensures that the end result of the marriage is ultimately not negative. So if you have chosen the right person (astrologically speaking), then the marriage will go well. This of course, does not mean that a good date will prevent divorce or separation. If you happen to choose the wrong person, divorce or separation can still occur but with a good date, at least your divorce may not be an acrimonious and messy affair.

As a general rule, Date Selection for marriage is of greater importance for individuals with BaZi charts that indicate problems with marriage compared to individuals with charts where there is less indication of marriage issues. By selecting a good date for marriage, the marital problems of the person are minimised.

Now, a good date or even the perfect date, will not mean that all problems will miraculously disappear or dissipate and the couple will live up to the vow of 'till death do us part'. What the positive energies of a good date will help do is help the parties to the marriage better weather the storms that lie in wait. It means the marriage is less likely to collapse at the first sign of trouble. It is especially important to get a good date for marriage if the BaZi charts of both the bride and groom indicate matrimonial challenges or problems.

Hence, a Date Selection specialist, when engaged to select a date for marriage, must not only take into account the usual Date Selection considerations, but must also evaluate the BaZi charts of both parties to ascertain what the matrimonial challenges between the couple are likely to be. For example, is it a problem due to the character of each party? Is it a challenge caused by adultery or the influence of a third party? Or is it a problem with an accident that takes place that puts pressure on the relationship?

Once the issue has been identified, the Date Selection specialist will select a date and identify a suitable hour that contains the elements needed to neutralise, pacify or combine away the obstacles and challenges that put pressure on the relationship.

This, of course, is Date Selection at its highest level and typically the Date Selection specialist has to be given at least one entire year's worth of dates to choose from; to find an ideal date. This is costly as it is time-consuming, requiring a great deal of time to plot the charts for individual dates. That's not an option for everyone.

So for most people, the perfect date (in the Date Selection context), is not necessary and most of the time, a good date will suffice. However, this still requires some time and calculation effort, especially if you are looking at a date well in advance of the current year.

Some people ask me if they should also get a BaZi consultation. Usually the Date Selection specialist will of course evaluate the BaZi of the bride and groom, but when a suitable date is communicated to the parties, it may not be explained to the clients why the particular date is chosen. Certainly there is value in having a BaZi consultation prior to choosing a good date, so that the couple understands what may be ahead on the road together and understands the extent of their compatibility with each other, but this is not necessary.

You might be thinking - wow, this is complex stuff! Should I even be selecting a marriage date for myself? Certainly, because the calculation involves more than one party, a little more work is required. However, it is possible to select a good wedding date for yourself, using the methods outlined in this book. Of course, the methods used by a Date Selection specialist will be more sophisticated and much more personalised to the couple's BaZi. But if you follow the method I have outlined, you will at least be sure you won't get married on a bad date, and if you apply the 12 Day Officers method, you will be sure of getting a reasonably good date.

What date constitutes the marriage date?

In the old days, when a Date Selection specialist was sought out to select a date for marriage, this date was usually the date that the marriage ceremony took place. The marriage ceremony consisted of the married couple praying to their ancestors, praying to Heaven and Earth at the altar and then paying their respects to their parents by serving them tea, what the Chinese refer to as the `tea ceremony'. The occasion signifies the man's family accepting the new wife into the family.

Today, the number of events involved in a marriage has increased. There may be a religious ceremony (in a church or a temple, depending on the religious preference), a cultural ceremony such as the tea serving session if the couple are Chinese, a legal registration ceremony where the relationship is formalised in law through the signing of legal documents, and of course, the wedding banquet. Sometimes, people choose to run the gauntlet of events in one day, but there are also those who prefer to separate the occasions.

People are often confused as to which date matters when it comes to selecting a date for marriage, especially if they spread out the festivities over a few days.

So which date really matters?

In a modern context, the date that you are recognised in the eyes of the law as husband and wife is the 'marriage date'. As such, the date that the husband and wife sign the marriage register or sign the requisite legal documents required to make them legally husband and wife is usually the date that matters.

The date of your wedding banquet, or your tea ceremony, strictly speaking, is not important and you can hold these activities at your convenience. I do appreciate that this may seem like a rather 'controversial' assertion. After all, the wedding banquet is usually the date when one's relatives and friends recognise the marriage. For individuals of notable or high standing in society, this is an important social occasion. Many traditional Chinese families often view the registration as a 'formality' and the banquet as the one that counts in terms of officiating the marriage.

From a strict Date Selection theory standpoint, as the wedding banquet involves no legal obligation or commitment, it is not as important as the date for the religious ceremony or the date for the marriage registration or legal ceremony. After all, Heaven comes first, followed by Earth, followed by Man according to the Cosmic Trinity.

So when it comes to a marriage date, the date of the religious ceremony should always be a good date, tailored to the BaZi of the couple. If the couple are not religious, then of course, the Earth component, represented by the laws of the state, must rank first. If your marriage involves both a religious and civil component, to be on the safe side, one should select a date for BOTH the legal registration and for the religious ceremony or prayer component, be it in a church, a temple or whatever your personal religious denomination.

However, if you and your prospective spouse and various family members intend to have a largely non-religious wedding, or if this aspect of the occasion is of only cultural significance to you and your prospective spouse, then the key date, the date where selection matters, is the date of the legal ceremony.

The religious and civil ceremony are the events that matter when it comes to a marriage date selection and it is these events that the couple should look to select a good date that is personalised to their individual BaZi.

For the wedding banquet, a generic good date (not a Year or Month Breaker Day for example) will usually suffice. You don't really need a personalised or extremely good date for the wedding banquet and using a generic good date for the wedding banquet affords a lot more flexibility in terms of dates. Save the really good date for the event that really matters in the eyes of Heaven, or the law!

The challenges in marriage Date Selection

Date Selection for marriages is often a complex affair, even for a Date Selection specialist, because everyone wants to get married on a weekend. Given that there are only 52 weeks in a year, and only so many hotels, coordinating everything together - from the availability of the hotel or church or temple, to finding a good date that is a weekend - is not easy.

It's an especially bigger challenge if the couple or family want to have the whole gamut of events on the same day and there is a need to find two usable hours, within the same day, for the religious ceremony and legal ceremony.

Frequently, time is often not something that many couples have the luxury of and few people are prepared to wait a long period for a good date. And then there are couples who want a good date for everything. Chinese couples in particular who go as far as wanting a good date and time to 'pick up their future wife' (a significant cultural aspect of a Chinese marriage).

Like all things, it boils down to a matter of priority. For my Chinese and Asian readers, do note that there are many parts of the Chinese marriage that require no Date Selection or selection of the hour because these are largely cultural aspects of the marriage. For example, the time to pick up your wife from her home or go to the groom's house to begin the tea ceremony is not really significant unless the tea ceremony includes religious practices or procedures.

Prioritising also means being willing to consider letting go of certain personal preferences (such as having all the events on the same day) if that is what you may need to do to get a good date. Some couples don't want the inconvenience of having the legal registration ceremony and the wedding banquet on a different day. But if it is difficult to coordinate the legal registration ceremony and banquet on the same day, couples must be prepared to be a little more flexible.

To many people, this may seem to be an unnecessary inconvenience or throwing of an unnecessary spanner in the works. Ultimately, a good date, while not something to hang the success of your entire marriage on, does give you a small cushion or slight advantage against any future problems during your life together. I prefer to view it as something small and not of huge inconvenience, which affords a positive benefit in the long run, especially when you consider that it is only the legal registration date that ultimately matters.

How to select a good marriage date

Bearing in mind now that the date of importance is the date of the legal ceremony (and religious ceremony, if you intend to include one), there is no need to restrict yourself to just weekends. I would suggest going for a broader scope of dates rather than a narrower scope. If possible, give yourself a 6-month window to find a date rather than say, a particular month.

Avoiding the Bad Days

It goes without saying that your marriage day should not be a Year Breaker or Month Breaker Day. Just in case you've forgotten, the Year Breaker is the Day that clashes with the Year, and the Month Breaker is the Day that clashes with the Month. So for example, in 2007, the year of the Pig 亥 (Hai), avoid all Snake 巳 (Si) Days. In the month of the Tiger 寅 (Yin) which is February 4 – March 5, avoid all Monkey 申 (Shen) Days.

Now, because getting married is an important personal activity involving great personal commitment, it is particularly important to avoid the Personal Breakers of both bride and groom. The Personal Breaker is the day that clashes with your year of birth. So for example, if either bride or groom or both are born in the year of the Dragon 辰(Chen), they should avoid getting married in a Dog 戌 (Xu) Year, or on ANY Dog Days and Dog Months (October 6 - November 6 of any given year). The rule on avoiding the Personal Breaker Days applies even if that particular day is a good day, according to the 12 Day Officers method.

When it comes to selecting the hour, avoid selecting an hour that clashes with the day. Remember, a Chinese hour equals 2 Western hours. So for example if you are getting married on a Pig Day, then you should avoid getting married during the Snake Hour (9am-11am) as the Snake clashes with the Pig.

Add in the Gods and Killings Method

There are certain stars that should not be present on marriage dates. In particular, you want to avoid two stars known as the Loneliness Star 寡宿 (Gua Su) and the Solitary Star 孤辰(Gu Chen). The names make it clear what the effect of these stars might be. As a marriage involves two people living together and for all intents and purposes, building a life together, you don't want a Loneliness Star or Solitary Star on your marriage date as this denotes a life of loneliness or solitude (read: one without the spouse present!).

The table below tells you which are the Loneliness and Solitary Stars, based on the year of birth.

Year 年	Solitary Star 孤辰	Loneliness Star 寡宿
寅 *Yin* **Tiger**, 卯 *Mao* **Rabbit**, 辰 *Chen* **Dragon**	巳 *Si* **Snake**	丑 *Chou* **Ox**
巳 *Si* **Snake**, 午 *Wu* **Horse**, 未 *Wei* **Goat**	申 *Shen* **Monkey**	辰 *Chen* **Dragon**
申 *Shen* **Monkey**, 酉 *You* **Rooster**, 戌 *Xu* **Dog**	亥 *Hai* **Pig**	未 *Wei* **Goat**
亥 *Hai* **Pig**, 子 *Zi* **Rat**, 丑 *Chou* **Ox**	寅 *Yin* **Tiger**	戌 *Xu* **Dog**

The Solitary Star is considered more disadvantageous towards the groom, whereas the Loneliness Star is less favourable for the bride. Since marriage involves two people, you want to avoid having both Stars present on the marriage date.

So, let's try an example. Let's say the groom is born in the year of the Rabbit 卯(Mao)and the bride is born in the year of the Rat子(Zi). Looking at the Loneliness and Solitary Star table, we know that the groom's personal Solitary Star is the Snake巳 (Si). So he should avoid getting married on a Snake Day - if he does get married on a Snake Day, this denotes that he will not spend a lot of time with his wife (perhaps due to work, the person is on the road a lot) and the relationship is not intimate. The relationship is likely to experience long-term problems which may lead to divorce.

The Dog 戌 (Xu) is the bride's Loneliness Star Day so she must avoid Dog Days for marriage as the Dog Days are her personal Loneliness Star. If the bride chooses to get married on a Dog Day, then she will find herself living in an empty house or there is very little communication between the couple even if they live together. The relationship will also be a lot less vibrant, which could also lead to long-term problems as it progresses.

Accordingly, in addition to the usual bad dates that must be avoided, the couple must avoid getting married on Snake and Dog Days, to ensure they do not get married on a day that contains their personal Solitary and Loneliness Star.

Finding the Good amongst the Usable and Neutral

Okay, all the bad days have been eliminated and so now we are left mostly with neutral or good days. So how do we find the best date amongst the goods and neutrals?

The 12 Day Officers method, discussed in Chapter 4, is the primary method we will use to find the good days amongst the leftover days. It is quite safe to ignore the 28 Constellations method as it is quite tedious and in any case, having plugged in the Gods and Killings Method, you should be quite safe. If you are industrious, you can of course cross check with the 28 Constellations method but this is not strictly necessary.

You have 12 Day Officers to choose from - which is the best day? For marriage, Date Selection specialists use the Success Day 成, Stable Day 定 and Open Day 開. The best are the Success Day and Stable Day.

Now, just as there are stars to avoid when it comes to selecting a marriage date, there are also stars we want to see. Where possible, it is good to get married on a day with a Sky Happiness Star 天喜星 (Tian Xi Xing) , to help keep 'that loving feeling' alive throughout the marriage. Now, unlike the Solitary and Loneliness Stars, which is unique to the person, the Sky Happiness Star is determined by the month. Every month, the Sky Happiness Star appears on a certain day.

Month 月		Sky Happiness Star 天喜星
寅 *Yin* **Tiger**	February 4th	戌 *Xu* **Dog**
卯 *Mao* **Rabbit**	March 5th	亥 *Hai* **Pig**
辰 *Chen* **Dragon**	April 5th	子 *Zi* **Rat**
巳 *Si* **Snake**	May 5th	丑 *Chou* **Ox**
午 *Wu* **Horse**	June 6th	寅 *Yin* **Tiger**
未 *Wei* **Goat**	July 7th	卯 *Mao* **Rabbit**
申 *Shen* **Monkey**	August 7th	辰 *Chen* **Dragon**
酉 *You* **Rooster**	September 8th	巳 *Si* **Snake**
戌 *Xu* **Dog**	October 8th	午 *Wu* **Horse**
亥 *Hai* **Pig**	November 7th	未 *Wei* **Goat**
子 *Zi* **Rat**	December 7th	申 *Shen* **Monkey**
丑 *Chou* **Ox**	January 6th	酉 *You* **Rooster**

For example, in the Goat 未 (Wei) Month, the Sky Happiness Star appears on each and every Rabbit 卯 (Mao) Day. In the Rooster 酉 (You) Month, the Sky Happiness Star appears on each and every Snake 巳(Si) Day.

You might have noticed a pattern to the calculation of this Star. Yes, the Sky Happiness Star appears on every Success Day in the month. That is why it is preferable for a marriage date to be a Success Day as far as possible. You will also notice that if you choose a Stable Day, you are getting married on a day that is part of the Three Harmony Combination. That is why the Success and Stable Days are preferred to the Initiate and Open Days.

日支 Day Branches / 月支 Month Branches	寅 *Yin* Tiger	卯 *Mao* Rabbit	辰 *Chen* Dragon	巳 *Si* Snake	午 *Wu* Horse	未 *Wei* Goat	申 *Shen* Monkey	酉 *You* Rooster	戌 *Xu* Dog	亥 *Hai* Pig	子 *Zi* Rat	丑 *Chou* Ox
寅 *Yin* Tiger Feb 4	建 *Jian* Establish	除 *Chu* Remove	満 *Man* Full	平 *Ping* Balance	定 *Ding* Stable	執 *Zhi* Initiate	破 *Po* Destruction	危 *Wei* Danger	成 *Cheng* Success	收 *Shou* Receive	開 *Kai* Open	閉 *Bi* Close
卯 *Mao* Rabbit Mar 6	閉 *Bi* Close	建 *Jian* Establish	除 *Chu* Remove	満 *Man* Full	平 *Ping* Balance	定 *Ding* Stable	執 *Zhi* Initiate	破 *Po* Destruction	危 *Wei* Danger	成 *Cheng* Success	收 *Shou* Receive	開 *Kai* Open
辰 *Chen* Dragon Apr 5	開 *Kai* Open	閉 *Bi* Close	建 *Jian* Establish	除 *Chu* Remove	満 *Man* Full	平 *Ping* Balance	定 *Ding* Stable	執 *Zhi* Initiate	破 *Po* Destruction	危 *Wei* Danger	成 *Cheng* Success	收 *Shou* Receive
巳 *Si* Snake May 6	收 *Shou* Receive	開 *Kai* Open	閉 *Bi* Close	建 *Jian* Establish	除 *Chu* Remove	満 *Man* Full	平 *Ping* Balance	定 *Ding* Stable	執 *Zhi* Initiate	破 *Po* Destruction	危 *Wei* Danger	成 *Cheng* Success
午 *Wu* Horse June 6	成 *Cheng* Success	收 *Shou* Receive	開 *Kai* Open	閉 *Bi* Close	建 *Jian* Establish	除 *Chu* Remove	満 *Man* Full	平 *Ping* Balance	定 *Ding* Stable	執 *Zhi* Initiate	破 *Po* Destruction	危 *Wei* Danger
未 *Wei* Goat Jul 7	危 *Wei* Danger	成 *Cheng* Success	收 *Shou* Receive	開 *Kai* Open	閉 *Bi* Close	建 *Jian* Establish	除 *Chu* Remove	満 *Man* Full	平 *Ping* Balance	定 *Ding* Stable	執 *Zhi* Initiate	破 *Po* Destruction
申 *Shen* Monkey Aug 8	破 *Po* Destruction	危 *Wei* Danger	成 *Cheng* Success	收 *Shou* Receive	開 *Kai* Open	閉 *Bi* Close	建 *Jian* Establish	除 *Chu* Remove	満 *Man* Full	平 *Ping* Balance	定 *Ding* Stable	執 *Zhi* Initiate
酉 *You* Rooster Sept 8	執 *Zhi* Initiate	破 *Po* Destruction	危 *Wei* Danger	成 *Cheng* Success	收 *Shou* Receive	開 *Kai* Open	閉 *Bi* Close	建 *Jian* Establish	除 *Chu* Remove	満 *Man* Full	平 *Ping* Balance	定 *Ding* Stable
戌 *Xu* Dog Oct 8	定 *Ding* Stable	執 *Zhi* Initiate	破 *Po* Destruction	危 *Wei* Danger	成 *Cheng* Success	收 *Shou* Receive	開 *Kai* Open	閉 *Bi* Close	建 *Jian* Establish	除 *Chu* Remove	満 *Man* Full	平 *Ping* Balance
亥 *Hai* Pig Nov 7	平 *Ping* Balance	定 *Ding* Stable	執 *Zhi* Initiate	破 *Po* Destruction	危 *Wei* Danger	成 *Cheng* Success	收 *Shou* Receive	開 *Kai* Open	閉 *Bi* Close	建 *Jian* Establish	除 *Chu* Remove	満 *Man* Full
子 *Zi* Rat Dec 7	満 *Man* Full	平 *Ping* Balance	定 *Ding* Stable	執 *Zhi* Initiate	破 *Po* Destruction	危 *Wei* Danger	成 *Cheng* Success	收 *Shou* Receive	開 *Kai* Open	閉 *Bi* Close	建 *Jian* Establish	除 *Chu* Remove
丑 *Chou* Ox Jan 6	除 *Chu* Remove	満 *Man* Full	平 *Ping* Balance	定 *Ding* Stable	執 *Zhi* Initiate	破 *Po* Destruction	危 *Wei* Danger	成 *Cheng* Success	收 *Shou* Receive	開 *Kai* Open	閉 *Bi* Close	建 *Jian* Establish

Right Day, Right Time

If you are able to accommodate it, it is also good to add a good hour to the good date, to complete the day. In general, it is good to select an hour that creates a Three Harmony combination. For example, you have selected a Pig 亥 (Hai) Day, in a Rabbit 卯 (Mao) Month, so a Goat 未 (Wei) Hour will complete the combination. However, you must always check against the Hour Table found in Chapter 5, to make sure that this hour is really good because the Combination will not neutralise any negative stars present in the hour.

However, sometimes a particular hour is not convenient to use or simply not practical. For example, who can get married in the Rabbit Hour (5am-7am) or the Pig Hour (9pm-11pm)? In that case, aim to avoid an hour that clashes with the day - for example, if you have chosen a Tiger 寅 (Yin) Day to get married, avoid selecting the Monkey 申 (Shen) Hour, which is 3pm-5pm.

Now, if you have some BaZi knowledge, you can add on the Heavenly Stems to the equation. Do not select an hour pillar where there is a Stem or Branch clash.

時 Hour	日 Day	月 Month	年 Year	
				天干 Heavenly Stems
申 Shen Monkey ← Clash →	寅 Yin Tiger			地支 Earthly Branches

Branch clash between Day and Hour Pillars

For example, if the day is a Jia 甲 Day, in a Dog 戌 (Xu) Month, if you select the Horse 午 (Wu) Hour, this gives you the Tiger-Horse-Dog 寅午戌 (Yin-Wu-Xu) Three Harmony Combination. However, the Horse Hour gives you Geng 庚 Metal in the Stem, which clashes with the Day. So, you don't want to select the Horse Hour.

戊 Wu Yang Earth 癸 Gui Yin Water	丁 Ding Yin Fire 壬 Ren Yang Water	丙 Bing Yang Fire 辛 Xin Yin Metal	乙 Yi Yin Wood 庚 Geng Yang Metal	甲 Jia Yang Wood 己 Ji Yin Earth	日 Day / 時 Hour	
甲子 Jia Zi Wood Rat	壬子 Ren Zi Water Rat	庚子 Geng Zi Metal Rat	戊子 Wu Zi Earth Rat	丙子 Bing Zi Fire Rat	夜子 Ye Zi Late Rat	11 pm - 11.59 pm
壬子 Ren Zi Water Rat	庚子 Geng Zi Metal Rat	戊子 Wu Zi Earth Rat	丙子 Bing Zi Fire Rat	甲子 Jia Zi Wood Rat	子 Zi Early Rat	12 am - 12.59 am
癸丑 Gui Chou Water Ox	辛丑 Xin Chou Metal Ox	己丑 Ji Chou Earth Ox	丁丑 Ding Chou Fire Ox	乙丑 Yi Chou Wood Ox	丑 Chou Ox	1 am - 2.59 am
甲寅 Jia Yin Wood Tiger	壬寅 Ren Yin Water Tiger	庚寅 Geng Yin Metal Tiger	戊寅 Wu Yin Earth Tiger	丙寅 Bing Yin Fire Tiger	寅 Yin Tiger	3 am - 4.59 am
乙卯 Yi Mao Wood Rabbit	癸卯 Gui Mao Water Rabbit	辛卯 Xin Mao Metal Rabbit	己卯 Ji Mao Earth Rabbit	丁卯 Ding Mao Fire Rabbit	卯 Mao Rabbit	5 am - 6.59 am
丙辰 Bing Chen Fire Dragon	甲辰 Jia Chen Wood Dragon	壬辰 Ren Chen Water Dragon	庚辰 Geng Chen Metal Dragon	戊辰 Wu Chen Earth Dragon	辰 Chen Dragon	7 am - 8.59 am
丁巳 Ding Si Fire Snake	乙巳 Yi Si Wood Snake	癸巳 Gui Si Water Snake	辛巳 Xin Si Metal Snake	己巳 Ji Si Earth Snake	巳 Si Snake	9 am -10.59 am
戊午 Wu Wu Earth Horse	丙午 Bing Wu Fire Horse	甲午 Jia Wu Wood Horse	壬午 Ren Wu Water Horse	庚午 Geng Wu Metal Horse	午 Wu Horse	11 am - 12.59 pm
己未 Ji Wei Earth Goat	丁未 Ding Wei Fire Goat	乙未 Yi Wei Wood Goat	癸未 Gui Wei Water Goat	辛未 Xin Wei Metal Goat	未 Wei Goat	1pm - 2.59 pm
庚申 Geng Shen Metal Monkey	戊申 Wu Shen Earth Monkey	丙申 Bing Shen Fire Monkey	甲申 Jia Shen Wood Monkey	壬申 Ren Shen Water Monkey	申 Shen Monkey	3 pm - 4.59 pm
辛酉 Xin You Metal Rooster	己酉 Ji You Earth Rooster	丁酉 Ding You Fire Rooster	乙酉 Yi You Wood Rooster	癸酉 Gui You Water Rooster	酉 You Rooster	5 pm - 6.59 pm
壬戌 Ren Xu Water Dog	庚戌 Geng Xu Metal Dog	戊戌 Wu Xu Earth Dog	丙戌 Bing Xu Fire Dog	甲戌 Jia Xu Wood Dog	戌 Xu Dog	7 pm - 8.59 pm
癸亥 Gui Hai Water Pig	辛亥 Xin Hai Metal Pig	己亥 Ji Hai Earth Pig	丁亥 Ding Hai Fire Pig	乙亥 Yi Hai Wood Pig	亥 Hai Pig	9 pm - 10.59 pm

時 Hour	日 Day	月 Month	年 Year	
庚 Geng ← Clash →	甲 Jia			天干 Heavenly Stems
午 Wu Horse	寅 Yin Tiger	戌 Xu Dog		地支 Earthly Branches

Don't worry if you can't plug in this information into your Date Selection - as long as you avoid the hour that clashes with the day, it is reasonably safe!

Marriage Date Selection Example

To help you figure out how to select a date for a marriage, I'm going to walk you through a working example, so you know how to select a date, step by step.

Step #1: Obtain the Personal BaZi Charts of both bride and groom.

First, you need the personal BaZi of the two people involved in the marriage. For this example, our groom, Jack, is born on September 7, 1976 and his bride-to-be, Diane, is born on March 6, 1978.

Here are their BaZi Charts.

時 Hour	日 Day	月 Month	年 Year	
	壬 *Ren* Yang Water	丙 *Bing* Yang Fire	丙 *Bing* Yang Fire	天干 Heavenly Stems
	戌 *Xu* **Dog** Yang Earth	申 *Shen* **Monkey** Yang Metal	辰 *Chen* **Dragon** Yang Earth	地支 Earthly Branches
	丁 *Ding* 戊 *Wu* 辛 *Xin*	戊 *Wu* 庚 *Geng* 壬 *Ren*	癸 *Gui* 戊 *Wu* 乙 *Yi*	藏干 Hidden Stems

Jack's BaZi Chart

時 Hour	日 Day	月 Month	年 Year	
	丁 *Ding* Yin Fire	乙 *Yi* Yin Wood	戊 *Wu* Yang Earth	天干 Heavenly Stems
	卯 *Mao* **Rabbit** Yin Wood	卯 *Mao* **Rabbit** Yin Wood	午 *Wu* **Horse** Yang Fire	地支 Earthly Branches
	乙 *Yi*	乙 *Yi*	丁 *Ding* 己 *Ji*	藏干 Hidden Stems

Diane's BaZi Chart

Step #2: Determine the Personal Breakers for the Groom and Bride.

Using the respective birth years of the groom and bride, we can determine their Personal Breakers. This will help determine which year is suitable for marriage.

In our example, Jack is born in the Year of the Dragon 辰 (Chen) while Diane is born in the Year of the Horse 午(Wu). So Jack's Personal Breaker is the Dog 戌 (Xu) and Diane's Personal Breaker is the Rat 子 (Zi). If you have forgotten why this is, check the Six Clashes table below.

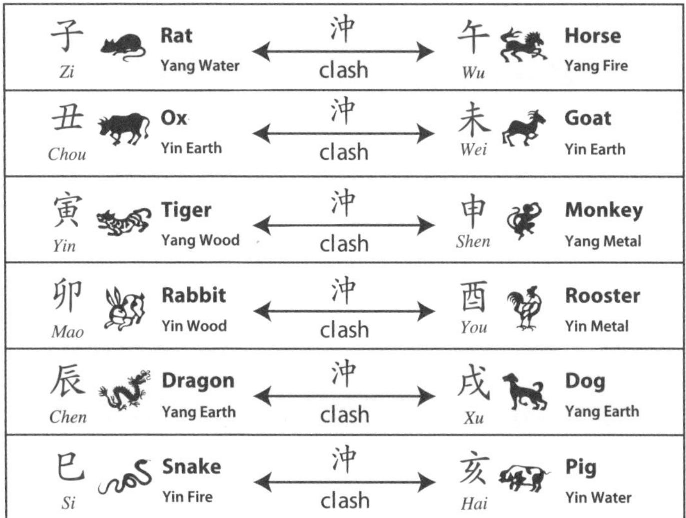

子 *Zi*	Rat	Yang Water	沖 clash	午 *Wu*	Horse	Yang Fire
丑 *Chou*	Ox	Yin Earth	沖 clash	未 *Wei*	Goat	Yin Earth
寅 *Yin*	Tiger	Yang Wood	沖 clash	申 *Shen*	Monkey	Yang Metal
卯 *Mao*	Rabbit	Yin Wood	沖 clash	酉 *You*	Rooster	Yin Metal
辰 *Chen*	Dragon	Yang Earth	沖 clash	戌 *Xu*	Dog	Yang Earth
巳 *Si*	Snake	Yin Fire	沖 clash	亥 *Hai*	Pig	Yin Water

If Jack and Diane had wanted to get married in 2006, a Date Selection specialist would advice against it as 2006 is the year of the Dog and the Dog clashes with Jack's year of birth, which is the Dragon. So what about 2007? 2007 is the year of the Pig and does not clash with either Jack or Diane's year of birth so this would be acceptable. However, if the couple want to get married in 2008, this is unwise as it is the year of the Rat and that clashes with Diane's year of birth.

Step #3: Cross off the bad dates

Let's assume Jack and Diane plan to get married in the year of the Pig 亥 (Hai), which is 2007. Let's also assume that they would like to get married in the month of June 2007. Let's take a look at the month of June.

JUNE 2007 丙午

SUNDAY	MONDAY	TUESDAY	WEDNESDAY	THURSDAY	FRIDAY	SATURDAY
					丙寅 1 十六	丁卯 2 十七
戊辰 3 十八	~~己巳 歲破日 Year Breaker Day 4 十九~~	庚午 5 二十	辛未 6 廿一	壬申 7 廿二	癸酉 8 廿三	甲戌 9 廿四
乙亥 10 廿五	~~丙子 月破日 Month Breaker Day 11 廿六~~	丁丑 12 廿七	戊寅 13 廿八	己卯 14 廿九	庚辰 15 五月初一	~~辛巳 歲破日 Year Breaker Day 16 初二~~
壬午 17 初三	癸未 18 初四	甲申 19 初五	乙酉 20 初六	丙戌 21 初七	丁亥 22 初八	~~戊子 月破日 Month Breaker Day 23 初九~~
己丑 24 初十	庚寅 25 十一	辛卯 26 十二	壬辰 27 十三	~~癸巳 歲破日 Year Breaker Day 28 十四~~	甲午 29 十五	乙未 30 十六

Remember at the start of Chapter 3, I said that the Art of Date Selection is as much about avoiding bad dates as it is about selecting good dates. So here, first, we cross out the dates that cannot be used. The priority would be to eliminate the Month Breaker and Year Breaker Days. June 4, 16, and 28 are Year Breakers and thus cannot be used. June 11 and 23 are Month Breaker Days so these also cannot be used.

Once we have eliminated the general bad dates, we must then cross out the personal bad dates for Jack and Diane. This means crossing out the Personal Breaker Days - in the case of our example, no Dog 戌 (Xu) Days as this is Jack's Personal Breaker, and no Rat 子 (Zi) Days as this is Diane's Personal Breaker.

So cross out June 9 and 21 as these are Dog Days. Coincidentally, the Month Breaker Days are also the Personal Breaker Days of Diane, so those days have already been eliminated.

Now, once all the bad dates have been crossed out, this is what we are left with:

JUNE 2007 丙午

SUNDAY	MONDAY	TUESDAY	WEDNESDAY	THURSDAY	FRIDAY	SATURDAY
					丙寅 1 十六	丁卯 2 十七
戊辰 3 十八	己巳 歲破日 Year Breaker Day 4 十九 (crossed out)	庚午 5 二十	辛未 6 廿一	壬申 7 廿二	癸酉 8 廿三	甲戌 Personal Breaker 9 廿四 (crossed out)
乙亥 10 廿五	丙子 月破日 Month Breaker Day 11 廿六 (crossed out)	丁丑 12 廿七	戊寅 13 廿八	己卯 14 廿九	庚辰 15 五月初一	辛巳 歲破日 Year Breaker Day 16 初二 (crossed out)
壬午 17 初三	癸未 18 初四	甲申 19 初五	乙酉 20 初六	丙戌 Personal Breaker 21 初七 (crossed out)	丁亥 22 初八	戊子 月破日 Month Breaker Day 23 初九 (crossed out)
己丑 24 初十	庚寅 25 十一	辛卯 26 十二	壬辰 27 十三	癸巳 歲破日 Year Breaker Day 28 十四 (crossed out)	甲午 29 十五	乙未 30 十六

Admittedly, there's not a lot of choice, but hey, flexibility is sometimes required when it comes to getting a good date, especially when it comes to a marriage date since the date selection process must consider both the bride and groom's BaZi.

Step #4: Pick the good day

To select a suitable date, we now deploy the 12 Day Officers method discussed in Chapter 4. For marriage, Date Selection specialists usually prefer a Success 成, Stable 定 or Open 開 Day. The Success Day is usually preferred over the other 3 days where possible, as this is the day that also contains the Sky Happiness Star, under the Gods and Killings Method.

So, how do we find the Success Days?

月支 Month Branches \ 日支 Day Branches	寅 Yin Tiger	卯 Mao Rabbit	辰 Chen Dragon	巳 Si Snake	午 Wu Horse	未 Wei Goat	申 Shen Monkey	酉 You Rooster	戌 Xu Dog	亥 Hai Pig	子 Zi Rat	丑 Chou Ox
午 Wu Horse June 6	成 Cheng Success	收 Shou Receive	開 Kai Open	閉 Bi Close	建 Jian Establish	除 Chu Remove	滿 Man Full	平 Ping Balance	定 Ding Stable	執 Zhi Initiate	破 Po Destruction	危 Wei Danger

Now, based on the 12 Day Officers method table, we can see that in June, all Tiger 寅 (Yin) Days are Success Days, all Dog 戌 (Xu) Days are Stable Days, and all Dragon 辰 (Chen) Days are Open Days.

Now, let's take a look at our usable days in June.

JUNE 2007 丙午

SUNDAY	MONDAY	TUESDAY	WEDNESDAY	THURSDAY	FRIDAY	SATURDAY
					丙寅 1 十六	丁卯 2 十七
戊辰 3 十八	己巳 歲破日 Year Breaker Day 4 十九	庚午 5 二十	辛未 6 廿一	壬申 7 廿二	癸酉 8 廿三	甲戌 Personal Breaker 9 廿四
乙亥 10 廿五	丙子 月破日 Month Breaker Day 11 廿六	丁丑 12 廿七	戊寅 成 Cheng Success 13 廿八	己卯 14 廿九	庚辰 開 Kai Open 15 五月初一	辛巳 歲破日 Year Breaker Day 16 初二
壬午 17 初三	癸未 18 初四	甲申 19 初五	乙酉 20 初六	丙戌 Personal Breaker 21 初七	丁亥 22 初八	戊子 月破日 Month Breaker Day 23 初九
己丑 24 初十	庚寅 成 Cheng Success 25 十一	辛卯 26 十二	壬辰 開 Kai Open 27 十三	癸巳 歲破日 Year Breaker Day 28 十四	甲午 29 十五	乙未 30 十六

What therefore are the available dates for Jack and Diane to get married on?

June 13 and 25 are Success Days so these dates should be considered by the couple if possible as these are the best dates for marriage. Stable Days are not usable as these are Dog Days and are eliminated by virtue of being Jack's Personal Breaker anyway. June 15 and 27 are Open Days and are also usable by both Jack and Diane.

Of course, a professional Date Selection specialist will consider the best date for the bride and groom, from this clutch of dates, by matching it in-depth to their personal BaZi charts. This is an additional layer of personalisation that those of you who have some knowledge of BaZi, may want to add on. However, for basic Date Selection, this, combined with Step #5 below on selecting a suitable hour, is sufficient to ensure a reasonably good date for marriage.

Step #5: Find the Right Hour

When selecting a time, we must first refer to the Hour Table found in Chapter 5. Now, assume that Jack and Diane have selected June 13 to get married. June 13, 2007 is a Wu Yin 戊寅 Day. Based on the Auspicious Hour Reference table, the Dragon 辰 (Chen) Hour, which is 7am-9am, is the best hour of the day as that hour has two auspicious stars present. Hence, this is the hour that should be used for a signing ceremony or religious ceremony.

戊寅 Wu Yin Day			Clash 沖	壬申 Water Ren Shen Monkey	甲申 Wood Jia Shen Monkey
11 pm - 12.59 am	1 am - 2.59 am	3 am - 4.59 am	5 am - 6.59 am	7 am - 8.59 am	9 am - 10.59 am
壬子 Water Ren Zi Rat	癸丑 Water Gui Chou Ox	甲寅 Wood Jia Yin Tiger	乙卯 Wood Yi Mao Rabbit	丙辰 Fire Bing Chen Dragon	丁巳 Fire Ding Si Snake
青 Green 龍 Dragon 路 Road 空 Emptiness	天 Heavenly 乙 Noble 路 Road 空 Emptiness	日 Day 建 Establish Star 不 Non 遇 Eligible Day	天 Heavenly 官 Officer 朱 Red 雀 Phoenix	喜 Happy 神 Spirit 金 Golden 匱 Lock	寶 Precious 光 Light 日 Day 刑 Punishment
11 am - 12.59 pm	1 pm - 2.59 pm	3 pm - 4.59 pm	5 pm - 6.59 pm	7 pm - 8.59 pm	9 pm - 10.59 pm
戊午 Earth Wu Wu Horse	己未 Earth Ji Wei Goat	庚申 Metal Geng Shen Monkey	辛酉 Metal Xin You Rooster	壬戌 Water Ren Xu Dog	癸亥 Water Gui Hai Pig
白 White 虎 Tiger	天 Heavenly 乙 Noble 玉 Jade 堂 Hall	福 Prosperity 星 star 日 Day 破 Breaker	旬 Group 空 Emptiness 元 Black 武 Tortoise	司 Life 命 Governor 路 Road 空 Emptiness	日 Day 合 Combine 路 Road 空 Emptiness

Now let's say June 13 is not convenient, being a weekday and the couple prefer the 15th as it is a Friday. Check the Auspicious Hour Reference table in Chapter 5 for a Geng Chen 庚辰 Day. You could use the Tiger 寅 (Yin) Hour which is 3am-5am, as it is a good hour with auspicious stars but obviously that is not practical - who would want to get married at 3am-5am in the morning? What then is the next best hour? Look at the Horse 午(Wu) Hour, which is 11am-1pm - it has the Heavenly Officer Star 天官 (Tian Guan) and this is good for marriage. The Goat 未 (Wei) Hour, which is 1pm-3pm, has the Heavenly Nobleman Star 天乙 (Tian Yi) so that hour is also auspicious for marriage.

庚辰 Geng Chen Day			Clash 沖	甲戌 Jia Xu Wood Dog	戊戌 Wu Xu Earth Dog
11 pm - 12.59 am	**1 am - 2.59 am**	**3 am - 4.59 am**	**5 am - 6.59 am**	**7 am - 8.59 am**	**9 am - 10.59 am**
丙子 Bing Zi Fire Rat	丁丑 Ding Chou Fire Ox	戊寅 Wu Yin Earth Tiger	己卯 Ji Mao Earth Rabbit	庚辰 Geng Chen Metal Dragon	辛巳 Xin Si Metal Snake
天牢 Sky Jail 不遇 Non Eligible Day	福星 Prosperity star 元武 Black Tortoise	日馬 Day Horse 司命 Life Governor	勾陳 Grappling Hook 日害 Day Harm	日建 Day Establish Star 日刑 Day Punishment	明堂 Bright Hall
11 am - 12.59 pm	**1 pm - 2.59 pm**	**3 pm - 4.59 pm**	**5 pm - 6.59 pm**	**7 pm - 8.59 pm**	**9 pm - 10.59 pm**
壬午 Ren Wu Water Horse	癸未 Gui Wei Water Goat	甲申 Jia Shen Wood Monkey	乙酉 Yi You Wood Rooster	丙戌 Bing Xu Fire Dog	丁亥 Ding Hai Fire Pig
天官 Heavenly Officer 路空 Road Emptiness	天乙 Heavenly Noble 路空 Road Emptiness	日祿 Day Wealth 旬空 Group Emptiness	日合 Day Combine 旬空 Group Emptiness	喜神 Happy Spirit 不遇 Non Eligible Day	玉堂 Jade Hall

Five steps were all it took to select a good date for marriage - not that hard, right?

2. Selecting a date to propose marriage

In this modern day and age, proposing marriage is no longer the sole prerogative of men. Ladies have become a little more forward and are not shy about trying to nudge the relationship forward by proposing marriage. It is no longer a case of waiting for February 29 to roll around before a lady can ask a man to marry her!

You might be wondering - is it necessary to select a good date for a marriage proposal? Well, in the old days, couples didn't court each other - their parents simply decided they would marry a certain person and would send a 'proposal' along to the family. Marriage was more like a business transaction and negotiation.

Today of course, marriage and proposals don't have that flavour any more but the need to select a good date still matters, especially if you want to make sure that you get a 'yes' answer, rather than a 'I'll think about it' or 'I'll ask my mother' or ' Let me get back to you'. In short, if you want to be that little bit more certain of success, a good date is what matters.

Unlike marriage Date Selection, when it comes to a marriage proposal, the proposing party (be it male or female) gets the priority. We want the energies of the day to favour the proposing party more because that is the party that is seeking success in the task of asking for their other half's hand in marriage. Ideally, we also want to make sure the date selected does not clash with the party that you are proposing to because this will cause the person to be agitated and annoyed and more inclined to say 'no'.

However, it can be a challenge to get the person's entire BaZi or sometimes, the time frame for the proposal is urgent, thus necessitating prioritisation. In such an instance, the party asking for marriage is always favoured. So if you are doing the asking, make sure the date is good for YOU personally first, if you don't have a choice.

Using the Combination

When selecting a date for a marriage proposal, a Date Selection specialist will favour a date where there is a combination between the Day Stem of the date and the Day Stem of the proposing party's Day Pillar, also known as the Day Master. Alternatively, the Date Selection specialist will look for a combination between the Day Branch of the date and the Day Branch of the proposing party's Day Pillar in the proposing party's BaZi.

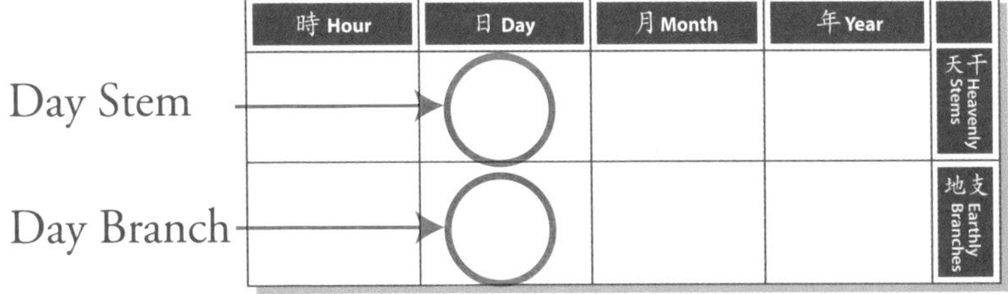

This method is not a guaranteed fail-safe method because the complete BaZi is not being considered. However, this method is reasonably effective in making sure the energies of the day favour a positive answer and the stars are on your side for this particular endeavour. Think of it as a layer of comfort and security when you pop THE question!

How to select a date for Marriage Proposal

You will need the BaZi of the proposing party and a time frame for the proposal i.e., which month they are planning to propose.

Step #1: Avoid all the bad days

Cross out any Year Breaker, Month Breaker and Personal Breaker Days for the proposing party in the month that they have chosen to make their proposal.

Step #2: Go for the Success 成 or Stable 定 Day

Once you have eliminated all the bad days, using the 12 Day Officers system, select a Success Day. If you cannot use a Success Day for some reason, then go for a Stable Day. This is because Stable Days denote favourable Qi for activities that are being set-up or pre-determined, hence, it can also be used for a marriage proposal.

Step #3: Match the date with the Combinations

Remember what I said about either the Stem or Branch of the date selected, combining with the proposing party's Day Branch or Day Stem? After you have your clutch of dates, you then need to find the date that provides the Combination.

Here's a quick reminder of the combinations.

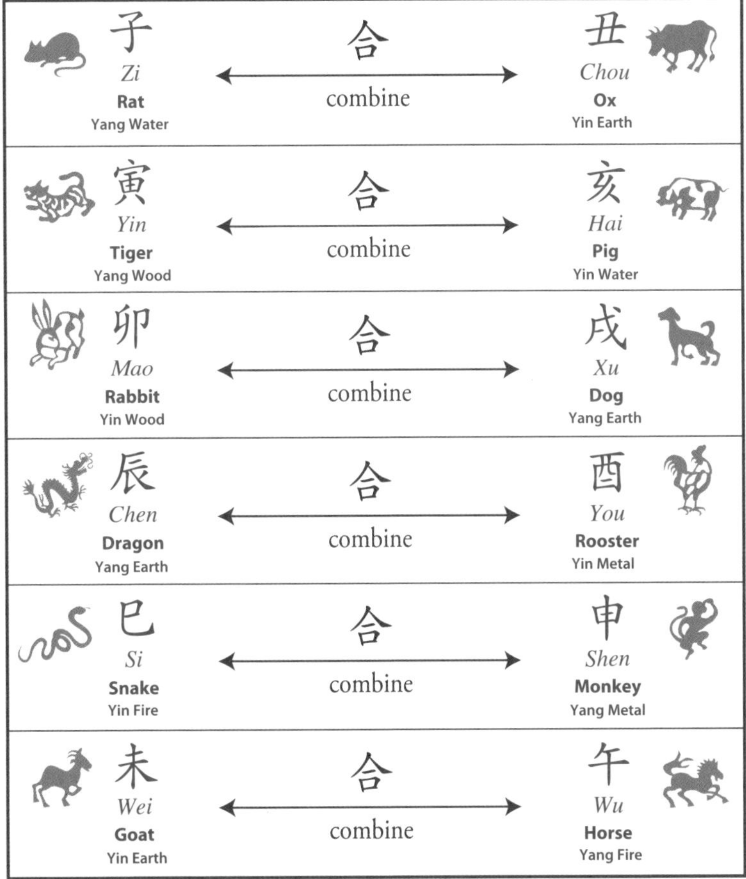

子 *Zi* **Rat** Yang Water	合 ←→ combine	丑 *Chou* **Ox** Yin Earth
寅 *Yin* **Tiger** Yang Wood	合 ←→ combine	亥 *Hai* **Pig** Yin Water
卯 *Mao* **Rabbit** Yin Wood	合 ←→ combine	戌 *Xu* **Dog** Yang Earth
辰 *Chen* **Dragon** Yang Earth	合 ←→ combine	酉 *You* **Rooster** Yin Metal
巳 *Si* **Snake** Yin Fire	合 ←→ combine	申 *Shen* **Monkey** Yang Metal
未 *Wei* **Goat** Yin Earth	合 ←→ combine	午 *Wu* **Horse** Yang Fire

Step #4: Find the favourable hour

Romance of course may be on the mind of the proposing party but that may not be the best hour to pop the question! Generally, we want to avoid an hour that clashes with either the Branch or Stem of the Day chosen for the proposal. Most of the time, this affords a reasonable measure of flexibility to the proposing party and if they can be flexible on the date, then it is much easier to ensure they can pop the question during that romantic candlelit dinner!

Marriage Proposal Date Selection Example

Let's take an old fashioned example and assume it is a man - Hugh - who is planning to propose marriage. Hugh's date of birth is April 23, 1976. His lady love, Liz, is born on July 28, 1974. Incidentally, if the proposing party doesn't know the birthday of the person they are proposing to, frankly, they deserve to be rejected!

時 Hour	日 Day	月 Month	年 Year	
	乙 Yi Yin Wood	壬 Ren Yang Water	丙 Bing Yang Fire	天干 Heavenly Stems
	巳 Si Snake Yin Fire	辰 Chen Dragon Yang Earth	辰 Chen Dragon Yang Earth	地支 Earthly Branches
	庚 Geng 丙 Bing 戊 Wu	癸 Gui 戊 Wu 乙 Yi	癸 Gui 戊 Wu 乙 Yi	藏干 Hidden Stems

Hugh's BaZi

時 Hour	日 Day	月 Month	年 Year	
	庚 Geng Yang Metal	辛 Xin Yin Metal	甲 Jia Yang Wood	天干 Heavenly Stems
	午 Wu Horse Yang Fire	未 Wei Goat Yin Earth	寅 Yin Tiger Yang Wood	地支 Earthly Branches
	丁 Ding 己 Ji	乙 Yi 己 Ji 丁 Ding	戊 Wu 甲 Jia 丙 Bing	藏干 Hidden Stems

Liz's BaZi.

Hugh is looking to propose in the month of March 2007. What day in March should he choose to minimise the possibility of being turned down?

Step #1: Avoid all the bad days

Cross out any Year Breaker, Month Breaker and Personal Breaker Days in the month that Hugh has chosen to make his proposal. In Hugh's case, as he is born in the year of the Dragon 辰 (Chen), he should avoid all Dog 戌 (Xu) Days as this is his Personal Breaker Day. He should also avoid all the Monkey 申 (Shen) Days as this is the Personal Breaker of Liz, the person he wants to propose to. Remember, we want the person to be in a good mood - it's all about making sure nothing goes wrong.

MARCH 2007 癸卯

SUNDAY	MONDAY	TUESDAY	WEDNESDAY	THURSDAY	FRIDAY	SATURDAY
				甲午 1 十二	乙未 2 十三	丙申 月破日 Month Breaker Day 3 十四
丁酉 4 十五	戊戌 Personal Breaker Day 5 十六	己亥 6 十七	庚子 7 十八	辛丑 8 十九	壬寅 9 二十	癸卯 10 廿一
甲辰 11 廿二	乙巳 歲破日 Year Breaker Day 12 廿三	丙午 13 廿四	丁未 14 廿五	戊申 Personal Breaker Day 15 廿六	己酉 月破日 Month Breaker Day 16 廿七	庚戌 Personal Breaker Day 17 廿八
辛亥 18 廿九	壬子 19 二月初一	癸丑 20 初二	甲寅 21 初三	乙卯 22 初四	丙辰 23 初五	丁巳 歲破日 Year Breaker Day 24 初六
戊午 25 初七	己未 26 初八	庚申 Personal Breaker Day 27 初九	辛酉 月破日 Month Breaker Day 28 初十	壬戌 Personal Breaker Day 29 十一	癸亥 30 十二	甲子 31 十三

Step #2: Go for the Success 成 or Stable 定 Day

Based on the 12 Day Officers Reference table, we know that in March, which is the Rabbit 卯 (Mao) Month, the Pig 亥 (Hai) Day is a Success Day and the Goat 未(Wei) Day is a Stable Day.

日支 Day Branches / 月支 Month Branches	寅 Yin Tiger	卯 Mao Rabbit	辰 Chen Dragon	巳 Si Snake	午 Wu Horse	未 Wei Goat	申 Shen Monkey	酉 You Rooster	戌 Xu Dog	亥 Hai Pig	子 Zi Rat	丑 Chou Ox
卯 Mao Rabbit Mar 6	閉 Bi Close	建 Jian Establish	除 Chu Remove	満 Man Full	平 Ping Balance	定 Ding Stable	執 Zhi Initiate	破 Po Destruction	危 Wei Danger	成 Cheng Success	收 Shou Receive	開 Kai Open

MARCH 2007 癸卯

SUNDAY	MONDAY	TUESDAY	WEDNESDAY	THURSDAY	FRIDAY	SATURDAY
				甲午 1 十二	乙未 2 十三	丙申 月破日 Month Breaker Day 3 十四
丁酉 4 十五	戊戌 Personal Breaker 5 十六	己亥 成 Cheng Success 6 十七	庚子 7 十八	辛丑 8 十九	壬寅 9 二十	癸卯 10 廿一
甲辰 11 廿二	乙巳 歲破日 Year Breaker Day 12 廿三	丙午 13 廿四	丁未 定 Ding Stable 14 廿五	戊申 Personal Breaker 15 廿六	己酉 月破日 Month Breaker Day 16 廿七	庚戌 Personal Breaker 17 廿八
辛亥 成 Cheng Success 18 廿九	壬子 19 二月初一	癸丑 20 初二	甲寅 21 初三	乙卯 22 初四	丙辰 23 初五	丁巳 歲破日 Year Breaker Day 24 初六
戊午 25 初七	己未 定 Ding Stable 26 初八	庚申 Personal Breaker 27 初九	辛酉 月破日 Month Breaker Day 28 初十	壬戌 Personal Breaker 29 十一	癸亥 成 Cheng Success 30 十二	甲子 31 十三

Step #3: Match the date with the Combinations

Now, the Success Day, being a Pig Day, does not Combine with Hugh's personal Day Branch. Worse, it Clashes with his BaZi's Day Branch, which is a Snake. So, although the Success Day is generally a good day, this date is not usable by Hugh personally. This is what we mean by personalisation in Date Selection and why it is an important aspect of Date Selection.

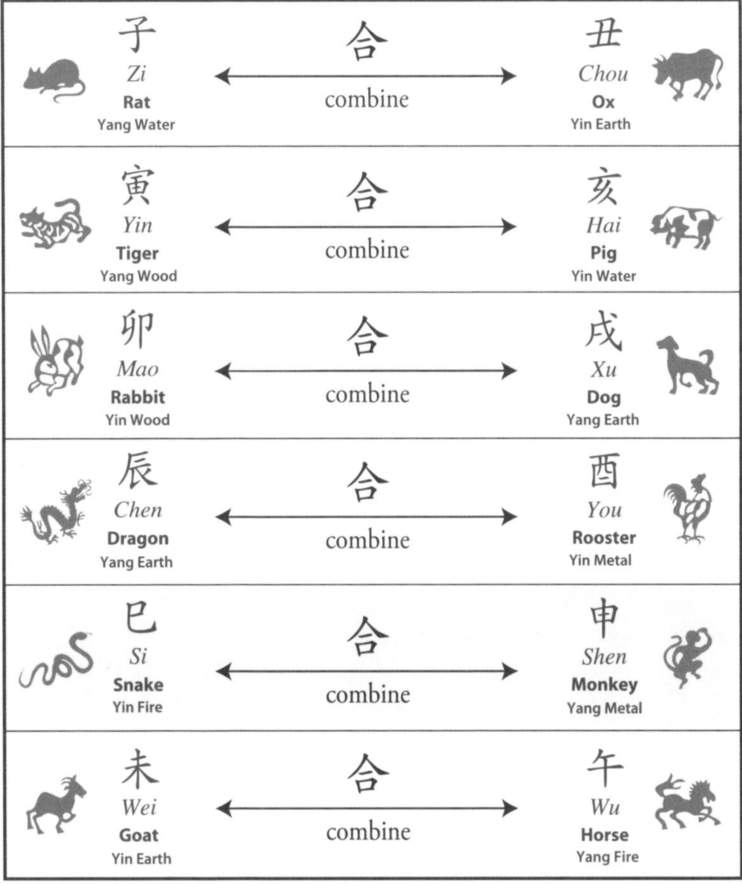

子
Zi
Rat
Yang Water
合
combine
丑
Chou
Ox
Yin Earth
寅
Yin
Tiger
Yang Wood
合
combine
亥
Hai
Pig
Yin Water
卯
Mao
Rabbit
Yin Wood
合
combine
戌
Xu
Dog
Yang Earth
辰
Chen
Dragon
Yang Earth
合
combine
酉
You
Rooster
Yin Metal
巳
Si
Snake
Yin Fire
合
combine
申
Shen
Monkey
Yang Metal
未
Wei
Goat
Yin Earth
合
combine
午
Wu
Horse
Yang Fire

By contrast, the Goat 未 (Wei) Day , which is March 14 and March 26, is usable because there is no clash, but of course, it is second-grade since there is no combination. It might be good for Hugh to reconsider proposing in March as the days available are not that good.

MARCH 2007 癸卯

SUNDAY	MONDAY	TUESDAY	WEDNESDAY	THURSDAY	FRIDAY	SATURDAY
				甲午 1 十二	乙未 2 十三	丙申 月破日 Month Breaker Day 3 十四
丁酉 4 十五	戊戌 Personal Breaker 5 十六	己亥 成 Cheng Success 6 十七	庚子 7 十八	辛丑 8 十九	壬寅 9 二十	癸卯 10 廿一
甲辰 11 廿二	乙巳 歲破日 Year Breaker Day 12 廿三	丙午 13 廿四	丁未 定 Ding Stable 14 廿五	戊申 Personal Breaker 15 廿六	己酉 月破日 Month Breaker Day 16 廿七	庚戌 Personal Breaker 17 廿八
辛亥 成 Cheng Success 18 廿九	壬子 19 二月初一	癸丑 20 初二	甲寅 21 初三	乙卯 22 初四	丙辰 23 初五	丁巳 歲破日 Year Breaker Day 24 初六
戊午 25 初七	己未 定 Ding Stable 26 初八	庚申 Personal Breaker 27 初九	辛酉 月破日 Month Breaker Day 28 初十	壬戌 Personal Breaker 29 十一	癸亥 成 Cheng Success 30 十二	甲子 31 十三

What do we do in the event Hugh remains adamant? Well, there are two usable days for Hugh to choose from: March 14 and March 26. Now these two days, despite both being Stable Days, are not created equal. If you have a bit of BaZi knowledge, you will notice that March 26 , a Ji Wei 己未 Day is the better date because that is a pure Wealth Star Day for Hugh. The Wealth Star, in the study of BaZi, represents not just money, but also the wife. Clearly, March 26 is better than March 14,

Let's say Hugh is not very confident and really wants to make sure things will go well with Liz. So he's prepared to be flexible for the right day. What would be an ideal date?

Let's look at what we know: we know we want a Success or Stable Day and we know we want it to be a day that combines with Hugh's Day Branch or Day Stem, which is a Snake.

The Snake 巳 (Si) Combines with the Rooster 酉 (You) under the Three Harmony Combination. So let's check the 12 Day Officers table to see in which months the Rooster has either a Success or a Stable Day.

日支 Day Branches / 月支 Month Branches	寅 Yin Tiger	卯 Mao Rabbit	辰 Chen Dragon	巳 Si Snake	午 Wu Horse	未 Wei Goat	申 Shen Monkey	酉 You Rooster	戌 Xu Dog	亥 Hai Pig	子 Zi Rat	丑 Chou Ox
寅 Yin Tiger Feb 4	建 Jian Establish	除 Chu Remove	満 Man Full	平 Ping Balance	定 Ding Stable	執 Zhi Initiate	破 Po Destruction	危 Wei Danger	成 Cheng Success	收 Shou Receive	開 Kai Open	閉 Bi Close
卯 Mao Rabbit Mar 6	閉 Bi Close	建 Jian Establish	除 Chu Remove	満 Man Full	平 Ping Balance	定 Ding Stable	執 Zhi Initiate	破 Po Destruction	危 Wei Danger	成 Cheng Success	收 Shou Receive	開 Kai Open
辰 Chen Dragon Apr 5	開 Kai Open	閉 Bi Close	建 Jian Establish	除 Chu Remove	満 Man Full	平 Ping Balance	定 Ding Stable	執 Zhi Initiate	破 Po Destruction	危 Wei Danger	成 Cheng Success	收 Shou Receive
巳 Si Snake May 6	收 Shou Receive	開 Kai Open	閉 Bi Close	建 Jian Establish	除 Chu Remove	満 Man Full	平 Ping Balance	定 Ding Stable	執 Zhi Initiate	破 Po Destruction	危 Wei Danger	成 Cheng Success
午 Wu Horse June 6	成 Cheng Success	收 Shou Receive	開 Kai Open	閉 Bi Close	建 Jian Establish	除 Chu Remove	満 Man Full	平 Ping Balance	定 Ding Stable	執 Zhi Initiate	破 Po Destruction	危 Wei Danger
未 Wei Goat Jul 7	危 Wei Danger	成 Cheng Success	收 Shou Receive	開 Kai Open	閉 Bi Close	建 Jian Establish	除 Chu Remove	満 Man Full	平 Ping Balance	定 Ding Stable	執 Zhi Initiate	破 Po Destruction
申 Shen Monkey Aug 8	破 Po Destruction	危 Wei Danger	成 Cheng Success	收 Shou Receive	開 Kai Open	閉 Bi Close	建 Jian Establish	除 Chu Remove	満 Man Full	平 Ping Balance	定 Ding Stable	執 Zhi Initiate
酉 You Rooster Sept 8	執 Zhi Initiate	破 Po Destruction	危 Wei Danger	成 Cheng Success	收 Shou Receive	開 Kai Open	閉 Bi Close	建 Jian Establish	除 Chu Remove	満 Man Full	平 Ping Balance	定 Ding Stable
戌 Xu Dog Oct 8	定 Ding Stable	執 Zhi Initiate	破 Po Destruction	危 Wei Danger	成 Cheng Success	收 Shou Receive	開 Kai Open	閉 Bi Close	建 Jian Establish	除 Chu Remove	満 Man Full	平 Ping Balance
亥 Hai Pig Nov 8	平 Ping Balance	定 Ding Stable	執 Zhi Initiate	破 Po Destruction	危 Wei Danger	成 Cheng Success	收 Shou Receive	開 Kai Open	閉 Bi Close	建 Jian Establish	除 Chu Remove	満 Man Full
子 Zi Rat Dec 7	満 Man Full	平 Ping Balance	定 Ding Stable	執 Zhi Initiate	破 Po Destruction	危 Wei Danger	成 Cheng Success	收 Shou Receive	開 Kai Open	閉 Bi Close	建 Jian Establish	除 Chu Remove
丑 Chou Ox Jan 6	除 Chu Remove	満 Man Full	平 Ping Balance	定 Ding Stable	執 Zhi Initiate	破 Po Destruction	危 Wei Danger	成 Cheng Success	收 Shou Receive	開 Kai Open	閉 Bi Close	建 Jian Establish

JANUARY 2007 辛丑

SUNDAY	MONDAY	TUESDAY	WEDNESDAY	THURSDAY	FRIDAY	SATURDAY
	乙未 1 十三	丙申 2 十四	丁酉 3 十五	戊戌 4 十六	己亥 5 十七	庚子 6 十八
辛丑 7 十九	壬寅 8 二十	癸卯 9 廿一	甲辰 歲破日 Year Breaker Day 10 廿二	乙巳 定 Ding Stable 11 廿三	丙午 12 廿四	丁未 月破日 Month Breaker Day 13 廿五
戊申 14 廿六	己酉 成 Cheng Success 15 廿七	庚戌 16 廿八	辛亥 17 廿九	壬子 18 三十	癸丑 19 十二月初一	甲寅 20 初二
乙卯 21 初三	丙辰 歲破日 Year Breaker Day 22 初四	丁巳 定 Ding Stable 23 初五	戊午 24 初六	己未 月破日 Month Breaker Day 25 初七	庚申 26 初八	辛酉 成 Cheng Success 27 初九
壬戌 28 初十	癸亥 29 十一	甲子 30 十二	乙丑 31 十三			

January is obviously a usable month for Hugh. So let's look at January 2007. After eliminating all the negative days, we are left with the following options: January 15 and January 27 which are both Success Days and January 11 and January 23, both of which are Stable Days. Clearly, we would prefer the Success Day - it is the better 12 Day Officers day and there is the Combination we want to see in the Branch.

So which of the two Rooster Days should Hugh chose? Remember, not all dates are created equal and minor elemental differences can make a difference. January 15 is an Earth Rooster 己酉 Day whilst January 27 is a Metal Rooster 辛酉 Day.

Now, for convenience the 27th of course is better as it is a Saturday. But Date Selection-wise, the 15th is a better day. Why? The 15th is a Wealth Day for Hugh, and the Ji 己Earth element, which represents his Wealth Star, appears on the Stem. This makes the 15th the superior date of the two - a proposal of marriage on this day is certain to receive a favourable reply.

JANUARY 2007 辛丑

SUNDAY	MONDAY	TUESDAY	WEDNESDAY	THURSDAY	FRIDAY	SATURDAY
	乙未 1 十三	丙申 2 十四	丁酉 3 十五	戊戌 4 十六	己亥 5 十七	庚子 6 十八
辛丑 7 十九	壬寅 8 二十	癸卯 9 廿一	甲辰 歲破日 Year Breaker Day 10 廿二	乙巳 11 廿三	丙午 12 廿四	丁未 月破日 Month Breaker Day 13 廿五
戊申 14 廿六	(己酉) 15 廿七	庚戌 16 廿八	辛亥 17 廿九	壬子 18 三十	癸丑 19 十二月初一	甲寅 20 初二
乙卯 21 初三	丙辰 歲破日 Year Breaker Day 22 初四	丁巳 23 初五	戊午 24 初六	己未 月破日 Month Breaker Day 25 初七	庚申 26 初八	(辛酉) 27 初九
壬戌 28 初十	癸亥 29 十一	甲子 30 十二	乙丑 31 十三			

時 Hour	日 Day	月 Month	年 Year	
	乙 Yi Yin Wood	壬 Ren Yang Water	丙 Bing Yang Fire	天干 Heavenly Stems
	巳 Si Snake Yin Fire	辰 Chen Dragon Yang Earth	辰 Chen Dragon Yang Earth	地支 Earthly Branches

Hugh's Bazi

Of course the March dates are usable and hardly bad dates in any sense, but if Hugh wants it to be perfect, then the January 15th date is the best. Ultimately, the best date is ideal but sometimes, it is better to have something, rather than nothing. Always remember that a decent date always trumps over a bad date, any time, when it comes to Date Selection.

Step #4: Find the favourable hour

As we have selected a Rooster 酉(You) Day for Hugh, obviously, he should avoid the Rabbit 卯(Mao) Hour to propose. However, since few people propose at 5am in the morning, this is not really a problem. Once you have eliminated the hour that clashes with the day you have selected, you need to find a good hour to pop the question.

The safest hour to select is an hour with a Heavenly Nobleman 天乙 (Tian Yi). However, if you are going for the ideal hour, look for an hour that contains the Happy Spirit 喜神 (Xi Shen) or the Prosperity Star 福星 (Fu Xing).

3. Selecting a date for a break-up

We've all been in situations where a relationship with someone, be it a business partner, a significant other or a supplier, is no longer comfortable and the level of cooperation is no longer beneficial. In such an instance, you may want to select a suitable date to bring the curtain down on the relationship, but without the nasty unpleasant feelings that are typical of the end of a relationship, be it working or personal. Selecting a date for a break-up is not just to be used for breaking-up with your significant other, but for corporate divorces or ending a business partnership.

Avoid the bad, even if things are...bad

Some Date Selection specialists use Personal Breaker Days or Month Breaker Days to break-off from a relationship but personally, I do not advocate the use of such days because on such days, the energies are disruptive. Bad days are just bad and no matter what the nature of the relationship is (rocky or still civil), your plan is to get out of the situation smelling of roses and with amicable feelings all around. Using negative days like Breaker Days is certainly not going to help everyone walk away with that `no hard feelings'!

Accordingly, the negative days should still be eliminated and not used for breaking off a relationship.

Remove 除 Day is best

You should use a Remove Day of course, to end the relationship. For those who want to go the extra mile, the Remove Day should also contain the Heavenly Virtue Noble Star 天德貴人 (Tian De Gui Ren)or the Monthly Virtue Noble Star 月德貴人 (Yue De Gui Ren). The Heavenly Virtue Noble Star is found either in the Stem or Branch of a day, based on the month in question. This Star has a pacifying effect on any negative activity and helps infuse the activity with positive energies. The Monthly Virtue Noble Star is always one of these four Heavenly Stems – Jia 甲, Bing 丙, Geng 庚 and Ren 壬. It is determined by referencing the month in question.

The Heavenly Virtue Noble Star has similar, but slightly weaker effects, compared to the Monthly Virtue Noble Star.

Month		Heavenly Virtue Noble Star 天德貴人	
寅 *Yin*	**Tiger**	丁 *Ding*	**Yin Fire**
卯 *Mao*	**Rabbit**	申 *Shen*	**Monkey**
辰 *Chen*	**Dragon**	壬 *Ren*	**Yang Water**
巳 *Si*	**Snake**	辛 *Xin*	**Yin Metal**
午 *Wu*	**Horse**	亥 *Hai*	**Pig**
未 *Wei*	**Goat**	甲 *Jia*	**Yang Wood**
申 *Shen*	**Monkey**	癸 *Gui*	**Yin Water**
酉 *You*	**Rooster**	寅 *Yin*	**Tiger**
戌 *Xu*	**Dog**	丙 *Bing*	**Yang Fire**
亥 *Hai*	**Pig**	乙 *Yi*	**Yin Wood**
子 *Zi*	**Rat**	巳 *Si*	**Snake**
丑 *Chou*	**Ox**	庚 *Geng*	**Yang Metal**

Day Stem	Monthly Virtue Noble Star 月德貴人		
丙 *Bing* **Yang Fire**	寅 *Yin* **Tiger**	午 *Wu* **Horse**	戌 *Xu* **Dog**
壬 *Ren* **Yang Water**	申 *Shen* **Monkey**	子 *Zi* **Rat**	辰 *Chen* **Dragon**
甲 *Jia* **Yang Wood**	亥 *Hai* **Pig**	卯 *Mao* **Rabbit**	未 *Wei* **Goat**
庚 *Geng* **Yang Metal**	巳 *Si* **Snake**	酉 *You* **Rooster**	丑 *Chou* **Ox**

The trick is to look for a day that contains either of these stars, in the month when you intend to announce the break-up. So for example, if you plan to drop the bombshell in February, which is a Tiger 寅 (Yin) Month, look for a Ding 丁 Day as the Heavenly Virtue Noble Star falls on a Ding Stem Day. If you are planning to break the news in March, a Rabbit 卯 (Mao) Month, the Heavenly Virtue Noble Star always falls on a Monkey 申 (Shen) Branch day.

If you cannot use the Heavenly Virtue Noble Star, then try the Monthly Virtue Noble Star instead. So following on the example above, if you plan to break-up with someone in February, which is the Tiger Month, the Monthly Virtue Noble Star falls on any Bing 丙 Day. If you want to break the news in March, which is the Rabbit Month, then the Monthly Virtue Noble Star falls on any Jia 甲 day.

Now, Yang energy denotes external matters, which is why it is preferable to have Yang energies for activities involving business break-ups, a partnership break up or corporate divorce. By contrast, Yin energy pacifies relationships that are internal in nature so it is best used for personal break-ups, like breaking up with a girlfriend or boyfriend, announcing you are seeking a divorce, or giving your pet away. So pick which of the two stars you want to use, based on whether the relationship is an 'external' one, or an 'internal' one.

Generally, using a Remove Day with the correct type of Heavenly Virtue Noble Star or Monthly Virtue Noble Star is sufficient. But if you want to perfect it, avoid an Hour that clashes with the Day and you should be quite safe.

Break-Up Date Selection Example

Sam wants out of an extra-marital relationship. However, he wants to make sure that when he does the deed, his mistress will not sing all the details of their relationship to every Tom, Dick and Harry and will be discreet and extricate herself from the situation without too much trouble. How should he go about selecting a date to tell her the news? Sam has decided to do this in the month of March 2007.

Sam's birthdate is 8 May 1965.

時 Hour	日 Day	月 Month	年 Year	
	壬 *Ren* Yang Water	辛 *Xin* Yin Metal	乙 *Yi* Yin Wood	天干 Heavenly Stems
	戌 *Xu* **Dog** Yang Earth	巳 *Si* **Snake** Yin Fire	巳 *Si* **Snake** Yin Fire	地支 Earthly Branches
	丁 *Ding* 戊 *Wu* 辛 *Xin*	庚 *Geng* 丙 *Bing* 戊 *Wu*	庚 *Geng* 丙 *Bing* 戊 *Wu*	藏干 Hidden Stems

Sam's BaZi chart

Step #1: Eliminate all bad days.

Look at the calendar for the month of March 2007 and cross out all Month Breaker and Year Breaker Days.

MARCH 2007 癸卯

SUNDAY	MONDAY	TUESDAY	WEDNESDAY	THURSDAY	FRIDAY	SATURDAY
				甲午 1 十二	乙未 2 十三	丙申 月破日 Month Breaker Day 3 十四
丁酉 4 十五	戊戌 5 十六	己亥 6 十七	庚子 7 十八	辛丑 8 十九	壬寅 9 二十	癸卯 10 廿一
甲辰 11 廿二	乙巳 歲破日 Year Breaker Day 12 廿三	丙午 13 廿四	丁未 14 廿五	戊申 15 廿六	己酉 月破日 Month Breaker Day 16 廿七	庚戌 17 廿八
辛亥 18 廿九	壬子 19 二月初一	癸丑 20 初二	甲寅 21 初三	乙卯 22 初四	丙辰 23 初五	丁巳 歲破日 Year Breaker Day 24 初六
戊午 25 初七	己未 26 初八	庚申 27 初九	辛酉 月破日 Month Breaker Day 28 初十	壬戌 29 十一	癸亥 30 十二	甲子 31 十三

Step #2: Find the Remove 除 Day

According to the 12 Day Officers Reference table, in the month of March, the Remove Days are all the Dragon 辰(Chen) Days. March 11 and March 23 are Dragon Days. So Sam can choose either one of these days to end the relationship.

日支 Day Branches / 月支 Month Branches	寅 Yin Tiger	卯 Mao Rabbit	辰 Chen Dragon	巳 Si Snake	午 Wu Horse	未 Wei Goat	申 Shen Monkey	酉 You Rooster	戌 Xu Dog	亥 Hai Pig	子 Zi Rat	丑 Chou Ox
卯 Mao Rabbit Mar 6	閉 Bi Close	建 Jian Establish	除 Chu Remove	滿 Man Full	平 Ping Balance	定 Ding Stable	執 Zhi Initiate	破 Po Destruction	危 Wei Danger	成 Cheng Success	收 Shou Receive	開 Kai Open

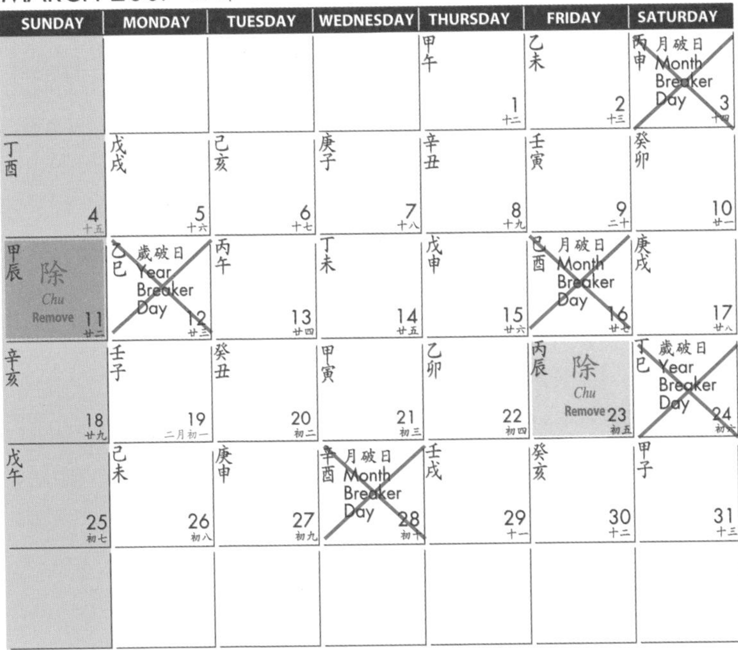

MARCH 2007 癸卯

SUNDAY	MONDAY	TUESDAY	WEDNESDAY	THURSDAY	FRIDAY	SATURDAY
				甲午 1 十二	乙未 2 十三	丙申 月破日 Month Breaker Day 3 十四
丁酉 4 十五	戊戌 5 十六	己亥 6 十七	庚子 7 十八	辛丑 8 十九	壬寅 9 二十	癸卯 10 廿一
甲辰 除 Chu Remove 11 廿二	乙巳 歲破日 Year Breaker Day 12 廿三	丙午 13 廿四	丁未 14 廿五	戊申 15 廿六	己酉 月破日 Month Breaker Day 16 廿七	庚戌 17 廿八
辛亥 18 廿九	壬子 19 二月初一	癸丑 20 初二	甲寅 21 初三	乙卯 22 初四	丙辰 除 Chu Remove 23 初五	丁巳 歲破日 Year Breaker Day 24 初六
戊午 25 初七	己未 26 初八	庚申 27 初九	辛酉 月破日 Month Breaker Day 28 初十	壬戌 29 十一	癸亥 30 十二	甲子 31 十三

Step #3: Factor in the Heavenly or Monthly Virtue Noble Star

Of the two days, the better day would be the day with the Monthly Virtue Noble Star, especially since Sam wants to end it nicely and discreetly.

Day Stem	Monthly Virtue Noble Star 月德貴人		
丙 *Bing* **Yang Fire**	寅 *Yin* **Tiger**	午 *Wu* **Horse**	戌 *Xu* **Dog**
壬 *Ren* **Yang Water**	申 *Shen* **Monkey**	子 *Zi* **Rat**	辰 *Chen* **Dragon**
甲 *Jia* **Yang Wood**	亥 *Hai* **Pig**	卯 *Mao* **Rabbit**	未 *Wei* **Goat**
庚 *Geng* **Yang Metal**	巳 *Si* **Snake**	酉 *You* **Rooster**	丑 *Chou* **Ox**

Based on the Monthly Virtue Noble Star table, we know that the Monthly Virtue Noble Star appears on all Jia 甲 Days, in the month of March, which is the Rabbit 卯(Mao) Month. Now, as it is an extra-martial affair, it is considered an 'external matter' and thus a Yang Day should be used.

March 11, 2007 is a Jia Chen 甲辰 Day and clearly a Yang Day. So he should break the news to her on this day.

Step #4: The right hour

Sam must avoid breaking the news to his mistress at an hour that clashes with the Day. Accordingly, as he has selected a Dragon 辰 (Chen) Day, he should not tell her he wants to break-up with her at the Dog 戌 (Xu) Hour, or between the hours of 7pm-9pm. This news therefore is best not delivered over dinner.

You might be wondering why I chose the example of a person looking to end a relationship with a mistress. After all, break-ups involve a variety of relationships, not just extra-marital ones, right? The extra-marital affair provides a sufficiently extreme example of a person who is looking to get out of a situation without causing embarrassment or problems for themselves or all the parties involved. It is an example of when Date Selection is not just practical, but prudent. It is also an example of a relationship where while ending it is necessary, ending it in an unpleasant manner is not.

In life, relationships are cyclical in nature. One can never be certain that there will never come a day when we will have to work with someone whom we ended a relationship with. Burning one's bridges is never wise and with Date Selection, you can be sure that the bridges are burned, but with the option to rebuild it in the future, if the need arises!

4. Selecting a date for a divorce

As divorce has now become a rather complicated legal affair that can be quite protracted in nature and complex in outcome, it has become a trend to seek a good date for the act of divorce itself.

As a personal rule, I do not advocate divorce unless the relationship is abusive, tormenting emotionally or physically or the parties are adamant about ending the relationship as they have simply found they have grown apart and have life directions that do not connect. I do try to see if the situation can be resolved through BaZi advice for example or Feng Shui techniques first, before resorting to offering a date for a divorce.

Nonetheless, it is a fact that divorce is on the rise. And many people would prefer a painless divorce rather than a nasty battle. And the key to this is doing the deed, on the right day. The process for selecting a date for divorce are a little different from selecting a day for a break-up because obviously, a divorce entails a legal break-up and may involve other activities such as negotiating a settlement.

It is important to note that the situations that may confront a person, upon seeking a divorce are very varied. The spouse may not be agreeable to the divorce. Or the spouse is agreeable to the divorce but only if a sizeable alimony payment is made. Or the spouse may fight you for custody of your children. Each scenario may or may not require a different form of Date Selection technique.

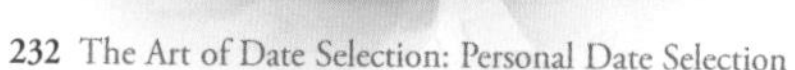

Now, what I am about to share with you may seem nasty. However, based on my extensive consulting experience in the West, divorce matters can be (but do not have to be) nasty. Sometimes, you do need to think of yourself first, before you think of the other person.

However, at all times, one should always seek to be the honourable person, do the right thing and not short-change others, including the ex or the children. I only advocate taking a selfish approach, if you find the situation to be very difficult to resolve as a result of the opposing party simply being outright unreasonable.

For the purposes of a divorce, the date selected is the date used to serve the divorce documents to the receiving party. It is not the date you see the lawyer or the date that you announce your intentions.

The best day to use for serving divorce papers is a Remove 除 Day. Now, you want this day to not just be a Remove Day, but also be a day that Clashes the receiving party's year or personal Day Branch. It is also permissible for this day to Clash your personal Day Branch but it should never Clash with your year.

Divorce Date Selection Example

Jennifer, having put up with Bradley's infidelity for sometime, decides she wants to serve her husband divorce papers. Bradley is born in May 2, 1968. Jennifer is born in June 11, 1970.

時 Hour	日 Day	月 Month	年 Year	
	壬 *Ren* Yang Water	丙 *Bing* Yang Fire	戊 *Wu* Yang Earth	天干 Heavenly Stems
	申 *Shen* **Monkey** Yang Metal	辰 *Chen* **Dragon** Yang Earth	申 *Shen* **Monkey** Yang Metal	地支 Earthly Branches
	戊 *Wu* 庚 *Geng* 壬 *Ren*	癸 *Gui* 戊 *Wu* 乙 *Yi*	戊 *Wu* 庚 *Geng* 壬 *Ren*	藏干 Hidden Stems

Bradley's BaZi Chart

時 Hour	日 Day	月 Month	年 Year	
	壬 *Ren* Yang Water	壬 *Ren* Yang Water	庚 *Geng* Yang Metal	天干 Heavenly Stems
	戌 *Xu* **Dog** Yang Earth	午 *Wu* **Horse** Yang Fire	戌 *Xu* **Dog** Yang Earth	地支 Earthly Branches
	丁 *Ding* 戊 *Wu* 辛 *Xin*	丁 *Ding* 己 *Ji*	丁 *Ding* 戊 *Wu* 辛 *Xin*	藏干 Hidden Stems

Jennifer's BaZi Chart

Step #1: Find the Clash Day

We first find a day that clashes with Jennifer's soon-to-be ex-husband's year or day - if possible, BOTH!

Bradley is born in a Monkey 申 (Shen) year and his Day Branch is also a Monkey. So, Jennifer just has to find a Tiger 寅 (Yin) Day and she would have achieved a double-whammy. This is because the Tiger Clashes with the Monkey.

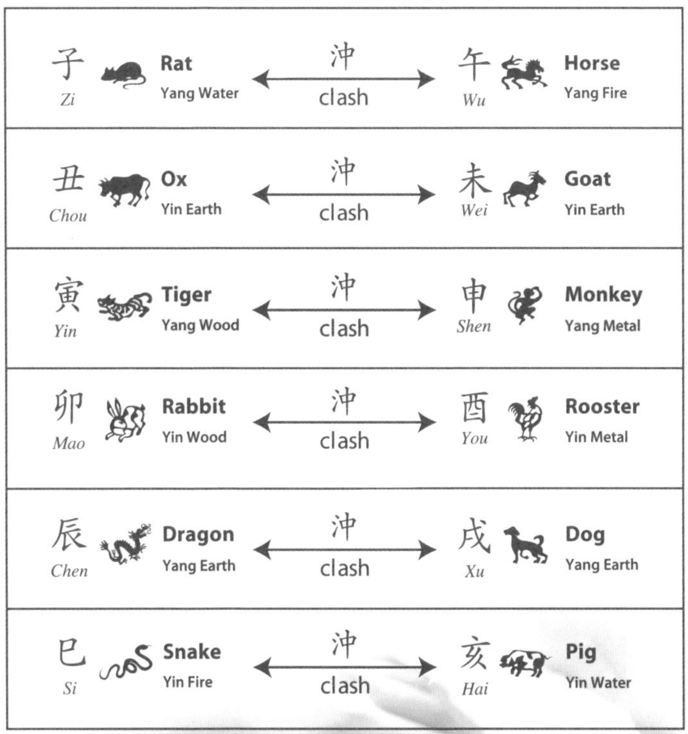

子 *Zi*	Rat	Yang Water	沖 ←→ clash	午 *Wu*	Horse	Yang Fire
丑 *Chou*	Ox	Yin Earth	沖 ←→ clash	未 *Wei*	Goat	Yin Earth
寅 *Yin*	Tiger	Yang Wood	沖 ←→ clash	申 *Shen*	Monkey	Yang Metal
卯 *Mao*	Rabbit	Yin Wood	沖 ←→ clash	酉 *You*	Rooster	Yin Metal
辰 *Chen*	Dragon	Yang Earth	沖 ←→ clash	戌 *Xu*	Dog	Yang Earth
巳 *Si*	Snake	Yin Fire	沖 ←→ clash	亥 *Hai*	Pig	Yin Water

Step #2: Find the Remove 除 Day

Having worked out that she has to use a Tiger 寅 (Yin) Day, Jennifer now just needs to find a Tiger Day that is also a Remove Day using the 12 Day Officers method.

日支 Day Branches / 月支 Month Branches	寅 Yin Tiger	卯 Mao Rabbit	辰 Chen Dragon	巳 Si Snake	午 Wu Horse	未 Wei Goat	申 Shen Monkey	酉 You Rooster	戌 Xu Dog	亥 Hai Pig	子 Zi Rat	丑 Chou Ox
寅 Yin Tiger Feb 4	建 Jian Establish	除 Chu Remove	滿 Man Full	平 Ping Balance	定 Ding Stable	執 Zhi Initiate	破 Po Destruction	危 Wei Danger	成 Cheng Success	收 Shou Receive	開 Kai Open	閉 Bi Close
卯 Mao Rabbit Mar 6	閉 Bi Close	建 Jian Establish	除 Chu Remove	滿 Man Full	平 Ping Balance	定 Ding Stable	執 Zhi Initiate	破 Po Destruction	危 Wei Danger	成 Cheng Success	收 Shou Receive	開 Kai Open
辰 Chen Dragon Apr 5	開 Kai Open	閉 Bi Close	建 Jian Establish	除 Chu Remove	滿 Man Full	平 Ping Balance	定 Ding Stable	執 Zhi Initiate	破 Po Destruction	危 Wei Danger	成 Cheng Success	收 Shou Receive
巳 Si Snake May 6	收 Shou Receive	開 Kai Open	閉 Bi Close	建 Jian Establish	除 Chu Remove	滿 Man Full	平 Ping Balance	定 Ding Stable	執 Zhi Initiate	破 Po Destruction	危 Wei Danger	成 Cheng Success
午 Wu Horse June 6	成 Cheng Success	收 Shou Receive	開 Kai Open	閉 Bi Close	建 Jian Establish	除 Chu Remove	滿 Man Full	平 Ping Balance	定 Ding Stable	執 Zhi Initiate	破 Po Destruction	危 Wei Danger
未 Wei Goat Jul 7	危 Wei Danger	成 Cheng Success	收 Shou Receive	開 Kai Open	閉 Bi Close	建 Jian Establish	除 Chu Remove	滿 Man Full	平 Ping Balance	定 Ding Stable	執 Zhi Initiate	破 Po Destruction
申 Shen Monkey Aug 8	破 Po Destruction	危 Wei Danger	成 Cheng Success	收 Shou Receive	開 Kai Open	閉 Bi Close	建 Jian Establish	除 Chu Remove	滿 Man Full	平 Ping Balance	定 Ding Stable	執 Zhi Initiate
酉 You Rooster Sept 8	執 Zhi Initiate	破 Po Destruction	危 Wei Danger	成 Cheng Success	收 Shou Receive	開 Kai Open	閉 Bi Close	建 Jian Establish	除 Chu Remove	滿 Man Full	平 Ping Balance	定 Ding Stable
戌 Xu Dog Oct 8	定 Ding Stable	執 Zhi Initiate	破 Po Destruction	危 Wei Danger	成 Cheng Success	收 Shou Receive	開 Kai Open	閉 Bi Close	建 Jian Establish	除 Chu Remove	滿 Man Full	平 Ping Balance
亥 Hai Pig Nov 7	平 Ping Balance	定 Ding Stable	執 Zhi Initiate	破 Po Destruction	危 Wei Danger	成 Cheng Success	收 Shou Receive	開 Kai Open	閉 Bi Close	建 Jian Establish	除 Chu Remove	滿 Man Full
子 Zi Rat Dec 7	滿 Man Full	平 Ping Balance	定 Ding Stable	執 Zhi Initiate	破 Po Destruction	危 Wei Danger	成 Cheng Success	收 Shou Receive	開 Kai Open	閉 Bi Close	建 Jian Establish	除 Chu Remove
丑 Chou Ox Jan 6	除 Chu Remove	滿 Man Full	平 Ping Balance	定 Ding Stable	執 Zhi Initiate	破 Po Destruction	危 Wei Danger	成 Cheng Success	收 Shou Receive	開 Kai Open	閉 Bi Close	建 Jian Establish

In the Ox 丑 (Chou) Month, the Tiger Day is a Remove Day. So Jennifer must either serve her soon-to-be ex-husband the divorce papers between January 7 - February 3, 2007 or January 7 - February 3, 2008.

JANUARY 2008 癸丑

SUNDAY	MONDAY	TUESDAY	WEDNESDAY	THURSDAY	FRIDAY	SATURDAY
		庚子 1 廿三	辛丑 2 廿四	壬寅 3 廿五	癸卯 4 廿六	甲辰 5 廿七
乙巳 歲破日 Year Breaker Day 6 廿八	丙午 7 廿九	丁未 月破日 Month Breaker Day 8 十二月初一	戊申 9 初二	己酉 10 初三	庚戌 11 初四	辛亥 12 初五
壬子 13 初六	癸丑 14 初七	甲寅 除 Chu Remove 15 初八	乙卯 16 初九	丙辰 17 初十	丁巳 歲破日 Year Breaker Day 18 十一	戊午 19 初十二
己未 月破日 Month Breaker Day 20 十三	庚申 21 十四	辛酉 22 十五	壬戌 23 十六	癸亥 24 十七	甲子 25 十八	乙丑 26 十九
丙寅 27 廿十	丁卯 28 廿一	戊辰 29 廿二	己巳 歲破日 Year Breaker Day 30 廿三	庚午 31 廿四		

January 15, 2008 is a Remove Day that is also a Jia Yin 甲寅 Day. This day clearly clashes with her soon-to-be-ex-husband's Day Branch so this day can be used to serve the divorce papers.

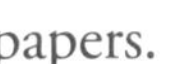

Let's say Jennifer cannot wait and wants the matter dealt with urgently. What should she do? In such a case, she can use a generic Remove Day but go for a month that clashes with Bradley's Day Branch or Year Branch. Accordingly, she can use any Remove Day, in February 2007 because February is a Tiger Month and this clashes with Bradley's personal Year Branch and Day Branch.

FEBRUARY 2007 壬寅

SUNDAY	MONDAY	TUESDAY	WEDNESDAY	THURSDAY	FRIDAY	SATURDAY
				丙寅 1 十四	丁卯 2 十五	戊辰 3 十六
己巳 4 十七	庚午 5 十八	辛未 6 十九	壬申 7 二十	癸酉 8 廿一	甲戌 9 廿二	乙亥 10 廿三
丙子 11 廿四	丁丑 12 廿五	戊寅 13 廿六	己卯 除 Chu Remove 14 廿七	庚辰 15 廿八	辛巳 16 廿九	壬午 17 三十
癸未 18 正月初一	甲申 19 初二	乙酉 20 初三	丙戌 21 初四	丁亥 22 初五	戊子 23 初六	己丑 24 初七
庚寅 25 初八	辛卯 除 Chu Remove 26 初九	壬辰 27 初十	癸巳 28 十一			

Bradley's BaZi Chart

5. Selecting a date for a business opening

Ideally, a business should commence on a day when there are Wealth Stars so that business begins on a positive and cash-register ringing note! After all, entrepreneurs are in business for the money and not just the fun of it, right?

There is often some confusion as to which date constitutes the official opening. This is because there are often many steps or stages in the process of starting a business, including the business registration process. Typically, Date Selection specialists use the day that you cut the ribbon - in other words, it is the day you officially open your doors for business to the public or the first official business transaction you conduct. The date that you apply for a business license, register your business or sign a contract for the rental of a premise, is not regarded as the official opening date.

Now, some of you may be wondering: why is it that the legal registration of a marriage is considered the starting point for the marriage, but the legal registration of a business is not the starting point for the business? The registration of a business simply indicates an intent to engage in business or start a business. It does not involve the conduct of business transactions, nor is it the point when you start to receive money for your work or accept clients. By contrast, the registration of a marriage generally does not indicate 'an intent to get married' but is the actual point that you are considered married.

When it comes to official openings or business openings, Date Selection involves selecting an appropriate 12 Day Officers day and also, using the right Gods and Killings stars.

It goes without saying that unless you plan to open and close in a short span of time, you should never have an official business opening on any of the Breaker Days, especially your own Personal Breaker Day. Once you have identified the month that you want to open your business and start selling or taking orders, you need to find either an Open 開, Success 成 or Stable 定 Day to officially open your doors. Between the three, generally we prefer the Open Day above the other two, where this can be accommodated.

Certainly, no business wants to just do 'one-time' business. You want repeat orders, customers who tell other customers about you, and customers who get you customers! These are known as your Noble People and to ensure you start business off on the right foot in the customer department, you want to find a date where the Yearly Prosperity Wealth Star 歲祿星 (Sui Lu Xing) is present.

Year Stem		Yearly Prosperity Star 歲祿星	
甲 *Jia*	Yang Wood	寅 *Yin*	Tiger
乙 *Yi*	Yin Wood	卯 *Mao*	Rabbit
丙 *Bing*	Yang Fire	巳 *Si*	Snake
丁 *Ding*	Yin Fire	午 *Wu*	Horse
戊 *Wu*	Yang Earth	巳 *Si*	Snake
己 *Ji*	Yin Earth	午 *Wu*	Horse
庚 *Geng*	Yang Metal	申 *Shen*	Monkey
辛 *Xin*	Yin Metal	酉 *You*	Rooster
壬 *Ren*	Yang Water	亥 *Hai*	Pig
癸 *Gui*	Yin Water	子 *Zi*	Rat

The Yearly Prosperity Star is based on the Year Stem. So in the year 2007, which is the year of Ding Hai 丁亥, the Yearly Prosperity Wealth Star resides in all Horse 午 (Wu) Days. In 2008, it is a Wu Zi 戊子 year, the Yearly Prosperity Wealth Star resides in the Snake 巳 (Si) Days.

歲祿星

Business Opening Date Selection Example

Hilary wishes to start a cake business. She has already rented a shop, done her renovations and applied for a business license. She is now ready to open the doors of her shop, to do business and get customers. So, what date would you tell Hilary to open for business?

First, we must have Hilary's personal BaZi details. Hilary was born on April 24, 1964. Her Day Master is Gui 癸 Water.

時 Hour	日 Day	月 Month	年 Year	
	癸 *Gui* Yin Water	戊 *Wu* Yang Earth	甲 *Jia* Yang Wood	天干 Heavenly Stems
	卯 *Mao* **Rabbit** Yin Wood	辰 *Chen* **Dragon** Yang Earth	辰 *Chen* **Dragon** Yang Earth	地支 Earthly Branches
	乙 *Yi*	癸 *Gui* 戊 *Wu* 乙 *Yi*	癸 *Gui* 戊 *Wu* 乙 *Yi*	藏干 Hidden Stems

Let's assume that Hilary wants to start business in 2007.

We know that for the year 2007, the Yearly Prosperity Wealth Star appears on all the Horse 午 (Wu) Days. The Horse is not her Personal Breaker so we know the Horse Days are quite safe for Hilary to use, as long as they are not Month Breaker Days.

So, Hilary must open her bakery in a month when the Horse Day is either an Open 開, Success 成, Full 満 or Stable 定 Day according to the 12 Day Officers method.

So, let's look at the 12 Day Officers Reference table and see what options are available.

日支 Day Branches / 月支 Month Branches	寅 Yin Tiger	卯 Mao Rabbit	辰 Chen Dragon	巳 Si Snake	午 Wu Horse	未 Wei Goat	申 Shen Monkey	酉 You Rooster	戌 Xu Dog	亥 Hai Pig	子 Zi Rat	丑 Chou Ox
寅 Yin Tiger Feb 4	建 Jian Establish	除 Chu Remove	満 Man Full	平 Ping Balance	定 Ding Stable	執 Zhi Initiate	破 Po Destruction	危 Wei Danger	成 Cheng Success	收 Shou Receive	開 Kai Open	閉 Bi Close
卯 Mao Rabbit Mar 6	閉 Bi Close	建 Jian Establish	除 Chu Remove	満 Man Full	平 Ping Balance	定 Ding Stable	執 Zhi Initiate	破 Po Destruction	危 Wei Danger	成 Cheng Success	收 Shou Receive	開 Kai Open
辰 Chen Dragon Apr 5	開 Kai Open	閉 Bi Close	建 Jian Establish	除 Chu Remove	満 Man Full	平 Ping Balance	定 Ding Stable	執 Zhi Initiate	破 Po Destruction	危 Wei Danger	成 Cheng Success	收 Shou Receive
巳 Si Snake May 6	收 Shou Receive	開 Kai Open	閉 Bi Close	建 Jian Establish	除 Chu Remove	満 Man Full	平 Ping Balance	定 Ding Stable	執 Zhi Initiate	破 Po Destruction	危 Wei Danger	成 Cheng Success
午 Wu Horse June 6	成 Cheng Success	收 Shou Receive	開 Kai Open	閉 Bi Close	建 Jian Establish	除 Chu Remove	満 Man Full	平 Ping Balance	定 Ding Stable	執 Zhi Initiate	破 Po Destruction	危 Wei Danger
未 Wei Goat Jul 7	危 Wei Danger	成 Cheng Success	收 Shou Receive	開 Kai Open	閉 Bi Close	建 Jian Establish	除 Chu Remove	満 Man Full	平 Ping Balance	定 Ding Stable	執 Zhi Initiate	破 Po Destruction
申 Shen Monkey Aug 8	破 Po Destruction	危 Wei Danger	成 Cheng Success	收 Shou Receive	開 Kai Open	閉 Bi Close	建 Jian Establish	除 Chu Remove	満 Man Full	平 Ping Balance	定 Ding Stable	執 Zhi Initiate
酉 You Rooster Sept 8	執 Zhi Initiate	破 Po Destruction	危 Wei Danger	成 Cheng Success	收 Shou Receive	開 Kai Open	閉 Bi Close	建 Jian Establish	除 Chu Remove	満 Man Full	平 Ping Balance	定 Ding Stable
戌 Xu Dog Oct 8	定 Ding Stable	執 Zhi Initiate	破 Po Destruction	危 Wei Danger	成 Cheng Success	收 Shou Receive	開 Kai Open	閉 Bi Close	建 Jian Establish	除 Chu Remove	満 Man Full	平 Ping Balance
亥 Hai Pig Nov 7	平 Ping Balance	定 Ding Stable	執 Zhi Initiate	破 Po Destruction	危 Wei Danger	成 Cheng Success	收 Shou Receive	開 Kai Open	閉 Bi Close	建 Jian Establish	除 Chu Remove	満 Man Full
子 Zi Rat Dec 7	満 Man Full	平 Ping Balance	定 Ding Stable	執 Zhi Initiate	破 Po Destruction	危 Wei Danger	成 Cheng Success	收 Shou Receive	開 Kai Open	閉 Bi Close	建 Jian Establish	除 Chu Remove
丑 Chou Ox Jan 6	除 Chu Remove	満 Man Full	平 Ping Balance	定 Ding Stable	執 Zhi Initiate	破 Po Destruction	危 Wei Danger	成 Cheng Success	收 Shou Receive	開 Kai Open	閉 Bi Close	建 Jian Establish

From the table, we can see that Hilary can either choose to start her bakery business in February, April, August or October 2007. These are the months when the Yearly Prosperity Wealth Star will be on a usable day for a business opening for Hilary.

Now, when it comes to Date Selection, we want to not just have a good day, but go for the best day possible, and as personalised a date as possible. So from our clutch of months, Hilary should try as far as possible, to go for August or October 2007 as these are the months where the Horse Day is an Open or Success Day, which is the better day to use for a business opening.

AUGUST 2007 戊申

SUNDAY	MONDAY	TUESDAY	WEDNESDAY	THURSDAY	FRIDAY	SATURDAY
			丁卯 1 十九	戊辰 2 二十	己巳 歲破日 Year Breaker Day 3 廿一	庚午 4 廿二
辛未 5 廿三	壬申 6 廿四	癸酉 7 廿五	甲戌 8 廿六	乙亥 9 廿七	丙子 10 廿八	丁丑 11 廿九
戊寅 月破日 Month Breaker Day 12 三十	己卯 13 七月初一	庚辰 14 初二	辛巳 歲破日 Year Breaker Day 15 初三	壬午 開 Kai Open 16 初四	癸未 17 初五	甲申 18 初六
乙酉 19 初七	丙戌 20 初八	丁亥 21 初九	戊子 22 初十	己丑 23 十一	庚寅 月破日 Month Breaker Day 24 十二	辛卯 25 十三
壬辰 26 十四	癸巳 歲破日 Year Breaker Day 27 十五	甲午 月食 Moon Eclipse 28 十六	乙未 29 十七	丙申 30 十八	丁酉 31 十九	

Note that August 28 is not a usable day as there is a moon eclipse.

OCTOBER 2007 庚戌

SUNDAY	MONDAY	TUESDAY	WEDNESDAY	THURSDAY	FRIDAY	SATURDAY
	戊辰 1 廿一	己巳 歲破日 Year Breaker Day 2 廿二	庚午 3 廿三	辛未 4 廿四	壬申 5 廿五	癸酉 6 廿六
甲戌 7 廿七	乙亥 8 廿八	丙子 9 廿九	丁丑 10 三十	戊寅 11 九月初一	己卯 12 初二	庚辰 月破日 Month Breaker Day 13 初三
辛巳 歲破日 Year Breaker Day 14 初四	壬午 成 Cheng Success 15 初五	癸未 16 初六	甲申 17 初七	乙酉 18 初八	丙戌 19 初九	丁亥 20 初十
戊子 21 十一	己丑 22 十二	庚寅 23 十三	辛卯 24 十四	壬辰 月破日 Month Breaker Day 25 十五	癸巳 歲破日 Year Breaker Day 26 十六	甲午 成 Cheng Success 27 十七
乙未 28 十八	丙申 29 十九	丁酉 30 二十	戊戌 31 廿一			

A complete Date Selection for a business opening requires an additional consideration of the personal BaZi and also Grand Master Dong's System for Date Selection. So in Hilary's case, we want as far as possible to open a date that is an Open or Success Day, where the Yearly Prosperity Wealth Star is present. Ideally, we also want the day to be her personal Wealth Day. However, that is icing on the cake. In Hilary's case, any of the dates selected are already quite good dates, even without applying Grand Master Dong's System or personalising the date to her BaZi.

6. Selecting a date for asset acquisition

In the old days, a person's wealth was frequently determined by their personal stocks. For a farmer, their stock was crops. For a jeweller, his stock was his merchandise or raw gems. So a full 'stockroom' or warehouse was regarded as an indication of wealth. It is for this reason that a lot of importance was placed on selecting a suitable date to buy a warehouse or a place to hold stock - what I call asset acquisition dates.

The modern equivalent of this practice is the purchasing of property to conduct one's business (such as a store or office) and the purchasing of property to store stock or valuables or manufacture items related to your business, such as a warehouse, storage space or a factory. The relevance of selecting a suitable date for this type of activity has not diminished over the years and there are certain dates that are best used for the acquisition of large commercial assets.

If you're not sure if something qualifies as an asset or not, follow the rule of thumb of size. If it is large, has storage capacity or room for stock, then it is an asset in the context of asset acquisition date selection. If it is merely a chattel (a car, a ring or a pet or computer), then it is not classified as an asset for the purposes of asset acquisition Date Selection.

Seeking Security in Earth

In the study of the Five Elements, Earth is described as 'the storage of ten thousand things'. In the study of BaZi, Earth Branches (Earthly Branches that contain the Earth element as the Main Qi) are referred to as `Graveyards', and also the storage for certain elements.

Hence, Earth is typically associated with assets and property. Four particular Earthly Branches - Ox 丑 (Chou), Dragon 辰 (Chen), Dog 戌 (Xu), Goat 未 (Wei) - are sometimes called the Earth Branches. The presence of Earth is preferred on a day that involves any activity that involves assets or property. Now, between the four - Ox, Dragon, Dog and Goat, how do we know which is the best day to use for asset acquisition?

There are two stars we use, to determine which Earth Branch to use - the Year Asset Star or the Month Asset Star. Personally, I prefer the Year Asset Star over the Month Asset Star as this Star has more long-lasting Qi and thus is better for long-term asset classes, such as property or large items.

Year Stem		Year Asset / Storage Star			
甲 *Jia* **Yang Wood**	乙 *Yi* **Yin Wood**	未 *Wei* **Goat**			
丙 *Bing* **Yang Fire**	丁 *Ding* **Yin Fire**	戌 *Xu* **Dog**			
戊 *Wu* **Yang Earth**	己 *Ji* **Yin Earth**	辰 *Chen* **Dragon**	戌 *Xu* **Dog**	丑 *Chou* **Ox**	未 *Wei* **Goat**
庚 *Geng* **Yang Metal**	辛 *Xin* **Yin Metal**	丑 *Chou* **Ox**			
壬 *Ren* **Yang Water**	癸 *Gui* **Yin Water**	辰 *Chen* **Dragon**			

The Year Asset Star Day is determined by the Year Stem of the year. So for example in a Jia 甲 or Yi 乙year, the Goat 未 (Wei) Day contains the Year Asset Star. For 2007, which is the year of Ding Hai 丁亥, the Year Asset Star for the year is in the Dog 戌 (Xu) Day.

For those who have some knowledge of BaZi or Feng Shui, you will note that the Year Asset Star is actually the storage of the Year Stem's element. Ding 丁 or Yin Fire has its storage in the Dog, hence the Year Asset Star in the Ding Hai year is the Dog. During Geng 庚 and Xin 辛 years, the Year Asset Star is in the Ox 丑 (Chou), because the Ox is the storage of Metal.

What about Earth years then? The Earth has no storage. So what is the Year Asset Star during a Wu 戊 or Ji 己 Earth year? Some schools argue that any of the four Earthly Branches is the storage of Wu or Ji Earth years. I personally do not agree with this view as none of the branches stores Earth. My view is that between the four Earths, I would favour the Goat Earthly Branch, as this contains the Fire element, which in BaZi, is the Resource Star for Earth.

To further personalise this day, try to match the date with your Personal Heavenly Wealth Star Day. This way, you can be sure that this asset would eventually appreciate, as well as contribute to your existing wealth.

Day Stem 日干		Heavenly Wealth Star 天財星	
甲 *Jia*	Yang Wood	戊 *Wu*	Yang Earth
乙 *Yi*	Yin Wood	己 *Ji*	Yin Earth
丙 *Bing*	Yang Fire	庚 *Geng*	Yang Metal
丁 *Ding*	Yin Fire	辛 *Xin*	Yin Metal
戊 *Wu*	Yang Earth	壬 *Ren*	Yang Water
己 *Ji*	Yin Earth	癸 *Gui*	Yin Water
庚 *Geng*	Yang Metal	甲 *Jia*	Yang Wood
辛 *Xin*	Yin Metal	乙 *Yi*	Yin Wood
壬 *Ren*	Yang Water	丙 *Bing*	Yang Fire
癸 *Gui*	Yin Water	丁 *Ding*	Yin Fire

Asset Acquisition Date Selection Example

In 2006, Mr Li decided to buy a new factory. How should he go about finding a good date to complete his purchase or to move his stock into the new factory?

Step #1: Avoid all bad days

It is unwise to acquire new assets during Month or Year Breaker Days.

Step #2: Look for the Year Asset Star.

In 2004, the Year Asset Star appears on Goat 未 (Wei) Days.

Step #3: Add in the 12 Day Officers Method

Ideally, for an asset acquisition, it is best to use Full 滿 Days - this signifies that you will have many more assets to acquire in the future. Now, Mr Li must make sure that the Goat Day he selects is also a Full Day.

日支 Day Branches / 月支 Month Branches	寅 Yin Tiger	卯 Mao Rabbit	辰 Chen Dragon	巳 Si Snake	午 Wu Horse	未 Wei Goat	申 Shen Monkey	酉 You Rooster	戌 Xu Dog	亥 Hai Pig	子 Zi Rat	丑 Chou Ox
寅 Yin Tiger Feb 4	建 Jian Establish	除 Chu Remove	滿 Man Full	平 Ping Balance	定 Ding Stable	執 Zhi Initiate	破 Po Destruction	危 Wei Danger	成 Cheng Success	收 Shou Receive	開 Kai Open	閉 Bi Close
卯 Mao Rabbit Mar 6	閉 Bi Close	建 Jian Establish	除 Chu Remove	滿 Man Full	平 Ping Balance	定 Ding Stable	執 Zhi Initiate	破 Po Destruction	危 Wei Danger	成 Cheng Success	收 Shou Receive	開 Kai Open
辰 Chen Dragon Apr 5	開 Kai Open	閉 Bi Close	建 Jian Establish	除 Chu Remove	滿 Man Full	平 Ping Balance	定 Ding Stable	執 Zhi Initiate	破 Po Destruction	危 Wei Danger	成 Cheng Success	收 Shou Receive
巳 Si Snake May 6	收 Shou Receive	開 Kai Open	閉 Bi Close	建 Jian Establish	除 Chu Remove	滿 Man Full	平 Ping Balance	定 Ding Stable	執 Zhi Initiate	破 Po Destruction	危 Wei Danger	成 Cheng Success
午 Wu Horse June 6	成 Cheng Success	收 Shou Receive	開 Kai Open	閉 Bi Close	建 Jian Establish	除 Chu Remove	滿 Man Full	平 Ping Balance	定 Ding Stable	執 Zhi Initiate	破 Po Destruction	危 Wei Danger
未 Wei Goat Jul 7	危 Wei Danger	成 Cheng Success	收 Shou Receive	開 Kai Open	閉 Bi Close	建 Jian Establish	除 Chu Remove	滿 Man Full	平 Ping Balance	定 Ding Stable	執 Zhi Initiate	破 Po Destruction
申 Shen Monkey Aug 8	破 Po Destruction	危 Wei Danger	成 Cheng Success	收 Shou Receive	開 Kai Open	閉 Bi Close	建 Jian Establish	除 Chu Remove	滿 Man Full	平 Ping Balance	定 Ding Stable	執 Zhi Initiate
酉 You Rooster Sept 8	執 Zhi Initiate	破 Po Destruction	危 Wei Danger	成 Cheng Success	收 Shou Receive	開 Kai Open	閉 Bi Close	建 Jian Establish	除 Chu Remove	滿 Man Full	平 Ping Balance	定 Ding Stable
戌 Xu Dog Oct 8	定 Ding Stable	執 Zhi Initiate	破 Po Destruction	危 Wei Danger	成 Cheng Success	收 Shou Receive	開 Kai Open	閉 Bi Close	建 Jian Establish	除 Chu Remove	滿 Man Full	平 Ping Balance
亥 Hai Pig Nov 7	平 Ping Balance	定 Ding Stable	執 Zhi Initiate	破 Po Destruction	危 Wei Danger	成 Cheng Success	收 Shou Receive	開 Kai Open	閉 Bi Close	建 Jian Establish	除 Chu Remove	滿 Man Full
子 Zi Rat Dec 7	滿 Man Full	平 Ping Balance	定 Ding Stable	執 Zhi Initiate	破 Po Destruction	危 Wei Danger	成 Cheng Success	收 Shou Receive	開 Kai Open	閉 Bi Close	建 Jian Establish	除 Chu Remove
丑 Chou Ox Jan 6	除 Chu Remove	滿 Man Full	平 Ping Balance	定 Ding Stable	執 Zhi Initiate	破 Po Destruction	危 Wei Danger	成 Cheng Success	收 Shou Receive	開 Kai Open	閉 Bi Close	建 Jian Establish

As you can see from the 12 Day Officer Reference table, in the month of May, which is the Snake 巳 (Si) Month, the Goat Day is a Full Day. Any Goat Day can be used for the purchase of or to move the stocks but if Mr Li wants to further personalise the date, he should look for a Goat Day that also is his Heavenly Wealth Star Day.

Notice that in this example, I used the Gods and Killings Method first, before turning to the 12 Day Officers technique to further qualify the day. In other examples, the 12 Day Officers technique came first, with Gods and Killings being used to qualify the day. This approach is sometimes used because it's simply practical. Rather than finding a Full Day in a month, only to discover it is not an Earth Branch Day, we get straight to the point. Date Selection techniques are not always set in stone and sometimes, certain short-cuts save time. The only step you should always perform first is to discard the Breaker Days. After that, remember that there is some measure of flexibility in how we go on to select the date.

7. Selecting a date for contract signing or commercial deals

When it comes to signing a contract, selecting a good date is about making sure that all the parties keep their promises to each other. It's less about money, and more about obligations and responsibilities. Selecting dates for contract signings and commercial deal signings is one of the most common types of Date Selection done by Date Selection specialists.

The complexity of Date Selection for contracts increases as the number of parties to the agreement increases. It also calls for an understanding on the part of the Date Selection specialist, of the nature of the contract, and the obligations within. As an introduction to selecting dates for contract signings, I will show you the most basic example - a contract signing between two parties.

The goal in any Date Selection for contract signings is harmony and wealth. By harmony, we mean the parties are one in purpose with each other, when they sign the contract. Wealth naturally is self-explanatory - the contract should enrich all the parties.

Not all contracts are suitable for this particular method of Date Selection. A loan agreement with a bank, for example, is a different kind of agreement and does not fall within the purview of this form of Date Selection.

Infusing Harmony and Wealth

From the clutch of usable and neutral dates, we want to find either an Initiate 執, Success 成 or Stable 定 Day. Of course, the Success Day would be the preferred day.

Now, to ensure harmony between the parties, we use the combination - specifically, we want to use the Three Harmony Combination. The reference point for the Three Harmony Combination is the Year Branch of the parties. Ideally, the day of the signing should form a Three Harmony Combination with the year. This indicates a good start and minimal botch-ups in the course of the parties executing the agreement.

Where possible, the day should also include a Combination with the other party to the contract. This means the contract is of mutual benefit. If there is a Three Harmony Combination but it is only for one party, then that party enters the transaction or agreement with a slight advantage.

Now, working out the Combinations can be hard, especially since you may not be familiar with them. But here are two quick and simple examples:

A and B are parties to a contract. A is born in the year of the Dragon 辰(Chen). B is born in the year of the Ox 丑(Chou). If a Rat 子 (Zi) Day is used to sign the contract, both parties go into the agreement on par with each other. This is because the Dragon and Rat form a Three Harmony Combination 申子辰 (Shen-Zi-Chen) and Rat and Ox share a Six Combination 六合 relationship.

X and Y are signing a contract. X is born in the year of the Dragon 辰(Chen), Y is born in the year of the Snake 巳 (Si). They choose to sign on a Rat 子 (Zi) Day. The Rat combines with X's year of birth but not Y's year of birth. So in this case, the contract favours X.

The Heavenly Wealth Star, please!

In addition to using the combinations, it is best to also make sure the day contains the signing party's Personal Heavenly Wealth Star 天財星 (Tian Cai Xing) Day, especially if the contract is of a commercial nature and involves money.

Day Stems 日干		Heavenly Wealth Star 天財星	
甲 *Jia*	Yang Wood	戊 *Wu*	Yang Earth
乙 *Yi*	Yin Wood	己 *Ji*	Yin Earth
丙 *Bing*	Yang Fire	庚 *Geng*	Yang Metal
丁 *Ding*	Yin Fire	辛 *Xin*	Yin Metal
戊 *Wu*	Yang Earth	壬 *Ren*	Yang Water
己 *Ji*	Yin Earth	癸 *Gui*	Yin Water
庚 *Geng*	Yang Metal	甲 *Jia*	Yang Wood
辛 *Xin*	Yin Metal	乙 *Yi*	Yin Wood
壬 *Ren*	Yang Water	丙 *Bing*	Yang Fire
癸 *Gui*	Yin Water	丁 *Ding*	Yin Fire

The reference point for your Personal Heavenly Wealth Star is your Day Master. Those who are familiar with BaZi will note that the Personal Heavenly Wealth Star is usually the Indirect Wealth Star. So for example, if your Day Master is Geng 庚, your Personal Heavenly Wealth Star is Jia 甲 wood. The day that you select should also have, on the Day Stem, your Personal Heavenly Wealth Star.

Contract Signing Date Selection Example

Bill is going to sign a contract with George. Bill's date of birth is June 5, 1970. George's date of birth is November 4, 1967. Here are their personal BaZi charts.

時 Hour	日 Day	月 Month	年 Year	
	丙 *Bing* Yang Fire	辛 *Xin* Yin Metal	庚 *Geng* Yang Metal	天干 Heavenly Stems
	辰 *Chen* **Dragon** Yang Earth	巳 *Si* **Snake** Yin Fire	戌 *Xu* **Dog** Yang Earth	地支 Earthly Branches
	癸 *Gui* 戊 *Wu* 乙 *Yi*	庚 *Geng* 丙 *Bing* 戊 *Wu*	丁 *Ding* 戊 *Wu* 辛 *Xin*	藏干 Hidden Stems

Bill's BaZi Chart

時 Hour	日 Day	月 Month	年 Year	
	壬 *Ren* Yang Water	庚 *Geng* Yang Metal	丁 *Ding* Yin Fire	天干 Heavenly Stems
	申 *Shen* **Monkey** Yang Metal	戌 *Xu* **Dog** Yang Earth	未 *Wei* **Goat** Yin Earth	地支 Earthly Branches
	戊 *Wu* 庚 *Geng* 壬 *Ren*	丁 *Ding* 戊 *Wu* 辛 *Xin*	乙 *Yi* 己 *Ji* 丁 *Ding*	藏干 Hidden Stems

George's BaZi Chart

Now, because Bill is your client, you need to not just find a good day for him to sign the contract, but one that is a little bit in his favour.

Step #1: Avoid the bad days

Avoid all the Breaker Days, including Personal Breakers.

Step #2: Find the Three Harmony Combination

Bill is born in the year of the Dog 戌 (Xu). The other two animals that make up the Three Harmony combination with the Dog are the Horse 午 (Wu) and the Tiger 寅 (Yin). Which do we favour? We go with the Horse, because the Horse is a Six Combination with George's year of birth, which is the Goat 未 (Wei). This will bind the parties together and ensure they both carry out their obligations.

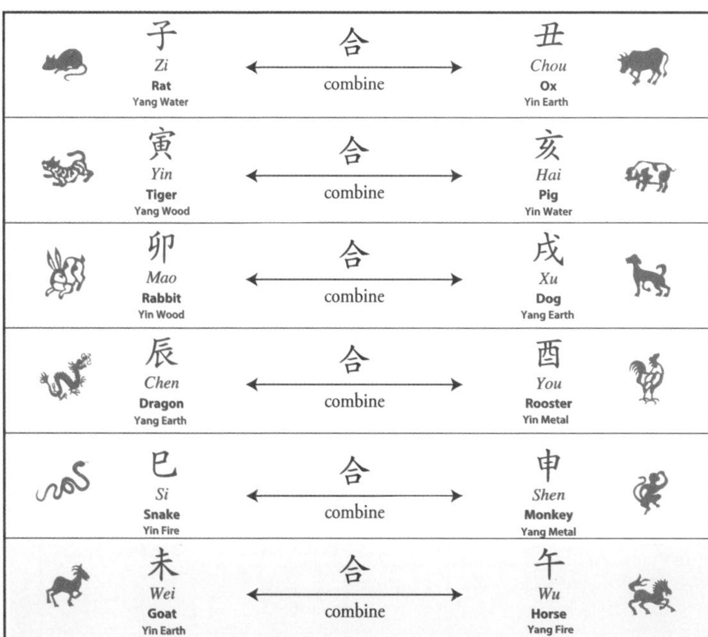

子 *Zi* **Rat** Yang Water	合 ←→ combine	丑 *Chou* **Ox** Yin Earth
寅 *Yin* **Tiger** Yang Wood	合 ←→ combine	亥 *Hai* **Pig** Yin Water
卯 *Mao* **Rabbit** Yin Wood	合 ←→ combine	戌 *Xu* **Dog** Yang Earth
辰 *Chen* **Dragon** Yang Earth	合 ←→ combine	酉 *You* **Rooster** Yin Metal
巳 *Si* **Snake** Yin Fire	合 ←→ combine	申 *Shen* **Monkey** Yang Metal
未 *Wei* **Goat** Yin Earth	合 ←→ combine	午 *Wu* **Horse** Yang Fire

Step #3: Pick a Balance 平, Success 成 or Stable 定 Day

Knowing that we want to use a Horse Day that is either a Balance, Success or Stable Day, we can now check the 12 Day Officers Reference table to determine the suitable months for the signing of the contract. In 2007, the Horse Day is a Balance, Success or Stable Day in February, March and October 2007. So Bill has a choice of dates. What's the best day that also favours him? We need to find a day that is also his personal Heavenly Wealth Star Day.

日支 Day Branches / 月支 Month Branches	寅 Yin Tiger	卯 Mao Rabbit	辰 Chen Dragon	巳 Si Snake	午 Wu Horse	未 Wei Goat	申 Shen Monkey	酉 You Rooster	戌 Xu Dog	亥 Hai Pig	子 Zi Rat	丑 Chou Ox
寅 Yin Tiger Feb 4	建 Jian Establish	除 Chu Remove	滿 Man Full	平 Ping Balance	定 Ding Stable	執 Zhi Initiate	破 Po Destruction	危 Wei Danger	成 Cheng Success	收 Shou Receive	開 Kai Open	閉 Bi Close
卯 Mao Rabbit Mar 6	閉 Bi Close	建 Jian Establish	除 Chu Remove	滿 Man Full	平 Ping Balance	定 Ding Stable	執 Zhi Initiate	破 Po Destruction	危 Wei Danger	成 Cheng Success	收 Shou Receive	開 Kai Open
辰 Chen Dragon Apr 5	開 Kai Open	閉 Bi Close	建 Jian Establish	除 Chu Remove	滿 Man Full	平 Ping Balance	定 Ding Stable	執 Zhi Initiate	破 Po Destruction	危 Wei Danger	成 Cheng Success	收 Shou Receive
巳 Si Snake May 6	收 Shou Receive	開 Kai Open	閉 Bi Close	建 Jian Establish	除 Chu Remove	滿 Man Full	平 Ping Balance	定 Ding Stable	執 Zhi Initiate	破 Po Destruction	危 Wei Danger	成 Cheng Success
午 Wu Horse June 6	成 Cheng Success	收 Shou Receive	開 Kai Open	閉 Bi Close	建 Jian Establish	除 Chu Remove	滿 Man Full	平 Ping Balance	定 Ding Stable	執 Zhi Initiate	破 Po Destruction	危 Wei Danger
未 Wei Goat Jul 7	危 Wei Danger	成 Cheng Success	收 Shou Receive	開 Kai Open	閉 Bi Close	建 Jian Establish	除 Chu Remove	滿 Man Full	平 Ping Balance	定 Ding Stable	執 Zhi Initiate	破 Po Destruction
申 Shen Monkey Aug 8	破 Po Destruction	危 Wei Danger	成 Cheng Success	收 Shou Receive	開 Kai Open	閉 Bi Close	建 Jian Establish	除 Chu Remove	滿 Man Full	平 Ping Balance	定 Ding Stable	執 Zhi Initiate
酉 You Rooster Sept 8	執 Zhi Initiate	破 Po Destruction	危 Wei Danger	成 Cheng Success	收 Shou Receive	開 Kai Open	閉 Bi Close	建 Jian Establish	除 Chu Remove	滿 Man Full	平 Ping Balance	定 Ding Stable
戌 Xu Dog Oct 8	定 Ding Stable	執 Zhi Initiate	破 Po Destruction	危 Wei Danger	成 Cheng Success	收 Shou Receive	開 Kai Open	閉 Bi Close	建 Jian Establish	除 Chu Remove	滿 Man Full	平 Ping Balance
亥 Hai Pig Nov 7	平 Ping Balance	定 Ding Stable	執 Zhi Initiate	破 Po Destruction	危 Wei Danger	成 Cheng Success	收 Shou Receive	開 Kai Open	閉 Bi Close	建 Jian Establish	除 Chu Remove	滿 Man Full
子 Zi Rat Dec 7	滿 Man Full	平 Ping Balance	定 Ding Stable	執 Zhi Initiate	破 Po Destruction	危 Wei Danger	成 Cheng Success	收 Shou Receive	開 Kai Open	閉 Bi Close	建 Jian Establish	除 Chu Remove
丑 Chou Ox Jan 6	除 Chu Remove	滿 Man Full	平 Ping Balance	定 Ding Stable	執 Zhi Initiate	破 Po Destruction	危 Wei Danger	成 Cheng Success	收 Shou Receive	開 Kai Open	閉 Bi Close	建 Jian Establish

Step #4: Find the Heavenly Wealth Star

Bill is a Bing 丙 Fire Day Master. His personal Heavenly Wealth Star is Geng 庚 Metal.

FEBRUARY 2007 壬寅

SUNDAY	MONDAY	TUESDAY	WEDNESDAY	THURSDAY	FRIDAY	SATURDAY
				丙寅 1 十四	丁卯 2 十五	戊辰 歲破日 Year Breaker Day 3 十六
己巳 歲破日 Year Breaker Day 4 十七	庚午 定 Ding Stable 5 十八	辛未 6 十九	壬申 月破日 Month Breaker Day 7 二十	癸酉 8 廿一	甲戌 9 廿二	乙亥 10 廿三
丙子 11 廿四	丁丑 12 廿五	戊寅 13 廿六	己卯 14 廿七	庚辰 15 廿八	辛巳 歲破日 Year Breaker Day 16 廿九	壬午 定 Ding Stable 17 三十
癸未 歲破日 月破日 Year & Month Breaker Day 18 正月初一	甲申 月破日 Month Breaker Day 19 初二	乙酉 20 初三	丙戌 21 初四	丁亥 22 初五	戊子 23 初六	己丑 24 初七
庚寅 25 初八	辛卯 26 初九	壬辰 27 初十	癸巳 歲破日 Year Breaker Day 28 十一			

MARCH 2007 癸卯

SUNDAY	MONDAY	TUESDAY	WEDNESDAY	THURSDAY	FRIDAY	SATURDAY
				甲午 定 Ding Stable 1 十二	乙未 2 十三	丙申 月破日 Month Breaker Day 3 十四
丁酉 4 十五	戊戌 5 十六	己亥 6 十七	庚子 7 十八	辛丑 8 十九	壬寅 9 二十	癸卯 10 廿一
甲辰 11 廿二	乙巳 歲破日 Year Breaker Day 12 廿三	丙午 平 Ping Balance 13 廿四	丁未 14 廿五	戊申 15 廿六	己酉 月破日 Month Breaker Day 16 廿七	庚戌 17 廿八
辛亥 18 廿九	壬子 19 二月初一	癸丑 20 初二	甲寅 21 初三	乙卯 22 初四	丙辰 23 初五	丁巳 歲破日 Year Breaker Day 24 初六
戊午 平 Ping Balance 25 初七	己未 26 初八	庚申 27 初九	辛酉 月破日 Month Breaker Day 28 初十	壬戌 29 十一	癸亥 30 十二	甲子 31 十三

Now, looking through all the months, you will notice that while there are quite a few usable Horse Days, only February 5, 2007 is a Horse Day and contains Bill's personal Heavenly Wealth Star, which is Geng 庚 Metal. It is a Stable Day, which while not the best day, is an acceptable day to use for contract signing. This is the best day to sign the contract to ensure Bill comes out of the deal with profit, and with a slight advantage.

Avoid the No Wealth Days 無祿日 (Wu Lu Ri)

There are certain days in a stream or group of 10 years that are known as No Wealth Days 無祿日 (Wu Lu Ri). These are days to avoid making important financial decisions or engaging in important wealth related activities such as investments.

According to the Book of Unifying Time and Discerning Dimensions 協紀辨方書 (Xie Ji Bian Fang Shu), there are ten days in the 60 Jia Zi Pillars where the "Lu" (Prosperous Qi) element is in the Void (Death and Emptiness) branch. On these days, Prosperous Qi (which can be regarded in modern contexts as wealth) is void or absent.

These ten days are also known as the The Ten Ferocious and Big Disaster Day 十惡大敗 (Shi E Da Bai). These 10 days are: Jia Chen 甲辰, Yi Si 乙巳, Bing Shen 丙申, Ding Hai 丁亥, Geng Chen 庚辰, Wu Xu 戊戌, Xin Si 辛巳, Ji Chou 己丑, Ren Shen 壬申 and Gui Hai 癸亥.

Ascertaining the ten No Wealth Days requires an understanding of the Prosperous stage of each of the Heavenly Stems, and calculating the Earthly Branch where that element's prosperous Qi is void. The first table tells you which is the Prosperous Branch for each of the ten Heavenly Stems. The second table shows you how each of the sixty Jia Zi are categorised into 10 streams or sets and the 10 year cycles for each of the streams or sets.

Now, as there are 10 Heavenly Stems and 12 Earthly Branches, there will be two Earthly Branches that do not 'belong' as it were. These are the branches that are void, or the 'Death and Emptiness' 空亡 (Kong Wang) Earthly Branches. Again, do not be spooked by the term 'Death and Emptiness'. It is just a technical term and doesn't carry any dire implications.

Table 1: 十干祿

Heavenly Stem 天干	Prosperous Branch 歲祿 (also known as Yearly Prosperous Star)
甲 *Jia* **Yang Wood**	寅 *Yin* **Tiger**
乙 *Yi* **Yin Wood**	卯 *Mao* **Rabbit**
丙 *Bing* **Yang Fire**	巳 *Si* **Snake**
丁 *Ding* **Yin Fire**	午 *Wu* **Horse**
戊 *Wu* **Yang Earth**	巳 *Si* **Snake**
己 *Ji* **Yin Earth**	午 *Wu* **Horse**
庚 *Geng* **Yang Metal**	申 *Shen* **Monkey**
辛 *Xin* **Yin Metal**	酉 *You* **Rooster**
壬 *Ren* **Yang Water**	亥 *Hai* **Pig**
癸 *Gui* **Yin Water**	子 *Zi* **Rat**

Table 2: The Six Streams of the 60 Jia Zi and the Death and Emptiness Branches 六十甲子空亡

Streams	The 60 Jia Zi 六十甲子	Death & Emptiness Branch 空亡
	Year 1984 - 1993	
甲子旬 *Jia Zi Xun* **Wood Rat Stream**	甲子, 乙丑, 丙寅, 丁卯, 戊辰, *Jia Zi, Yi Chou, Bing Yin, Ding Mao, Wu Chen* 己巳, 庚午, 辛未, 壬申, 癸酉 *Ji Si, Geng Wu, Xin Wei, Ren Shen, Gui You*	**Dog Pig** 戌亥 *Xu Hai*
	Year 1994 - 2003	
甲戌旬 *Jia Xu Xun* **Wood Dog Stream**	甲戌, 乙亥, 丙子, 丁丑, 戊寅, *Jia Xu, Yi Hai, Bing Zi, Ding Chou, Wu Yin* 己卯, 庚辰, 辛巳, 壬午, 癸未 *Ji Mao, Geng Chen, Xin Si, Ren Wu, Gui Wei*	**Monkey Rooster** 申酉 *Shen You*
	Year 2004 - 2013	
甲申旬 *Jia Shen Xun* **Wood Monkey Stream**	甲申, 乙酉, 丙戌, 丁亥, 戊子, *Jia shen, Yi You, Bing Xu, Ding Hai, Wu Zi* 己丑, 庚寅, 辛卯, 壬辰, 癸巳 *Ji Chou, Geng Yin, Xin Mao, Ren Chen, Gui Si*	**Horse Goat** 午未 *Wu Wei*
	Year 2014 - 2023	
甲午旬 *Jia Wu Xun* **Wood Horse Stream**	甲午, 乙未, 丙申, 丁酉, 戊戌, *Jia Wu, Yi Wei, Bing Shen, Ding You, Wu Xu* 己亥, 庚子, 辛丑, 壬寅, 癸卯 *Ji Hai, Geng Zi, Xin Chou, Ren Yin, Gui Mao*	**Dragon Snake** 辰巳 *Chen Si*
	Year 2024 - 2033	
甲辰旬 *Jia Chen Xun* **Wood Dragon Stream**	甲辰, 乙巳, 丙午, 丁未, 戊申, *Jia Chen, Yi Si, Bing Wu, Ding Wei, Wu Shen* 己酉, 庚戌, 辛亥, 壬子, 癸丑 *Ji You, Geng Xu, Xin Hai, Ren Zi, Gui Chou*	**Tiger Rabbit** 寅卯 *Yin Mao*
	Year 2034 - 2043	
甲寅旬 *Jia Yin Xun* **Wood Tiger Stream**	甲寅, 乙卯, 丙辰, 丁巳, 戊午, *Jia Yin, Yi Mao, Bing Chen, Ding Si, Wu Wu* 己未, 庚申, 辛酉, 壬戌, 癸亥 *Ji Wei, Geng Shen, Xin You, Ren Xu, Gui Hai*	**Rat Ox** 子丑 *Zi Chou*

From Table 1, you can see that Jia's Prosperous branch is Yin 寅 (Tiger), Yi's Prosperous Earthly Branch is Mao 卯 (Rabbit), Bing's Prosperous Earthly Branch is Si 巳 (Snake) and so fourth. In Table 2, if you look at the Wood Rat stream 甲子旬, the Dog 戌 (Xu) and Pig 亥 (Hai) Earthly Branches are the Death and Emptiness Earthly Branches. Similarly, in the Wood Dragon stream 甲辰旬, the Tiger and Rabbit are the Death and Emptiness Earthly Branches.

To compute the No Wealth Day, you must use the two tables together.

First, you determine the Annual Pillar of the year in question. Let's take the example of Ren Shen 壬申 year. Ren Shen in the Chinese Solar Calendar is 1992. Now, the Ren Shen pillar is part of the Wood Rat stream 甲子旬 and is a part of the 1984-1993 10 year streams.

The table above tells us that in the Wood Rat stream, Pig 亥 (Hai) and Dog 戌 (Xu) are the Death and Emptiness Earthly Branches. If you look at Table 1, you will see that the Pig Earthly Branch is the Prosperous Branch of Ren Water. As Ren's Prosperous Earthly Branch is in the void during the years 1984-1993, the Ren Shen pillar is the pillar when the prosperous energies of the element are void.

So, between the years of 1984-1993, all Ren Shen Days are No Wealth Days.

By the same token, this means from 2004 – 2013, all the Ding Hai 丁亥 and Ji Chou 己丑 Days are considered No Wealth Days. And during the following stream, 2014 to 2023, all the No Wealth Days are Bing Shen 丙申 and Wu Xu 戊戌.

Mark the No Wealth Days out in your calendar each year. Do not undertake or enter into any financial agreements, sign contracts or engage in any form of important commercial activities on these days. As the calculation of the No Wealth Day is quite complicated, I have calculated out all the No Wealth Days for the years 2007-2012 for your convenience here.

No Wealth Days 無祿日		
Year	**丁亥 Ding Hai Day**	**己丑 Ji Chou Day**
2007	February 22	February 24
	April 23	April 25
	June 22	June 24
	August 21	August 23
	October 20	October 22
	December 19	December 21
2008	February 17	February 19
	April 17	April 19
	June 16	June 18
	August 15	August 17
	October 14	October 16
	December 13	December 15
2009	February 11	February 13
	April 12	April 14
	June 11	June 13
	August 10	August 12
	October 9	October 11
	December 8	December 10

No Wealth Days 無祿日		
Year	**丁亥 Ding Hai Day**	**己丑 Ji Chou Day**
2010	February 6	February 8
	April 7	April 9
	June 6	June 8
	August 5	August 7
	October 4	October 6
	December 3	December 5
2011	February 1	February 3
	April 2	April 4
	June 1	June 3
	July 31	August 2
	September 29	October 1
	November 28	November 30
2012	January 27	January 29
	March 27	March 29
	May 26	May 28
	July 25	July 27
	September 23	September 25
	November 22	November 24

8. Selecting a date for business travel

A special or particularly ideal date is not required for business travel, especially since it is so common these days. In the old days however, dates were usually selected because it was usually rare for anyone to travel out of their home village and on the rare occasion that this was required, it usually involved some measure of danger or peril, hence the need for Date Selection. In the old days, people also usually travelled only to conduct business transactions such as to sell their wares or crops, hence it was important to select a good date to ensure the transaction went smoothly and profitably.

If you are travelling for a particularly important business deal or transaction and can accommodate Date Selection, then you may want to incorporate the methods I will be discussing here.

Find the Wealth Sky Horse 祿馬貴人 (Lu Ma Gui Ren)

When travel involves business, we like to select a day that has a Wealth Sky Horse Star present. Your personal Wealth Sky Horse is determined with reference to your year of birth.

Year			Wealth Sky Horse 祿馬貴人
寅 *Yin* **Tiger**	午 *Wu* **Horse**	戌 *Xu* **Dog**	申 *Shen* **Monkey**
巳 *Si* **Snake**	酉 *You* **Rooster**	丑 *Chou* **Ox**	亥 *Hai* **Pig**
申 *Shen* **Monkey**	子 *Zi* **Rat**	辰 *Chen* **Dragon**	寅 *Yin* **Tiger**
亥 *Hai* **Pig**	卯 *Mao* **Rabbit**	未 *Wei* **Goat**	巳 *Si* **Snake**

So if you are born in the Horse 午(Wu) year, then your Wealth Sky Horse is a Monkey 申(Shen) Day. If you are born in the Rabbit 卯(Mao) year, then your Wealth Sky Horse is a Snake 巳 (Si) Day.

Now, you might have noticed that a problem arises for persons born in a Tiger 寅(Yin) Year. Their personal Wealth Sky Horse is also their Personal Breaker. And remember what I said in the earlier sections about avoiding Personal Breakers as far as possible?

This is one of those exceptions but only of course, applicable to the Personal Breaker. You should still avoid travelling on a Month and Year Breaker Day as far as possible.

When you travel on a day that is both your Wealth Sky Horse and your Personal Breaker, this means that the situation is unfavourable and favourable at the same time. The trip will be financially fruitful, thanks to the effect of the Wealth Sky Horse, but because the Personal Breaker comes into play, there are either lots of obstacles involved in the trip (passport stolen, money lost, delays in flight) or the money is not 'bankable' money. You reap a profit from the deal but something comes along that eats into that profit. However, the presence of other auspicious daily stars may alleviate this matter.

Generally, when such an instance occurs, my advice is to select a good hour to depart or to begin the journey. Stars like Day Horse 日馬 (Ri Ma), Heavenly Noble 天乙 (Tian Yi) or Heavenly Officers 天官 (Tian Guan) are good stars for this activity.

If you can accommodate the dates or if the deal is of great importance, then look to select a day with your Wealth Sky Horse present that is also a Balance 平, Success 成 or Full 满 Day as well.

Flight plan

As for the time to fly or travel, generally avoid selecting an hour that clashes with the day where possible. So for example, if you are travelling on a Tiger 寅(Yin) Day, avoid flying at the Monkey 申(Shen) Hour or 3pm-5pm. However, as I have said, this should really only be used for major deals or a significant transaction because you are really restricting your travel options and dates, as well as the time you can fly, which can be tiresome and inconvenient in other ways.

Moving to another house or a new house is also considered a form of travel in the context of Date Selection. However as it relates more to Feng Shui and requires that the house information be incorporated into the equation, I will talk about how to select a date to move to a new home in my second *Art of Date Selection* book, ***Feng Shui Date Selection***.

9. Selecting a date for a medical procedure

In the old days, Date Selection was used to determine a good day to seek treatment and to prepare medication for consumption to treat an ailment.

I must state at the onset that in the event the medical procedure involves a 50 percent or higher risk of failure, or it is a very serious medical procedure that involves hospitalisation (such as but not limited to a heart bypass or brain surgery), I do not at all recommend you engage in DIY Date Selection, be it for yourself or a relative or friend! It is best in such cases to consult a professional Date Selection specialist rather than attempt to select a date yourself.

In such situations, it is also important to employ some common sense - if the surgery is urgent but your only good date is 9 months down the line, really, taking your doctor's advice should trump over Date Selection. If Date Selection is within the time frame and you can safely, from a medical standpoint, wait, then fine. But if you have to wait half a year to undergo the procedure and might not live to that point, a good date might not be the priority. In such cases, a Date Selection specialist might simply try to avoid having you go under the knife on a bad day.

However, if it is an elective surgery (such as Lasik, cosmetic surgery, wisdom tooth removal) or a non-risky operation (such as removal of cysts, non-malignant growths, keyhole surgery), then selecting a good date is helpful because it speeds up recovery, minimise the possibility of complications or post-operative problems. For an ordinary check up or very minor procedure (such as removing warts) a good date is not really necessary.

Not today, Doctor!

There are some days when a visit to the doctor should be avoided unless it is extremely urgent or an emergency. These are the days that contain your personal Extinction Star 絕星(Jue Xing) and usually do not bode well for medical procedures or treatment. It is possible that you may receive an incorrect diagnosis, misdiagnosis, wrong medication or experience mistakes and mishaps in the hands of the doctor if you see one on a day with your personal Extinction Star.

Each person's Extinction Star Day is different. It derived from what is known as the 12 Stages 十二長生 (Shi Er Chang Sheng), a principle that runs through Feng Shui and BaZi. Each of the 12 Stems goes through 12 Stages, one of which is known as the Extinction stage. At this stage, the Qi is old, and worn out. It is from here that the personal Extinction Star is derived.

Day Master		Extinction Star 絕星	
甲 *Jia*	Yang Wood	申 *Shen*	Monkey
乙 *Yi*	Yin Wood	酉 *You*	Rooster
丙 *Bing*	Yang Fire	亥 *Hai*	Pig
丁 *Ding*	Yin Fire	子 *Zi*	Rat
戊 *Wu*	Yang Earth	亥 *Hai*	Pig
己 *Ji*	Yin Earth	子 *Zi*	Rat
庚 *Geng*	Yang Metal	寅 *Yin*	Tiger
辛 *Xin*	Yin Metal	卯 *Mao*	Rabbit
壬 *Ren*	Yang Water	巳 *Si*	Snake
癸 *Gui*	Yin Water	午 *Wu*	Horse

The year of birth is used to ascertain the Extinction Star Days but my personal research into the ancient classics on Date Selection indicates that it is more accurate to follow the day of birth or Day Master.

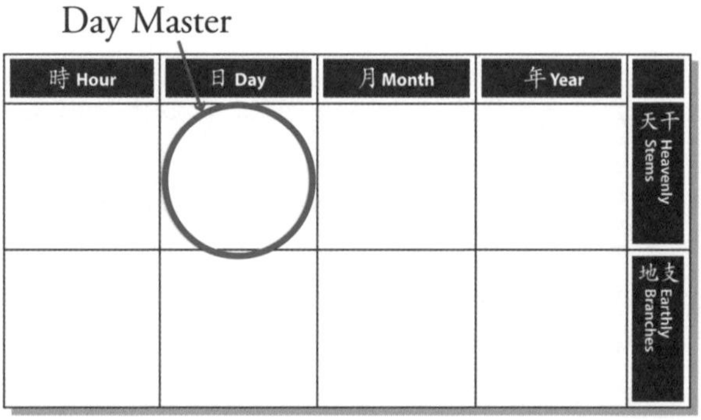

時 Hour	日 Day	月 Month	年 Year	
	(Day Master)			天干 Heavenly Stems
				地支 Earthly Branches

If you are a Geng 庚 Day Master, your Extinction Star resides in Tiger 寅(Yin) Days. If you are a Gui 癸 Day Master, your Extinction Star resides in the Horse 午 (Wu) Days. On these days, try to avoid seeing a doctor if it is not absolutely necessary.

Matching the treatment to the 12 Day Officers

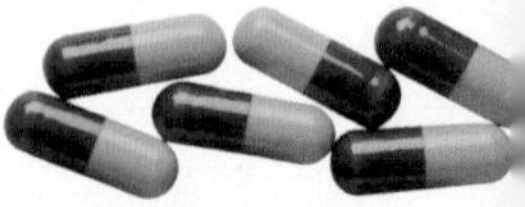

For minor medical procedures, the most suitable of the 12 Day Officers days to use is the Success 成 Day. By using the Qi of the Success Day, you will be striving to ensure the procedure will be successful. The Grand Master Dong system is frequently added to further ensure the day is a good day, but you can safely just use the 12 Day Officers method. The Success Day is best for simple procedures or treatments that don't involve removing something from your body.

If the procedure involves the removal of something (e.g. cyst, appendix, benign growth) a Remove 除 Day is more suitable. As a final resort, the Stable 定 Day is also usually quite safe for minor medical procedures that involve removing something from your body.

You should always avoid having surgery or any form of medical procedure or treatment performed on a Danger 危 or Close Day 閉. In addition to it being unsuitable for such activities under the 12 Day Officers method, the Gods and Killings Method indicates that the Close Day also usually contains the Monthly Illness Star 病符星(Bing Fu Xing). It is for this reason that the Danger and Close Days should not be used to seek medical treatment, diagnosis or for the performing of any medical procedure.

Year Branch	Illness Star 病符星
子 *Zi* **Rat**	亥 *Hai* **Pig**
丑 *Chou* **Ox**	子 *Zi* **Rat**
寅 *Yin* **Tiger**	丑 *Chou* **Ox**
卯 *Mao* **Rabbit**	寅 *Yin* **Tiger**
辰 *Chen* **Dragon**	卯 *Mao* **Rabbit**
巳 *Si* **Snake**	辰 *Chen* **Dragon**
午 *Wu* **Horse**	巳 *Si* **Snake**
未 *Wei* **Goat**	午 *Wu* **Horse**
申 *Shen* **Monkey**	未 *Wei* **Goat**
酉 *You* **Rooster**	申 *Shen* **Monkey**
戌 *Xu* **Dog**	酉 *You* **Rooster**
亥 *Hai* **Pig**	戌 *Xu* **Dog**

For added strength, the date should contain the person's Personal Heavenly Doctor Star 天醫星 (Tian Yi Xing). The Personal Heavenly Doctor Star is not the same as the Heavenly Doctor direction in Eight Mansions Feng Shui. The Personal Heavenly Doctor Star appears on certain dates and is determined by your personal Month of Birth. The table below tells you how to find your Personal Heavenly Doctor Star, based on your Month of Birth.

Birth Month		Heavenly Doctor Star 天醫星
寅 *Yin* **Tiger**	February 4th	丑 *Chou* **Ox**
卯 *Mao* **Rabbit**	March 5th	寅 *Yin* **Tiger**
辰 *Chen* **Dragon**	April 5th	卯 *Mao* **Rabbit**
巳 *Si* **Snake**	May 5th	辰 *Chen* **Dragon**
午 *Wu* **Horse**	June 6th	巳 *Si* **Snake**
未 *Wei* **Goat**	July 7th	午 *Wu* **Horse**
申 *Shen* **Monkey**	August 7th	未 *Wei* **Goat**
酉 *You* **Rooster**	September 8th	申 *Shen* **Monkey**
戌 *Xu* **Dog**	October 8th	酉 *You* **Rooster**
亥 *Hai* **Pig**	November 7th	戌 *Xu* **Dog**
子 *Zi* **Rat**	December 7th	亥 *Hai* **Pig**
丑 *Chou* **Ox**	January 6th	子 *Zi* **Rat**

**At a glance, the Heavenly Doctor and Illness Star seem to share the same table. But take note that their reference points are different. Your personal Heavenly Doctor star references your month of birth. It is a personal star.*

If you are born in the Tiger 寅 (Yin) Month, your Personal Heavenly Doctor Star appears during each Ox 丑 (Chou) Day. If you are born in the Horse 午 (Wu) Month, your Personal Heavenly Doctor Star appears on all the Snake 巳 (Si) Days.

If you cannot use your Personal Heavenly Doctor Star, every month has a Heavenly Doctor Star and this Star typically appears on the Success Day. This can be used if for some reason, you cannot use the Personal Heavenly Doctor Star Days.

In some situations, you may find your Personal Heavenly Doctor Star and your Extinction Star appear on the same day. In such a case, it is still best to avoid such a day. Where you have a day that has both good and bad stars, it is always better to err on the side of caution, and go with another day.

It's all about scheduling

When it comes to selecting a date for a medical procedure, the trick is to schedule the procedure on a day that is BOTH a Success Day, and a day where your Personal Heavenly Doctor Star appears.

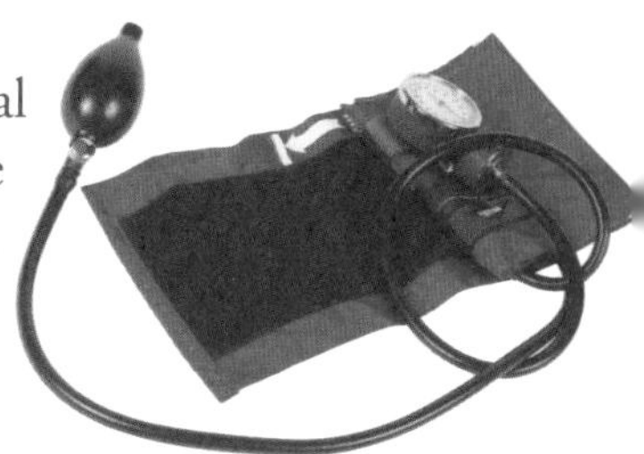

So the trick is to schedule your procedure on a day that has your Personal Heavenly Doctor Star and is also a Success Day. There aren't of course that many days for you to choose from, especially when you have excluded the unusable and bad days. It is necessary to be prepared to use Stable and Balance Days, so long as these days also contain your Personal Heavenly Doctor Star.

Medical Procedure Date Selection Example

John has been told by his doctor that his bum knee can only be improved through surgery. He now needs to select a date to undergo the surgical procedure to fix his bad knee. John's birthday is June 20, 1958. This is John's BaZi chart.

時 Hour	日 Day	月 Month	年 Year	
	戊 *Wu* Yang Earth	戊 *Wu* Yang Earth	戊 *Wu* Yang Earth	天干 Heavenly Stems
	辰 *Chen* **Dragon** Yang Earth	午 *Wu* **Horse** Yang Fire	戌 *Xu* **Dog** Yang Earth	地支 Earthly Branches
	癸 *Gui* 戊 *Wu* 乙 *Yi*	丁 *Ding* 己 *Ji*	丁 *Ding* 戊 *Wu* 辛 *Xin*	藏干 Hidden Stems

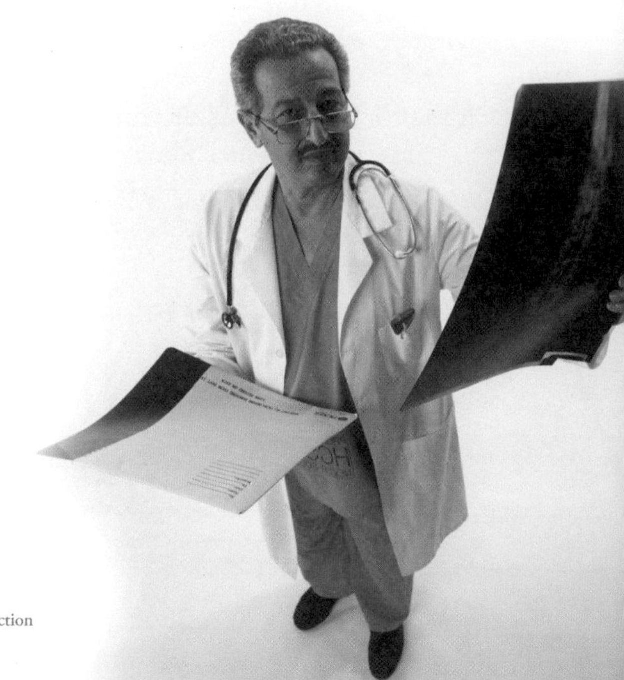

Step #1: Avoid all the bad days

Within the time frame that John has to have his procedure done, eliminate all Breaker Days (Month Breaker, Year Breaker and Personal Breaker).

Step #2: Find the Personal Heavenly Doctor Star

John is born in a Horse 午 (Wu) Month, which means his personal Heavenly Doctor Star appears on all Snake 巳 (Si) Days. Now, we double check against the Extinction Star table to make sure that the Snake is not his personal Extinction Star. John is a Wu 戊 Earth Day Master. From the table below, we can see that his personal Extinction Star is the Pig 亥 (Hai) Earthly Branch. So it is safe for John to use the Snake Day.

Birth Month			Heavenly Doctor Star 天醫星	
寅 *Yin*	**Tiger**	February 4th	丑 *Chou*	**Ox**
卯 *Mao*	**Rabbit**	March 5th	寅 *Yin*	**Tiger**
辰 *Chen*	**Dragon**	April 5th	卯 *Mao*	**Rabbit**
巳 *Si*	**Snake**	May 5th	辰 *Chen*	**Dragon**
午 *Wu*	**Horse**	June 6th	巳 *Si*	**Snake**
未 *Wei*	**Goat**	July 7th	午 *Wu*	**Horse**
申 *Shen*	**Monkey**	August 7th	未 *Wei*	**Goat**
酉 *You*	**Rooster**	September 8th	申 *Shen*	**Monkey**
戌 *Xu*	**Dog**	October 8th	酉 *You*	**Rooster**
亥 *Hai*	**Pig**	November 7th	戌 *Xu*	**Dog**
子 *Zi*	**Rat**	December 7th	亥 *Hai*	**Pig**
丑 *Chou*	**Ox**	January 6th	子 *Zi*	**Rat**

Day Master			Extinction Star 絕星		
甲 *Jia*	Yang Wood		申 *Shen*		Monkey
乙 *Yi*	Yin Wood		酉 *You*		Rooster
丙 *Bing*	Yang Fire		亥 *Hai*		Pig
丁 *Ding*	Yin Fire		子 *Zi*		Rat
戊 *Wu*	Yang Earth		亥 *Hai*		Pig
己 *Ji*	Yin Earth		子 *Zi*		Rat
庚 *Geng*	Yang Metal		寅 *Yin*		Tiger
辛 *Xin*	Yin Metal		卯 *Mao*		Rabbit
壬 *Ren*	Yang Water		巳 *Si*		Snake
癸 *Gui*	Yin Water		午 *Wu*		Horse

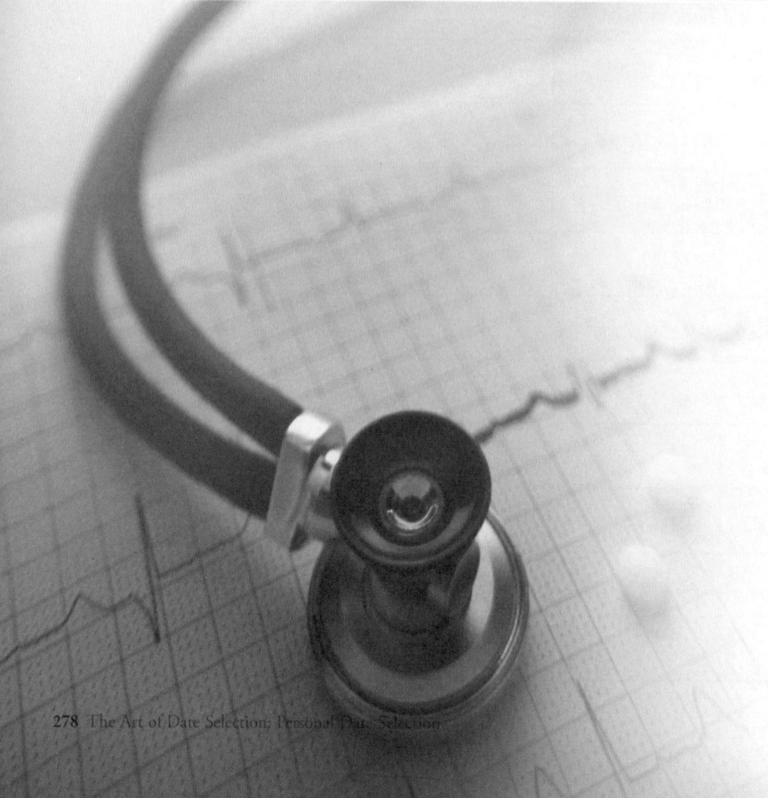

Step #3: Add-in the 12 Day Officers

The best days in the 12 Day Officers method for an operation are Success 成, Stable 定 and Remove 除 Days. So we must find a Success, Stable or Remove Day, which is also a Snake 巳 (Si) Day. Look at the 12 Day Officers table below:

日支 Day Branches / 月支 Month Branches	寅 Yin Tiger	卯 Mao Rabbit	辰 Chen Dragon	巳 Si Snake	午 Wu Horse	未 Wei Goat	申 Shen Monkey	酉 You Rooster	戌 Xu Dog	亥 Hai Pig	子 Zi Rat	丑 Chou Ox
寅 Yin Tiger Feb 4	建 Jian Establish	除 Chu Remove	滿 Man Full	平 Ping Balance	定 Ding Stable	執 Zhi Initiate	破 Po Destruction	危 Wei Danger	成 Cheng Success	收 Shou Receive	開 Kai Open	閉 Bi Close
卯 Mao Rabbit Mar 6	閉 Bi Close	建 Jian Establish	除 Chu Remove	滿 Man Full	平 Ping Balance	定 Ding Stable	執 Zhi Initiate	破 Po Destruction	危 Wei Danger	成 Cheng Success	收 Shou Receive	開 Kai Open
辰 Chen Dragon Apr 5	開 Kai Open	閉 Bi Close	建 Jian Establish	除 Chu Remove	滿 Man Full	平 Ping Balance	定 Ding Stable	執 Zhi Initiate	破 Po Destruction	危 Wei Danger	成 Cheng Success	收 Shou Receive
巳 Si Snake May 6	收 Shou Receive	開 Kai Open	閉 Bi Close	建 Jian Establish	除 Chu Remove	滿 Man Full	平 Ping Balance	定 Ding Stable	執 Zhi Initiate	破 Po Destruction	危 Wei Danger	成 Cheng Success
午 Wu Horse June 6	成 Cheng Success	收 Shou Receive	開 Kai Open	閉 Bi Close	建 Jian Establish	除 Chu Remove	滿 Man Full	平 Ping Balance	定 Ding Stable	執 Zhi Initiate	破 Po Destruction	危 Wei Danger
未 Wei Goat Jul 7	危 Wei Danger	成 Cheng Success	收 Shou Receive	開 Kai Open	閉 Bi Close	建 Jian Establish	除 Chu Remove	滿 Man Full	平 Ping Balance	定 Ding Stable	執 Zhi Initiate	破 Po Destruction
申 Shen Monkey Aug 8	破 Po Destruction	危 Wei Danger	成 Cheng Success	收 Shou Receive	開 Kai Open	閉 Bi Close	建 Jian Establish	除 Chu Remove	滿 Man Full	平 Ping Balance	定 Ding Stable	執 Zhi Initiate
酉 You Rooster Sept 8	執 Zhi Initiate	破 Po Destruction	危 Wei Danger	成 Cheng Success	收 Shou Receive	開 Kai Open	閉 Bi Close	建 Jian Establish	除 Chu Remove	滿 Man Full	平 Ping Balance	定 Ding Stable
戌 Xu Dog Oct 8	定 Ding Stable	執 Zhi Initiate	破 Po Destruction	危 Wei Danger	成 Cheng Success	收 Shou Receive	開 Kai Open	閉 Bi Close	建 Jian Establish	除 Chu Remove	滿 Man Full	平 Ping Balance
亥 Hai Pig Nov 7	平 Ping Balance	定 Ding Stable	執 Zhi Initiate	破 Po Destruction	危 Wei Danger	成 Cheng Success	收 Shou Receive	開 Kai Open	閉 Bi Close	建 Jian Establish	除 Chu Remove	滿 Man Full
子 Zi Rat Dec 7	滿 Man Full	平 Ping Balance	定 Ding Stable	執 Zhi Initiate	破 Po Destruction	危 Wei Danger	成 Cheng Success	收 Shou Receive	開 Kai Open	閉 Bi Close	建 Jian Establish	除 Chu Remove
丑 Chou Ox Jan 6	除 Chu Remove	滿 Man Full	平 Ping Balance	定 Ding Stable	執 Zhi Initiate	破 Po Destruction	危 Wei Danger	成 Cheng Success	收 Shou Receive	開 Kai Open	閉 Bi Close	建 Jian Establish

John can opt to have his knee operation done in either the Ox 丑 (Chou) Month which is January 6 to February 3, the Dragon 辰 (Chen) Month which is April 5 - May or the Rooster 酉 (You) Month which September 7 - October 7. Within these months, John can choose any Snake Day for the procedure.

Step #4: Avoid the negative hour

The procedure should not be performed at an hour that clashes with the day.

Further personalisation can be done through adding on Grand Master Dong's System and of course, selecting the day that is best based on John's personal BaZi.

10. Selecting a good day to start a diet

Now you might be wondering - why on earth has Joey chosen to include this as a working example? Surely this seems a bit frivolous? Not really.

The diet offers an example of how Date Selection has moved with the times and how an ancient practice can be successfully transplanted into a modern context effectively. In the age of the GI, Atkins, South Beach, Low-Carb, Blood Type diet, it is rare to meet people who haven't tried some form of diet, in order to lose weight or simply gain better health. Yet it's also a personal endeavour that very few people are actually successful at on the first go. Some people 'yo-yo' on a diet, some people lose very little despite their efforts and some people even gain weight!

So, it's the perfect activity to tackle with the help of Date Selection and the power of a good date!

Avoid the bad days

Although a diet naturally involves some measure of discomfort, I would still not recommend using any Breaker Days. If you use a Breaker Day, you're more likely to fall off the wagon after a few days or find your diet doesn't go very far.

Go for Remove 除 or Success 成 Days

Now, because a diet is an activity that involves getting rid of something, I would recommend using a Remove Day - this is one of the rare instances where the Remove Day is the preferred choice. Alternatively, you may also want to select a Success Day, thus infusing your weight loss efforts with success.

Do not start a diet on a Danger 危 Day as you might have health problems as a result of your diet. You should also avoid a Receive 收 Day as the Receive Day denotes 'getting something' and not 'losing something' and unless your diet involves putting on weight , this is not a good day to use.

Use the Clash

In addition, I would select a Remove or Success Day that also clashes with the Day Branch of the person's BaZi. The Day Branch represents the person's home and also their sense of comfort. I have yet to meet a person who enjoyed going on diet or was comfortable with the idea of a diet so using a Clash is appropriate and in line with the nature of the activity. In addition, a Clash usually denotes a loss of something hence by using a Remove or Success Day that Clashes with your Day Branch, you stand a better chance of 'losing' unwanted fat.

Diet Commencement Date Selection Example

Rene would like to lose some weight so she has decided to go on a diet. Rene is born on August 5, 1972.

時 Hour	日 Day	月 Month	年 Year	
	戊 *Wu* Yang Earth	丁 *Ding* Yin Fire	壬 *Ren* Yang Water	天干 Heavenly Stems
	辰 *Chen* **Dragon** Yang Earth	未 *Wei* **Goat** Yin Earth	子 *Zi* **Rat** Yang Water	地支 Earthly Branches
	癸 *Gui* 戊 *Wu* 乙 *Yi*	乙 *Yi* 己 *Ji* 丁 *Ding*	癸 *Gui*	藏干 Hidden Stems

Rene's BaZi

As we can see from her BaZi chart, Rene is a Wu 戊 Earth Day Master.

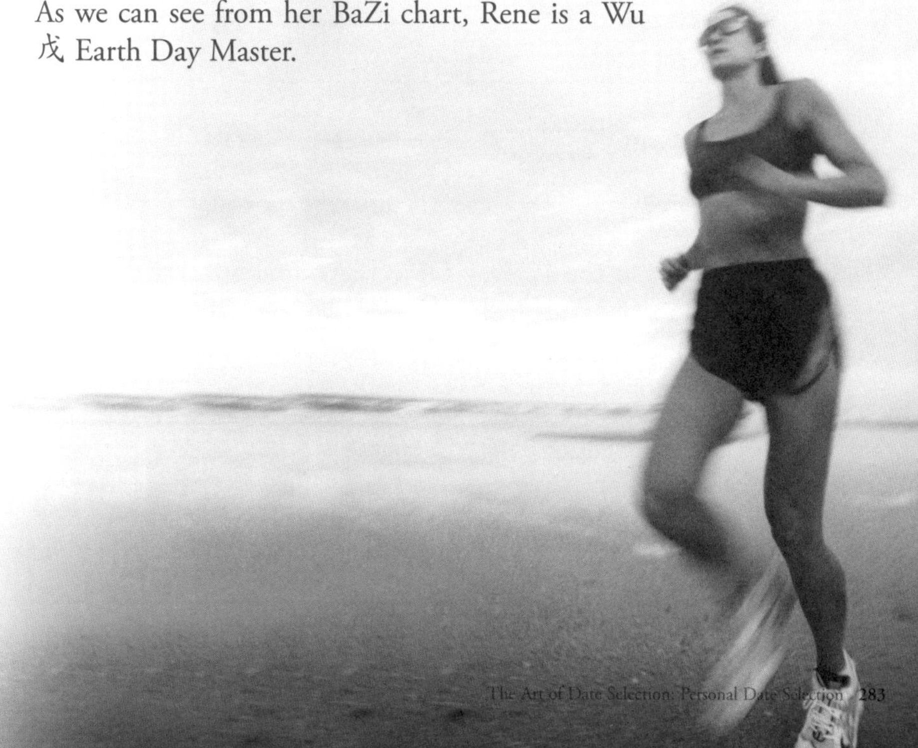

First we want to find a Remove 除 Day that also clashes with her Day Branch. Rene's Day Branch is the Dragon 辰(Chen), so we must find a Remove Day that is a Dog 戌 (Xu) Day as the Dog and Dragon has a Clash relationship.

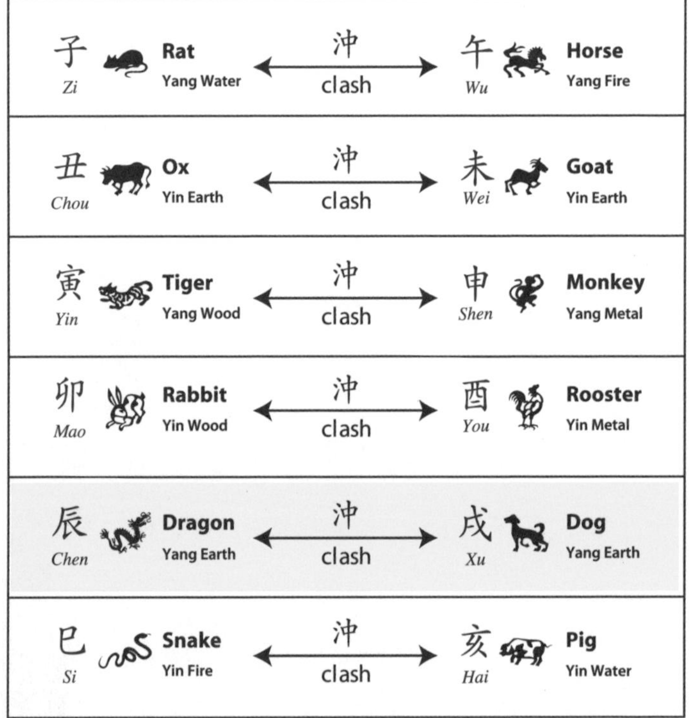

Now, refer to the 12 Day Officers method table. We can see from the table that in the Rooster 酉(You) Month, the Dog Day is also a Remove Day. So Rene should start her diet on either October 7, 19 or 31.

日支 Day Branches / 月支 Month Branches	寅 Yin Tiger	卯 Mao Rabbit	辰 Chen Dragon	巳 Si Snake	午 Wu Horse	未 Wei Goat	申 Shen Monkey	酉 You Rooster	戌 Xu Dog	亥 Hai Pig	子 Zi Rat	丑 Chou Ox
酉 You Rooster Sept	執 Zhi Initiate	破 Po Destruction	危 Wei Danger	成 Cheng Success	收 Shou Receive	開 Kai Open	閉 Bi Close	建 Jian Establish	除 Chu Remove	滿 Man Full	平 Ping Balance	定 Ding Stable

OCTOBER 2007 庚戌

SUNDAY	MONDAY	TUESDAY	WEDNESDAY	THURSDAY	FRIDAY	SATURDAY
	戊辰 1 廿一	己巳 歲破日 Year Breaker Day 2 廿二	庚午 3 廿三	辛未 4 廿四	壬申 5 廿五	癸酉 6 廿六
甲戌 除 Chu Remove 7 廿七	乙亥 8 廿八	丙子 9 廿九	丁丑 10 三十	戊寅 11 九月初一	己卯 12 初二	庚辰 月破日 Month Breaker Day 13 初三
辛巳 歲破日 Year Breaker Day 14 初四	壬午 15 初五	癸未 16 初六	甲申 17 初七	乙酉 18 初八	丙戌 除 Chu Remove 19 初九	丁亥 20 初十
戊子 21 十一	己丑 22 十二	庚寅 23 十三	辛卯 24 十四	壬辰 月破日 Month Breaker Day 25 十五	癸巳 歲破日 Year Breaker Day 26 十六	甲午 27 十七
乙未 28 十八	丙申 29 十九	丁酉 30 二十	戊戌 除 Chu Remove 31 廿一			

Ideally, you want to personalise the Date Selection further using BaZi. A diet is all about discipline and following the 'rules' of the diet. So the star that we ideally will want to use is the Direct Officer 正官 or Seven Killings 七殺 Star, based on the person's BaZi. So the date that you select, in addition to being a Remove or Success Day that clashes the Day Branch should also be a day that contains the person's Direct Officer or Seven Killings Stars.

11. Selecting a good date for negotiations

Business negotiations are an important part of any business and for a particularly important deal or transaction, you may want to select a date to commence negotiations. But negotiations are not just for business people or entrepreneurs. The average person, you and I included, engages in negotiations all the time. Whether it's haggling at the market, bargaining for a better deal at the supermarket or asking for a pay rise, negotiations are a constant in our lives.

Now of course, I'm not suggesting you select a date to haggle over chicken in the market or to buy a carpet in a shop. But for something like say a pay rise (or for the ladies, if you want to ask for something special from your Other Half), selecting a date can provide that crucial little extra push that ensures you don't just get what you want, but get a good deal too!

Of course, if you expect to be negotiating with someone whom you think may give you a hard time (such as a stingy boss, or perhaps, a difficult mother-in-law), then a good date may be just what you need to even up the odds, in your favour of course!

Step #1: Avoid the bad dates

It goes without saying that any kind of Breaker Day (Month Breaker, Year Breaker, Personal Breaker) is not to be used, unless your plan is to have negotiations fail before you even get your foot in the door.

Step 2: Go for Success 成, Stable 定, Full 滿 or Receive 收 Days

The Success, Stable, Full or Receive Days in the 12 Day Officers method, are the best days to use for negotiation or any form of activity that involves having to ask for something and justifying your request. By using any of these four days, you will be able to get what you want, without giving away too much (always essential in a negotiation) and also, not having to grovel or work too hard for it!

Step #3: Add in the Combination and use the Nobleman

Now, negotiations are only fun when you have the upper hand or you know you have leverage and thus are certain of success. How then do you acquire 'leverage' in the Date Selection context?

Using the power of the Combination will help you acquire this Qi leverage. Look for a Success, Stable, Full or Receive Day that combines with your Year Branch.

This is because the Year Branch not only signifies assets or items acquired or received, but is also regarded as the Grand Duke. By choosing a day that combines with your Grand Duke, you are tapping into the energies of the Grand Duke so that in the course of the negotiation, you are being supported and watched over all the way.

For example, if your personal Year Branch is Dragon 辰 (Chen), then select a Success, Stable, Full or Receive Day that is a Rooster 酉 (You) Day. The Rooster and Dragon form a Combination, remember?

Let's say you're facing a particularly challenging or uphill negotiation and you want to make sure as much is weighed in your favour as possible. To enhance your advantage to the maximum, you can tap into your Personal Nobleman 貴人 (Gui Ren), in the Day and Hour.

甲戊庚牛羊

乙己鼠猴鄉

丙丁豬雞位

壬癸兔蛇藏

六辛逢馬虎

此是貴人方

The Nobleman Star can be simply described as a star that brings "helpful people". This particular star enables you to not only meet the right person at the right time, but also a person who will be able to help you get what you want or need.

To determine your Personal Nobleman, the reference point is your Day Master. So for example, if you are a Xin 辛 Metal Day Master, your Nobleman is the Horse 午 (Wu) and Tiger 寅 (Yin). So you want to use a Horse or Tiger Day that is also a Success, Stable, Receive or Full Day and if possible, combines with your Year Branch.

Day Stems 日干	Nobleman Star 貴人
甲 *Jia* Yang Wood, 戊 *Wu* Yang Earth, 庚 *Geng* Yang Metal	丑 *Chou* **Ox**, 未 *Wei* **Goat**
乙 *Yi* Yin Wood, 己 *Ji* Yin Earth	子 *Zi* **Rat**, 申 *Shen* **Monkey**
丙 *Bing* Yang Fire, 丁 *Ding* Yin Fire	亥 *Hai* **Pig**, 酉 *You* **Rooster**
壬 *Ren* Yang Water, 癸 *Gui* Yin Water	卯 *Mao* **Rabbit**, 巳 *Si* **Snake**
辛 *Xin* Yin Metal	午 *Wu* **Horse**, 寅 *Yin* **Tiger**

Step #4: Deploy the Nobleman Hour

For a super-important negotiation, you also want to use the right hour to ensure nothing will be against you on that day. Once you have selected your date, look for an hour that contains either the Heavenly Noble 天乙 (Tian Yi) or the Heavenly Officer 天官 (Tian Guan) Stars, using the Auspicious Hour Reference table in Chapter 5.

Going Forward...

The Art of Date Selection extends significantly beyond the activities and examples given here although these are some of the more common types of activities that people frequently seek a Date Selection specialist to assist them with. Date Selection is a very different kettle of fish and vastly more sophisticated for business activities for example, or where a transaction involves multiple parties. There are always greater levels of personalisation that can be used to cut out and narrow down the available dates, to ensure the best date is used.

There are also other methods of Date Selection that add further sophistication and refinement to the methods I have discussed here, such as Grand Master Dong's System 董公 (Dong Gong) and in particular, the Mystical Doors Method 奇門盾甲 (Qi Men Dun Jia) , when it comes to using the hour to offset disadvantages in certain days. Also, by having some knowledge of BaZi, narrowing down the best date for a particular activity, particularly personal endeavours, becomes easier.

Through my *Art of Date Selection* series, I will share with you more techniques and methods on how you can use a good date, to help your personal and business activities and endeavours achieve success. For now, have fun doing some Date Selection for yourself, try out these methods and give your personal actvities and endeavours the best possible start you can through the power of a good date.

About Joey Yap

Joey Yap is the Founder and Master Trainer of the Mastery Academy of Chinese Metaphysics, a global organisation devoted to the worldwide teaching of Feng Shui, BaZi, Mian Xiang, Yi Jing and other Chinese Metaphysics subjects. Joey is also the Chief Consultant of Yap Global Consulting, an international Feng Shui and Chinese Astrology consulting firm offering audit and consultation services to corporations and individuals all over the world.

Joey received his formal education in Malaysia and Australia. He has combined the best of Eastern learning and Western education systems in the teaching methodology practiced at the Academy. Students of the Mastery Academy study traditional syllabuses of Chinese Metaphysics but through Western-style modular programs that are structured and systematic, enabling individuals to easily and quickly learn, grasp and master complex Chinese Metaphysics subjects like Feng Shui and BaZi. These unique structured learning systems are also utilized by Mastery Academy instructors all over the world to teach BaZi and Feng Shui.

The Mastery Academy is also the first international educational organisation to fully utilize the benefits of the Internet to promote continuous education, encourage peer-to-peer learning, enable mentoring and distance learning. Students interact with each other live, and continue to learn and improve their knowledge.

Despite his busy schedule, Joey continues to write for the Mastery Journal, a monthly eZine on Feng Shui and Astrology devoted for world-wide readers and the production of the world's first bilingual *Ten Thousand Year Calendar*. He is also the best selling author of *Stories and Lessons on Feng Shui, Mian Xiang- Discover Face Reading, Tong Shu Diary, BaZi - The Destiny Code, BaZi - The Destiny Code Revealed, Feng Shui for Homebuyers-Interior, Feng Shui for Homebuyers-Exterior* and the *Mini Feng Shui Compass*. Besides being a regular guest of various radio and TV talk shows, Joey is also a regular columnist for a national newspaper and various magazines in Malaysia. In fact, he hosted his own *TV series, Discover Feng Shui with Joey Yap*, on Malaysia's 8TV channel in 2005; a popular program that focused on heightening awareness of Feng Shui and Chinese Metaphysics.

A firm believer in innovation being the way forward, Joey recently released the BaZi Ming Pan 2.0 software, which allows users to generate configurable, detailed BaZi charts.

Author's personal website: www.joeyyap.com
Academy website: www.masteryacademy.com | www.masteryjournal.com | www.maelearning.com

EDUCATION

The Mastery Academy of Chinese Metaphysics: the first choice for practitioners and aspiring students of the art and science of Chinese Classical Feng Shui and Astrology.

For thousands of years, Eastern knowledge has been passed from one generation to another through the system of discipleship. A venerated master would accept suitable individuals at a young age as his disciples, and informally through the years, pass on his knowledge and skills to them. His disciples in turn, would take on their own disciples, as a means to perpetuate knowledge or skills.

This system served the purpose of restricting the transfer of knowledge to only worthy honourable individuals and ensuring that outsiders or Westerners would not have access to thousands of years of Eastern knowledge, learning and research.

However, the disciple system has also resulted in Chinese Metaphysics and Classical Studies lacking systematic teaching methods. Knowledge garnered over the years has not been accumulated in a concise, systematic manner, but scattered amongst practitioners, each practicing his/her knowledge, art and science, in isolation.

The disciple system, out of place in today's modern world, endangers the advancement of these classical fields that continue to have great relevance and application today.

At the Mastery Academy of Chinese Metaphysics, our Mission is to bring Eastern Classical knowledge in the fields of metaphysics, Feng Shui and Astrology sciences and the arts to the world. These Classical teachings and knowledge, previously shrouded in secrecy and passed on only through the discipleship system, are adapted into structured learning, which can easily be understood, learnt and mastered. Through modern learning methods, these renowned ancient arts, sciences and practices can be perpetuated while facilitating more extensive application and understanding of these classical subjects.

The Mastery Academy espouses an educational philosophy that draws from the best of the East and West. It is the world's premier educational institution for the study of Chinese Metaphysics Studies offering a wide range and variety of courses, ensuring that students have the opportunity to pursue their preferred field of study and enabling existing practitioners and professionals to gain cross-disciplinary knowledge that complements their current field of practice.

Courses at the Mastery Academy have been carefully designed to ensure a comprehensive yet compact syllabus. The modular nature of the courses enables students to immediately begin to put their knowledge into practice while pursuing continued study of their field and complementary fields. Students thus have the benefit of developing and gaining practical experience in tandem with the expansion and advancement of their theoretical knowledge.

Students can also choose from a variety of study options, from a distance learning program, the Homestudy Series, that enables study at one's own pace or intensive foundation courses and compact lecture-based courses, held in various cities around the world by Joey Yap or our licensed instructors. The Mastery Academy's faculty and make-up is international in nature, thus ensuring that prospective students can attend courses at destinations nearest to their country of origin or with a licensed Mastery Academy instructor in their home country.

The Mastery Academy provides 24x7 support to students through its Online Community, with a variety of tools, documents, forums and e-learning materials to help students stay at the forefront of research in their fields and gain invaluable assistance from peers and mentoring from their instructors.

Introducing...
The Mastery Academy's E-Learning Center!

The Mastery Academy's goal has always been to share authentic knowledge of Chinese Metaphysics with the whole world.

Nevertheless, we do recognize that distance, time, and hotel and traveling costs – amongst many other factors – could actually hinder people from enrolling for a classroom-based course. But with the advent and amazing advance of IT today, NOT any more!

With this in mind, we have invested heavily in IT, to conceive what is probably the first and only E-Learning Center in the world today that offers a full range of studies in the field of Chinese Metaphysics.

Convenient

Study from Your Own Home

Easy Enrollment

The Mastery Academy's E-Learning Center

Now, armed with your trusty computer or laptop, and Internet access, knowledge of classical Feng Shui, BaZi (Destiny Analysis) and Mian Xiang (Face Reading) are but a literal click away!

Study at your own pace, and interact with your Instructor and fellow students worldwide, from anywhere in the world. With our E-Learning Center, knowledge of Chinese Metaphysics is brought DIRECTLY to you in all its clarity – topic-by-topic, and lesson-by-lesson; with illustrated presentations and comprehensive notes expediting your learning curve!

Your education journey through our E-Learning Center may be done via any of the following approaches:

1. Online Courses

There are 3 Programs available: our Online Feng Shui Program, Online BaZi Program, and Online Mian Xiang Program. Each Program consists of several Levels, with each Level consisting of many Lessons in turn. Each Lesson contains a pre-recorded video session on the topic at hand, accompanied by presentation-slides and graphics as well as downloadable tutorial notes that you can print and file for future reference.

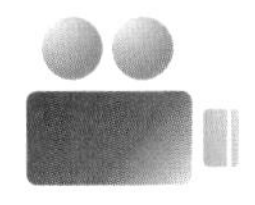

Video Lecture

Presentation Slide

Downloadable Notes

2. MA Live!

MA Live!, as its name implies, enables LIVE broadcasts of Joey Yap's courses and seminars – right to your computer screen. Students will not only get to see and hear Joey talk on real-time `live', but also participate and more importantly, TALK to Joey via the MA Live! interface. All the benefits of a live class, minus the hassle of actually having to attend one!

1.

Our Live Classes

2.

You at Home

3. Video-On-Demand (VOD)

Get immediate streaming-downloads of the Mastery Academy's wide range of educational DVDs, right on your computer screen. No more shipping costs and waiting time to be incurred!

Instant VOD Online

1.

2.

Choose From Our list of Available VODs!

Click "Play" on Your PC

Welcome to **www.maelearning.com**; the web portal of our E-Learning Center, and YOUR virtual gateway to Chinese Metaphysics!

Mastery Academy around the world

Canada
United States
Mexico
Brazil
United Kingdom
Switzerland
Netherlands
France
Cyprus
Italy
Germany
Austria
Poland
Hungary
Greece
South Africa
Russian Federation
Ukraine
Turkey
India
China
Japan
Philippines
Kuala Lumpur
Malaysia
Indonesia
Singapore
Australia
New Zealand
MASTERY ACADEMY OF CHINESE METAPHYSICS

YAP GLOBAL CONSULTING

Joey Yap & Yap Global Consulting

Headed by Joey Yap, Yap Global Consulting (YGC) is a leading international consulting firm specializing in Feng Shui, Mian Xiang (Face Reading) and BaZi (Destiny Analysis) consulting services worldwide. Joey - an internationally renowned Master Trainer, Consultant, Speaker and best-selling Author - has dedicated his life to the art and science of Chinese Metaphysics.

YGC has its main offices in Kuala Lumpur and Australia, and draws upon its diverse reservoir of strength from a group of dedicated and experienced consultants based in more than 30 countries, worldwide.

As the pioneer in blending established, classical Chinese Metaphysics techniques with the latest approach in consultation practices, YGC has built its reputation on the principles of professionalism and only the highest standards of service. This allows us to retain the cutting edge in delivering Feng Shui and Destiny consultation services to both corporate and personal clients, in a simple and direct manner, without compromising on quality.

Across Industries: Our Portfolio of Clients

Our diverse portfolio of both corporate and individual clients from all around the world bears testimony to our experience and capabilities.

Virtually every industry imaginable has benefited from our services - ranging from academic and financial institutions, real-estate developers and multinational corporations, to those in the leisure and tourism industry. Our services are also engaged by professionals, prominent business personalities, celebrities, high-profile politicians and people from all walks of life.

YAP GLOBAL GONSULTING

Name (Mr./Mrs./Ms.):

Contact Details

Tel: ______________ Fax: ______________

Mobile : ______________

E-mail: ______________

What Type of Consultation Are You Interested In?

☐ Feng Shui ☐ BaZi ☐ Date Selection ☐ Yi Jing

Please tick if applicable:

☐ Are you a Property Developer looking to engage Yap Global Consulting?

☐ Are you a Property Investor looking for tailor-made packages to suit your investment requirements?

Please attach your name card here.

Thank you for completing this form.
Please fax it back to us at:

Singapore
Fax: +65-3125 7131
Tel : +65-6722 8775

Australia
Fax: +618-9479 3388
Tel : +618-9467 3626

Malaysia & the rest of the world
Fax: +603-2284 2213
Tel : +603-2284 1213

www.joeyyap.com

www.joeyyap.com

Feng Shui Consultations

For Residential Properties
- Initial Land/Property Assessment
- Residential Feng Shui Consultations
- Residential Land Selection
- End-to-End Residential Consultation

For Commercial Properties
- Initial Land/Property Assessment
- Commercial Feng Shui Consultations
- Commercial Land Selection
- End-to-End Commercial Consultation

For Property Developers
- End-to-End Consultation
- Post-Consultation Advisory Services
- Panel Feng Shui Consultant

For Property Investors
- Your Personal Feng Shui Consultant
- Tailor-Made Packages

For Memorial Parks & Burial Sites
- Yin House Feng Shui

BaZi Consultations

Personal Destiny Analysis
- Personal Destiny Analysis for Individuals
- Children's BaZi Analysis
- Family BaZi Analysis

Strategic Analysis for Corporate Organizations
- Corporate BaZi Consultations
- BaZi Analysis for Human Resource Management

Entrepreneurs & Business Owners
- BaZi Analysis for Entrepreneurs

Career Pursuits
- BaZi Career Analysis

Relationships
- Marriage and Compatibility Analysis
- Partnership Analysis

For Everyone
- Annual BaZi Forecast
- Your Personal BaZi Coach

Date Selection Consultations

- **Marriage Date Selection**
- **Caesarean Birth Date Selection**
- **House-Moving Date Selection**
- **Renovation & Groundbreaking Dates**
- **Signing of Contracts**
- **Official Openings**
- **Product Launches**

Yi Jing Assessment

A Time-Tested, Accurate Science

- With a history predating 4 millennia, the Yi Jing - or Classic of Change - is one of the oldest Chinese texts surviving today. Its purpose as an oracle, in predicting the outcome of things, is based on the variables of Time, Space and Specific Events.

- A Yi Jing Assessment provides specific answers to any specific questions you may have about a specific event or endeavor. This is something that a Destiny Analysis would not be able to give you.

Basically, what a Yi Jing Assessment does is focus on only ONE aspect or item at a particular point in your life, and give you a calculated prediction of the details that will follow suit, if you undertake a particular action. It gives you an insight into a situation, and what course of action to take in order to arrive at a satisfactory outcome at the end of the day.

Please Contact YGC for a personalized Yi Jing Assessment!

Tel: +603-2284 1213 Email: consultations@joeyyap.com

www.joeyyap.com

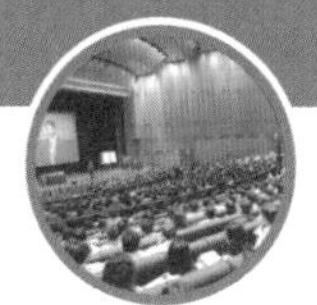

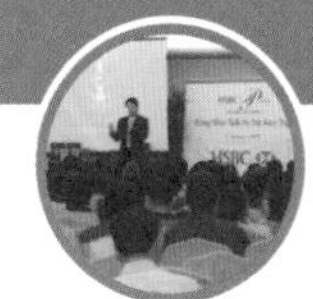

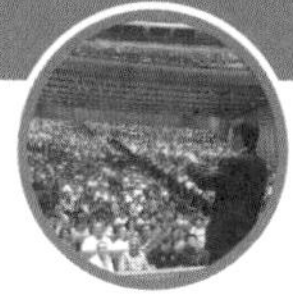

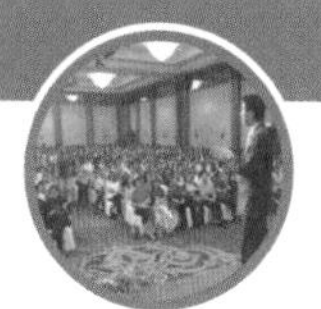

Inviting us to Your Corporate Events

Many reputable organizations and institutions have worked closely with YGC to build a synergistic business relationship by engaging our team of consultants, led by Joey Yap, as speakers at their corporate events. Our seminars and short talks are always packed with audiences consisting of clients and associates of multinational and public-listed companies as well as key stakeholders of financial institutions.

We tailor our seminars and talks to suit the anticipated or pertinent group of audience. Be it a department, subsidiary, your clients or even the entire corporation, we aim to fit your requirements in delivering the intended message(s).

Tel: +603-2284 1213 **Email: consultations@joeyyap.com**

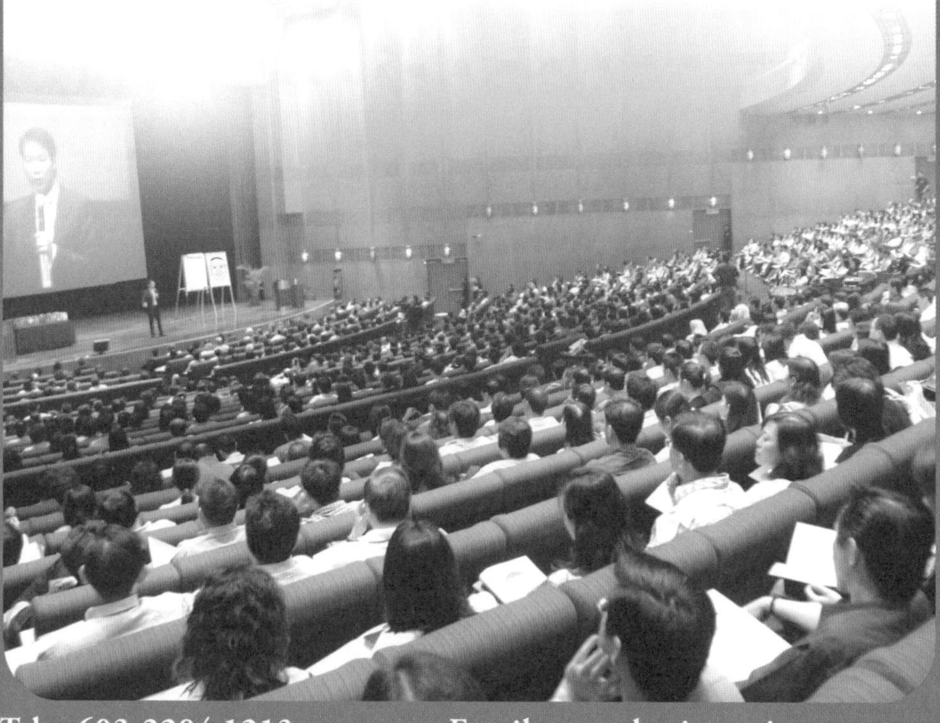

Latest DVDs Release by Joey Yap
Feng Shui for Homebuyers DVD Series

Best-selling Author, and international Master Trainer and Consultant Joey Yap reveals in these DVDs the significant Feng Shui features that every homebuyer should know when evaluating a property.

Joey will guide you on how to customise your home to maximise the Feng Shui potential of your property and gain the full benefit of improving your health, wealth and love life using the 9 Palace Grid. He will show you how to go about applying the classical applications of the Life Gua and House Gua techniques to get attuned to your Sheng Qi (positive energies).

In these DVDs, you will also learn how to identify properties with good Feng Shui features that will help you promote a fulfilling life and achieve your full potential. Discover how to avoid properties with negative Feng Shui that can bring about detrimental effects to your health, wealth and relationships.

Joey will also elaborate on how to fix the various aspects of your home that may have an impact on the Feng Shui of your property and give pointers on how to tap into the positive energies to support your goals.

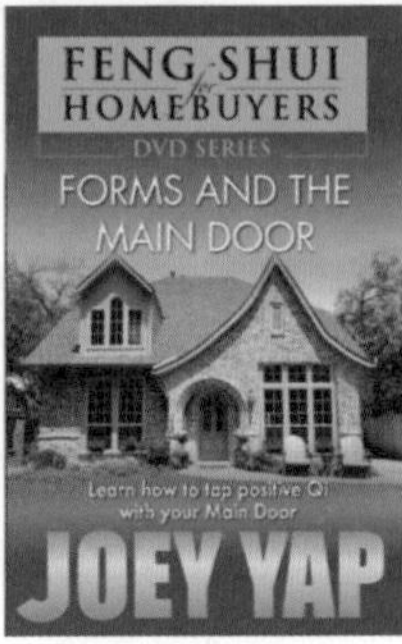

Feng Shui for Homebuyers Series

Feng Shui For Homebuyers - Exterior

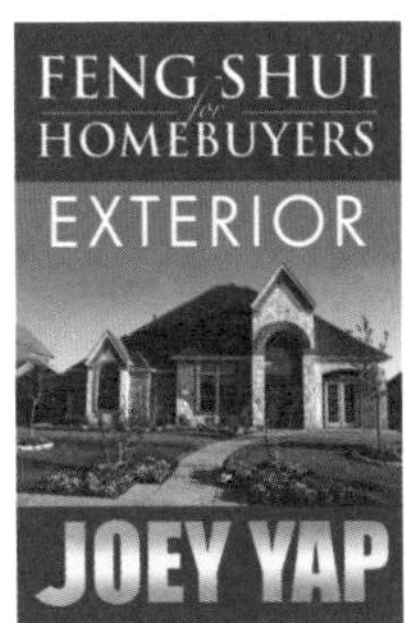

Best selling Author and international Feng Shui Consultant, Joey Yap, will guide you on the various important features in your external environment that have a bearing on the Feng Shui of your home. For homeowners, those looking to build their own home or even investors who are looking to apply Feng Shui to their homes, this book provides valuable information from the classical Feng Shui theories and applications.

This book will assist you in screening and eliminating unsuitable options with negative FSQ (Feng Shui Quotient) should you acquire your own land or if you are purchasing a newly built home. It will also help you in determining which plot of land to select and which to avoid when purchasing an empty parcel of land.

Feng Shui for Homebuyers - Interior

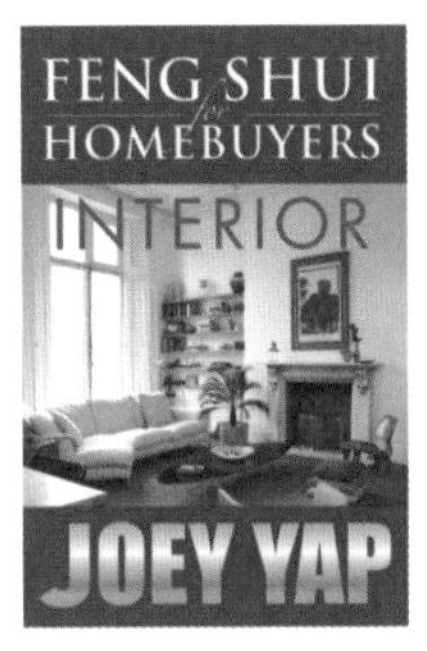

A book every homeowner or potential house buyer should have. The Feng Shui for Homebuyers (Interior) is an informative reference book and invaluable guide written by best selling Author and international Feng Shui Consultant, Joey Yap.

This book provides answers to the important questions of what really does matter when looking at the internal Feng Shui of a home or office. It teaches you how to analyze your home or office floor plans and how to improve their Feng Shui. It will answer all your questions about the positive and negative flow of Qi within your home and ways to utilize them to your maximum benefit.

Providing you with a guide to calculating your Life Gua and House Gua to fine-tune your Feng Shui within your property, Joey Yap focuses on practical, easily applicable ideas on what you can implement internally in a property.

Discover Feng Shui with Joey Yap (TV Series)

Discover Feng Shui with Joey Yap: Set of 4 DVDs

Informative and entertaining, classical Feng Shui comes alive in *Discover Feng Shui with Joey Yap!*

Dying to know how you can use Feng Shui to improve your house or office, but simply too busy attend for formal classes?

You have the questions. Now let Joey personally answer them in this 4-set DVD compilation! Learn how to ensure the viability of your residence or workplace, Feng Shui-wise, without having to convert it into a Chinese antiques' shop. Classical Feng Shui is about harnessing the natural power of your environment to improve quality of life. It's a systematic and subtle metaphysical science.

And that's not all. Joey also debunks many a myth about classical Feng Shui, and shares with viewers Face Reading tips as well!

Own the series that national channel 8TV did a re-run of in 2005, today!

Educational Tools & Software

Mini Feng Shui Compass

This Mini Feng Shui Compass with the accompanying Companion Booklet written by leading Feng Shui and Chinese Astrology Master Trainer Joey Yap is a must-have for any Feng Shui enthusiast.

The Mini Feng Shui Compass is a self-aligning compass that is not only light at 100gms but also built sturdily to ensure it will be convenient to use anywhere. The rings on the Mini Feng Shui Compass are bi-lingual and incorporate the 24 Mountain Rings that is used in your traditional Luo Pan.

The comprehensive booklet included will guide you in applying the 24 Mountain Directions on your Mini Feng Shui Compass effectively and the 8 Mansions Feng Shui to locate the most auspicious locations within your home, office and surroundings. You can also use the Mini Feng Shui Compass when measuring the direction of your property for the purpose of applying Flying Stars Feng Shui.

BaZi Ming Pan Software Version 2.0

Professional Four Pillars Calculator for Destiny Analysis

The BaZi Ming Pan Version 2.0 Professional Four Pillars Calculator for Destiny Analysis is the most technically advanced software of its kind in the world today. It allows even those without any knowledge of BaZi to generate their own BaZi Charts, and provides virtually every detail required to undertake a comprehensive Destiny Analysis.

This Professional Four Pillars Calculator allows you to even undertake a day-to-day analysis of your Destiny. What's more, all BaZi Charts generated by this software are fully printable and configurable! Designed for both enthusiasts and professional practitioners, this state-of-the-art software blends details with simplicity, and is capable of generating 4 different types of BaZi charts: **BaZi Professional Charts, BaZi Annual Analysis Charts, BaZi Pillar Analysis Charts and BaZi Family Relationship Charts.**

Additional references, configurable to cater to all levels of BaZi knowledge and usage, include: • Dual Age & Bilingual Option (Western & Chinese) • Na Yin narrations • 12 Life Stages evaluation • Death & Emptiness • Gods & Killings • Special Days • Heavenly Virtue Nobles

This software also comes with a Client Management feature that allows you to save and trace clients' records instantly, navigate effortlessly between BaZi charts, and file your clients' information in an organized manner.

The BaZi Ming Pan Version 2.0 Calculator sets a new standard by combining the best of BaZi and technology.

Accelerate Your Face Reading Skills With Joey Yap's Face Reading Revealed DVD Series

Mian Xiang, the Chinese art of Face Reading, is an ancient form of physiognomy and entails the use of the face and facial characteristics to evaluate key aspects of a person's life, luck and destiny. In his Face Reading DVDs series, Joey Yap shows you how the facial features reveal a wealth of information about a person's luck, destiny and personality.

Mian Xiang also tell us the talents, quirks and personality of an individual. Do you know that just by looking at a person's face, you can ascertain his or her health, wealth, relationships and career? Let Joey Yap show you how the 12 Palaces can be utilised to reveal a person's inner talents, characteristics and much more.

Each facial feature on the face represents one year in a person's life. Your face is a 100-year map of your life and each position reveals your fortune and destiny at a particular age as well as insights and information about your personality, skills, abilities and destiny.

Using Mian Xiang, you will also be able to plan your life ahead by identifying, for example, the right business partner and knowing the sort of person that you need to avoid. By knowing their characteristics through the facial features, you will be able to gauge their intentions and gain an upper hand in negotiations.

Do you know what moles signify? Do they bring good or bad luck? Do you want to build better relationships with your partner or family members or have your ever wondered why you seem to be always bogged down by trivial problems in your life?

In these highly entertaining DVDs, Joey will help you answer all these questions and more. You will be able to ascertain the underlying meaning of moles, birthmarks or even the type of your hair in Face Reading. Joey will also reveal the guidelines to help you foster better and stronger relationships with your loved ones through Mian Xiang.

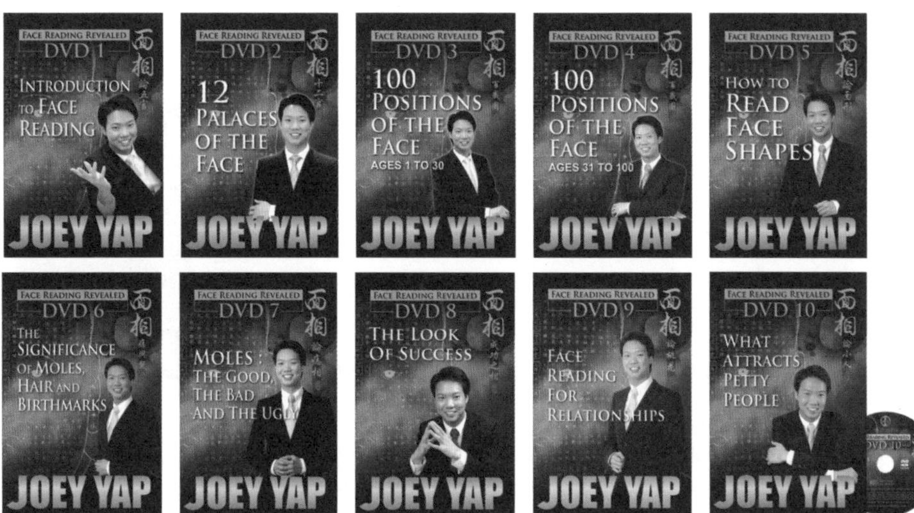

Continue Your Journey with Joey Yap's Books

BaZi - The Destiny Code (English & Chinese versions)

Leading Chinese Astrology Master Trainer Joey Yap makes it easy to learn how to unlock your Destiny through your BaZi with this book. BaZi or Four Pillars of Destiny is an ancient Chinese science which enables individuals to understand their personality, hidden talents and abilities as well as their luck cycle, simply by examining the information contained within their birth data. *The Destiny Code* is the first book that shows readers how to plot and interpret their own Destiny Charts and lays the foundation for more in-depth BaZi studies. Written in a lively entertaining style, the Destiny Code makes BaZi accessible to the layperson. Within 10 chapters, understand and appreciate more about this astoundingly accurate ancient Chinese Metaphysical science.

BaZi - The Destiny Code Revealed

In this follow up to Joey Yap's best-selling *The Destiny Code*, delve deeper into your own Destiny chart through an understanding of the key elemental relationships that affect the Heavenly Stems and Earthly Branches. Find out how Combinations, Clash, Harm, Destructions and Punishments bring new dimension to a BaZi chart. Complemented by extensive real-life examples, *The Destiny Code Revealed* takes you to the next level of BaZi, showing you how to unlock the Codes of Destiny and to take decisive action at the right time, and capitalise on the opportunities in life.

The Ten Thousand Year Calendar

The Ten Thousand Year Calendar or 萬年曆 Wan Nian Li is a regular reference book and an invaluable tool used by masters, practitioners and students of Feng Shui, BaZi (Four Pillars of Destiny), Chinese Zi Wei Dou Shu Astrology (Purple Star), Yi Jing (I-Ching) and Date Selection specialists.

JOEY YAP's *Ten Thousand Year Calendar* provides the Gregorian (Western) dates converted into both the Chinese Solar and Lunar calendar in both the English and Chinese language.

It also includes a comprehensive set of key Feng Shui and Chinese Astrology charts and references, including Xuan Kong Nine Palace Flying Star Charts, Monthly and Daily Flying Stars, Water Dragon Formulas Reference Charts, Zi Wei Dou Shu (Purple Star) Astrology Reference Charts, BaZi (Four Pillars of Destiny) Heavenly Stems, Earthly Branches and all other related reference tables for Chinese Metaphysical Studies.

Annual Releases

Chinese Astrology for 2008

This information-packed annual guide to the Chinese Astrology for 2008 goes way beyond the conventional `animal horoscope' book. To begin with, author Joey Yap includes a personalized outlook for 2008 based on the individual's BaZi Day Pillar (Jia Zi) and a 12-month micro-analysis for each of the 60 Day Pillars – in addition to the annual outlook for all 12 animal signs and the 12-month outlook for each animal sign in 2008. Find out what awaits you in 2008 from the four key aspects of Health, Wealth, Career and Relationships... with Joey Yap's **Chinese Astrology for 2008**!

Feng Shui for 2008

Maximize the Qi of the Year of the Earth Rat for your home and office, with Joey Yap's **Feng Shui for 2008** book. Learn how to tap into the positive sectors of the year, and avoid the negative ones and those with the Annual Afflictions, as well as ascertain how the annual Flying Stars affect your property by comparing them against the Eight Mansions (Ba Zhai) for 2008. Flying Stars enthusiasts will also find this book handy, as it includes the monthly Flying Stars charts for the year, accompanied by detailed commentaries on what sectors to use and avoid – to enable you to optimize your Academic, Relationships and Wealth Luck in 2008.

Tong Shu Diary 2008

Organize your professional and personal lives with the **Tong Shu Diary 2008**, with a twist... it also allows you to determine the most suitable dates on which you can undertake important activities and endeavors throughout the year! This compact Diary integrates the Chinese Solar and Lunar Calendars with the universal lingua franca of the Gregorian Calendar.

Tong Shu Monthly Planner 2008

Tailor-made for the Feng Shui or BaZi enthusiast in you, or even professional Chinese Metaphysics consultants who want a compact planner with useful information incorporated into it. In the **Tong Shu Monthly Planner 2008**, you will find the auspicious and inauspicious dates for the year marked out for you, alongside the most suitable activities to be undertaken on each day. As a bonus, there is also a reference section containing all the monthly Flying Stars charts and Annual Afflictions for 2008.

Tong Shu Desktop Calendar 2008

Get an instant snapshot of the suitable and unsuitable activities for each day of the Year of the Earth Rat, with the icons displayed on this lightweight Desktop Calendar. Elegantly presenting the details of the Chinese Solar Calendar in the form of the standard Gregorian one, the **Tong Shu Desktop Calendar 2008** is perfect for Chinese Metaphysics enthusiasts and practitioners alike. Whether it a business launching or meeting, ground breaking ceremony, travel or house-moving that you have in mind, this Calendar is designed to fulfill your information needs.

Tong Shu Year Planner 2008

This one-piece Planner presents you all the essential information you need for significant activities or endeavors...with just a quick glance! In a nutshell, it allows you to identify the favorable and unfavorable days, which will in turn enable you to schedule your year's activities so as to make the most of good days, and avoid the ill-effects brought about by inauspicious ones.

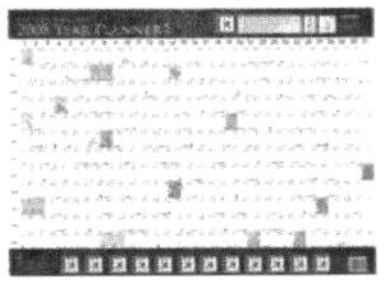

Continue Your Journey with Joey Yap's Books

Mian Xiang - Discover Face Reading

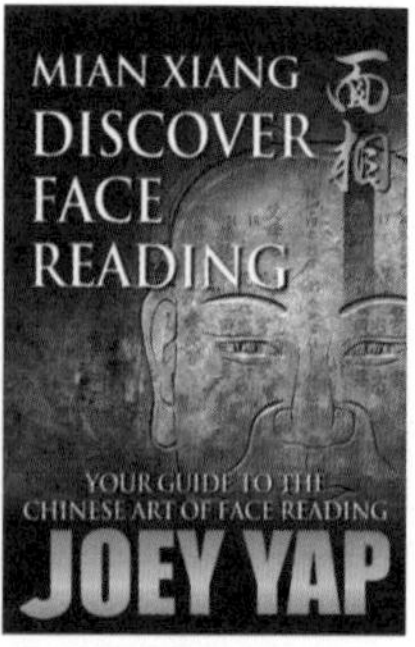

Need to identify a suitable business partner? How about understanding your staff or superiors better? Or even choosing a suitable spouse? These mind boggling questions can be answered in Joey Yap's introductory book to Face Reading titled *Mian Xiang – Discover Face Reading*. This book will help you discover the hidden secrets in a person's face.

Mian Xiang – Discover Face Reading is comprehensive book on all areas of Face Reading, covering some of the most important facial features, including the forehead, mouth, ears and even the philtrum above your lips. This book will help you analyse not just your Destiny but help you achieve your full potential and achieve life fulfillment.

Stories and Lessons on Feng Shui (English & Chinese versions)

Stories and Lessons on Feng Shui is a compilation of essays and stories written by leading Feng Shui and Chinese Astrology trainer and consultant Joey Yap about Feng Shui and Chinese Astrology.

In this heart-warming collection of easy to read stories, find out why it's a myth that you should never have Water on the right hand side of your house, the truth behind the infamous 'love' and 'wealth' corners and that the sudden death of a pet fish is really NOT due to bad luck!

More Stories and Lessons on Feng Shui

Finally, the long-awaited sequel to *Stories & Lessons on Feng Shui*!

If you've read the best-selling Stories & Lessons on Feng Shui, you won't want to miss this book. And even if you haven't read *Stories & Lessons on Feng Shui*, there's always a time to rev your Feng Shui engine up.

The time is NOW.

And the book? *More Stories & Lessons on Feng Shui* – the 2nd compilation of the most popular articles and columns penned by Joey Yap; **specially featured in national and international publications, magazines and newspapers.**

All in all, *More Stories & Lessons on Feng Shui* is a delightful chronicle of Joey's articles, thoughts and vast experience - as a professional Feng Shui consultant and instructor - that have been purposely refined, edited and expanded upon to make for a light-hearted, interesting yet educational read. And with Feng Shui, BaZi, Mian Xiang and Yi Jing all thrown into this one dish, there's something for everyone...so all you need to serve or accompany *More Stories & Lessons on Feng Shui* with is your favorite cup of tea or coffee!

Continue Your Journey with Joey Yap's Books

Xuan Kong: Flying Stars Feng Shui

Xuan Kong Flying Stars Feng Shui is an essential introductory book to the subject of Xuan Kong Fei Xing, a well-known and popular system of Feng Shui, written by International Feng Shui Master Trainer Joey Yap.

In his down-to-earth, entertaining and easy to read style, Joey Yap takes you through the essential basics of Classical Feng Shui, and the key concepts of Xuan Kong Fei Xing (Flying Stars). Learn how to fly the stars, plot a Flying Star chart for your home or office and interpret the stars and star combinations. Find out how to utilise the favourable areas of your home or office for maximum benefit and learn 'tricks of the trade' and 'trade secrets' used by Feng Shui practitioners to enhance and maximise Qi in your home or office.

An essential integral introduction to the subject of Classical Feng Shui and the Flying Stars System of Feng Shui!

Xuan Kong Flying Stars: Structures and Combinations

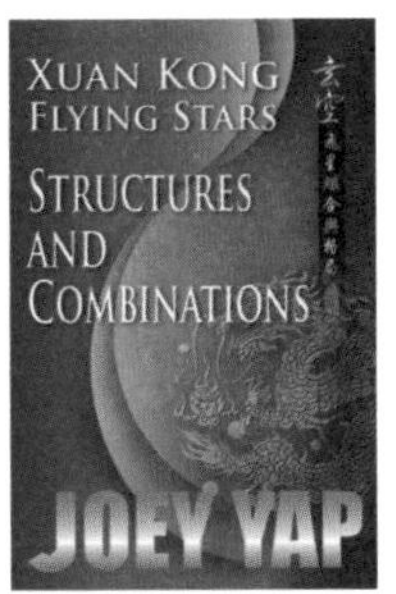

(Available in 2008)

Delve deeper into Flying Stars through a greater understanding of the 81 Combinations and the influence of the Annual and Monthly Stars on the Base, Sitting and Facing Stars in this 2nd book in the Xuan Kong Feng Shui series. Learn how Structures like the Combination of 10, Up the Mountain and Down the River, Pearl and Parent String Structures are used to interpret a Flying Star chart.

Xuan Kong Flying Stars: Advanced Techniques

(Available in 2009)

Take your knowledge of Xuan Kong Flying Stars to a higher level and learn how to apply complex techniques and advanced formulas such as Castle Gate Technique, Seven Star Robbery Formation, Advancing the Dragon Formation and Replacement Star technique amongst others. Joey Yap also shows you how to use the Life Palace technique to combine Gua Numbers with Flying Star numbers and utilise the predictive facets of Flying Stars Feng Shui.

Continue Your Journey with Joey Yap's Books

The Art of Date Selection: Personal Date Selection

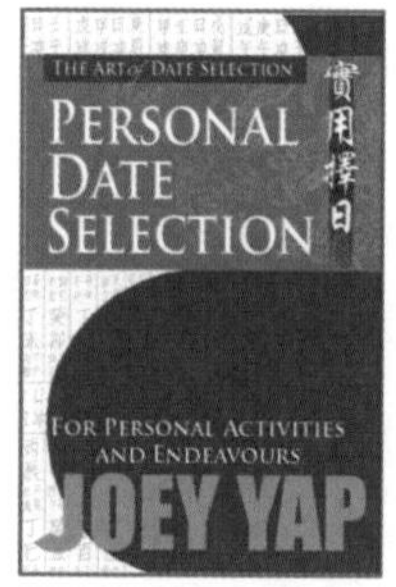

In today's modern world, it is not good enough to just do things effectively – we need to do them efficiently, as well. From the signing of business contracts and moving into a new home, to launching a product or even tying the knot; everything has to move, and move very quickly too. There is a premium on Time, where mistakes can indeed be costly.

The notion of doing the Right Thing, at the Right Time and in the Right Place is the very backbone of Date Selection. Because by selecting a suitable date specially tailored to a specific activity or endeavor, we infuse it with the most positive energies prevalent in our environment during that particular point in time; and that could well make the difference between `make-and-break'! With the *Art of Date Selection: Personal Date Selection*, learn simple, practical methods you can employ to select not just good dates, but personalized good dates. Whether it's a personal activity such as a marriage or professional endeavor such as launching a business, signing a contract or even acquiring assets, this book will show you how to pick the good dates and tailor them to suit the activity in question, as well as avoid the negative ones too!

The Art of Date Selection: Feng Shui Date Selection

(Available in 2008)

Date Selection is the Art of selecting the most suitable date, where the energies present on the day support the specific activities or endeavors we choose to undertake on that day. Feng Shui is the Chinese Metaphysical study of the Physiognomy of the Land – landforms and the Qi they produce, circulate and conduct. Hence, anything that exists on this Earth is invariably subject to the laws of Feng Shui. So what do we get when Date Selection and Feng Shui converge?

Feng Shui Date Selection, of course! Say you wish to renovate your home, or maybe buy or rent one. Or perhaps, you're a developer, and wish to know WHEN is the best date possible to commence construction works on your project. In any case – and all cases – you certainly wish to ensure that your endeavors are well supported by the positive energies present on a good day, won't you? And this is where Date Selection supplements the practice of Feng Shui. At the end of the day, it's all about making the most of what's good, and minimizing what's bad.

Elevate Your Feng Shui Skills With Joey Yap's Home Study Course And Educational DVDs

Xuan Kong Vol.1

An Advanced Feng Shui Home Study Course

Learn the Xuan Kong Flying Star Feng Shui system in just 20 lessons! Joey Yap's specialised notes and course work have been written to enable distance learning without compromising on the breadth or quality of the syllabus. Learn at your own pace with the same material students in a live class would use. The most comprehensive distance learning course on Xuan Kong Flying Star Feng Shui in the market. Xuan Kong Flying Star Vol. 1 comes complete with a special binder for all your course notes.

Feng Shui for Period 8 - (DVD)

Don't miss the Feng Shui Event of the next 20 years! Catch Joey Yap LIVE and find out just what Period 8 is all about. This DVD boxed set zips you through the fundamentals of Feng Shui and the impact of this important change in the Feng Shui calendar. Joey's entertaining, conversational style walks you through the key changes that Period 8 will bring and how to tap into Wealth Qi and Good Feng Shui for the next 20 years.

Xuan Kong Flying Stars Beginners Workshop - (DVD)

Take a front row seat in Joey Yap's Xuan Kong Flying Stars workshop with this unique LIVE RECORDING of Joey Yap's Xuan Kong Flying Stars Feng Shui workshop, attended by over 500 people. This DVD program provides an effective and quick introduction of Xuan Kong Feng Shui essentials for those who are just starting out in their study of classical Feng Shui. Learn to plot your own Flying Star chart in just 3 hours. Learn 'trade secret' methods, remedies and cures for Flying Stars Feng Shui. This boxed set contains 3 DVDs and 1 workbook with notes and charts for reference.

BaZi Four Pillars of Destiny Beginners Workshop - (DVD)

Ever wondered what Destiny has in store for you? Or curious to know how you can learn more about your personality and inner talents? BaZi or Four Pillars of Destiny is an ancient Chinese science that enables us to understand a person's hidden talent, inner potential, personality, health and wealth luck from just their birth data. This specially compiled DVD set of Joey Yap's BaZi Beginners Workshop provides a thorough and comprehensive introduction to BaZi. Learn how to read your own chart and understand your own luck cycle. This boxed set contains 3 DVDs and 1 workbook with notes and reference charts.

Interested in learning MORE about Feng Shui? Advance Your Feng Shui Knowledge with the Mastery Academy Courses.

Feng Shui Mastery Series™

LIVE COURSES (MODULES ONE TO FOUR)

Feng Shui Mastery – Module One

Beginners Course

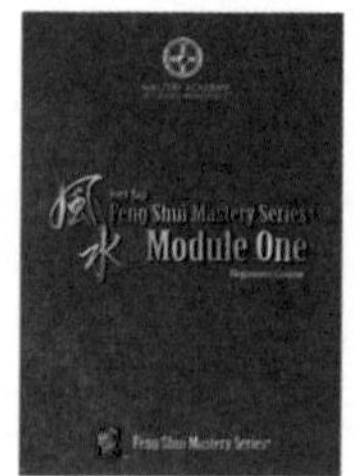

Designed for students seeking an entry-level intensive program into the study of Feng Shui , Module One is an intensive foundation course that aims not only to provide you with an introduction to Feng Shui theories and formulas and equip you with the skills and judgments to begin practicing and conduct simple Feng Shui audits upon successful completion of the course. Learn all about Forms, Eight Mansions Feng Shui and Flying Star Feng Shui in just one day with a unique, structured learning program that makes learning Feng Shui quick and easy!

Feng Shui Mastery – Module Two

Practitioners Course

Building on the knowledge and foundation in classical Feng Shui theory garnered in M1, M2 provides a more advanced and in-depth understanding of Eight Mansions, Xuan Kong Flying Star and San He and introduces students to theories that are found only in the classical Chinese Feng Shui texts. This 3-Day Intensive course hones analytical and judgment skills, refines Luo Pan (Chinese Feng Shui compass) skills and reveals 'trade secret' remedies. Module Two covers advanced Forms Analysis, San He's Five Ghost Carry Treasure formula, Advanced Eight Mansions and Xuan Kong Flying Stars and equips you with the skills needed to undertake audits and consultations for residences and offices.

Feng Shui Mastery – Module Three

Advanced Practitioners Course

Module Three is designed for Professional Feng Shui Practitioners. Learn advanced topics in Feng Shui and take your skills to a cutting edge level. Be equipped with the knowledge, techniques and confidence to conduct large scale audits (like estate and resort planning). Learn how to apply different systems appropriately to remedy situations or cases deemed inauspicious by one system and reconcile conflicts in different systems of Feng Shui. Gain advanced knowledge of San He (Three Harmony) systems and San Yuan (Three Cycles) systems, advanced Luan Tou (Forms Feng Shui) and specialist Water Formulas.

Feng Shui Mastery – Module Four

Master Course

The graduating course of the Feng Shui Mastery (FSM) Series, this course takes the advanced practitioner to the Master level. Power packed M4 trains students to 'walk the mountains' and identify superior landform, superior grade structures and make qualitative evaluations of landform, structures, Water and Qi and covers advanced and exclusive topics of San He, San Yuan, Xuan Kong, Ba Zhai, Luan Tou (Advanced Forms and Water Formula) Feng Shui. Master Internal, External and Luan Tou (Landform) Feng Shui methodologies to apply Feng Shui at every level and undertake consultations of every scale and magnitude, from houses and apartments to housing estates, townships, shopping malls and commercial districts.

BaZi Mastery Series™

LIVE COURSES (MODULES ONE TO FOUR)

BaZi Mastery – Module One

Intensive Foundation Course

This Intensive One Day Foundation Course provides an introduction to the principles and fundamentals of BaZi (Four Pillars of Destiny) and Destiny Analysis methods such as Ten Gods, Useful God and Strength of Qi. Learn how to plot a BaZi chart and interpret your Destiny and your potential. Master BaZi and learn to capitalize on your strengths, minimize risks and downturns and take charge of your Destiny.

BaZi Mastery – Module Two

Practical BaZi Applications

BaZi Module Two teaches students advanced BaZi analysis techniques and specific analysis methods for relationship luck, health evaluation, wealth potential and career potential. Students will learn to identify BaZi chart structures, sophisticated methods for applying the Ten Gods, and how to read Auxiliary Stars. Students who have completed Module Two will be able to conduct professional BaZi readings.

BaZi Mastery – Module Three

Advanced Practitioners Program

Designed for the BaZi practitioner, learn how to read complex cases and unique events in BaZi charts and perform Big and Small assessments. Discover how to analyze personalities and evaluate talents precisely, as well as special formulas and classical methodologies for BaZi from classics such as Di Tian Sui and Qiong Tong Bao Jian.

BaZi Mastery – Module Four

Master Course in BaZi

The graduating course of the BaZi Mastery Series, this course takes the advanced practitioner to the Masters' level. BaZi M4 focuses on specialized techniques of BaZi reading, unique special structures and advance methods from ancient classical texts. This program includes techniques on date selection and ancient methodologies from the Qiong Tong Bao Jian and Yuan Hai Zi Ping classics.

Xuan Kong Mastery Series™

LIVE COURSES (MODULES ONE TO THREE)

* Advanced Courses For Master Practitioners

Xuan Kong Mastery – Module One

Advanced Foundation Program

This course is for the experienced Feng Shui professionals who wish to expand their knowledge and skills in the Xuan Kong system of Feng Shui, covering important foundation methods and techniques from the Wu Chang and Guang Dong lineages of Xuan Kong Feng Shui.

Xuan Kong Mastery – Module Two A

Advanced Xuan Kong Methodologies

Designed for Feng Shui practitioners seeking to specialise in the Xuan Kong system, this program focuses on methods of application and Joey Yap's unique Life Palace and Shifting Palace Methods, as well as methods and techniques from the Wu Chang lineage.

Xuan Kong Mastery – Module Two B

Purple White

Explore in detail and in great depth the star combinations in Xuan Kong. Learn how each different combination reacts or responds in different palaces, under different environmental circumstances and to whom in the property. Learn methods, theories and techniques extracted from ancient classics such as Xuan Kong Mi Zhi, Xuan Kong Fu, Fei Xing Fu and Zi Bai Jue.

Xuan Kong Mastery – Module Three

Advanced Xuan Kong Da Gua

This intensive course focuses solely on the Xuan Kong Da Gua system covering the theories, techniques and methods of application of this unique 64-Hexagram based system of Xuan Kong including Xuan Kong Da Gua for landform analysis.

MIAN XIANG MASTERY SERIES™
LIVE COURSES (MODULES ONE AND TWO)

Mian Xiang Mastery – Module One
Basic Face Reading

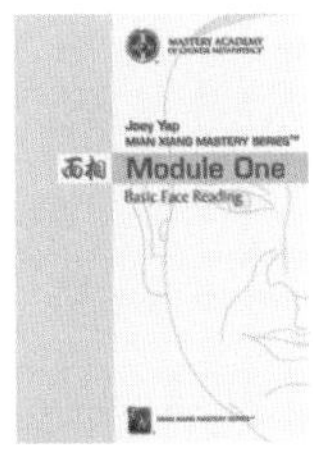

A person's face is their fortune – learn more about the ancient Chinese art of Face Reading. In just one day, be equipped with techniques and skills to read a person's face and ascertain their character, luck, wealth and relationship luck.

Mian Xiang Mastery – Module Two
Practical Face Reading

Mian Xiang Module Two covers face reading techniques extracted from the ancient classics Shen Xiang Quan Pian and Shen Xiang Tie Guan Dau. Gain a greater depth and understanding of Mian Xiang and learn to recognize key structures and characteristics in a person's face.

Yi Jing Mastery Series™
LIVE COURSES

Traditional Yi Jing

'Yi', relates to change. Change is the only constant in life and the universe, without exception to this rule. The Yi Jing is hence popularly referred to as the Book or Classic of Change. Discoursed in the language of Yin and Yang, the Yi Jing is one of the oldest Chinese classical texts surviving today. With Traditional Yi Jing, learn how this Classic is used to divine the outcomes of virtually every facet of life; from your relationships to seeking an answer to the issues you may face in your daily life.

Plum Blossom Numerology

Shao Yong, widely regarded as one of the greatest scholars of the Sung Dynasty, developed Mei Hua Yi Shu (Plum Blossom Numerology) as a more advanced means for divination purposes using the Yi Jing. In Plum Blossom Numerology, the results of a hexagram are interpreted by referring to the Gua meanings, where the interaction and relationship between the five elements, stems, branches and time are equally taken into consideration. This divination method, properly applied, allows us to make proper decisions whenever we find ourselves in a predicament.

Ze RI Mastery Series™

LIVE COURSES (MODULES ONE AND TWO)

Ze Ri Mastery Series Module 1

The Mastery Academy's Date Selection Mastery Series Module 1 is specifically structured to provide novice students with an exciting introduction to the Art of Date Selection. Learn the rudiments and tenets of this intriguing metaphysical science. What makes a good date, and what makes a bad date? What dates are suitable for which activities, and what dates simply aren't? And of course, the mother of all questions: WHY aren't all dates created equal. All in only one Module – Module 1!

Ze Ri Mastery Series Module 2

In Module 2, discover advanced Date Selection techniques that will take your knowledge of this Art to a level equivalent to that of a professional's! This is the Module where Date Selection infuses knowledge of the ancient metaphysical science of Feng Shui and BaZi (Chinese Astrology, or Four Pillars of Destiny). Feng Shui, as a means of maximizing Human Luck (i.e. our luck on Earth), is often quoted as the cure to BaZi, which allows us to decipher our Heaven (i.e. inherent) Luck. And one of the most potent ways of making the most of what life has to offer us is to understand our Destiny, know how we can use the natural energies of our environment for our environments and MOST importantly, WHEN we should use these energies and for WHAT endeavors!

You will learn specific methods on how to select suitable dates, tailored to specific activities and events. More importantly, you will also be taught how to suit dates to a person's BaZi (Chinese Astrology, or Four Pillars of Destiny), in order to maximize his or her strengths, and allow this person to surmount any challenges that lie in wait. Add in the factor of `place', and you would have satisfied the notion of `doing the right thing, at the right time and in the right place'! A basic knowledge of BaZi and Feng Shui will come in handy in this Module, although these are not pre-requisites to successfully undergo Module 2.

Walk the Mountains! Learn Feng Shui in a Practical and Hands-on Program.

Feng Shui Mastery Excursion Series™ : CHINA

Learn landform (Luan Tou) Feng Shui by walking the mountains and chasing the Dragon's vein in China. This Program takes the students in a study tour to examine notable Feng Shui landmarks, mountains, hills, valleys, ancient palaces, famous mansions, houses and tombs in China. The Excursion is a 'practical' hands-on course where students are shown to perform readings using the formulas they've learnt and to recognize and read Feng Shui Landform (Luan Tou) formations.

Read about China Excursion here:
http://www.masteryacademy.com/Education/schoolfengshui/fengshuimasteryexcursion.asp

Mastery Academy courses are conducted around the world. Find out when will Joey Yap be in your area by visiting **www.masteryacademy.com** or call our office at +603-2284 8080.